Growing Prosperity

Books by Barry Bluestone and Bennett Harrison
The Deindustrialization of America
The Great U-Turn: Corporate Restructuring and the
    Polarizing of America

Books by Barry Bluestone
Low Wages and the Working Poor
Aircraft Industry Dynamics
The Retail Revolution
Negotiating the Future: A Labor Perspective on American
    Business
The Prosperity Gap

Books by Bennett Harrison
The Economic Development of Harlem
Education, Training and the Urban Ghetto
Urban Economic Development
Lean and Mean: The Changing Landscape of Corporate
    Power in the Age of Flexibility

Growing Prosperity

*The Battle for Growth with Equity
in the Twenty-first Century*

Barry Bluestone and
Bennett Harrison

A Century Foundation Book

UNIVERSITY OF CALIFORNIA PRESS
Berkeley · Los Angeles · London

The Century Foundation, formerly the Twentieth Century Fund, sponsors and supervises timely analyses of economic policy, foreign affairs, and domestic political issues. Not-for-profit and nonpartisan, it was founded in 1919 and endowed by Edward A. Filene.

University of California Press
Berkeley and Los Angeles, California

University of California Press, Ltd.
London, England

First Paperback Printing 2001

Published by arrangement with Houghton Mifflin Company.

Library of Congress Cataloging-in-Publication Data
Bluestone, Barry.
Growing prosperity : the battle for growth with equity in the
twenty-first century / Barry Bluestone and Bennett Harrison.
p.   cm.
Includes bibliographical references and index.
ISBN 0-520-23070-1 (alk. paper)
1. Income distribution—United States.   2. United States—Economic
conditions—1981–   3. United States—Economic policy.
I. Harrison, Bennett.   II. Title.
HC110.I5 B539   2001
339.2'0973—dc21   00-051167

Book design by Joyce C. Weston

Printed in the United States of America

08 07 06 05 04 03 02 01
9 8 7 6 5 4 3 2 1

The paper used in this publication is both acid-free and totally chlorine-free (TCF).
It meets the minimum requirements of ANSI/NISO Z39.48-1992 (R 1997)
(*Permanence of Paper*). ∞

To my best friend and cherished colleague,
Bennett Harrison (1942–1999)

Contents

Foreword ix

Preface xiii

Preface to the Paperback Edition xvii

1 Growth with Equity 1

2 A History of American Growth 27

3 America's New Growth Potential 50

4 The Wall Street Model 102

5 The Wall Street Model: Too Little Long-Term Growth 138

6 The Wall Street Model: Too Much Long-Term Inequality 182

7 The Main Street Model for Growth with Equity 205

8 From Wall Street to Main Street: Economic Policy for
   the Twenty-first Century 237

Notes 265

Bibliography 311

Index 329

Foreword

Americans generally have had good reason to believe that the future would always be better than the past. This persistent optimism rose to a new level with the extraordinary economic growth of the post–World War II years. From 1960 to 1973, gross domestic product (GDP) grew by an average of 4.2 percent per year. Americans also had reason to assume that the expanding pie would be fairly shared, with all income groups moving up the economic ladder together. In fact, over that same thirteen-year period, income for all segments of the population grew at roughly similar rates.

For reasons that have not been altogether clear, this pattern of rapid and egalitarian economic growth came to a rather sudden halt in 1973. For the quarter-century ending in 1998, GDP growth fell to an average of about 2.6 percent annually. Moreover, the gains in personal income from this slower growth have not been shared by all. Strikingly, every income segment except the highest has had smaller advances than occurred during the 1960s and early 1970s. Indeed, 60 percent of families experienced declines in real income, with the poorest fifth hardest hit, losing 15 percent, on average, in purchasing power.

Twenty-five years is a long time in terms of economic memory. And while Americans clung as long as possible to the dreams of an earlier era of rosy hopes, by the mid-1990s they had come to expect their children to have a tougher time, economically speaking, than they did. Many economists, too, were convinced that slower and more unequal growth might be inevitable for the foreseeable future. Key elements of public policy are currently debated in terms of this new conventional economic wisdom. In this sense, low expectations can become more than technical projections; they can reduce the scope and vision of the political debate about economic policy. For example, even more than the size of the baby-boom generation, slow growth is the underlying explanation for much of the anticipated pressure on Social Security and for projections of a future crisis in financing health care for the elderly.

In 1997, when work on this book started, there was early evidence of a shift in these patterns of growth and income. The more rapid and equitable growth of GDP in the last years of the twentieth century has caused others to share Bluestone and Harrison's outlook. But only a few observers were bold enough to suggest that the latest numbers are more than random variations from the previous pattern and that something important may have changed. Fewer still predicted that such changes would emerge toward the end of the twentieth century. In that last group of brave and thoughtful scholars are the authors of this volume.

Barry Bluestone, Sterns Trustee Professor of Political Economy at Northeastern University, and the late Bennett Harrison, who was an economist at the New School for Social Research, have argued for several years that the expectations of low growth might be based on too truncated a view of history. They took a longer historical perspective, and in so doing learned that major technological breakthroughs in the past often led to decades of slow growth before the productivity premium of the new discoveries was fully realized. This pattern, they argue, not only best explains the diminished productivity and growth in the United States beginning in the early 1970s, it also tells us why we are experiencing a surge in growth today and have the potential for continued rapid growth.

Moreover, Bluestone and Harrison separate out some of the factors that affect growth, highlighting those that, in their view, have not received sufficient attention. In this book, they note that although public sector expenditures on infrastructure, education, and other matters are generally recognized as important to growth, their contribution is often simply rolled into the overall figures on productivity and growth credited to the private sector. This lack of specificity may lead us to underspend — or even, theoretically, to overspend — on the public sector without understanding the implications of that spending for overall growth. If we try to imagine a country with no public school system or interstate highway network, we realize that the impact of large-scale public investment must be significant, but a mental experiment is no substitute for the analytical work that will tell us whether or how economic policy should be adjusted to take full account of the role of government spending in growth.

As a startling example of the recent decline in public investment, Bluestone and Harrison point out that federal expenditures on education and training have dropped as a percent of GDP "an astounding 50 percent" since their peak in 1976. In this and other ways, this book jerks our attention back to policies that perhaps could change the bleak forecasts of slow growth into a more promising reality. Overall, Bluestone and Harrison see the role of government as neither inevitable nor necessarily positive. Rather, they make a strong case for learning more about the implications of public sector budget policy.

Bluestone and Harrison are also concerned about the increase in inequality: the stagnation of wages for a large share of workers and the exceptional concentration of financial assets in the hands of those in the top 10 percent of income. They point out that the unusual and widely noted upward race of the Dow Jones and Standard & Poor's averages has not meant a greater sharing of wealth. Nor has the run-up in mutual fund assets meant an increase in the share of equity wealth owned by the bottom 90 percent of the wealth distribution. In a low-growth future, the failure of most Americans to participate in the prosperity of the 1990s would have potentially somber implications.

The Century Foundation seeks authors who push beyond the conventional wisdom; therefore, we are especially pleased to sponsor this book. It is a superb addition to our growing body of work in this area, which includes Robert Kuttner, *Everything for Sale: The Virtues and Limits of Markets*; James K. Galbraith, *Created Unequal: The Crisis in American Pay*; Edward Wolff, *Top Heavy: The Increasing Inequality of Wealth in America*; Stephen A. Herzenberg, John A. Alic, and Howard Wial, *New Rules for a New Economy: Employment and Opportunity in Postindustrial America*; Theda Skocpol, *The Missing Middle: Working Families and the Future of American Social Policy*; Paul Osterman, *Securing Prosperity: The American Labor Market*; and John D. Donahue, *Hazardous Crosscurrents: Confronting Inequality in an Era of Devolution*. We also sponsor, with the Russell Sage Foundation, an ongoing task force studying sustainable employment, as well as Simon Head's study of the impact of technology on economic prosperity. Jonas Pontusson's look at the policies aimed at inequality that have been pursued in other nations, and Jeff Madrick's exploration of factors that influence productivity growth and its relation to income.

Bennett Harrison's untimely loss will deny us his rare combination of economic knowledge and imagination — as well as his fine personal character and commitment to doing good. His colleague, Barry Bluestone, however, saw this work through to conclusion in a fashion that, I am sure, would leave Ben well satisfied with this last jointly authored publication. On behalf of the foundation, I thank them both for adding to our understanding of the present and future of the American economy.

Richard C. Leone, President
The Century Foundation
December 2000

Preface

Some years ago, just after Ben Harrison and I had completed our book *The Great U-Turn,* documenting America's veer toward economic and social inequality, we were introduced to a large college audience by a moderator who closed his otherwise enthusiastic remarks with "And now I give you Dr. Doom and Dr. Gloom." Our earlier book together, *The Deindustrialization of America,* had presented extraordinary statistics about the numbers of workers who had lost their jobs to plant closings and the adverse effects those losses had on both their families and their communities. Now, in our second book, we were explaining how globalization and the restructuring of American business were creating a socially and economically polarized nation. The conditions we were warning about in the 1970s and 1980s easily could have earned us the honorary sobriquets that moderator bestowed upon us.

This new book is quite different. In fact, some may accuse us of being Pollyannas. In 1995, when Ben and I first talked of doing a third book together to investigate the possibility of another era of American prosperity like the one we grew up in during the 1950s and 1960s, there was scant evidence that America had reversed direction from its more than two decades of declining growth rates, frustratingly high unemployment, and a general feeling of malaise about the economy's potential. But as we burrowed deeper into the literature regarding the sources of economic growth, we realized that many of the elements needed for an economic renaissance were coming together. Improvements in productivity in the manufacturing sector, based on the utilization of new information technologies, hinted at what was to come in the service sector, where productivity growth had been dismal. We also came to understand that if the American economy could sustain red-hot growth, we would begin to see a reversal in the long-standing trend of falling wages and stagnating incomes — and even some closing of the income gap between rich and poor.

Still, it is only fair to say that we had moments when we questioned the entire premise of our work. Only as more and more data came to light, and as one quarter of good economic news led to another, did we gain real faith in our project.

At the same time, we became ever more acutely aware that the prosperity we forecast could be sabotaged by misguided economic policy. And the more we saw the political establishment along Pennsylvania Avenue adopt the nostrums of Wall Street, the more we worried that the potential for a more equally shared long-term prosperity could be compromised by an obsession with keeping financial markets happy and the stock market booming.

In the end, we remain optimistic about the economy's potential but deeply concerned that the newly evolving Wall Street–Pennsylvania Avenue policy accord will not permit that potential to be realized. We are not quite back to being Dr. Doom and Dr. Gloom, but there are days when those titles might still fit.

Tragically, as we worked to complete this book, Ben became ill with cancer, and his health deteriorated at an alarming rate. We finished a full draft of the manuscript only a couple of days before his death in January of this year. Since then I have painstakingly worked to refine the manuscript into a book that might precipitate some debate within our profession and, even more important, in public forums across the country. Whether the economy can achieve the goal of long-term growth with equity is the question at the center of virtually every major public policy debate today. We hope that this book, now in Ben's memory, can contribute to the debate by raising important questions for all to consider. Nothing would have made Ben happier. And nothing would have made me happier than to have had more years of collaborating with my very best friend and colleague. Ben and I always enjoyed walking in each other's shadow because it meant we could share each other's sunshine.

Many, if not most, of the ideas discussed here draw on the work of scholars and thinkers who have come before us. There are simply too many to thank, but their insights are well documented in the notes and bibliography. We wish to acknowledge the assistance of the scholars who were kind enough to read earlier drafts of our work and to provide us with a stream of comments that helped us refine our ideas. They include Eileen Applebaum, Bob Kuttner, Gerald Adams, Dick Nelson, Michael Bölle, Alan Blinder, Rafael Múnoz de Bustillo, Richard Leone, Greg Anrig, Steve Fraser, and our Houghton Mifflin editor, Anton Mueller. Lee Simmons did a magnificent job of copy editing the manuscript. We also benefited from the opportunities we had to present some of our ideas at seminars at the Economic Policy Institute in Washington, D.C., at the Wissenschaftscentrum and the Freie Universität in Berlin, at LASAIRE in Lyon, France, and at the Centro Internazionale di Studi Sociali (CISS) in Rome, Italy. At every seminar, a great many individuals added a thought here and a thought there that improved our understanding.

Finally, I must thank my lovely and patient wife, Mary Ellen Colten, and our eight-year-old son, Joshua, for putting up with the long gestation period of this book. Whether Joshua's budding soccer career was damaged by the inattention of his too often absent father will be a matter of some controversy for years to come.

Barry Bluestone
Cambridge, Massachusetts
July 1999

Preface to the Paperback Edition

After the publication of the first edition of *Growing Prosperity* in January 2000, the American economy soared to even greater heights than the original volume predicted. With surging economic growth pushing unemployment down to four percent, earnings and income inequality continued to wane. Then, in early 2001, the economy began to slow dramatically. The first hint of the downturn came just months before the new year as one dot.com company after another went belly-up. Corporate profit reports began to show red ink for the first time in years, spooking the stock market. NASDAQ, where the hot new technology stocks were housed, saw its price index plummet, eerily reminiscent of the Dow Jones Industrial Average in 1929. Consumer confidence began to tumble, leading to the fear that families would soon reduce their spending in anticipation of bad times. Such a reduction in household consumption could easily become a self-fulfilling prophecy. For the first time in nearly a decade, the word "recession" was muttered.

The slowdown in the economy was not totally unexpected. Beginning in late 1999, the Federal Reserve Board piled on seven quarter-point interest rate hikes in a row. It did this ostensibly to counteract the stock market's "irrational exuberance" and to bring the soaring economy to a soft landing rather than a hard crash. Clearly, by early 2001, Alan Greenspan and the Board recognized their early efforts amounted to overkill with a lag. An emergency cut of one half point in short-term interest rates in January was followed within weeks with another half point cut. But everyone knew that just as the original interest rate hikes took months to take effect, the rate cuts would entail a long lag too. By February, dozens of major companies were announcing layoffs and the official unemployment rate was on the rise. Now the concern was whether we were in for a brief period of economic stagnation or a full-blown recession. The optimists hoped we would be growing again by the second half of 2001. The pessimists hinted that the late 1990s economic boom was a joyful, but short-lived, aberration. A return to anemic growth with rising unemployment and increased inequality would be almost inevitable for years to come.

Is the boom over? Or does the economy have the wherewithal to overcome the current downturn and resume three percent or better annual economic growth into the foreseeable future?

The answer to these questions, we believe, lies in whether we have the wisdom to understand what brought us newfound prosperity in the first place and the political savvy to implement appropriate economic policy in light of that knowledge. Without a better idea of what has been responsible for the economic resurgence we have enjoyed, there is little hope that we will do the right things to keep the economic engine humming and assure the gains are equitably shared.

The recent U.S. presidential campaign, not to mention the bizarre culmination to the national election, did not help very much in this regard. Despite Ralph Nader's contention that George W. Bush and Al Gore resembled tweedledee and tweedledum, the two candidates expressed very different views on how to promote economic prosperity. Following in the tradition of Ronald Reagan's supply-side nostrums, President Bush continues to champion a huge tax cut (admittedly benefiting the rich the most) to keep America growing. Tax cuts would presumably stimulate both spending and saving, spurring the economy in the short run and boosting private investment over the long term. For his part, Mr. Gore claimed, to the day he conceded defeat, that he would make America "even better" by saving the lion's share of the projected federal government surplus in order to quickly eliminate the nation's entire multi-trillion dollar privately-held federal debt. Debt reduction, he affirmed, would help sustain American prosperity by keeping interest rates low and inflation at bay, boosting private investment.

The problem, as this book attempts to explain, is that neither candidate provided much insight into the real sources of economic growth. Indeed, both the tax policy that Bush promised to implement and Gore's debt retirement pledge could do more to sabotage long-term prosperity than promote it. Since both candidates shared a fundamental misconception of why the American economy began to grow again in the mid-1990s, both failed to offer an appropriate public policy to sustain this growth.

This volume tries to explain why America experienced such a profound and exhilarating economic renaissance in the 1990s and what it will take to maintain this newfound prosperity. It challenges the conventional wisdom that President Clinton's commitment to deficit reduction and the Fed's obsession with inflation containment were the keys to economic revival. The book reviews a great deal of growth theory—emanating from economists who work in the neo-classical tradition as well as from those who are their critics—so that students and others can judge what factors promote economic growth in an information age. It also lays out a set of policies aimed at promoting growth and greater economic equity based on this exploration of theory.

The paperback version is virtually identical to the original book with one exception. Since the original appeared, new data have been issued by the government on productivity and growth. Using more sophisticated techniques, statistics for past years have been revised and we now have more recent data documenting the nation's economic progress. As a result, the tables and charts in Chapters 2 and 3 have been updated. If anything, the new and revised statistics make the argument for growth presented in this book even stronger.

One last note. Soon after this book first appeared in hardcover, I was invited to a number of high level conferences in Europe and in Japan to explain the ideas Ben and I had captured in this latest book of ours. With their nations' unemployment rates in double-digits, German and Italian audiences wanted to know the secret of America's economic success. Mired in recession, the Japanese were even more curious. Almost universally, those in the audience assumed that balancing the federal budget, reining in inflation, and increasing labor market "flexibility" through weaker unions, freer international trade, and welfare reform were the sine qua non of America's economic renaissance. They were therefore more than a little surprised when I disabused them of this idea. After all, they had been told this tale in virtually every business publication they had read in English or in their own language. When I told them the roots of the current prosperity could be traced to public investment policies of the 1960s and 1970s, they were more than mildly interested.

To challenge the conventional wisdom by identifying various streams of growth theory is the purpose of this volume as it was in those lectures. If this book helps to broaden the discourse in the U.S. and abroad about the sources of growth and appropriate public policy, we will know that this effort was ultimately a success.

Barry Bluestone
Cambridge, Massachusetts
February 19, 2001

Growing Prosperity

Chapter 1

Growth with Equity

F ROM THE END of World War II until the early 1970s, America reveled in its "glory days." The economy grew so swiftly that by 1973 the typical family had more than twice as much income as it did in 1947. On the strength of the economy and Lyndon Johnson's War on Poverty, those at the bottom of the economic ladder enjoyed improvements in income that were proportionately greater than those of the most wealthy. As a result, we experienced economic growth with at least a modicum of improved social equity. There was great turmoil in the land, but its root cause was political, not economic. In the midst of the great civil rights struggle, the assassinations of John and Robert Kennedy, Martin Luther King, Jr., and Malcolm X, the tragedy of Vietnam, and the persistent underlying fear of nuclear obliteration, few worried about the overall strength of the economy. Growth seemed assured, and the nation was at least trying to address the question of social inequality.

Then, quite suddenly, the bottom fell out. The glory days ended with the 1973 oil embargo, but even after gas and oil prices stabilized and then fell, the economy continued to stagnate. Over a period of more than three decades, the nation's growth rate moved inexorably downward, from 4.4 percent in the 1960s and 3.2 percent in the 1970s to 3.0 percent in the 1980s, and finally only 2.3 percent in the early 1990s. Average wages and family incomes stopped growing, and for many actually declined. Inequality in earnings, income, and wealth — the gap between the best- and the worst-off among us — intensified without letup. Experts, while never quite understanding why the glory days came to such an abrupt end, worried that we had lost our competitive edge and wondered if we could ever catch up with the Europeans, let alone the Japanese. American productivity growth had slipped to less than one percent a year. Ordinary people told journalists and pollsters, and whoever else would listen, of their growing sense of insecurity and of their fears for the future — if not for themselves, then for their children.

By the early 1990s, many had come to the conclusion that we Americans had better get used to slow growth, for it was now going to be a more or less permanent condition of life for most of us. We would do well to learn to accept modest improvements in the economy, counseled MIT's distinguished economist Paul Krugman in his popular tract, *The Age of Diminished Expectations*. The much admired journalist Jeffrey Madrick admonished us to begin to deal with *The End of Affluence*. Those who reached this conclusion seemed to be on reasonably strong ground, for there appeared to be no indication of a recovery in the nation's labor productivity — output per hour worked — despite the proliferation of computers into every aspect of life.[1] Without more productivity, there could not be much more growth.

Indeed, those who had been optimistic about the nation's economic future found their forecasts going badly awry. In *The Coming Boom*, published in 1982, the conservative futurist Herman Kahn (who had previously thought the unthinkable about thermonuclear war in the 1960s) assured us that we could expect relatively high and sustained growth rates throughout the 1980s and 1990s. He based this upbeat prediction on the fact that "a whole host of new technologies and technological improvements are now (or soon will be) ripe for large-scale exploitation."[2] Two years before Kahn's book appeared, Alvin Toffler's blockbuster best-seller *The Third Wave* promised a new economic epoch of unparalleled prosperity nearly at hand. Supply-side economists promised faster growth as the payoff for Reagan era tax cuts and the wholesale repeal of government regulations. Alas, they all had it wrong. Subsequent to these heady pronouncements, growth rates continued to slide downhill, and we ended up suffering for the next decade and a half the slowest average growth since the Great Depression.

Then, just when we were on the verge of accepting slow growth as our lot, the economy surged again. The first inkling of a revival was felt in the mid-1990s, and for the rest of the decade we enjoyed a renaissance economy that bordered on giddy exuberance. The nation's gross domestic product (GDP) — the broadest measure of economic output —

expanded by 3.4 percent in 1996 and then turned in spectacular back-to-back 3.9 percent performances in both 1997 and 1998.[3] By 1999, growth was beginning to be reminiscent of the postwar glory days. In President Clinton's famous phrase, "we are growing the economy" once more — at a pace considerably faster than any expert or policymaker could have expected, predicted, or counseled even a few years ago.

Growth was paying off in newfound prosperity. By the end of the 1990s, a larger share of Americans were working than at any time in the twentieth century: almost two-thirds of all Americans sixteen years of age or older.[4] Officially measured unemployment fell to levels not seen since the early 1970s. Even so, inflation remained firmly in check, slipping to under 2 percent per year. The stock market boomed, reflecting a sustained burst in corporate profits. The Dow Jones industrial average rose at an annual rate of better than 20 percent for an unprecedented three years running and closed out the fourth (1998) up another 16 percent. By early 1999 it had broken through the 10,000 mark and was marching quickly toward 11,000. For the first time in two decades, the median real (or inflation-adjusted) wage rate stopped falling and actually rose slightly, even for those at the bottom of the scale.[5] At the root of these improvements was a recovery in productivity growth far beyond what anyone could have imagined would again be feasible. With all of this good economic news, consumer confidence soared, hitting a thirty-two-year high in early 1999, and we began to imagine a new virtuous cycle of growth where good times augured more of the same.[6]

A New Era of Prosperity?

How did this wondrous turnabout occur? And can it last? After wandering in the economic desert for twenty-five years, have we finally reached the promised land — or is this just a tiny oasis? Were the great glory days following World War II the anomaly, or the subsequent quarter century of slow growth? As we enter the twenty-first century, the paramount question is whether we shall have the wherewithal to convert a short-term boom into lasting prosperity — and find a way to share the bounty more equitably.

We believe an optimistic view of our nation's *potential* is warranted. Indeed, we are substantially more upbeat about the economy's future growth potential than are the official forecasts of the White House and congressional agencies charged with charting the economy. The information revolution, now more than a quarter century in the making, is finally bearing a much richer economic harvest than most mainstream economists ever believed possible, while fundamental changes in the labor market are adding to the nation's growth rate. Moreover, there is growing evidence that a red-hot economy is the sine qua non for reversing the economic polarization of America.

We are a lot less sanguine, however, about whether we can turn the economy's potential and its recent short-term success into long-run prosperity. Much of this book explains why. The problem, essentially, is that in the 1990s we as a nation adopted a model of economic growth and a set of economic policies that, while seeming to turn economic gloom into glory, will likely end up sabotaging the very prosperity we might otherwise enjoy.

The story we are about to tell involves a momentous clash between two big ideas about what makes economies prosper. One is about financial markets, private investment, savings, inflation, and interest rates. The beauty of this model is that it rests on a simple Cartesian logic elegantly tying the rate of economic growth to just two controllable factors: the *rate of inflation* and the *national savings rate*. In this view, now dominant in the land, if the government focuses its full attention on assuring price stability and encouraging private and public savings, interest rates will fall, financial markets will respond with a flood of investment funds, business will boom, and prosperity will be the result. In line with this new conventional wisdom, the government's role in the economy shrinks tremendously compared with what it had been from the time of Franklin Roosevelt to that of Richard Nixon.[7]

The competing big idea about the source of economic growth is considerably more controversial. It focuses on the central importance of *technological innovation* and *public investment,* and on how economic and political *institutions* relate to each other in the production of economic growth. According to this theory, growth depends more on successful innovation than on any other factor. It requires the public sector to ensure an adequate level of research and development, infrastructure investment, education, and training in order to foster new technologies and prepare the labor force to take advantage of them. In this view, the government should invest more in the economy, not less, and should do everything it can to keep the economy running red-hot.

The battle between these two economic models would be irrelevant if it had remained in the province of arcane academic journals, but it has not. In the decade of the 1990s, the new conventional wisdom tying growth to price stability and savings rates triumphed on both ends of Pennsylvania Avenue in Washington, and it is now having enormous influence on public policy in other capitals around the world. And why not? When inflation was low in the 1950s and 1960s, and households and governments were more parsimonious, the economy soared. When inflation took off in the 1970s and savings rates fell, the economy soured. Only when we regained price stability in the 1990s and the government boosted national savings by moving toward fiscal surplus did growth return. The simple logic of *post hoc, ergo propter hoc* (after this, therefore because of this) was too obvious to ignore. It seemed to follow that if government focused its attention mainly on getting prices under control and boosting public savings, all kinds of good things would follow.

The original conception of the new conventional wisdom was the work of economists working within the standard "neoclassical" paradigm, but its most ardent proponents were those who earn their living on Wall Street. Low inflation and high savings rates have always been good for the stock market and those who play it. Thus, when the seemingly dispassionate truth of economic theory met the passion of Wall Street, there was a phalanx of support for economic policies driven by the commitment to price stability. What made the 1990s different was not so much the theory or Wall Street's adherence to it but the fact that both the White House and Congress bought into it — hook, line, and sinker.[8] In this new era, as Secretary of the Treasury Larry Summers puts it, "Financial markets don't just oil the wheels of economic growth; they are the wheels."[9] What is good for Wall Street is good for America.

As the wisdom of this proposition began to sink in, the outlines of a new *Wall Street–Pennsylvania Avenue "policy accord"* began to take form. With Wall Street's backing and political support from both ends of Pennsylvania Avenue, federal policy would be redirected toward the twin goals of subduing inflation and reducing government deficits in order to stimulate growth. This commitment ultimately would shape not only government budget policy, but trade legislation, labor market initiatives, and monetary policy as well. In a short period of time, a neoclassical growth model developed by economists, a conception of a virtuous growth cycle espoused by financial leaders, and the new policy accord would come to dominate global thinking about what makes economies prosper. Almost as soon as the new elixir — what we shall call the *Wall Street model* — was tried, the economy seemed to spring miraculously to life, exactly as the proponents of the new conventional wisdom had advertised. GDP soared, millions of jobs were created, and unemployment plummeted. Who could argue with such extraordinary success, so immediately at hand?

We shall. What we will endeavor to prove is that the theory behind the new conventional wisdom is badly flawed, that its elaborate model of growth is based on the most unstable and speculative of market forces, and that the public policies consistent with it will almost inevitably undermine the very growth it is supposed to generate. To be sure, we ignore the threat of inflation at our peril, but we also suffer if we become too obsessed with it. In this moment of economic ebullience, we are betting our future on a panacea that seemingly offers sustained growth with equity, but which in the end will provide us neither.

The Nation's Growth Potential

The first question we need to ask is just how fast the economy can grow. This is, in fact, a matter of great debate. Recently, conservative politicians and some of America's leading business groups have tended to gaze into more promising crystal balls. In his unsuccessful bid for the Republican presidential nomination in 1992, Steve Forbes battered George Bush for being too pessimistic about growth, arguing that if we only had another round of large tax cuts and a further slashing of government budgets, the economy could grow at 5 percent a year. Former congressman Jack Kemp has never doubted the ability of the economy to expand at this pace, regardless of the fact that the economy has done this well in only a handful of years out of the last two hundred.[10]

The National Association of Manufacturers (NAM) has taken a more cautious tack but inveighs against anything less than 3 percent growth as too pessimistic.[11] Supporting that position, *Business Week,* the leading journal of American enterprise, has been touting a new era of growth ever since 1994, when the economy still seemed unable to grow at any more than half that rate. The good news, according to their economic analysts, is that America's "new economy" — based on the revolution in information technologies, the growth of global markets, the privatization of government functions, and changes in the organization of America's leading companies — is capable of reviving the growth we enjoyed during the glory days.[12] *Wall Street Journal* reporters Bob Davis and David Wessel have signed on to the new prosperity bandwagon as well.[13] In addition to praising the new technologies, they see the growth in community colleges as now producing a labor force that can take full advantage of what the new technologies have wrought.

Ironically, the government's own number crunchers are among the least optimistic about the economy. Chief among the "realists" counseling modest growth, even after four years of a booming economy, is no less eminent a group than the president's Council of Economic Advisers (CEA). Among its many roles, the CEA is charged with developing the official White House growth forecasts for the economy. At the other end of Pennsylvania Avenue is the Congressional Budget Office (CBO), which regularly grinds out predictions for Congress. In their 1999 Report, the CEA forecasts GDP growth of no more than 2.3 *percent* per year well into the next decade — exactly the same forecast it has made every year since 1996, regardless of the *fin-de-siècle* boom we have enjoyed.[14] The CBO estimate is virtually identical.

This 2.3 percent "speed limit" for the economy is based on the belief that no matter how well the economy may have performed in the second half of the 1990s, labor productivity will not grow any faster than 1.2 percent a year in the foreseeable future, while expansion of the labor force will add no more than 1.1 percent to annual output.[15] Even this forecast is downright rosy compared to what the actuaries at the Social Security Administration foresee. They predict that growth will retreat from 2.3 percent to no more than 1.5 percent over the next seventy-five years.[16]

Growth at 2.3 percent per year is obviously better than no growth, but it surely reflects an "age of diminished expectations" and an "end of affluence" given America's history. It pales in comparison with the average annual growth record of over 3 percent that we have enjoyed throughout most of the nineteenth and twentieth centuries (1800–1989). Indeed, if the nation's GDP grows by only 2.3 percent over the next decade, it will not even come close to the average 3.2 percent growth we experienced between World War II and the beginning of the present decade, a period that includes two decades of slow growth after 1973.[17] Is this really the best we can do?

Based on a great deal of new research, much of it reported in this book, we believe that labor productivity growth can be maintained at a new, higher rate, which, in turn, will permit faster growth. We agree with those who think a 3 percent growth rate in GDP well into the future is within the realm of possibility. Once you begin to understand the dynamics of the current revolutions in both technology and labor supply and consider them in light of history and emerging new theories of growth, sustained economic expansion at a 3 percent or better annual rate becomes quite plausible after all.

At this point, one might ask, "What's the big deal here?" The pessimists predict 2.3 percent; these cockeyed optimists predict a mere 0.7 percentage points higher. Why quibble over such a small difference? Don't economists have something better to do with their time?

In fact, the difference is enormous. When that small increment of 0.7 percentage points *per year* cumulates over time, thanks to compound growth rates, the impact on GNP is massive.[18] Between 1999 and 2008, that difference amounts to more than $3.2 *trillion* in total real output — better than $320 billion per year. That $3.2 trillion in otherwise foregone output would turn the Social Security "crisis" into a quite manageable affair and still make possible a sizable down payment on rebuilding America's cities, improving education, and cleaning up the environment — not to mention what it could mean for employment, wages, and family incomes.[19] If we did not want to take the added growth in the form of material goods and services, we could take it in added leisure. Every worker in America could take the equivalent of a five-month fully paid sabbatical sometime during the decade.

Faster Growth, More Equity

But that is only part of the good fortune that faster growth could provide. History reveals that sustained pedal-to-the-metal economic growth is critical to accomplish another long sought goal: the reversal of the enormous inequalities in income and wealth that have developed since the early 1970s. During the postwar glory days, rapid growth brought jobless rates to below 4 percent for the last four years of the 1960s, permitting many workers who had been denied access to the job market a more-or-less regular stream of wage income. The result was that nearly every measure of income inequality showed improvement, as those at the bottom were finally able to participate in the cornucopia of jobs and income provided by the economy. To be sure, large numbers of Americans did not prosper, including many in the nation's black community. The wage gap between women and men also remained stubbornly high. Still, the movement toward narrowing the gulf between the rich and the poor was hardly insignificant.

When the economy slowed, inequality surged. Just as mainstream economists have never been able to fully explain the post-1973 slowdown in growth, they have failed to account for the sharp increase in inequality that began at the same time and continued right into the mid-1990s. Most concluded that technological change was to blame, benefitting those with skills and punishing those without. Others saw globalization and competition from less developed countries as the culprit. Still others blamed the weakening of such social protections as the minimum wage.[20] In any case, nearly all perceived no end in sight for the inexorable rise in inequality. Indeed, on this particular forecast the Left and the Right found themselves in agreement.

Now there is mounting evidence that both may be wrong. During the late 1990s, when growth rates broke through the 3 percent barrier, median annual household income finally stopped falling and began rising again. The most recent census data we have show modest improvements between 1994 and 1996, followed by stronger growth in 1997 and 1998. In the private sector, overall compensation (including benefits as well as wages and salaries) increased by 3.4 percent in 1997. Wages and salaries alone rose even faster, up 3.9 percent from the year before. This was the largest annual increase in seven years.[21] In 1998, median weekly wages finally regained the ground lost in the 1990 recession, with incomes at the low end of the distribution growing faster than those in the middle or at the top.[22]

With the recovery in income growth, the overall dispersion in annual household incomes flattened out after 1993, following a full quarter century of increasing inequality. An examination of the share of all household income going to the bottom 60 percent of the population shows the same thing: a sharp decline up to 1993 and then essentially no worsening since then.[23] The story about the poverty rate is even a little better. The share of individuals with incomes below the poverty line has been falling throughout the current expansion, from 15.1 percent in 1993 to 11.8 percent in 1999, the most recent year for which the Census Bureau provides information. For families, the levels of poverty are slightly different, but the trajectory is the same. Moreover, even the historic gap in poverty rates between whites and blacks closed slightly during this period.[24]

The lesson is becoming clear. Growth rates matter when it comes to reducing inequality in general and racial and ethnic inequality in particular. But it takes a red-hot economy, sustained over a long period of time, to make a difference. While the skills and social capital of workers, the enforcement of antidiscrimination laws and regulations, and other institutional structures make a difference, without sustained growth, none of these antipoverty, antidiscrimination policies are likely to work very well. Rapid growth is a necessary condition.

And there's the catch. If we are stuck at no better than 2.3 percent growth over the long term, it is hard to fathom how we can make any more than a tiny dent in inequality, let alone substantially reverse it.

From the Main Street Model of Growth to the Wall Street Model

Whether the U.S. economy can break through the 2.3 percent speed limit, leading us to a new era of prosperity more equally shared, will ultimately depend on what model of growth we decide to pursue.

Historically, periods of exceptional economic growth have been stimulated by the opening of vast tracts of land, by the discovery of rich deposits of oil and ore, or by new inventions — from the spinning jenny that launched the industrial revolution to the steam engine and the railroad that marked the full realization of the industrial age. Each of these discoveries and inventions gave new impetus to economic growth.

So too has been the mighty influence of the *demand* side of the market. Mountains of World War II household savings, for example, fueled a postwar buying spree, not only inducing new capital investment to satisfy it, but creating the incentive for business to invest in a vast array of new consumer product innovations. If ordinary workers and consumers had not felt as well off as they did at the end of World War II, it is doubtful whether the 1950s would have become the golden age of the automobile, whether television would have exploded onto the American scene quite as fast as a new medium for news and entertainment, or whether by the end of the decade, Boeing jet airliners would have been setting a new standard for speed and comfort in commercial air travel.

Figure 1.1. The Post–World War II Virtuous Cycle

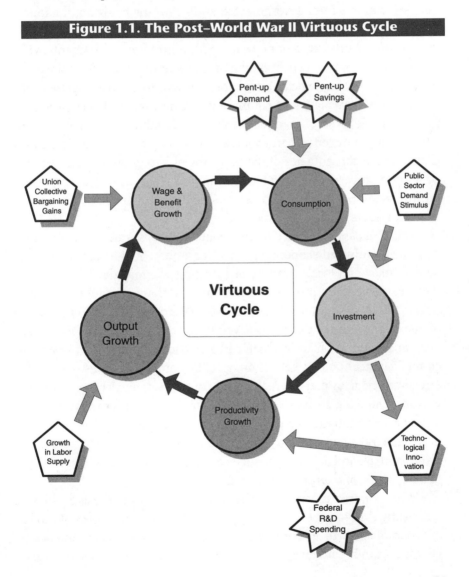

11

In retrospect, we can discern the key factors that stimulated the sustained GDP growth rates in excess of 4 percent that we enjoyed in the first two decades following the war. Together, they provide the essential ingredients of what we might call the *Main Street model* of economic growth. As Figure 1.1 depicts, a combination of enormous pent-up demand and pent-up savings after the war set off a consumption boom the likes of which no country had ever seen. The consumption boom, along with additional stimulus from government spending on the cold war, the interstate highway system, the GI Bill, and the expansion of public amenities in city and suburb led to unprecedented levels of new investment. With demand for new products booming and capital expenditures rising, the incentive for technological innovation was extraordinary. Together, investments in new plant and equipment and new technologies provided for remarkable levels of productivity growth. Combined with increases in labor supply, induced in part by a ready access to jobs, economic growth took off. As a consequence of the prodding of strong unions and the imposition of government-mandated minimum wage requirements, faster growth meant rising wages and benefits, so that workers benefited as well as stockholders, and income inequality declined.

This *virtuous cycle,* based on rising family incomes and consumption, continually refueled economic growth for a quarter of a century. So did federal, state, and local government spending. We may not have relished the idea of spending profuse amounts of tax dollars on national defense during the cold war, but the research and development (R&D) generated by the Department of Defense on everything from synthetic rubber, plastics, radar, and sonar to jet fighter planes had an enormous impact on commercial technology. Television, satellite communications, and modern commercial airliners were just a few of the benefits. The government was an invaluable partner with the private sector in producing technological breakthroughs in all manner of industry. Similarly, the construction of the interstate highway system and a national system of airports, air traffic control, and aircraft guidance beacons ushered in a whole new era of auto, truck, and airline transportation.

What is extraordinary about the new growth spurt of the late 1990s is that nearly everyone believes it has been based on a very different model of economic growth. According to the new *Wall Street model,* America is growing again because we have the best, most varied, and most pervasive set of instruments for accumulating and distributing finance capital of any country in the world. Economic success — the maintenance of steady growth — depends first and foremost, according to this new model of growth, on assuring a rising stock market. Anything that helps do this is basically good; anything that might put a damper on the accumulation of paper wealth is bad. In a nutshell, keeping Wall Street happy is now considered the surest way to help Main Street, not the other way round.

A Primer on the Wall Street Model

The mechanics of the Wall Street model have been elucidated best by Alan Greenspan, chairman of the Federal Reserve Board. It all begins not with the demand of consumers and governments or with new technology, as in the Main Street model, but with what is now seen as the successful government-led war against inflation. As Greenspan testified before the Joint Economic Committee of Congress in mid-1998, "The essential *precondition* for the emergence, and persistence, of this virtuous cycle is arguably the decline in the rate of inflation to near price stability" — which, in turn, provides the precondition for a stock market boom. [25]

Wall Street's version of the virtuous cycle works something like what we see in Figure 1.2. Bringing inflation under control allows interest rates to fall. This stimulates more capital investment, but most important, it provides a huge incentive for wealth holders to invest in equities. As financial portfolios appreciate, owners of stock feel wealthier. This leads to more discretionary spending — mostly by those of means, given their disproportionate ownership of stocks and mutual funds. Increased spending then leads to expanded output, higher employment, and further investments in productivity-enhancing capital — more machines, more factories, and more office towers. In turn, more productive capital means higher corporate profits. Profits ratify the higher stock prices and send them even higher. And so it goes. In the process, Main Street gets a share of the growth as higher employment levels and higher productivity permit faster wage growth and rising family incomes.

What we earlier termed the Wall Street–Pennsylvania Avenue policy accord gets the credit for this wonderful turn of events. The most important element of the new accord was the balancing of the federal budget.

Figure 1.2. Wall Street Virtuous Cycle

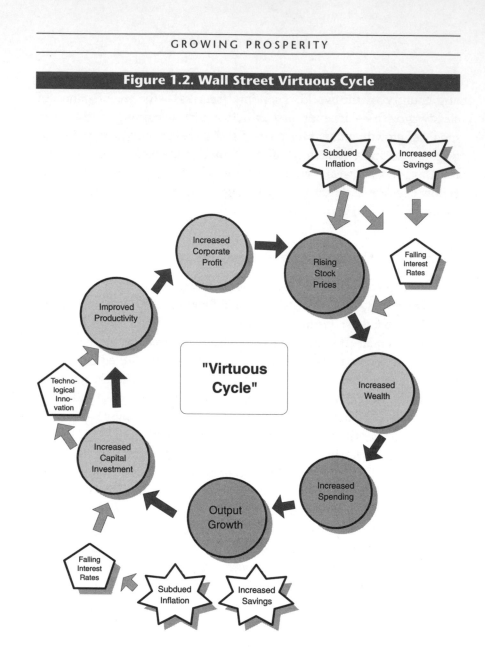

The White House and Congress committed themselves in principle and then in practice to bringing government spending into line with government revenue; having done this faster than expected, they then moved on to accruing a large budget surplus. This, according to the new conventional wisdom, would add to the national savings rate, reduce competition for consumption goods (thus reducing demand pressure on prices), and reduce competition for investment funds (by taking the government out of the borrowing business). This would help keep inflation under control, drive down long-term interest rates, and presumably stimulate growth.

But there was more to the anti-inflation aspect of the accord than budget balance. A second weapon in the war on inflation was a renewed and heightened commitment to free trade. This led to the passage of the North American Free Trade Agreement (NAFTA) with Canada and Mexico and a host of other bilateral and multilateral tariff reductions. While these trade agreements were enacted ostensibly to increase U.S. exports, their real objective was to keep downward pressure on wages and prices by spurring even more global competition.

Increasing the "flexibility" of labor markets became the third principle in the accord. Arguing that strong trade unions, periodic hikes in minimum wage laws, and overly generous welfare programs coddle labor and drive up wages, the accord frowned on any form of labor law reform that might help unions organize more workers. Minimum wages were increased, but by a trivial amount. Welfare reform focused on forcing millions of nonworking people into the paid labor force. Each of these policies may have been sold to the White House and Congress for different reasons, but the single underlying theme behind all of them was to encourage growth by increasing labor market "flexibility" and thereby curbing inflation.

Reinforcing all of this was the Federal Reserve's commitment to backstopping all efforts at holding the line on inflation. The Federal Reserve Board gained the confidence of Wall Street by demonstrating its vigilance at maintaining price stability, raising short-term interest rates in 1994 and again in 1995 as an inoculation against inflation. Since then, the Fed has practiced a more patient monetary policy, much to the credit of Chairman Greenspan. It has refrained from raising interest rates even as the unemployment rate came down below a level considered unsafe just a few years ago. Still, on numerous occasions the Fed has warned of impending inflationary pressure and has made it clear that interest rates would be raised at the slightest sign of upward movement in prices.

This new accord — based on balanced federal budgets, free trade, flexible labor markets, and a firm monetary policy — seems to have worked like a charm. As America continues to pull ahead of Europe in growth and employment, and as the once booming Asian economies struggle to regain their economic momentum, the wisdom of the Wall Street model is being acclaimed by an increasingly large and vocal chorus of economists, policymakers, pundits, and journalists, not only in the United States but also abroad. Prime Minister Tony Blair in England and Chancellor Gerhard Schroeder in Germany have taken on the mantle of Bill Clinton and embraced the Wall Street model. In Europe, it is now called "the Third Way."[26] As acceptance of the new paradigm grows, we are being cautioned that any deviation from its precepts or the government policies that support it could be fatal to continued prosperity. Keeping Wall Street happy is not only *a* road to prosperity — it is now seen as the *only* road. All others are detours to economic stagnation.

What's Wrong with This Picture?

Have we finally discovered the true path to sustained growth and renewed prosperity? All the signs look positive, but impressions can be deceiving. On the verge of the twenty-first century, the economy is indeed performing exceptionally well and has the potential to perform even better. But contrary to what has become nearly universal opinion, there is mounting evidence that this success has had little to do with the Wall Street model or the accommodations the government has made to conform with it. In fact, there are reasons to fear that the policies prescribed in the Wall Street–Pennsylvania Avenue accord will ultimately undermine future prosperity if we continue to rely on them to guide the economy.

How can we be so optimistic about the prospects for growth yet so critical of the Wall Street model that most economists credit for those prospects? Here, in summary, is our brief against the new conventional wisdom.

First, the underlying theory behind the Wall Street model is itself badly flawed, and it has cause and effect reversed. Low inflation no doubt contributes to faster growth by providing a stable financial base for investment. But low inflation did not come about because we balanced the federal budget, passed NAFTA, blocked labor law reform, or raised short-term interest rates early in the decade. What caused inflation to disappear in the late 1980s and throughout the 1990s was a return to high productivity growth that was long in coming, augmented by extraordinarily low oil prices and a labor force numbed by years of employment insecurity.[27]

Understanding the path of productivity growth during the past half century and what caused it is crucial to this story. Just as productivity growth seemed to instantaneously vanish at the beginning of the 1970s, it seems to have suddenly returned by the mid-1990s. Rising productivity has enabled businesses to increase their profits without having to raise prices. This is the main reason that stocks have soared in value and the key reason why inflation has vanished. Similarly, faster growth based on revived productivity has been the chief reason that federal budget deficits have disappeared, improving the national savings rate. The much acclaimed balanced budgets and vigilant Federal Reserve actions provided little more than the felicitous incantations over an already recovering economy. Even if we had not so quickly reduced the budget deficit, even if we had not passed NAFTA, even if we had legislated labor law reform and hiked the minimum wage more aggressively, and even if the Fed had not boosted short-term interest rates in the early 1990s, we would have had pretty much the same economic growth spurt we have experienced since the middle of the 1990s.

The Real Sources of Long-Run Growth

Such a cavalier dismissal of the Wall Street model would seem to overlook one important detail. If renewed productivity growth is the real root cause of economic growth, where did *it* come from? If Wall Street did not establish the preconditions for a productivity renaissance, what did?

A careful reading of the historical record demonstrates that the major reason for the surge in growth can be found in the long awaited coming of age of the *information revolution,* which is now spreading from one sector of the economy to another and *finally* boosting productivity and growth in its wake, even in the long-stagnant service sector. The newest productivity data indicate that companies have finally been working their way down the "learning curves" of a host of new technologies, gradually introducing organizational and other complementary institutional changes needed to take fuller advantage of the new hardware and software. All of this predates balanced budgets, NAFTA, welfare reform, and the Fed's vigilant anti-inflationary policy. In other words, it predates the implementation of the Wall Street model.

The history of technological innovation teaches us that what is happening now is not at all unusual; it typically takes decades for ideas to be translated into practical applications and diffuse throughout the economy. Indeed, when a revolutionary new technology is first introduced, it normally *reduces* productivity and growth for decades. Moreover, we now know that the process of technological innovation does not run in only one direction, from the laboratory to the workplace. There is frequent feedback from the workplace to the design stage as well, driven by the need to solve problems that arise in application, eventually improving what had begun as practical tinkering. Such lags and feedbacks are the norm, not the exception.[28] The point is that the long promised but seemingly elusive productivity premium from information technology is finally being realized, and it would have arrived even if fiscal and monetary policies had not been so focused on price stability and raising savings rates.

It is also important to recognize what initiated the information revolution in the first place. One might think that it was the brainchild of scientists and engineers toiling away in university laboratories and in the research facilities of private business. This is generally true, but the initiative for this research and a good part of the funds that underwrote it came from the government. It was the need for massive computing power to run modern defense systems that led to the construction of powerful mainframe computers. It was the need for miniaturized guidance systems for ICBMs and NASA rockets that led to the development of microprocessors and the software that they use. It was the federal government's investment in the ARPANET that led to the modern day Internet and the World Wide Web. In the private sector, firms believed they had to invest in the new technologies even though the payoff was unsure and perhaps many years away. Being left behind in the technology derby, corporate leaders feared, could leave a company out of the race altogether.

Without these investments, today's ubiquitous E-commerce might never have come about — or might have been delayed by decades. It is no wonder that the United States is doing so well today in computers and information technology relative to even our most advanced trading partners. The investments the federal government made in these technologies, mainly through the Department of Defense, put American firms such as Intel, Microsoft, Sun, Dell, Apple, Hewlett-Packard, and Compaq well ahead of the global pack. Similarly, medical research in government-funded laboratories has provided us with a leg up in biotechnology, scanning devices, and a range of pharmaceuticals.

Even Europe has learned this lesson. For a long time, U.S. government investments in military aircraft provided the basic and applied research for American dominance in commercial aircraft. Europe answered with large-scale government subsidies to the multinational Airbus consortium and to fly-by-wire technologies.[29] As a result, Airbus is now winning sales away from Boeing at an accelerating rate. Not surprisingly, economists find that $1 of federal basic research leverages an estimated $3 of private investment in the elements of economic growth.[30] This was good for the United States and it has been good for Europe.

While historians have been responsible for helping us to understand technology's role in economic growth and government's role in technology, a group of young economists has been taking these historical insights and creating a rigorous new model of growth that rejects many of the notions in the Wall Street model. Instead of seeing economic growth coming mainly from piling up ever larger stocks of factories, machines, and equipment in response to low interest rates, the New Growth theory sees technological innovation as the primary engine of growth. This alternative growth theory is consistent with a very different set of government policies.

As Paul Romer, one of the originators of the New Growth theory, has written, if we subscribe to the new model,

> We will be able to rejoin the ongoing policy debates about tax subsidies for private research, antitrust exemptions for research joint ventures, the activities of multinational firms, the effects of government procurement, the feedback between trade policy and innovation, the scope of protection for intellectual property rights, the links between private firms and universities, the mechanisms for selecting the research areas that receive public support, and the costs and benefits of an explicit government-led technology policy.[31]

It is precisely such public intervention in the economy — more federal spending, more tax incentives for research, more private sector-

public sector joint ventures, and more guidance of technology policy —
that the proponents of the Wall Street model vociferously oppose, in the
interest of balancing the federal books and sending reassuring signals to
the financial markets.

The Key Role of Demand

Still, new technology by itself can never bring about more growth. The
New Growth theorists have focused almost all of their attention on the
supply side of the economy; they are concerned with promoting productivity growth by accelerating technological innovation. But attention is
also needed on the demand side of the market. Without the expectation
of growth, innovation will be slow to evolve. Low expectations become
self-fulfilling prophecies.

In direct contradiction to the Wall Street model, the government has
a positive, activist role to play in stimulating aggregate demand. It can do
this by encouraging wage growth through stronger trade unions, regular
increases in the minimum wage, and deliberate antipoverty programs.
Spending more on education, highways, and health care can help as well.
Only with the anticipation of sufficient sales of new goods and services is
there adequate incentive for private sector innovation and investment to
take place at levels sufficient to maintain faster growth.[32] By marrying the
New Growth theory's passion for technology with the older Keynesian
theory's idea that government can help sustain aggregate demand, we
have the building blocks for a twenty-first century Main Street model of
growth with equity. A combination of innovative investment *plus* a commitment to running the economy as hot as possible amounts to a viable
alternative to the Wall Street model. If we can make the transition from
Wall Street to Main Street, we can sustain 3 percent or better economic
growth and assure that this faster growth is more equitably shared.

Will following this new Main Street model of growth ultimately permit us to repeal the business cycle, providing regular year-in, year-out improvements in our standard of living? That would be too much to ask for.
Volatility in the economy is here to stay, for successful innovation does
not flow smoothly but comes in spurts. We cannot expect that every time
the economy begins to slow some new invention will come along in the

nick of time to buoy productivity and enhance aggregate demand. What the new Main Street model will do is lift the nation's average growth rate so that periodic softness in the economy represents a decline from loftier heights, and it promises to make both the highs and the lows more fairly shared.

Rejecting the Wall Street Model

If the arrival of the productivity premium from early investments in information technologies is really the source of the 1990s growth spurt, would it not still be wise to follow the precepts of the Wall Street model when it comes to public policy? Would this not help sustain the growth we have already enjoyed?

This turns out to be bad advice for several reasons. First, we might ask, what if the Wall Street model actually did work as advertised? Would this give us cause to rejoice? The answer is no. Nothing in the economy (with the possible exception of hedge funds) is more unstable than the stock market. Does it make sense to bet our future on something as uncertain, as mercurial as stock prices? If the process really worked as the Wall Street model presumes, then when bull markets inevitably turn bearish, the virtuous cycle becomes a vicious cycle. After years of rocketing stock market prices, history tells us that the market will eventually level off or, more likely, take a dive. If we follow the precepts of a model that ties prosperity inextricably to the price of such equities as Amazon.com, we are likely to get in trouble.

Falling stock prices would lead to a sharp contraction in consumer confidence and spending and in business investment which in turn would lead to plummeting growth, spiraling unemployment, a further contraction of investment, and finally lower productivity. As Princeton economist Burton Malkiel puts it, "A very sharp decline in [stock] prices could deal a serious blow to America's long economic expansion. . . . So Wall Street and Main Street are closely related."[33] Surely, real prosperity should be based on something more durable than volatile capital markets and the bankers, financial managers, and hedge fund speculators who run them.

But even if instability were not an issue, there is something still more fundamental about the Wall Street model that undermines its ability to produce the kind of growth we believe attainable: Wall Street's unconditional need for stable prices. Following this model requires that everything possible be done to keep inflation under control. In practice this means that long-term monetary policy as practiced by the Fed is necessarily biased toward moderate growth. The same is true of fiscal policy as practiced by the president and the Congress. Running the economy "hot" risks unacceptable inflation. Thus, the Fed might permit rapid growth for a short time, as it has under Greenspan, but over the long run it would rather run a slower race, periodically stepping on the monetary brakes, than risk price instability by tapping on the accelerator. Similarly, the White House and Congress are now obsessed with running surpluses rather than deficits, even if the economy were to slow down. No wonder then that the official forecasts for growth are only in the 2.3 percent range. Implicitly, the conventional wisdom *imposes,* rather than detects, a strict speed limit on growth, and in the process we lose the $3.2 trillion growth dividend we might otherwise enjoy.

And who is ultimately imposing slow growth on America? Writing in 1994, Louis Uchitelle of the *New York Times* had it generally right: Behind the Federal Reserve and those responsible for fiscal policy is "the bond market — a loose confederation of wealthy Americans, bankers, financiers, money managers, rich foreigners, executives of the insurance companies, presidents of universities and nonprofit foundations, pensioners and people who once kept their money in passbook savings accounts (or under the bed) and now buy shares in mutual funds. While some would recoil at being called enemies of growth, the fact is that the confederation has ruled in recent [time] that the economy should lose strength, not gain it. . . . The national interest, these people believe, is smothering inflation — even at the cost of growth."[34]

That "loose confederation" is willing to accept slower growth because it does not penalize everyone equally.[35] Official data indicate that during the slow-growth 1970s and 1980s, when incomes were falling for the bottom two-fifths of the income distribution and hardly rising at all for most of the top half, the richest 5 percent of U.S. families did not suffer at all. They saw their incomes rise at precisely the same annual rate as during the glory days of the 1950s and 1960s, receiving a larger slice of a smaller pie. Virtually all of the growth in a slow-growth economy goes to the economic elite; even when the economy is just plodding along, there is enough to keep them happy.[36] But because slow growth means higher unemployment and depressed wages and benefits, workers and their families get little of the slowly expanding pie. That is why those who run financial markets do not care whether the economy runs at or below its potential and why the Wall Street model with its recipe for modest growth virtually assures an economically polarized society far into the future.

What is more, the Wall Street model precludes the possibility of going back to the Main Street virtuous cycle, if the former fails. A single-minded focus on budget balance (or budget surplus) constrains the nation's ability to invest sufficiently in public sector infrastructure, government-financed R&D, education, and training, all of which are needed to produce the kind of technology-driven productivity consistent with the Main Street model of growth. President Clinton may see himself as the "education President," but his desire to boost investment in the nation's future workforce is trumped by the commitment to keep the budget balanced and taxes low. Putting aside most of the federal budget surplus to "save" Social Security and Medicare may not be a very good idea either, according to Alan Murray of the *Wall Street Journal*. Instead of "building a bridge to the twenty-first century" through investments in R&D, infrastructure, education, and training, he writes, "the real Clinton legacy may turn out to be just the opposite," undermining the prospects for growth.[37]

The Republicans in Congress would go even further. Their year 2000 budget plan showcases support for Social Security, the Pentagon, and a new round of tax cuts, all resulting in continued reductions in discretionary funding, including new money for public investment.[38] The fallout from this policy stance is already showing up in an "innovation index" created by Michael Porter of the Harvard Business School and Scott Stern of MIT. Tracking R&D funding and investment in technical training across countries, they find that the United States topped the charts in the 1980s and 1990s. But if current trends continue, by 2005 the U.S. will trail Japan and a number of other countries, including Finland, Denmark, and Sweden.[39] Thus, as we do everything to expand the budget surplus, we actually reduce the very investments we need to assure sustained prosperity.

Why Faster Growth Is Better

There are those, of course, who will question this entire enterprise. Haven't we grown enough? Won't faster growth destroy the environment? Aren't we satiated with material goods already? These are not unreasonable questions. But they assume that faster growth is the culprit in environmental and cultural destruction. Here we respectfully disagree. Growth certainly can compromise the natural environment. Expansion in the built environment can lead, for example, to faster deforestation in order to fill the demand for wood products. And growth certainly can lead to a cultural wasteland where satisfying private material wants takes precedence over mutual needs and a spirit of community. Indeed, the Wall Street model implicitly feeds the get-rich-quick mentality of the stock market, and its glorification of the private market leads to a world in which it seems every garment and product blares out the name of the business that produced it.

But history tells us that the pace of economic growth, the rate of environmental destruction, and the nature of civil society are not highly correlated. Perhaps no country has suffered worse environmental or cultural degradation than the former Soviet Union. In trying to stem its increasing poverty as its growth rate slowed, the leaders of that nation deliberately jettisoned any pretension to environmental protection in order to meet the material needs of its people. Lake Baikal became the most polluted large body of water in the world.

On the other hand, rapid growth in the United States has permitted us to demand that business meet strict environmental guidelines, and it has generated the extra profits out of which firms could pay for these improvements. Indeed, faster growth provides engineers and business leaders with the incentive to develop new technologies for implementing cleanup. As a result, Lake Erie is cleaner today than twenty-five years ago, and Boston Harbor is now home to an array of fish species that had once practically disappeared. One of the benefits of faster growth, therefore, is the potential for a *cleaner* environment. When growth is slow, environmentalists have a much harder time convincing people to care about things green — except perhaps for what's in their pay envelopes.

The same is true of the social environment. When the economy is growing quickly and people find it easier to make a living, they tend to be more selfless. During the glory days, when employment growth was strong and real wages were rising rapidly, it was not difficult to convince the American people that the federal government should provide more for those who could not care for themselves. We could mount a War on Poverty and willingly spend hundreds of billions of dollars on it. President Kennedy's plea that we should "ask not what our country can do for us, but what we can do for our country" was much easier to sell politically when the economy was booming than it would have been later, when families suffered a quarter century of stagnating incomes and growing job insecurity. Indeed, slow growth gave us the "me generation"; faster growth could give us back the "we generation." As the pollster Stanley Greenberg has noted, "Progressives need to make the case for real growth and push economic policymakers to create it. *The citizen in a growing country may not feel so alone and may be able to contemplate what people can achieve together.*" (Italics added)[40]

Policies for Growth with Equity

At the turn of the millennium, America faces a momentous clash between two different models of growth. One emphasizes balanced budgets, tight monetary policy, industry deregulation, privatization, and generally smaller and weaker government. The other stresses the importance of public sector investments in research and development, in public infrastructure, in workforce education and development, and in reducing urban poverty and underemployment, along with a commitment to expansionary fiscal and monetary policies. While the government cannot ignore Wall Street, it need not be subservient to it. The government would cease tying domestic and global economic strategy to an ideology that makes trying to satisfy financial markets the very centerpiece of government policy.

As part of the Main Street model of growth with equity, the government balances the drive for greater trade stimulation with judicious regulation of financial capital flows and promotion of international labor standards and labor rights, in order to improve the conditions of working people at home and abroad. The government encourages unionization and provides greater labor market protection for workers and their families. All of this helps to stimulate the aggregate demand needed to grow the economy and assure a more equitable sharing of the dividends. The new growth economy has been described as a "high-risk society," one in which we must be willing to accept substantial risks in order to obtain the benefits.[41] The Main Street model suggests that it is possible — with appropriate government policies — to have faster growth with at least a modicum of economic security and a good deal more equity.

While the trajectory of the economy will depend critically on which model of growth we choose, the real choice is a political one. To make this choice soundly, we need nothing less than a full national debate over our growth strategy alternatives and their implications for the quality of life for all of our people. We hope this book contributes constructively to that debate.

Chapter 2

A History of American Growth

E VERY YEAR Boston Red Sox fans turn out fully expectant that *this* year will see an end to the "curse of the Bambino." If the Sox win five games in a row in early spring, pennant fever grips the city for months. Back in 1918, Babe Ruth led the Sox to a World Series victory before being sold to the team's arch rival, the New York Yankees. Ever since, the Red Sox have been incapable of pulling off another championship. For their fans, however, hope springs eternal: No matter how poor the pitching or hitting might be, if the team wins three games in a row, pennant fever returns.

What's true about Red Sox baseball does not seem to apply to the economy — or at least not to economists. After batting the equivalent of a .230 average for two decades, the American economy finally began to hit a string of home runs beginning in the second quarter of 1996. In one remarkable quarter after another, the nation's gross domestic product (GDP) expanded at an average rate of 4.2 percent a year — better than double the average rate of the previous six years (see Table 2.1). With faster growth, unemployment fell sharply to only 3.9 percent, while inflation remained in check. Not since the 1960s had we enjoyed a combination of such favorable economic conditions. A mounting Asian financial crisis and the collapse of the Russian economy gave brief pause to the steep climb in the value of the U.S. stock market in the second half of 1998. But surprisingly, the foreign crises had no adverse impact on the GDP growth rate, and unemployment remained near record-low levels.

Despite the spate of good economic news — indeed, even before the string of foreign financial crises surfaced — the majority of economists and political leaders refused to believe that the economy was capable of

Table 2.1. Growth in Real Gross Domestic Product			
Year	Change (%)	Year/Quarter	Annualized Change (%)
		1996	3.6%
1989	3.4%	1997	4.4
1990	1.8	1998:I	6.5
1991	−0.5	1998:II	2.9
1992	3.0	1998:III	3.4
1993	2.7	1998:IV	5.6
1994	4.0	1999:I	3.5
1995	2.7	1999:II	2.5
		1999:III	5.7
		1999:IV	8.3
		2000:I	4.8
		2000:II	5.6
1989–1995		1996:I–2000:II	
Annual Average	2.3%	Annual Average	4.2%

Source: Council of Economic Advisers, *Economic Indicators,* September, 2000.

sustained growth much faster than the modest rates of the early 1990s. The few who now believe we can return to growth rates close to those of the post–World War II glory days are viewed as cockeyed optimists. Both the official forecasts of the government and the unofficial forecasts of economists project quite modest growth well into the future. Before the economy took off in early 1996, President Clinton's Council of Economic Advisers projected a 2.3 percent average yearly growth rate for 1995 through 2002. Two years later, in their 1998 *Economic Report,* the council saw no reason to raise their forecast by even a tenth of a percent, even though the economy was running well ahead of expectations.[1] Certainly, by the 1999 *Economic Report* we might have expected a little more optimism. But, alas, three years of accelerated growth continued to be seen as little more than an anomaly.[2]

Generally, both the Federal Reserve Board and the Congressional Budget Office (CBO) have agreed with this assessment — even when it drew the ire of House Speaker Newt Gingrich, who threatened retaliation against his own agency for publishing such pessimistic GDP estimates.[3] Economists who advise the Social Security Administration are an even gloomier lot. They project a slowing of the nation's growth rate to 1.4 percent per year for most of the twenty-first century.[4] Not surprisingly then, Americans are warned that we face a looming Social Security "crisis" instead of a not very scary and quite manageable deficit in the program's trust fund, not even manifest until sometime after the middle of the new century.

Those who bemoan such a slow-growth future are told they had better get used to the idea. Every few years there may be a growth spurt for a few quarters, but these will be rare enough to keep the long-term annual growth rate only a fraction above 2 percent ad infinitum.

But is this really the best we can do? Even if the U.S. economy cannot sustain 4 to 5 percent growth indefinitely — a credible conclusion in our opinion — is it still possible to attain something significantly better than the official government forecast of 2.3 percent? Have we set our expectations too low, or is the $3.2 trillion growth dividend that accompanies a 3 percent growth rate simply pie in the sky? To answer such questions, we need to understand what is realistically feasible, what is unnecessarily gloomy, and what is sheer fantasy. To do this, it helps to take a brief look at America's long-term growth record and then consider what factors have been responsible for growth in the post–World War II era. In this chapter and the next, this is what we shall do. What the record will show is that growth rates as low as the official Washington projections are much more the anomaly than rates considerably faster.

Trying to Extrapolate the Future from the Past

Literally billions of tiny events join together every day to determine the size of the national economy and how fast it expands. If we had the equivalent of a scanning electronic microscope to view each of these events, we could detect the fact that buying a McDonald's Big Mac for lunch boosts the nation's GDP by the economic equivalent of an angstrom. Of course, tremendous events like the 1994 Los Angeles earthquake have a much bigger impact on output, large enough to show up in the national accounts without the need for even a dime store magnifying glass. Repairs to the city following the quake added $15 billion to national income, about two-tenths of one percent of the entire nation's income that year.[5]

To understand our prospects for growth, however, we are concerned not with the small or even middle-sized perturbations in the level of national output from day to day or even from year to year. Our interest lies in the economy's long-term historical trends, which conveniently, if not entirely accurately, summarize the changes in our material standard of living and our sense of economic security. From this perspective, the superb performance of the U.S. economy beginning in the mid-1990s could be nothing more than an isolated peak in an otherwise barren landscape — or it could be the beginning of a whole new era of prosperity. Using history as our guide, we will see that the buoyant growth rates we have enjoyed in the 1996–1999 period come closer to the long-term trend than the sluggish growth we experienced in the two decades preceding.

The nearly universal pessimism about future growth is based, in large part, on extrapolating from the post–World War II GDP record. If we had nothing to go on other than the information in Figure 2.1, predictions of more buoyant growth would certainly seem to be out of line. Since the 1960s, the economy's growth rate slipped from 4.4 percent to 2.3 percent in the early 1990s, in an almost unbroken downhill slide. Given the

Figure 2.1. Real GDP Growth in the United States, 1959–1995

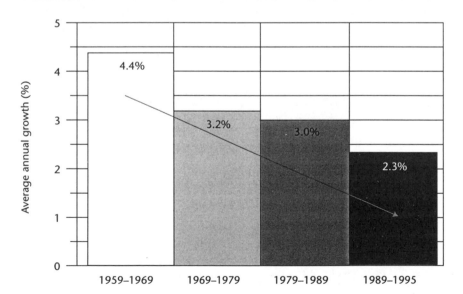

Sources: *Economic Report of the President,* 1987, 2000.

steady downward trend in the data, even the modest growth projections of the Council of Economic Advisers, the Federal Reserve, and the Congressional Budget Office might seem to be too optimistic.

However, a longer view of the matter provides a very different picture. Based on the yeoman work of economic historians Paul David, Robert Gallman, and Angus Maddison, Figure 2.2 traces the average annual growth rate of GDP from the early dissemination of the steam engine in the early 1800s to the present era of the microchip.[6] Over the course of nearly two centuries, the American economy grew by 3.8 percent per year — almost double what we experienced from 1989 through 1995 and nearly as well as the growth rate we have experienced during the post-1995 economic surge.

Inspection of these historical data suggests a remarkable resemblance between the trend in the long 1800–1929 period and the experience in

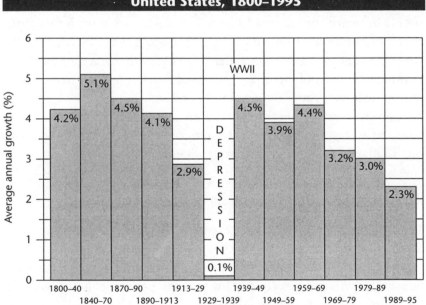

Figure 2.2. Long-Term Real GDP Growth in the United States, 1800–1995

Sources: for 1800–40, David, "The Growth of Real Product in the United States Before 1940"; 1840–70, Gallman, "Gross National Product in the United States, 1834–1909"; 1870–1929, Maddison, "Growth and Slowdown in Advanced Capitalist Economies"; 1929–50, *Economic Report of the President,* 1987; 1959–89, *Economic Report of the President,* 1997; 1989–2000, *Economic Indicators,* October 2000.

the post–World War II era, particularly from 1959 through 1995 — with the Great Depression separating the two. In both cases, growth rates of better than 4 percent at the beginning of each epoch gave way to slower GDP growth in succeeding decades. Overall, the long-term trend looks more like a roller coaster ride than one long unbroken downhill ski run. We bounced back from the decline in growth rates that eventually bottomed out in the Great Depression. If history provides a lesson, it is that we are not doomed to continued slow growth or endlessly declining growth in the future.

Those who accept slow growth as America's fate view the glory days following World War II as a unique period in American history — an ever so brief era when we were able to sustain unusually high growth. But in the long view, the glory days do not seem particularly unusual at all. If anything, the average growth rate from 1949 through 1969 is a bit lower than what was typical for much of the nineteenth century. In light of Figure 2.2, the postwar boom years certainly do not appear to be the "massive freak" that journalist Michael Elliott has dubbed them.[7] If anything should be seen as uncommon, it is the extremely slow growth we experienced beginning in 1990 and lasting through 1995. Only during the Great Depression did America suffer slower growth. Hence, in the short-term, myopic view of Figure 2.1, raising the economy back to a 2.3 percent growth rate seems like a real improvement. But over the long term, 2.3 percent seems rather paltry — barely three-fifths as well as we have done, on average, over the past two hundred years. Extrapolating the future from only the most recent past is what makes one a pessimist.

Economic Growth: The Lessons of the Postwar Boom

The long-term trends we saw in Figure 2.2 conceal an important story. The GDP trend for the 1800–1929 period may look similar to the trend for the much shorter 1959–1989 period, but the underlying causes of the buoyant growth and subsequent slowing of the economy in the two periods reflect somewhat different dynamics.

As in most things economic, it is useful to divide the world into supply-side and demand-side factors. Changes in the price of a given item can be initiated from either side. In 1973, when the *supply* of oil was curtailed by the Organization of Petroleum Exporting Countries (OPEC), the price of gasoline went through the roof. In contrast, when the Red Sox are on a winning streak, the scalper's price for bleacher tickets doubles or even triples because of increased *demand.*

Similarly, we can talk about supply-side and demand-side factors initiating a new round of economic growth. On the supply side are such things as industrial "revolutions," which provide a supply of new products, and exogenous increases in available labor, which might be due to an increased birthrate, more immigration, or higher labor force participation. On the demand side are factors like pent-up consumer demand and exogenous infusions of public sector spending. In this case, supply factors determine the economy's *potential* output, while demand factors determine how much of the potential is actually realized. In the short run, the two can be quite independent of each other. Supply can outstrip demand. In the long run, however, the two are interdependent. If supply continues to outdistance demand, firms will cut back on investment, reducing potential as well as current output. If demand remains buoyant for a long enough period, firms will take this as a sign to expand their investments, boosting the potential output of the economy.

In this context, the rapid growth of the mid-nineteenth century was heavily influenced by supply-side factors. The opening up of arable western lands for intensive farming, successful explorations for iron ore and oil, and the industrial revolution brought new technologies and new products that created a foundation for growth. The full utilization of steam power in factories and mills, the expansion of the railroad to meet the nation's need for long-haul transportation, and the later introduction and diffusion of electric power throughout industry led the growth during much of the nineteenth century and the early part of the twentieth.[8] So did wave after wave of immigrants who supplied the skilled and semi-skilled workforce for the expanding manufacturing sector. Of course, if there had been no expansion in demand for the vast new supplies of foodstuffs, clothes, and steel, the growth initiated by the supply side would very quickly have dried up. But demand accommodated supply, and the economy boomed.

In contrast, what initially energized the post–World War II economic boom had much less to do with supply-side factors and more to do with extraordinarily buoyant demand. To be sure, the introduction and rapid spread of air conditioning was a supply-side factor that helped open up the South and Southwest to economic growth. The swift spread of television was another important supply-side phenomenon. But the key ingredient for the economic boom following World War II was the release of an unprecedented level of pent-up private sector demand combined with public sector investment and spending. With military victory secured in Europe and the Pacific, America popped the cork and went on a buying spree.

After four years of war-imposed scarcity and a preceding decade of depression-induced belt-tightening, Americans looked forward to replacing worn-out household appliances and prewar automobiles. They wanted new homes in the suburbs. Moreover, their pent-up demand was matched by enormous savings they had accumulated during the war. All told, between Pearl Harbor and V-J Day, Americans socked away nearly $125 billion in war bonds, savings accounts, credit unions, pillow cases, and mattresses — the equivalent of more than $1.1 trillion in today's prices. These savings instantly turned consumption desire into real consumer demand and initiated a new epoch of economic growth.

Of course, to satisfy all of the new consumer demand, America's factories needed to be retooled. Conversion from war production to consumer products required enormous investment in new plant and equipment — a supply-side factor. In *real* (i.e., inflation-adjusted) terms, over $330 billion (in 1996 dollars) was spent on new factories and office buildings between 1946 and 1950 alone. Another $460 billion of real-dollar investment was poured into these plants in the form of new machinery and business equipment, from typewriters to open-hearth furnaces.[9] This new investment created millions of jobs and helped feed the economic boom.

Government too played a central role as a generator of aggregate demand. After the war, federal spending for the military collapsed, but it soon recovered as a result of the Korean conflict and the emergence of the cold war. And new government spending was hardly limited to defense work. Under the GI Bill, the federal government provided $14 billion in education and job-training benefits to over 7 million returning servicemen and -women.[10] Today that would be equivalent to spending nearly $125 billion on higher education. New subsidized housing was constructed under the Federal Housing Administration (FHA) and the Veterans Administration, and billions more were spent on urban renewal.

The interstate highway system was begun. Meanwhile, state and local governments were contributing to aggregate demand at an even faster clip, spending nearly $200 billion ($1.5 trillion in 1999 dollars) between 1947 and the end of the 1960s to build and maintain streets, roads, and highways, and spending more than twice this amount to build schools and hire teachers to educate a generation of baby boomers who began to arrive in kindergarten in 1950.[11]

As if this were not enough to spur an economic boom, the Marshall Plan boosted export demand. The United States committed over $13 billion ($115 billion in 1999 dollars) in foreign aid between 1947 and 1953 to help rebuild Europe, in a deliberate attempt to contain Soviet expansion.[12] As much as 80 percent of this aid came back to the United States in the form of orders for American exports, including food, building supplies, trucks, road-building equipment, and aircraft. On the other side, the one demand component that could have limited GDP expansion, the U.S. demand for imports, all but disappeared. Following World War II, our potential competitors were having a tough enough time feeding and clothing their own people, let alone producing goods for export abroad.

The Post–World War II Virtuous Cycle

The postwar boom was remarkable in a number of ways, not the least of which was its longevity: it lasted for a quarter of a century without letup. Between 1947 and 1973 output continued to surge, marred by what, in retrospect, were only minor recessions in 1954, 1961, and 1971. In a single generation, real GDP grew by more than two and a half times in value. Economic growth quickly attained critical mass and began to feed a self-sustaining *virtuous cycle* (in technical terms, a positive feedback loop). To be sure, pent-up demand and savings accumulated during World War II served as the initial stimulus for the growth cycle. But as Figure 1.1 in the first chapter illustrated, once the postwar consumption boom began, growth was sustained by investment, which in turn promoted technological innovation, which in turn promoted productivity improvements and ultimately a new round of growth. Economic expansion cycled upward from there.

On its own, however, postwar growth would likely have petered out in a decade or so if it were not for three critically important factors, all of which contributed to sustaining the virtuous cycle: One was the spread of organized labor and collective bargaining. The second was the explicit role of the federal government in stimulating aggregate demand whenever the pace of economic growth appeared to slacken. And the third was the unexpectedly strong expansion in labor supply as women entered the labor force in record numbers.

During and after World War II, workers joined unions in droves. By 1953, organized labor represented more than a third of the paid work-force. In addition, perhaps another third benefited from union-inspired wages and benefits, often because employers raised wages and offered health insurance and pensions to persuade their workers that they would be well cared for in a union-free environment. Beginning in the auto in-dustry and spreading like a prairie fire across many industries, successful union demands for annual wage increases and cost-of-living protection boosted take-home pay, contributing to consumption-led growth. Ex-panding "fringe benefits" to include health insurance, life insurance, and pensions reduced the workers' need to save every last penny for the in-evitable rainy day. Seniority provisions and formal grievance procedures added immeasurably to the workers' sense of job and income security. All of these provisions, established in what became the standard workplace contract, provided recurring booster shots to the economy and kept the virtuous growth cycle spinning.[13] Rising wages combined with job secu-rity became the centerpiece of a consumer-led postwar boom, a kind of "Main Street" model of economic growth.

Inoculations against economic stagnation during this period came from the deliberate use of government fiscal policy. The Employment Act of 1946, enacted in response to the widespread fear that the end of World War II military spending would return the country to prewar-type de-pression days, mandated the federal government to do everything within its power to create and maintain employment opportunities, sustain growth, and provide stable prices. The act provided the grounds for using tax and expenditure policy as well as monetary policy to encourage growth and employment. Fifteen years later, when the economic boom showed initial signs of aging, President Kennedy, acting under the 1946 legislation, stimulated the economy with his famous tax cut. President Johnson further boosted demand with War on Poverty spending and, of course, a flood of funds for the Vietnam War. Deficit financing to maintain economic growth came so far out of the closet that even a conservative president, Richard Nixon, would proclaim in his battle against unemployment in 1972 that "we are all Keynesians now."

Finally, growth was augmented by a fresh supply of labor as women entered the labor force in numbers unprecedented in peacetime. In 1948 fewer than one-third of all women participated in the labor force and most of these worked part-time. By 1979 more than half of all women were in the labor force and a rising proportion had taken up full-time work.[14] The dual-earner couple would come to replace the typical "Ozzie and Harriet" family where dad worked and mom stayed home with the kids. What mom brought home was no longer simply "pin money" but an important addition to the family's income. It helped pay for the second car as well as the two-car garage where that car was parked.

Thus, the post–World War II boom was driven by private and public sector demand along with an increased pool of workers to satisfy the economy's growing appetite for labor. There was no great technological breakthrough on the supply side like the steam engine or electrification. The computer did not enter the workplace to any significant degree until the 1980s and 1990s, well after the postwar virtuous cycle had run out of gas.

The Key Ingredients of Economic Growth

The story we have told so far provides a good summary of how we grew so fast in the first quarter century after World War II. But to really understand what powers growth in any society, we need to drill down through several layers of economic sediment, beginning with those nearest the surface and proceeding to those that lie much deeper in the bedrock of growth dynamics. It is good practice to pause at every layer, much as a geologist might, to ask, "And what caused *that* to occur?" By working through this process, we can gain not only a better understanding of economic history but perhaps also a better sense of what might be in store for the future. Merely extrapolating from history can be misleading; this type of economic archeology gets at the underlying forces driving growth.

A good place to begin this excavation is with Figure 2.3. It reveals the surface strata we need to probe in order to decipher the variation in post-

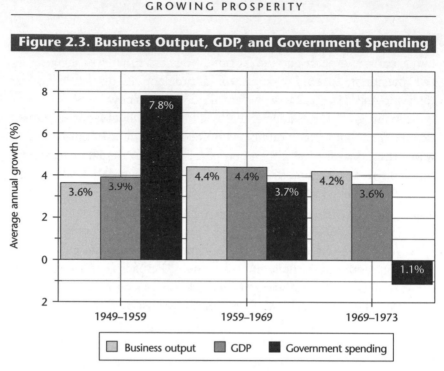

Figure 2.3. Business Output, GDP, and Government Spending

Sources: *Economic Report of the President,* 1959, 1996; *Economic Indicators,* February 1997.

war growth rates we saw in Figure 2.2. This chart shows the separate contributions of the private and public sectors to overall GDP growth. Recall that during the 1950s GDP grew by 3.9 percent per year. This was actually faster than the 3.6 percent average growth in the private sector. GDP grew more rapidly than private business output because government consumption of goods and services plus government investment at the federal, state, and local levels grew by a staggering 7.8 percent per year. This spending generated additional output directly, in the form of government services, and indirectly, in the form of demand for output from the rest of the economy. Total government employment grew by more than 3 percent per year during the 1950s and more than 4 percent per year in the 1960s, generating in the process substantial increases in direct government output. By contrast, total government employment grew by little more than 1 percent during the slow-growth 1980s and early 1990s.[15] The Korean War, the development of what President Eisenhower would call the "military-industrial complex," the initial construction of the vast interstate highway system, and enormous state and local government investment in urban renewal, suburban sprawl, and entire new towns and cities in the South and Southwest all contributed to the powerful economic thrust emanating from government.

In the 1960s, the private sector propelled the economy to even greater heights and the public sector obliged. Annual government growth slowed from 7.8 percent to a more reasonable rate of 3.7 percent, but it was sufficient in combination with the robust business sector to power GDP growth to a postwar record of 4.4 percent a year for the decade.

Overall GDP growth *would* have been sustained at something closer to this record clip in the early 1970s were it not for a total collapse in public sector growth. The private sector continued to zip along at a 4.2 percent growth rate, but the public sector actually contracted as a result of disengagement from the Vietnam War and a slowdown in domestic spending. The result was that GDP growth slowed from 4.4 percent throughout the 1960s to 3.6 percent between 1969 and 1973. In essence, the end of the government spending boom knocked more than a half point off the economy's growth path each year.

Still, what government spending contributes directly and indirectly to GDP growth pales in comparison with what are indisputably the two bedrock determinants of growth in the private business sector: the growth in the size of the employed labor force and the rate of productivity improvement — the increased output obtained from using labor more efficiently. Together, these two determine the rate at which private business output can expand — not by chance, but by algebra. And it is private business output, as we saw in Figure 2.3, that dominates overall economic growth.

The best measure of employed labor is *total hours of work*. Labor productivity is measured by *output per hour of work*. Thus, total output in the business sector can be expressed as employed labor times labor productivity, or

$$Y = (Y/H) \times H,$$

where Y is total private sector output, H is total hours worked by the private sector labor force, and Y/H is, by definition, productivity.[16]

It follows mathematically that the percentage change in private sector output over any period of time is equal to the percentage change in productivity *plus* the percentage change in hours of work. Simply put, output growth equals productivity growth plus employment growth, measured in total hours worked. If you know how fast the employed supply of labor is growing and how fast productivity is improving, you know precisely how fast business output is expanding. This plus the rate of growth in government output (properly weighted for the relative sizes of the private and public sectors) gives you the GDP growth rate. There is nothing fancy here — just the building blocks of the economy.

What all of this tells us is that instead of trying to forecast the future of growth from the entrails of the past, we need to focus our attention on three factors: the expected growth in *productivity,* the rate of growth in *labor supply,* and changes in *government spending* — particularly in terms of the public production of goods and services (e.g., public schools and sanitation services). If we can estimate what these will be in the future, we can predict GDP growth with decent accuracy.

What Caused Postwar Economic Growth in the Private Sector?

Let's begin by looking at the past. The postwar history of private business output, by far the largest component of GDP, clearly reflects the mathematical tautology that growth in private sector output equals growth in productivity plus growth in labor supply as measured by total hours worked (see Figure 2.4).

As the figure demonstrates, from 1949 through 1959, the first full decade of the postwar boom, virtually all of the growth in the private economy was the consequence of a remarkable increase in productivity. Total hours of work increased by only 0.2 percent per year — the slowest employment growth in the postwar era. Employment grew slowly because of a sharp decline in labor force participation among men, which was not fully offset by the increase in women's participation, and because of a decline in the length of the average workweek.[17] Dramatic efficiency improvement, pure and simple, drove the economy.

In the succeeding decade, which recorded the high-water mark of post-war economic growth, the annual rate of productivity improvement fell slightly, but a sharp upturn in employment more than compensated for it. With the economy booming, almost anyone and everyone who wanted to work was given a chance — and with rising wages, many took

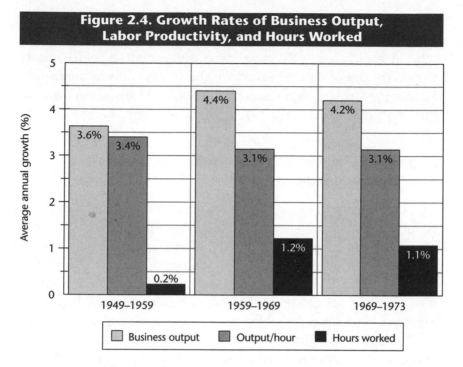

Figure 2.4. Growth Rates of Business Output, Labor Productivity, and Hours Worked

Sources: *Economic Report of the President,* 1987, 1996; *Economic Indicators,* February 1997.

the opportunity. The ratio of civilian employment to total population (age 16 and above) rose by 2 full percentage points during the 1960s, particularly as a consequence of women flooding the job market. For four years in a row, from 1966 through 1969, the national unemployment rate remained below 4 percent. In 1959 just over 53 million Americans were at work; a decade later the employment rolls stood at better than 70 million. In a single decade, the American workforce had increased by nearly a third. This explosion in employment, translated into total hours of work, contributed 1.2 percentage points to the decade's business output growth rate of 4.4 percent.

In the subsequent business cycle, running from 1969 to 1973, the last years of America's postwar glory days, both productivity growth and growth in annual hours continued at near-record pace. As a result, private sector output continued to churn along at better than 4 percent growth each year. In the years following 1973, output plummeted as productivity quite suddenly and mysteriously disappeared. Comparing 1969–73 with

41

1989–96 makes clear what happened. Output growth fell by half, from 4.2 percent to 2.1 percent, despite the fact that the supply of work (measured in hours) grew by the same rate in both periods. All of the massive drop in the rate of output growth was due to a collapse in productivity growth. Productivity was expanding in the early 1990s at less than one-third the rate achieved in the 1950s, 1960s, and early 1970s.

Digging Still Deeper into the Growth Process: The Production Function

That productivity and labor supply are the proximate sources of growth is surely important to understand, but this knowledge gets us only so far toward understanding why America did so well during the glory days and so badly thereafter. We must continue drilling deeper into the substrate to find out what these two factors themselves depend upon. Presumably, if we can find a way to forecast these ultimate factors, we will finally be in a position to construct a reliable forecast about the future of growth itself.

A useful way to generate a taxonomy of the sources of growth is to consider what economists call a *production function*. A production function is nothing more than a model of how economic inputs such as labor, capital, and land are transformed into outputs like wheat, cement, luxury automobiles, and restaurant meals. We could determine how much labor of what type goes into wheat farming, what types of tractors and mechanical reapers are used, and how much land and other natural resources are consumed in cultivating the crop. We could then see how increasing the supply of just one of these inputs adds to the size of the wheat harvest, holding everything else constant. In this way, the increment in productivity of each factor can be determined. For example, an investment in a modern mechanical harvester that cuts a wider swath increases the productivity of the farmer by permitting him to harvest a given field in less time. In this case, adding more physical capital increases the productivity of the farm worker and total output.

Increasing the wheat harvest, however, depends on more than just what kind of machinery the farmer uses in his fields. Over any period of time, increased yields also reflect the use of better seed, the application of more fertilizer, the amount of rainfall, the skills of the farmer, and dozens, if not hundreds, of other factors. For example, the more technology embedded in the harvester — or in the computer programs used to analyze the farmer's soil — the greater the wheat yields can be, even with the same dollar investment in the harvester and computer. Parsing out how much of the added yield can be attributed to each of these factors is the job of growth accounting.

Finally, there is one more element we must add to our basic growth accounting model. It has to do with what economists call *disembodied technical change*. This ghostly term refers to changes in the organization of existing inputs and the introduction of added knowledge *not* directly incorporated in plant and equipment or in workers themselves. This is hard to fathom in the abstract, but simply put, if two firms or two economies have the same level of physical and human capital, but the managers in one firm or economy find a better way of organizing how their employees and machines work together, their output will be higher — despite having no more capital than their neighbor. These factors can be neatly summarized, as follows.

The Ultimate Determinants of Economic Growth

1. Labor supply
2. Labor productivity
   a. Physical capital
   b. Technical change embodied in physical capital
   c. Human capital
3. Disembodied changes in technology and organization of production

Economic growth is therefore ultimately a function of labor supply, labor productivity, and technical change — with labor productivity, in turn, a function of the amount of physical capital workers have at their disposal, the level of technical sophistication built into those factories, machines, and tools, and the amount of human capital the workers themselves possess.[18] With this simple taxonomy as a guide, we finally are in position to determine what ultimately was responsible for the rapid growth of output we experienced from the end of World War II through 1973 as well as the slowdown that followed. This will give us the additional tools we need to consider any forecast of future American growth.

An Empirical Look at the Sources of Postwar Economic Growth

No economist has devoted more of his professional life to this type of economic archaeology than the Brookings Institution's late Edward Denison. In a series of painstakingly detailed volumes published between 1962 and 1985, Denison trained a statistical microscope on a mountain of economic data, examining every ridge and peering into every valley for any and every factor that might influence growth.[19] Then, with as much precision as he could muster, he endeavored to provide a rough idea of how much weight to assign to each boulder and pebble that might contribute to national output.

In this business of growth accounting, properly defining the object to be measured is critical. For the purpose at hand, Denison chose just about the most cumbersome definition possible: "potential national income per person potentially employed in the non-residential business sector."[20] This mouthful of a measure tracks what the changes would be in private business output (per employee) if the economy were at "full employment." By using potential rather than actual output, Denison could examine economic growth between any two years without worrying about the confounding factor of whether the economy was at the peak of a business cycle, in a trough, or in-between. This is important because the factors responsible for growth vary, depending on whether the economy is growing fast, growing slowly, or not growing at all. In addition, by measuring output on a per person basis, his figures come close to a measure of labor productivity. They are shy of a pure measure only because hours of work per employee are not held constant. Instead, changes in labor hours are counted as one of the growth factors in the accounting framework itself.[21]

In one of his many studies, Denison took aim at explaining the sources of growth during the glory days. His conclusions about the sources of U.S. growth for the period 1948 through 1973 are summarized in Table 2.2. According to his calculations, aggregate output *per employee* in this period, adjusted for the business cycle, increased by 2.3 percent per year.[22] The table provides an indication of what brought about this rapid growth.

Assuming the method is roughly accurate, one thing is certain about this period: growth in output per worker was not due to individual employees working longer or harder. During the late nineteenth century, output grew rapidly in part because factory bosses forced their employees to work more and more hours per day or week and to work at a faster pace. This was not the case during the glory days after World War II. Hours per worker declined so much that if it were not for other factors, we would have experienced only about 85 percent as much growth as we actually did. Workers were now enjoying rising earnings *and* more leisure.

One of the factors that permitted faster growth was the increased skill of the labor force, as measured by its formal education. About 20 percent of postwar growth in output per worker can be explained by this one factor. Smarter workers produce more output in the same time. Another 15 percent of the growth came from the fact that workers had more machinery at their disposal. Construction workers had bigger and more powerful cranes; secretaries now had electric typewriters.

Improved resource allocation and economies of scale also appear to account for sizable improvements in output per employee during this era. *Improved resource allocation* refers to the transfer of labor from low-productivity industries to higher-productivity lines of work. One particular

Table 2.2. Contributions to Growth in National Income per Person Employed, 1948–1973

Source of Growth	Percentage of Growth Rate
All Sources	100.0%
Change in hours per worker	−15.8
(with account taken of age-sex composition)	
Increased education per worker	20.0
More capital per worker	14.6
More land per worker	−1.9
Advances in knowledge	54.2
Improved resource allocation	15.0
Changes in legal and human environment	−1.9
Economies of scale	16.2
Irregular factors	−0.4

Source: Denison, *Accounting for Slower Economic Growth*, p. 97.

group uprooted was the black cotton farmer who had lived for decades in the Mississippi Delta. As new cotton-picking machinery was introduced on a wide scale in the early 1950s, black farmers and their families were forced to find other means of survival. Many moved north, where they took jobs in the high-productivity auto and steel industries. These families had to abandon a rural lifestyle they may have enjoyed, but they and the country benefited, at least materially, from the resulting higher output.

A full 15 percent of the increase in labor productivity during the glory days can be attributed to such employment reallocation — an element of what the great Austrian-American institutional economist Joseph Schumpeter called the dynamic of "creative destruction." Every time a worker moves from a low-productivity, low-wage job to a higher-productivity, higher-wage job, GDP goes up a tad. If enough workers experience this type of vertical mobility, the impact on growth is large enough to measure. Alternatively, if large numbers of workers are downwardly mobile, moving to jobs with lower productivity and wages, overall economic growth suffers. Moving from a southern cotton farm to a General Motors plant in Flint, Michigan, raises labor productivity and economic output. Losing one's job at the GM plant and ending up at the local McDonald's does just the opposite.

Economies of scale also played an important role in postwar growth. These represent efficiency gains from the increased use of mass production techniques and longer production runs, both of which allowed additional units of output to be produced with the same input. This was, after all, the heyday of manufacturing, when the Ford Motor Company was still building autos in its enormous River Rouge complex near Detroit, and America's steel companies were expanding their gigantic mills on the banks of Lake Michigan and along the Ohio, Allegheny, and Monongahela Rivers. In mass production markets, sheer size carries an efficiency premium, and Denison was able to quantify it. Apparently, another 16 percent of the overall increase in output per worker was due to this phenomenon of bigger plants and longer production runs.

Unfortunately, combining all of these factors (plus tiny effects on growth from changes in land utilization, changes in government regulation, and irregular factors such as weather) still left a large share of growth to be explained. This residual Denison attributed to *advances in knowledge* — the disembodied technical change that economists speak of. Denison found that the most important factor contributing to output per employee was something he could not directly measure. This one factor covers a profuse array of possible growth sources, from pure innovations and inventiveness to the organization and reorganization of production, the nature of labor-management relations, and pure managerial savvy. According to Denison's calculations, this residual accounted for a little over half (54 percent) of total growth in output per worker during the postwar glory days. If you add together the estimated contributions of advances in knowledge and increased education, the two by themselves account for nearly three-quarters of increased output per worker between 1948 and 1973. The key to growth during the postwar era appears then to have been a confluence of powerful demand met by sufficient supply, the latter arising from improved national productivity fueled by a more educated labor force, reallocation of labor to higher-productivity industries, improved organization of capital and labor, larger production facilities, and some more machinery and equipment for workers to use.

The Basis for Current Growth Projections

With all of this as prologue, we now have the building blocks needed to reconstruct the logic behind the current government growth forecasts. For the sake of comparison, we can contrast the growth parameters of the 1960s with those projected for 1998 through 2007 (see Table 2.4). What is abundantly clear is that the official growth projections for much of the next decade are so much lower than the 1960s because of one overriding factor: *productivity growth.* During the postwar glory days productivity rose by better than 3 percent per year. Projections for the near future expect growth in output per hour of no more than 1.3 percent. By itself, slower productivity growth accounts for over 85 percent of the difference in GDP growth rates between America's glory days and official Washington's vision of America's future.

The other factor expected to reduce economic growth is the shrinking size of the farm sector and government. Instead of adding a fraction to the growth rate, farming and, more importantly, government spending are expected to grow so much slower than the private business sector that when properly weighted, overall GDP growth is slower than the increase

Table 2.4. What Drives Growth? The 1960s vs. 1998–2007 (Projected)		
Source	1959–1969	1998–2007
Growth in labor force, Nonfarm business sector	1.2%	1.2%
Growth in labor productivity, Nonfarm business sector	3.1	1.3
Growth in output, farm and government sectors	0.1	−0.2
Growth in real GDP	4.4%	2.3%

Source: Figure 2.4, Figure 2.5, and *Economic Report of the President*, February 1999, Table 2.3, p. 85.

in nonfarm business output. In the 1960s these two sectors added to GDP growth. In the future they will detract from it.

The substantial slowdown in the growth of government spending reflects what might be considered the triumph of Reaganism. In his 1997 State of the Union Address, President Clinton adopted a slogan that would have fit well into a speech by Ronald Reagan: "The era of big government is over." The current official projections for economic growth are based on a continued shrinkage of the federal government as a share of total GDP. During the 1960s government spending was responsible for nearly 15 percent of total growth in national output. Since 1991 it has accounted for less than 2 percent.[23] The contribution from government is expected to be no greater in the future, given the new political ideology that claims small government is good government, echoing the nineteenth century ideology that "that government which governs best governs least."

That we cannot get more growth from labor supply is based on the assumptions that unemployment is already as low as it can be, that labor force participation cannot rise very much more, and that the average number of hours that workers labor each year will remain flat or decline. Thus, we cannot expect much growth stimulus from either the government or the workforce, according to the official forecasts. That leaves the whole burden for future GDP growth on productivity, and here the official forecast is rather gloomy.

But is this really the best we can do? Have we really entered an era of permanently slower economic growth — or is this simply a faulty extrapolation from an anomalous period that saw a sudden collapse in productivity?

To answer this question, we need to use our archaeological tools to investigate what really happened to the American economy beginning in 1973. Why did the United States suddenly stop growing? If we could understand that, perhaps it would give us a clue about the true potential for more rapid growth in the future. That is what we shall investigate in the next chapter.

Chapter 3

America's New Growth Potential

SINCE THE LATE nineteenth century, *natura non facit saltum* has been the guiding principle of standard economics. This bit of Latin, originally attributed to Linnaeus, appears on the frontispiece of what many consider to be the first modern economics textbook, Alfred Marshall's *Political Economy*, published in 1890. The phrase means "nature makes no leaps." In the Marshallian tradition, economic analysis has focused on such questions as how small changes in demand and supply affect prices "at the margin." Abrupt shifts in the economy usually leave economists scratching their heads, their particular tools of the trade useless to decipher such events.

Yet one of the great, lingering mysteries of the postwar American economy has been the sudden collapse of productivity growth after 1973. For the entire postwar era until then, productivity had improved by better than 3 percent per year, as we noted in the previous chapter. And then, quite suddenly and unexpectedly, it plummeted and failed to recover. Beginning in the same year as the first oil embargo, annual advances in productivity fell by more than half. Economists have been trying to unravel the causes of its mysterious disappearance ever since — with breathtakingly little success. Failing in their quest, most have concluded that the decline in productivity was no mere transitory aberration, but a permanent shift downward in America's growth prospects.

Other social scientists, including sociologists and political scientists, have tried their hand at the same enigma with not much more luck. Fortunately, as we shall see, historians have saved the day. Examining data from the nineteenth and early twentieth centuries, they detected a curious pattern in the long-term productivity trend that stems from the introduction of revolutionary new technologies. What they found explains why we could have expected a drop in productivity growth beginning sometime in the early 1970s, and why we should be expecting a resurgence just about now. Indeed, we shall present evidence that backs up the historians' claim, providing hope for faster growth and a future of greater prosperity.

The Productivity Slowdown after 1973

What saved overall economic growth (at least for a while during the 1970s and early 1980s) from declining as steeply as productivity was the baby boom generation. Recall that economic growth equals productivity growth plus growth in labor supply. What we lost in efficiency gains, we made up in sheer work effort. The boomers came of age in the nick of time, swelling the ranks of the workforce and contributing to GDP growth. In an amazingly brief period — between 1973 and 1979 — total nonagricultural employment increased from 77 million workers to nearly 90 million. As a result, private sector output grew at a healthy 3.1 percent annual rate, even though productivity grew at only 1.3 percent. Stunning as it may seem, if productivity growth after 1973 had been as strong as it was before, this remarkable increase in labor supply would have enabled American output to grow by nearly 5 percent a year — faster than at any time since at least 1870, excluding World War II.

Again in the 1980s another expansion in the workforce rescued the nation's growth rate. This time it was driven by the unprecedented peacetime entry of women into the labor market. Productivity growth, at only 1.2 percent a year for the decade, was crawling along. Nevertheless, GDP still grew by nearly 3 percent, with more than half the growth coming once again from increases in total hours worked, rather than from improved output per hour. Right through 1989, the potentially devastating impact of falling productivity growth was offset by more Americans going to work, and when at work, working longer days and often nights. Americans were "working harder, not smarter."

Productivity growth continued to weaken right through the mid-1990s. Between 1989 and 1995, growth in output per worker-hour fell to only 1.1 percent a year (see Figure 3.1). Now it was poking along at one-third the rate that prevailed from 1949 through 1973. This was

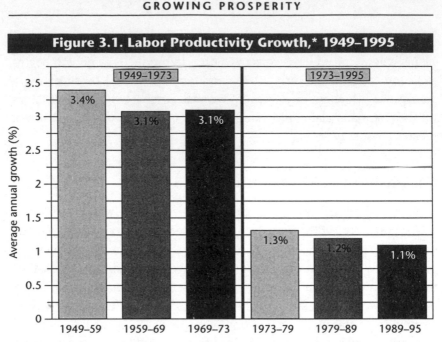

Figure 3.1. Labor Productivity Growth,* 1949–1995

Sources: for 1949–59, Krugman, *Age of Diminished Expectations;* 1959–89, *Economic Report of the President,* 2000.

*Growth in output per hour of work in business sector.

not merely a new record low for the postwar period — it was a record low for the century. Even during the Great Depression, productivity growth averaged 1.6 percent (see Table 3.1). This time, the growth in labor supply could not compensate for the dismal productivity performance, and economic growth slowed to only 2.3 percent per year — the lowest rate on record since the 1930s. Indeed, the surge of inexperienced workers into the labor force was partly responsible for bringing productivity growth rates down.

Explaining the Productivity Slowdown

Until recently, the official projections for economic growth into the next century were based on extrapolating the performance of productivity since 1973. Indeed, the official Washington forecast for much of the next decade was precisely equal to the 1.2 percent average productivity growth rate experienced between 1973 and 1995. In making this forecast, the government and most economists, in effect, decided to disre-

Table 3.1. Annual Labor Productivity Growth Rates, 1870–1995	
1870–1890	2.2%
1890–1913	1.8
1913–1929	2.4
1929–1939	1.6
1939–1949	2.6
1949–1959	3.4
1959–1969	3.1
1969–1973	3.1
1870–1973	2.4%
1973–1979	1.3
1979–1989	1.2
1989–1995	1.1
1973–1995	1.2%

Sources: for 1870–1929, Maddison, "Growth and Slowdown in Advanced Capitalist Economies": 1929–49, Krugman, *Age of Diminished Expectations;* 1949–59, *Economic Report of the President,* 1987; 1959–95, *Economic Report of the President,* 2000.

gard the productivity record for the entire preceding century — and, for that matter, the measured improvement since 1995. This was tantamount to suggesting that the productivity stagnation was permanent, that something fundamental was changed in the economy that will no longer permit us to grow as fast as we did before 1973.

This should prompt us to ask what has changed so dramatically. Why did productivity growth collapse when it did, and why should the post-1973 record suggest such an unalterable change in the nature of the economy?

In searching for answers to these important questions, it is instructive to begin by once again turning to the work of Edward Denison. After so carefully studying the factors responsible for the rapid growth in output per worker in the postwar era, Denison turned his attention to the subsequent initial period of depressed productivity growth — the period from 1973 through 1979. Denison's goal was to contrast the sharp drop-off

Table 3.2. The Sources of Decline in Productivity Growth,* 1964–73 versus 1973–79

Source of Productivity Decline	% point
All Sources	−2.05
Age-sex composition of the labor force	0.03
Hours of work per person	−0.08
Capital structures and equipment	−0.16
Land	−0.02
Reallocation from nonfarm self-employment	−0.16
Worker safety and health	−0.03
Dishonesty and crime	−0.06
Weather in farming	0.00
Labor disputes	0.00
Inventories	−0.08
Reallocation from farming	−0.08
Pollution abatement	−0.06
Economies of scale	−0.16
Education	0.01
Advances in knowledge	−1.20

Source: Denison, *Trends in American Economic Growth, 1929–1982*, p. 38.

*Potential national income per person potentially employed in nonresidential business.

in productivity growth in this period with productivity's boom years, 1964–73, to see if he could locate what went wrong in the economy. His comparison of growth between these two periods is reproduced in Table 3.2. This time he pulled out all the stops, investigating every possible factor he could think of that might explain the productivity slowdown.

Average annual growth in output per worker (measured at potential full employment) had dropped by 2.05 percentage points between these two periods. What surprised Denison and his readers was just how *unimportant* were some of the key factors that had played such central roles in explaining past growth. Of the 2.05–percentage point drop in labor productivity growth, capital spending on plant and equipment turned out to explain only 0.16 percentage points of the total. What that meant was that investment continued to grow after 1973, but its impact on productivity did not.

Economies of scale no longer mattered very much either. As small firms proliferated in the economy, economies of scale turned into "diseconomies." But the impact of this factor on productivity was also very small (−0.16 percentage points). Reallocation of the labor force between industrial sectors also did not account for much.

Bewildered by the fact that "nothing seemed to explain anything," Denison probed still deeper. Businesses had been complaining bitterly that they were being drowned in a sea of new regulations aimed at improving worker safety and health and at curbing pollution. Complying with these new regulations, they argued, hurt not only their profits but also their productivity. Putting expensive scrubbers on their smokestacks would make the air cleaner but add nothing to output as traditionally measured. A safer workplace would improve and extend workers' lives, but it would not readily show up in improved enterprise efficiency.

So Denison added measures to the productivity accounting model to capture the cost of these new regulations. Indeed, they were responsible for some of the decline in productivity growth, but their contribution was minuscule. Less than 0.1 of the 2.05-point decline in productivity growth could be attributed to these two forms of regulation combined.

When this line of inquiry proved fruitless, measures were added to the model for the impact of increased crime, the prevalence of labor disputes, and even changes in the weather, but none of these proved any more useful in explaining the mystery.

So what finally did explain the productivity slowdown? The answer seemed to lie in the residual term, what Denison had earlier called "advances in knowledge." This factor, so important in explaining pre-1973 growth, seemed again to be the Holy Grail. By itself, it was responsible for "explaining" nearly 60 percent of the total interperiod difference in labor productivity growth.

Unfortunately, this answer only added to the riddle. The influence of the residual was surely big enough, but what were we to make of its *negative* sign? If the residual really measured "advances in knowledge," then the negative sign suggested a near total collapse in the nation's technological and organizational prowess after 1973! Is it conceivable that American business fell prey to amnesia, suddenly forgetting much of what it had known about how to improve the efficiency of assembly lines or the use of electric power? Were we suddenly entering a dark age, something akin to what befell western civilization after the fall of ancient Rome and Greece?

One possibility, of course, was that Denison's new estimates were simply faulty. But when the equally renowned growth expert Angus Maddison tried to explain the post-1973 growth deceleration using his own methodology, he came up with a residual virtually identical to Denison's.[1] The same was true when Harvard's growth expert, Dale Jorgenson, tried his hand at the problem. Jorgenson's model generated the largest residual of all for this period: 80 percent.[2] Something astonishing seems to have happened after 1973 that could not be explained by any of the usual suspects in the economists' lineup.

A Rogue's Gallery of Suspects

With the usual suspects out of the picture, Denison searched for factors that previously had been ignored or left unmeasured. From a practically unlimited list of possible influences, he ended up investigating everything from research spending, big government, and Arab oil sheiks to the possibility that it could all be blamed on a generation of lazy workers and incompetent managers.

Declining R&D Spending. One possibility was a reduction in expenditures for research and development (R&D), a factor that can be directly associated with advances in knowledge. Economists who had been studying expenditures on formal R&D for years had found that these play an important role in economic growth, adding as much as 0.3 percentage points to the annual growth rate during the mid-1960s.[3] If R&D expenditures were critical to growth but had declined significantly after 1973, this would almost surely be one of the prime suspects in the productivity mystery.

It was a sound enough hypothesis, but the evidence was simply not there. Private sector R&D had not slumped during the 1970s. As a percentage of gross national product, total R&D expenditure rose from slightly less than 1 percent in 1955 to nearly 3 percent in 1964. During the 1970s it slipped to 2.3 percent of GNP. All of this relative decline, however, turned out to be due to cuts in federal government R&D spending following the completion of the Apollo space program and the end of the Vietnam War. Private sector R&D during the mid-1970s was just as high, as a percentage of GDP, as in the mid-1960s. From a growth accounting perspective, one was forced to conclude that measured R&D could not be responsible for much of the productivity slowdown after 1973.[4]

Of course, organized, measured R&D is only one source of advances in knowledge. The statistics do not count the efforts of individual workers and managers working to improve the production process or the research of individual inventors tinkering in their garages (or today on their notebook computers). These end up in Denison's residual category, like everything else not specifically identified in the growth model. Is it somehow possible that there was a decline in this source of growth beginning in the early 1970s? Did we simply run out of new ideas after a quarter century of postwar ingenuity? If this were true and somehow permanent, then we would indeed have to live with the consequences for years to come.

Indeed, there seemed to be some concrete evidence for this idea. It turns out that the number of patents issued to domestic corporations had peaked in 1971 and then began to decline.[5] Perhaps the falloff in new patents could be an indication of this decline in inventiveness and thus responsible for a slowing of productivity growth. Less innovation, less growth. But the timing was all out of synch. It is hard to believe that an erosion in Yankee ingenuity, if it occurred at all, would have had such a swift impact on measured output per worker, even if it could bear some responsibility for the sluggish productivity growth a decade or two later. Since Denison's accounting ended in 1982, it is hard to blame the first decade of the productivity slump on a sudden dearth of inventiveness as measured by patent applications.

Government Red Tape, Taxes, and Spending. Pollution abatement expenditures and the costs of implementing worker health and safety measures were directly accounted for in Denison's model. But what of consumer product safety regulations, fuel economy regulations, including the national 55 mph speed limit, and compliance costs for meeting Equal Employment Opportunity Commission (EEOC) mandates — none of which were specifically included in Denison's calculations? And what of all the government-imposed paperwork, which, according to one 1978 government report, required businesses to spend more than 500 million hours a year just to comply with government reporting standards?[6] Surely, the growth in regulation forced companies to devote more hours of work to activities which do not contribute to measured output. Maybe big government was to blame after all.

Again, this line of reasoning seemed plausible, but even if we allow for an enormous mountain of red tape, it is unlikely that much of the sharp decline in annual output growth after 1973 can be attributed to this factor. Half a billion hours devoted to government paperwork sounds like a huge waste of productive effort, but in 1973 the total number of hours worked in America was in the neighborhood of 140 billion. Even if the time spent complying with government reporting requirements doubled after 1973, at most we can attribute 0.18 points of the 2.05-point decline in productivity growth to this factor.

If government did not destroy productivity growth by tangling business up in red tape, did it do so by taxing it to death? Tax burdens on business, including levies on capital gains, theoretically could reduce investment levels below what they would be in a no-tax world. The only problem with this explanation is that there was *no* increase in taxation of business or increased levies on capital gains in the 1970s when productivity growth plunged, nor was a torrent of new investment unleashed in the 1980s when corporate taxes were slashed. It is hard, therefore, to blame much, if any, of the problem on the IRS.

Perhaps, then, it was not red tape and taxes, but the overall level of government spending? A long line of economists have argued before the House Committee on Ways and Means that big government is to blame for the slowdown in economic growth because public spending diverts resources into less productive pursuits.[7] A dollar spent on a public park is a dollar that cannot be spent on a new turret lathe by some manufacturing company. This argument is not only made by political conservatives; liberals have long argued the same in opposing the enormous spending on the Pentagon, especially during the cold war.[8]

There is a certain plausibility to this argument, but once again the timing is all wrong. Almost all of the great expansion in government spending occurred *before* 1973, when the U.S. economy was growing at a record pace. The slowdown in productivity occurred only after expansion in government spending had ceased. If anything, the raw historical data suggest a positive correlation between government outlays and productivity, not an inverse one. The economy boomed between 1947 and 1973, when the government share of total GDP was nearly doubling from 11 to 20 percent. In the subsequent period of economic stagnation (1973–95), government spending actually declined a bit as a share of GDP, to 19 percent.[9] This is one of the reasons that even Nixon's chairman of the Council of Economic Advisers put little stock in this argument. Studying the boom period from 1956 to 1973, Herbert Stein concluded that the alleged debilitating effects of government spending and taxes on economic growth were "at least uncertain and probably small."[10] Denison was quickly running out of suspects. What or who was left?

OPEC. A seemingly obvious culprit was the cabal of oil sheiks in the Middle East. After 1973, as the nation tried to grapple with oil and gas prices that went through the roof following the Yom Kippur war and the subsequent oil embargo, it seemed reasonable to blame the decline in productivity growth on OPEC. The timing in this case was perfect. Both the oil embargo and the beginning of the productivity slump happened almost simultaneously.

Moreover, there was a plausible theory to back up the contention that the energy crisis was the proximate cause for the end of the productivity boom. For decades, companies had built their production systems on the assumption of cheap oil. Now, suddenly, they were forced to convert their operations to work in an environment of expensive fuel. This meant that new investment had to be diverted away from productivity improvement to foster energy conservation.[11]

No one could easily argue with this theory as long as OPEC had the power to raise oil prices at will. But once the cartel's monopoly was shattered in the early 1980s, one would have expected productivity to surge. By the late 1980s the price of a barrel of crude was down to less than half of what it had been just five years earlier. Productivity growth, however, continued to erode. Again, theory was trumped by reality.

Baumol's Disease. Exasperated by the apparent fruitlessness of his search, Denison turned his attention to two final suspects. One was the shift of labor from the manufacturing sector to services. Such an interindustry shift could affect overall productivity if workers were moving from industries where productivity growth was generally high into sectors where productivity growth was much harder to achieve. Denison was searching for a measure of what had come to be known as "Baumol's disease."

In a seminal article appearing in 1967, Princeton's William Baumol, now at New York University, argued that the nature of production in manufacturing made it possible to increase labor productivity almost without limit.[12] As wage rates rose, manufacturers could progressively automate their operations, continuously reducing labor input. In contrast, he argued, the labor-intensive nature of retail trade and service industries almost assures stagnant productivity, since there are limits to how much technology can be used as a substitute for real human beings. Can a robot really replace a nurse in a hospital or a doorman at a luxury hotel?

Following this logic, it seemed obvious that as nations develop and the balance of consumption shifts from manufactured goods to trade and services, national productivity growth rates must inevitably slip. Cities would be hardest hit, as manufacturing fled to the suburbs, leaving core trade and service activities behind. Here was an argument that the fateful drop in productivity growth was permanent. A postindustrial society would have to settle for diminished growth.

The theory seems sound enough. After all, how much more efficient can the New York Philharmonic get at performing Beethoven's Ninth Symphony, even after playing it over and over again? Playing it in much less than sixty-six minutes or without a violin section would improve measured productivity, but one doubts that audiences would regard it as an improvement.

Yet empirical studies appear to rule out interindustry shifts as a major culprit. In fact, new information technologies may ultimately have their greatest impact not on industries like autos and steel but on banking and insurance, and in retail and wholesale trade. Indeed, while some expanding service sector industries have poor productivity records, others have reasonably good ones — as we shall document later in this chapter. In any case, while we have clearly moved toward a "service-based" economy, the shift has not been as dramatic as it might appear, and the ability of nonmanufacturing sectors to avoid Baumol's disease turns out to be greater than originally believed.[13] So the mystery of falling productivity remains unsolved, despite this intriguing possibility. That leaves one last suspect.

Lazy Workers and Incompetent Managers. Perhaps the ultimate cause of the productivity drought was not postindustrial society or wealthy Arab oil sheiks, but the American worker and the American manager. Perhaps, as some complained, "people didn't want to work any more." If younger workers are not as committed to their jobs as workers of an earlier generation, then output will doubtless suffer. Similarly, the quality of corporate management may have deteriorated so that resources have become inefficiently organized. Unfortunately, such human behavior is much too difficult to measure, so this idea can only remain conjecture. That people are working more overtime than ever before and that the labor force is better educated than ever before are two reasons to believe that blaming the productivity collapse on lousy workers and dumb managers is much too facile.

Surveying the wreckage at the end of his long inquiry, Denison concluded that "no single hypothesis seems to provide a probable explanation of the sharp change [in productivity growth] after 1973."[14] Concluding such a laborious and frustrating search for the productivity-robbing culprits of the post-1973 era, Denison signed off with a refreshingly candid conclusion (at least for an economist): "What happened is, to be blunt, a mystery."[15] Most economists scratched their heads and concurred.

This is quite a confession. The most significant and dismal reversal in the nation's economic prospects in half a century, and economists were at a total loss to explain it.

Searching Beyond Economics

To their credit, that the economics profession was not able to solve the mystery of America's lost productivity growth was not for lack of trying. A special MIT Commission on Industrial Productivity, comprising distinguished engineers and economists, made another valiant attempt at the end of the 1980s. But the commissioners came up as empty-handed as Denison. They concluded their long and detailed study by suggesting that hard-to-measure factors including "outdated competitive strategies," "short time horizons," "technological weaknesses," "neglect of human resources," "failures of cooperation," and "government and industry working at cross purposes" were responsible.[16] All of these fall into Denison's category of advances in knowledge — the 60 percent of the productivity conundrum left unexplained by his long bill of particulars.

The MIT commission report, though compiled by a cast of stellar scholars, suggested that if the productivity mystery were ever to be solved, it would be necessary to shift attention away from the narrow discipline of economics to consideration of the broader social and political environment within which the economy operates. Sociology and political science, often dismissed by economists as being too fuzzy-headed for scientific purposes, now seemed the best place to search for answers that had eluded the number crunchers.

Among economists who crossed jurisdictional lines in the renewed quest for an explanation was the late Mancur Olson of the University of Maryland. Olson noted that the "estimates of the sources of growth, however meticulous, subtle, and useful, do not tell us about the ultimate causes of growth. They do not tell us what incentives made the saving and investment occur, or what explained the innovations, or why there was more innovation and capital accumulation in one society or period than another."[17] Understanding social and political behavior might help.

In previous work, Olson had made the case that because of the gains to be made from collective action by individuals sharing a common condition, special-interest groups will inevitably proliferate in a democracy.[18] In his new work, Olson tried to show how the spread of special-interest groups ultimately subverts economic growth.

All rational individuals, he argued, have a powerful incentive to join organizations that work to assure their members higher incomes. Workers join unions, if they can; professionals form associations; and companies create their own trade organizations. Special-interest groups proliferate like rabbits, and they lobby government for special privileges. This might not be so destructive of growth if there were some countervailing power that supported the public interest against such organizations. But this is unlikely to occur, for whereas special interests have a powerful incentive to fight for their own members, the incentive for any one member of the public at large to resist is much weaker.

A good example is trade protection. A tariff or quota on imported steel benefits steelworkers and steel company stockholders greatly. On the other hand, despite the upward pressure such protection puts on steel prices, the purchasers of automobiles built only partly of steel hardly notice the marginally higher prices they pay for their cars.[19] Therefore, there is little inducement to mount and pay for a concerted counterattack on the special interests who engage dozens of lobbyists and spend millions of dollars to influence trade legislation.

Such asymmetrical incentives affect economic growth because special interests are oriented toward struggles over the *distribution* of income and wealth rather than toward the production of additional output. Olson called such special-interest groups "distributional coalitions." As the web of such organizations grows over time, Olson suggests, more of society's energy is devoted to distribution and less is devoted to production. Instead of expanding the economic pie, effort is focused on fighting over its division. Lawyers and financial advisers — those who create no new value but exist merely to redistribute existing output — replace scientists and engineers in the ranks of the best-paid professionals.

Occasionally, special-interest groups will serve the purpose of economic efficiency and growth by canceling out the negative influence of other special-interest groups, such as when the auto industry lobby opposes special tariff protection for the industry's steel suppliers. But on balance, Olson concluded, special-interest organizations reduce efficiency and national income and make political life more divisive.

According to this logic, by the early 1970s the organizational quicksand of special-interest groups had finally deepened sufficiently to impede further economic growth in America. A decade later the same argument was being made about Europe and even Japan. On the continent, it is called "Eurosclerosis." In the far east, it is "Japan, Inc." The slowdown in the growth rate of virtually every developed country is presumably the price we pay for democracy. Extrapolating from this theory, the slowdown in productivity and economic growth after 1973 must be seen as an inevitable and permanent state, something akin to Baumol's disease.

Intriguing as it may be, this theory is difficult to test. Olson reviewed European history and observed that Britain, which has the oldest stable democracy in the region, has also developed the most intricate web of collusive organizations, from trade unions to professional associations and trade groups, and has had (until recently) the lowest growth rate among developed countries. After World War II, most of Germany's and Japan's special-interest groups lay in ruins. It would take several decades for their special interests to regroup to the point that their actions hindered economic growth. For the United States, Olson shows that after the Civil War, it was the New South that grew faster than the old North, and southern and western cities grew faster than those of the earlier-established northeast, where special interests were already entrenched. All of this provides circumstantial evidence for the theory.[20]

But, we might ask, if the theory is correct, why did growth rates collapse so suddenly rather than slowly recede? How is it that growth was especially rapid in the 1950s and 1960s, when special interests like organized labor were most powerful, and it slowed only *after* unions had lost membership and political clout in the 1970s and 1980s?

The same can be said of business. Industry was particularly powerful in the immediate postwar era, when government regulation conferred virtual monopoly status on such sectors as telecommunications and air travel. The lack of global competition permitted virtual monopolies even in large parts of the unregulated sector. Yet this is precisely when the economy grew the fastest. For nearly two decades, business was able to use its considerable clout to forestall social regulation pertaining to the environment, civil rights, and workplace safety and health. It was only later, in the slow-growth period after 1973, that broad-based public lobbying groups such as the Sierra Club and the Children's Defense Fund gained the political power to check special interests in the logging, mining, and tobacco industries.

As a result, it is difficult to tell from the historical record whether the development of powerful special-interest groups in the form of virtual monopolies enhances or retards economic growth. The redistributionalist, sclerotic behavior of certain groups cannot be discounted as a factor influencing growth in certain sectors of the economy (such as in railroads, when rail unions insisted on keeping coal firemen on diesel locomotives). But the evidence suggests that it is hard to blame much of the post-1973 collapse in economic growth on the proliferation of special-interest groups. We might get special pleasure from blaming our problems on lawyers and lobbyists, but it is hard to make the case.

Blame It on the Data!

When all else fails, there is one last refuge for the forensic detective: rein-vestigate whether a crime actually took place. Perhaps the reason why the experts have not been able to locate the sources of the productivity deba-cle is that no such debacle actually occurred. A number of prominent economists have suggested just that. The problem might lie in the data, not in the economy.

Productivity, it is argued, may be increasing in key sectors, but stan-dard measures are failing to detect it. The statistics may have become more problematic over time, as output shifts from manufacturing, where it is relatively easy to measure tangible output, to service industries, where measurement is confounded by subtle changes in output quality and where the output itself is sometimes even hard to recognize. In the health care industry, how do you count the productivity gain from a medical procedure that reduces the recovery period from surgery? Fewer hospital days per patient may capture part of the resulting productivity gain. But what of the productivity gain if the patient returns to work a week sooner than otherwise? Measuring the efficiency gain in the plastics extrusion industry or in meat packing is surely easier.

Harvard economist Zvi Griliches suggests that by 1990 the fraction of the American economy consisting of sectors in which it is hard to mea-sure productivity improvement had increased to 69 percent from only 51 percent in 1947.[21] Generally, this reflects the shift in the U.S. economy from goods production to services. If so, it is possible that our productiv-ity measures are getting worse and worse over time. Productivity growth may have declined, but maybe not.[22]

In one industry, at least, this is almost surely the problem. According to the official government numbers, there has been practically no growth in output in the financial services industry — in banking, mutual fund firms, and consumer credit agencies — since 1990. That seems impossi-ble given the explosion in the value of outstanding consumer credit, the number of ATM transactions, the quintupling of mortgage applications, and the sheer number of stocks trading on multiple stock exchanges.[23] The reason for the flat growth line in financial services is that the govern-ment has not figured out a good way to measure its value. Indeed, output in the banking sector is measured by the number of employee hours worked. As such, productivity in this large component of financial services is effectively *defined* to be flat. By one set of calculations, the mismeasurement of this one sector of the economy is responsible for undercounting GDP by $25 billion a year and undercounting productivity growth by 0.3 percentage points.[24]

Even Alan Greenspan, chairman of the Federal Reserve Board, has strong reservations about the official productivity statistics. Few can recite them more effortlessly than Greenspan, who is known to have an encyclopedic knowledge of economic data in general. When the overall productivity statistics are disaggregated by sector, he notes, many service industries show up as having *negative* productivity growth. When averaged in with other sectors, this brings the aggregate productivity numbers down sharply. But Greenspan asks whether we can really believe that firms are actually becoming less efficient over time. Since he finds this unlikely, he has instructed his own data crunchers at the Fed to simply ignore such data points and convert negative productivity statistics into zeros before calculating the aggregate numbers in their spreadsheets.[25] Presto! Much of the productivity growth collapse disappears.

Nevertheless, it would be hard to convince millions of workers and their families that over the past two decades their standard of living improved just about as fast as it did during the glory days. Is it possible that productivity continued to rise at 2 percent or better each year, but none of it showed up in rising wages or family incomes? Clearly, this would entail an enormous amount of extra income that went to someone — but not to anyone we personally know.

Historians to the Rescue

As it turns out, there is every reason to believe that the productivity slowdown of 1973–95 was real enough. And, indeed, there is an explanation for it. The explanation comes not from economists, political scientists, sociologists, or psychologists, but from historians. By looking at economic history in the nineteenth and early twentieth centuries, they have been able to propound a theory of a *productivity cycle* that appears to fit the current era.

The story begins with a paradox. How could it be that the computer and information technology revolution could have done so little for productivity? Just think of the telecommunications revolution that has given us virtually instantaneous communication worldwide without the need for a telephone operator. Or consider the widespread use of fax, voice mail, and e-mail. It is hard to believe that these innovations have not increased productivity. The same can be said, of course, of the large mainframe computers that now run every major business in the country and of the networked PCs on nearly everyone's desk.

Certainly, there has been a great deal of investment in these modern tools (see Table 3.3). Recent years have seen a rapid diffusion of new technology, as investment has moved away from traditional machinery and transportation equipment into information technologies, computers, and other "high-tech" products and services. With nearly half of all new equipment investment now in modern information processing equipment — up from only a quarter in 1979 — the technology is spreading rapidly throughout the economy. So why has the vaunted high-tech revolution not paid off in economic growth? This "productivity paradox" has stumped social scientists for at least a decade. Is it not peculiar, as the economist Robert Solow has remarked, that computers are showing up everywhere but in the productivity statistics?

One possibility is that we have pinned our hopes falsely on the computer revolution. Today computers are ubiquitous in virtually every industry from agriculture to zipper manufacture. Microprocessors are found in many of the consumer products we buy and in nearly every piece of machinery that produces them. These tiny bits of silicon and copper have become amazingly more powerful in the twenty-five years

Table 3.3. Composition of New Investment in Private Sector Producers' Durable Equipment

Year	Information Processing Equipment	Industrial Equipment	Transportation Equipment
1959	12.8%	50.7%	36.6%
1969	14.7	46.5	38.8
1979	24.2	39.6	36.1
1989	39.4	34.1	26.5
1995	46.5	26.3	27.2

Source: *Economic Report of the President*, 1996, Table B-15, p. 297.

they have been around. The first Intel 4004 chip, produced in late 1971, was capable of processing about 60,000 instructions per second. The latest, introduced in 1998, is capable of 300 million.[26] Yet it is over almost the same period of time that national productivity nose-dived.

The original industry-level studies of productivity during the 1980s were fully consistent with the aggregate national trend. They almost unanimously concluded that, for all the hoopla about the "information age," there was little increased productivity to show for it. Using data on sixty business units of large firms from 1978 to 1984, one researcher could find no evidence whatsoever that computers added *anything* to total output.[27] Other researchers, surprised at this counterintuitive result, reinvestigated the data. No matter how much they tried, they ended up with the same discouraging results. At best, the introduction of computers influenced inventory turnover but not overall company performance.[28] Around the same time, a series of studies using industry-level data for 1968 through 1986 found that a dollar spent on information technology returned only eighty cents in revenue to the firm.[29] Essentially, those firms and industries that spent lavishly on computers and information systems saw their productivity rise by less than at firms that retained more traditional methods in their operations. Investment in information technology was *negatively* correlated with productivity!

These studies have prompted many to ask whether information technology (IT) investment has gone into the wrong applications or whether the productivity contributions of IT are being offset or frittered away within firms.

Using the work of Stephen Roach, a well-respected financial analyst, sociologist Paul Attewell of the City University of New York suggests that company managers became so bewitched by the alleged capabilities of computers that they failed to consider the cost-benefit ratios of adopting new technologies and installed them en masse despite their lack of a proven performance record.[30] In Roach's words, "We have over-MIP'd ourselves."[31] The result is that instead of getting more productivity from computerizing, many industries have seen their productivity shrink as they threw more and more money into computers, networks, and related technology. Studies of capital productivity in the banking industry in the late 1980s appear to confirm this conjecture. While labor productivity has risen modestly with the introduction of computer technologies, the productivity of capital in the banking industry has actually dropped pre-cipitously since the mid-1950s.[32] ATMs may have been a boon for the customer, but, ironically, not for the banks — at least through the 1980s. The number of bank tellers has declined, but not anywhere near as much as one might have expected given the rush to put ATMs on what seems like every street corner.

How can we explain this counterintuitive finding? For one thing, the new machines need lots of care and feeding from human beings. Instead of tellers, banks now must hire hundreds of couriers to pick up deposits at the scattered ATMs and restock the machines with cash. It also takes a small army of repair technicians to keep these wonderfully efficient ma-chines on the job. There are a number of other possibilities, however, as to why the new technologies did not boost measured productivity when they were introduced. For example, the benefits of word processing may be showing up in "quality" rather than quantity. Anyone who has spent much time working at a computer keyboard (rather than a typewriter) recognizes the urge to reformat and reedit text over and over again in order to make a document not only read better but look better. While this may indulge a writer's pride in his or her own work, it is altogether possi-ble that this has gone well beyond the point of diminishing returns.[33] A related problem is that despite the promise that the electronic revolution would save entire forests, just the opposite seems to have occurred. With IT we are generating mountains of paper and paperwork, much of which may have little value at all. In the process, instead of reducing the need for labor, the new technology is creating a huge volume of new work, much of it producing little measurable output. In one of his own studies of a sample of New York firms, Attewell found that only 19 percent of IT applications led to shrinkage in employment, 20 percent led to increases, and 61 percent showed no change.[34] If total output did not change very much after introduction of the new technologies, then these employment figures would suggest virtually no change in average productivity.

Learning Curves and Lags

But perhaps the most straightforward reason for why the new technology has not paid off is simply that it is changing so rapidly. Companies are constantly updating their information technology hardware and the software that goes with it. Firms are essentially expensing their IT capital stock, not depreciating it. This is a far cry from the past, when new capital had useful lives of ten to fifteen years or even more.

The problem is that new machines and new software are not perfect substitutes for the old. Updated operating systems must be debugged, and employees must be trained in their peculiar characteristics. Just when workers are gaining proficiency on one system, it is replaced with another. Before they can move up the steep section of the "learning curve," where large productivity gains are made, workers are bumped onto the next curve, corresponding to a new, yet to be mastered technology. Instead of one long-term learning curve, there is a succession of curves, as depicted in Figure 3.2. Productivity increases along the learning curve associated with technology release 1.0 in this figure. But rather than continuing to move up this curve, release 2.0 of the technology is introduced. For a while, productivity actually declines, until a significant share of the new technique's users learn the new routines. If new versions of the technology are entering the market at a rapid clip, it may take years before the full productivity premium of the technology is achieved.

In this way, the speed of the technology revolution is actually a hin-

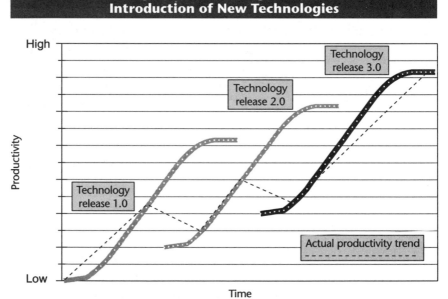

**Figure 3.2. Learning Curves:
Introduction of New Technologies**

drance to short-term productivity growth, not a contributor. The benefits may show up only when the new technology reaches a state of maturity, once many of its users have gained proficiency in the mature version.

This, at last, could provide the key to unlock the mystery of the productivity paradox: The arrival of the information age will *eventually* pay off in increased economic growth through improved productivity, but its initial impact on growth is trivial or even negative. It may take decades for a new technology — or a string of technological improvements — to finally bear fruit. This may explain why researchers found little productivity improvement in such industries as banking when they studied them some years ago.

Here is where the historians come in. Their studies tell us that a productivity lag is a common, if not universal, technological phenomenon. Farming provides just one example. No sector is more famous for its productivity improvement than American agriculture. At the turn of the century, 30 percent of the U.S. labor force worked on farms. Today less than 3 percent of the workforce is needed to feed the entire nation, with a surplus left over to export to other countries. This massive improvement in agricultural productivity did not happen suddenly or smoothly. Instead, very much like the learning curves we saw in Figure 3.2, productivity growth was initially quite modest and hit its stride only after several decades.

Economic historian Nathan Rosenberg of Stanford has used U.S. government agricultural statistics to compile estimates of the average man-hours needed to grow such crops as corn, wheat, and cotton.[35] As Figure 3.3 demonstrates, in each of these cases, productivity grew slowly from 1910 through 1935. Only in the following two decades, well after new farming techniques were first introduced, did crop yields flourish. World War II marks the transition to much higher yields per acre and per worker-hour. As Rosenberg documents, the productivity premium finally materialized only after several interrelated factors came together: the widespread use of herbicides, insecticides, and synthetic nitrogenous fertilizers, the development of hybrid seeds, greater use of irrigation facilities, and shifting patterns of regional crop specialization.[36] The development of chemical engineering and the declining cost of electrical energy needed to produce synthetic fertilizer were the critical preconditions permitting labor productivity to double each decade following World War II. One could have asked where the productivity dividend was

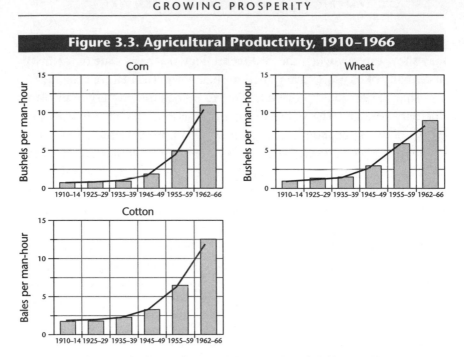

Figure 3.3. Agricultural Productivity, 1910–1966

Source: Rosenberg, *Technology and American Economic Growth,* Table 7, p. 136.

from all of the modern agricultural techniques applied in the first decades of the new century. Only after the war was the answer obvious.

Lags in the introduction and diffusion of new technology help explain the initial sluggishness in productivity growth. Agricultural machinery suffered long lags in its introduction. The mechanical reaper, for example, had been invented in the 1830s, yet not until fully two decades later did Midwestern farmers adopt the new machine en masse. According to economic historian Paul David, the delay occurred because it was only when farms reached a certain size threshold that the new technology had a clear benefit over the earlier labor-intensive methods of reaping.[37] Others suggest that only with numerous small improvements in the basic design did the reaper become commercially feasible.[38]

The introduction of electric motors into manufacturing provides another example of the slow diffusion of a new innovation and, consequently, the slow improvement in productivity. Electric motors were available at the end of the last century, but by 1899 less than 5 percent of the total installed horsepower in U.S. manufacturing enterprises came from the new power source.[39] Most businesses continued to rely on steam or water power to turn lathes, drills, and saws. A decade later only a quarter of manufacturing horsepower came from electric motors, and as late as World War I, less than half of the machinery used in American factories and plants was powered by electricity. In the very next decade, however, this ratio would jump to over 80 percent.

What made the difference was that electric motors supplanted steam and water power only when firms were prepared to make all of the concomitant changes needed in the basic layout of their factories. When steam and water were king, power from a central turbine was distributed throughout the mill by overhead shafts and belts connected to each individual machine. When electric power was first introduced, large, inefficient motors were simply substituted for the steam turbine or water wheel. When it finally became clear that each machine could be powered by its own small electric motor, electricity finally came into its own. Downtime was reduced since the failure of one motor took only one machine out of commission, not all of them, and much less energy was wasted simply in turning long, heavy shafts and miles of leather belt. Each machine could now be more easily and accurately controlled and could be relocated within the factory more readily.[40] Historians claim that the large boost in labor productivity after World War I is directly tied to the diffusion of the electric motor a quarter century after its invention; but the initial introduction produced a drop in labor productivity before its potential could be realized.

If we take history back even further, we learn that the productivity lag from the industrial revolution extended over generations. Economic historian Joel Mokyr of Northwestern University informs us that while the industrial revolution is usually dated between about 1760 and 1830, "the fruits of the industrial revolution were slow in coming. Per capita consumption and living standards increased little initially. . . . Large sectors of the economy, employing the majority of the labor force and accounting for at least half of the gross national product were, for all practical purposes, unaffected by innovation before the middle of the nineteenth century."[41]

That technological revolutions, in general, take time to work themselves through — to move from infancy to primacy — may be due to any number of factors. The steam engines built by Thomas Newcomen and used to pump water out of Welsh coal mines were first introduced in

1712. Because of their construction, they had a voracious appetite for fuel and thus were expensive to operate. Even after numerous improvements, the Newcomen steam engine of 1769 required 30 pounds of coal per horsepower-hour. Only in 1776, after James Watt separated the condenser from the piston cylinder so that the cylinder could be kept hot indefinitely, did the fuel consumption of the steam engine improve markedly, dropping to 7.5 pounds per horsepower-hour. For the first time, a steam engine was sufficiently fuel efficient to permit it to be used where coal was not as bounteously plentiful as at the bottom of coal mines.[42]

There are, in fact, numerous reasons why new technologies spread slowly, with their productivity benefits achieved only after a long gestation period. New techniques have many "bugs" that must be ironed out before large-scale adoption is worthwhile. The capital goods sector which produces the new machinery must learn how to produce the new tools efficiently. Complementary skills must be honed and a labor force trained to produce goods using the new technology.[43]

Based on these historical studies, Jeremy Greenwood, an economist at the University of Rochester, now tells a simple, but elegant, story that connects the rate of technological progress to the level of income inequality and productivity growth.[44] According to Greenwood, the adoption of a new technology involves a significant cost in terms of learning new processes and procedures. The lack of experience with a new technology almost surely means that it will be used inefficiently at first. Productivity growth may appear to stall as the economy undertakes the investment in knowledge needed to operate the new technology closer to its full potential. Since initially only highly skilled and specialized workers understand how to use the new technology, the demand for their skills rises, often sharply. As a result, the earnings gap between skilled and unskilled workers widens in the early stage of a technological revolution. Eventually, once this early phase is complete, productivity soars. But this will take years, perhaps even decades.

As a complement to this argument, when a new technology finally matures, lesser-skilled workers can be trained to operate it. Indeed, labor cost considerations will encourage this. Over the long run, then, new innovations generate both higher productivity and a lessening of income inequality, as newly trained, lesser-skilled workers are brought into the production loop.

Greenwood provides considerable evidence that this is precisely what happened during the British industrial revolution. Prior to 1760, labor productivity in England improved at an average rate of about 0.4 percent per year.[45] With the onset of the industrial revolution, annual productivity growth fell to about 0.2 percent and remained there for nearly four decades. Only after 1800, as the steam engine was perfected and other new manufacturing techniques became more commonplace, did productivity growth return to its pre-1760 levels. By 1830 the industrial revolution was in full bloom; workers had learned to use the new technologies, and productivity growth soared to 1.1 percent a year for much of the rest of the century (see Figure 3.4).

This U- or V-shaped pattern of productivity growth is seen again in the United States in the antebellum period. The industrial revolution arrived in America around 1840. Annual growth in the real stock of equipment on a per capita basis rose sharply from just 0.7 percent between 1775 and 1815 to 2.8 percent between 1815 and 1860. One indication of this explosion in investment is found in the railroad industry. In 1830

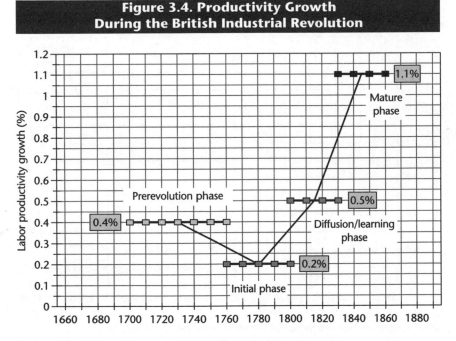

Figure 3.4. Productivity Growth During the British Industrial Revolution

Source: Adapted from Greenwood, "The Third Industrial Revolution."

there were just 30 miles of railroad track in the entire nation. Ten years later it had grown to only about 2,800. But in the next twenty years, the track bed grew by a factor of ten, reaching 30,000 by 1860. In the same 1840–1860 period, the aggregate capacity of steam locomotives quadrupled. Nevertheless, it was precisely during this period of massive investment in new technology that the productivity growth rate *declined* by nearly half (see Figure 3.5). Only after the mid-1850s did productivity take off, partly as a result of the growing (although still not complete) standardization of track gauges across different lines. This allowed more rapid transfer of freight, with less time wasted loading and reloading from the cars of one company to another.

When productivity in the United States did take off, it eclipsed the old prerevolution growth rate by better than two to one and the early diffusion/learning phase by better than four to one.[46] As in Britain, the premium paid to skilled workers rose sharply during the early phases of the industrial revolution. In the United States the skill premium increased

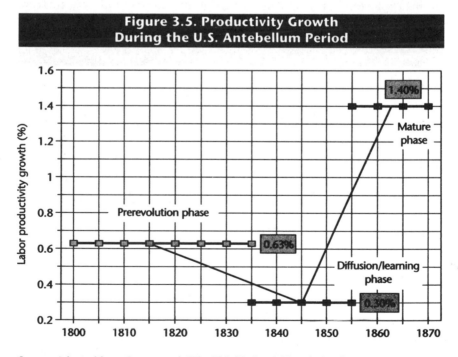

Figure 3.5. Productivity Growth During the U.S. Antebellum Period

Source: Adapted from Greenwood, "The Third Industrial Revolution."

from about 15 percent in the 1820s to 70 percent during the mature phase of the industrial cycle. It then settled down at the new, higher level just before the Civil War.[47]

The considerable lag in the productivity bonus from new technologies is thus due to two factors. One has to do with learning effects; the other with diffusion. More than thirty years ago, Stanford University's Kenneth Arrow published his seminal article on the economic implications of "learning by doing."[48] His point was quite simple: Much of learning does not precede going to work but is accomplished in the course of work. In an industrial setting, most learning takes place *after* the R&D stage is complete and *after* a product has been designed. Increasing skill in the course of production reduces real labor cost per unit of output and therefore is a critical component in the advancement of productivity. Case studies of airframe production, shipbuilding, machine tools, and textiles provide evidence of the importance of this form of productivity improvement.[49] The key point is that learning by doing takes time to spread throughout a vast economy.

Nathan Rosenberg identifies a slightly different form of the learning experience, something he calls "learning by using," but the implication is the same.[50] Productivity improvements come about mainly as the result of "individually small, but cumulatively very large, changes in technique that can only be learned from direct participation in the production process." This is the domain not of the product developer, but of the product user — the blue-collar worker finding ways to optimize the throughput of his machine, or the white-collar worker developing a better filing system or a better computerized database.

These improvements typically "require intimate familiarity with the minutiae of the productive sequence."[51] Especially in the case of complex, sophisticated technology, the performance characteristics of such equipment often cannot be understood until there has been prolonged experience with it. Thus, long bouts of trial and error are often required to get the most out of a complex new technology. This was certainly true of the steam engine and the cotton reaper, but it is just as true today for computer hardware and software. Moreover, improved productivity only comes as the result of a feedback loop between users and designers — between machine operators and machine designers, between airline pilots and aircraft manufacturers, and between prose writers and computer code writers who develop the software for word processing programs. Only with extensive feedback can reliability be built into new products — a major concern for banks that operate ATMs, almost as much as for airlines concerned with the safety of their passengers. Improving reliability in new models of aircraft and new releases of software also improves productivity, by reducing labor-intensive maintenance and repair costs. Fault-tolerant service has been particularly important in boosting the overall operating efficiency of telephone equipment.[52] But getting there takes time.[53]

The other cause of the productivity lag is the slow adoption of new technologies. Economic historians refer to a *diffusion curve,* similar to the S-shaped function we associate with learning curves. Like so many other things we have reviewed here, there is a feedback loop between learning curves and diffusion curves. The more costly it is for workers to master a new technology, the more slowly it will be adopted throughout the economy. Thus, the cost of adoption and the extent of adoption are interrelated. Especially with complex new technologies, elongated learning curves will lead to elongated diffusion curves, and the two operating in tandem will constrain productivity dividends for quite a long time.

The rate of diffusion depends especially on government- or industry-imposed standards, as in the example we gave of rail track gauges. The most dramatic contemporary examples come from the personal computer industry. The perception of real profitability — and therefore the burst of third-party hardware and software development — came only after the victory of the open IBM PC-compatible architecture over other operating systems such as the Apple Macintosh, and after the virtually complete standardization of computer environments due to the near monopoly of Intel microprocessors and Microsoft operating systems.

As a result of these multiple lags and feedback loops, it is common for the diffusion of modern techniques to take a long time. Using evidence from a study of 265 innovations, one research team found that it took a typical new innovation forty-one years, on average, to move from the 10 percent to the 90 percent diffusion level.[54] The diesel locomotive was clearly superior to the steam locomotive, yet twenty years after the first diesel was introduced to railroading in 1925, there were still nearly ten steam locomotives in service for every diesel-powered engine. Not until after World War II, between 1945 and 1955, did the diesel finally replace the old steam engine.[55] Five years later, in 1960, steam engines accounted for only 0.5 percent of all locomotives in America.

The Productivity Paradox Reassessed

This brings us back to the information age and the productivity paradox. The history we have reviewed suggests that we should not be surprised by the initially meager payoff on the massive investment in information technology (IT). Indeed, given what is now known about previous technological revolutions, it would actually be unusual if we were to have already seen a big productivity payoff from the computer revolution. For the introduction of computers and their offspring represents at least as much of a revolution in the workplace as the introduction of steam power, electric power, or the diesel locomotive. The payoff should be expected to be slow in coming because of the lags introduced in both the learning process and the diffusion process. In fact, rapid innovation in computers actually dampens the productivity dividend in the short run, as computer users move from one learning curve to the next before fully achieving the potential benefits of the first.

The information age is now in its fourth decade. Is there any evidence that we are finally reaping the rewards for the hundreds of billions of dollars spent on hardware and software and on the changes in organizational structure accompanying its introduction? The preliminary answer is yes. In a series of important studies by MIT's Erik Brynjolfsson and his colleague Lorin Hitt of the University of Pennsylvania, concrete evidence of the productivity dividend is beginning to appear. Using annual surveys of several hundred large firms over the period 1987–91, these two researchers have found that the marginal product for computers now exceeds 50 percent, and for many firms, investment in computers and associated IT pays off more handsomely than investments in conventional forms of capital.[56]

Brynjolfsson and Hitt's results differ from the findings of previous research for a number of reasons. First, they are looking at a later period. They note that the amount of computer power in the firms they studied was at least an order of magnitude greater than that in comparable firms studied in the 1980s. More important, they argue that what has really changed is not so much the new technology itself as the business processes and organizational structures needed to take full advantage of the technology's potential. These organizational changes normally lag behind implementation of the hardware and software and often are encouraged only after the technology is in place. As Lester Thurow put it, "to computerize the office, you have to reinvent the office."[57]

More generally, as Richard Nelson of Columbia and Sidney Winter of the University of Pennsylvania have long argued, old managerial routines (and sometimes experienced managers themselves) have to be undermined, scrapped, replaced, or skirted before new technologies can fully diffuse and thinking in new paradigms can take place.[58] Firms that are extensive users of information technology tend to adopt a complementary set of organizational practices, including decentralization of decision authority, emphasis on nonmonetary incentives, and a greater reliance on employee skills and human capital.[59] Such practices will become key elements in a new model of economic growth that we will develop in Chapter 7.

In short, companies are moving up the learning curve and are finally seeing a good return on their investments.[60] If the productivity trend in the current technological revolution follows the pattern of the technological revolutions in late eighteenth- and nineteenth-century England and in the nineteenth-century United States, then we may just be on the cusp of a productivity breakthrough.

An End to the Productivity Drought

Indeed, we can see the turning point in the most recent data. Labor productivity growth, which had so suddenly collapsed back in 1973, just as suddenly turned around in late 1995. Figure 3.6, which extends Figure 3.1 through the end of 1998, shows this clearly. For the last three years depicted, productivity in the private business sector grew by 2.6 percent per year — more than double the rate in the first half of the decade and substantially better than the rates of the 1970s and 1980s. While this improvement does not get us all the way back to the productivity performance of the glory days, it certainly should give pause to those who continue to counsel that we can never return to faster economic growth rates.

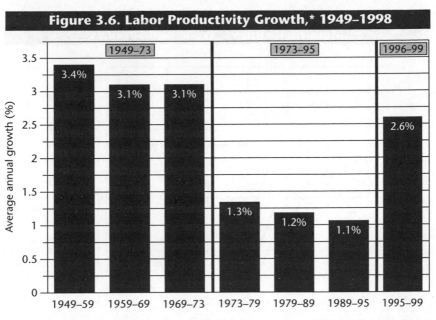

Figure 3.6. Labor Productivity Growth,* 1949–1998

Sources: for 1949–59, Krugman, *Age of Diminished Expectations;* 1959–99, *Economic Report of the President,* 2000.

*Growth in output per hour of work in business sector.

Admittedly, three years of exceptionally strong productivity growth provide a slender basis on which to proclaim the end of the productivity drought. But few economists would have forecast such strong growth a few years ago, and even today most are surprised that the economy has done as well as it has. If this strength *can* be sustained, and if labor force growth continues at a little better than 1 percent a year, GDP could grow at 3 percent or more a year, a quarter to a third better than recent official forecasts.

What makes this turnaround especially significant is that it reflects improved productivity in the *nonmanufacturing* sectors of the economy for the first time in two decades. As Figure 3.7 indicates, manufacturing productivity had already begun to recover soon after the 1973–79 period. Throughout the 1980s and early 1990s, productivity growth in this sector was as strong as it had been during the 1960s and faster than during the 1950s. By 1996–98, manufacturers were improving their efficiency by a remarkable 4.6 percent per year, the best record in the entire postwar era.

But it is the recovery in such industries as retail and wholesale trade, and transportation, communication, and financial services that is most

Figure 3.7. Labor Productivity Growth: Manufacturing vs. Trade and Services

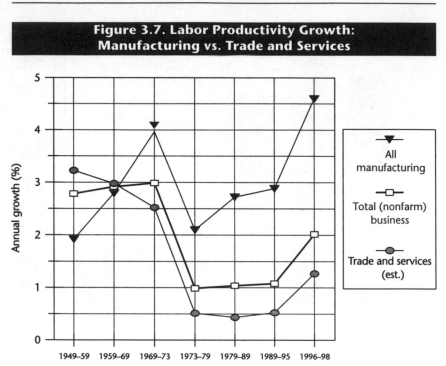

Sources: Bureau of Labor Statistics, Trade and services productivity interpolated from total business and all manufacturing series.

surprising and most helpful to the economy. The trade and services sector had performed tremendously immediately after World War II; indeed, productivity advances in this sector exceeded those in the goods-producing sectors. But already by the 1950s, efficiency gains in trade and services were on the wane, and they would continue to plummet through the early 1970s, when they reached a depressingly low 0.5 percent improvement per year. Productivity growth in this sector of the economy was so anemic that it dragged total business productivity growth down to less than 1 percent per year, despite a solid performance in the manufacturing sector.

The strong recovery in many of these trade and service industries can be seen in Table 3.4. In a few of these, there never was a productivity problem. Thanks to the continual introduction of new technologies in railroad transportation (particularly in tracing rail cars) and telephone communications, productivity growth in these industries has for decades

Table 3.4. The Productivity Turnaround* in Selected Trade and Service Industries, 1973–1996

Industry	1973–79	1979–90	1990–96	Direction of Change '90–96 vs. '79–90
Railroad transportation	2.6	7.4	7.1	–
Air transportation	5.6	1.9	3.1	+
Petroleum pipelines	0.7	0.5	2.8	+
Telephone communications	6.8	5.4	6.2	+
Gas utilities	−0.5	−3.6	3.2	+
Electric utilities	1.2	1.3	4.8	+
Department stores	3.3	2.2	2.7	+
Apparel and accessory stores	2.0	3.3	3.7	+
Home furnishings stores	2.0	2.3	5.7	+
Commercial banks	0.6	2.0	3.4	+
Hotels and motels	1.2	−1.2	2.2	+
Laundries and cleaning services	−0.1	−0.8	1.0	+
Beauty and barber shops	1.5	0.8	1.9	+
Automotive repair shops	−0.7	0.2	1.7	+

Sources: U.S. Bureau of Labor Statistics, *Industry Productivity Statistics*, Table 1, April 22, 1997; *Monthly Labor Review*, February 1999, Table 42.

*Average annual percentage change.

outperformed even the high flyers in the manufacturing sector. But the big story is about those industries that have been the laggards for the better part of the last twenty years. Some of these, such as gas utilities or laundries and cleaning services, now show positive productivity growth after years of apparently becoming less efficient over time. Others, such as electric utilities, apparel and accessory stores, home furnishings stores, commercial banks, and automotive repair shops show continuous improvement in productivity growth since the early 1970s. And still others, including petroleum pipelines, department stores, and hotels and motels, have reversed a slipping productivity trend. Led by these industries productivity growth in the trade and services sector as a whole rose to 1.3 percent per year after 1995, nearly tripling the rate of the early 1970s through the mid-1990s. Industries that are allegedly subject to Baumol's disease seem to have found an antidote, if not a cure.

Reviewing the record of the complete set of individual industries that the U.S. Bureau of Labor Statistics (BLS) tracks on a periodic basis provides additional reason for optimism about productivity. Altogether, the BLS follows 156 industries, ranging from those in mining and manufacturing to those in services and trade.[61] Of these, half (53 percent) saw a rebound in productivity growth in the early 1990s from their rates of the 1980s. The other half either saw no improvement or lost ground. What is more important, however, is how the once lagging trade and services sector made out. Of the 156 industries tracked, 37 are outside of manufacturing. Among these, half (51 percent) showed a positive trend in their productivity performance. Ten grew by better than 3 percent per year in the first half of the 1990s, while another five grew by at least 2 percent. This is the strongest evidence yet that trade and services are beginning to rebound, adding to overall productivity growth rather than subtracting from it.

To be sure, some industries have still not found a way to turn around their poor performance. Food stores, drugstores, liquor stores, and restaurants, for example, still show negative productivity growth. Whether these industries will rebound in the same way that department stores or hotels and motels have, we cannot tell with any certainty. But enough service and trade industries have improved their productivity growth records that one need no longer conclude that, as the economy becomes increasingly "postindustrial," we must settle inevitably for permanently slower growth. Those who counsel that we have entered an "age of diminished expectations" and face an "end to affluence" now must consider some data points that do not fit their neat, but pessimistic, view of America.

The Potential for U.S. Economic Growth

We now have in place most of the pieces needed to consider one of the key issues addressed in this book: How fast *can* the American economy grow? Beginning in 1992 we experienced higher growth in short, rapid spurts, almost as though the economic engine were trying to turn over like an old piston engine. In the first quarter of 1992, real GDP revved at a 4.7 percent annual clip, nearly matched by the 4.3 percent in the fourth quarter. Then the engine seemed to die until the last quarter of the following year. The economy turned in a stirring performance throughout most of 1994, only to falter for much of the next year.

Only in the spring of 1996 did the engine roar to life. The economy grew by 6 percent on an annual basis in the second quarter, a burst of economic activity nearly matched again in the first and last quarters of 1998. Indeed, growth exceeded 4 percent for a full year from the last quarter of 1996 through the last quarter of 1997, and it came close to this record again in 1998. For five years in a row now, the economy has been purring along much as it did during the glory days.

Still, the overall average annual growth rate between 1989 and 2000 was only 3.1 percent.[62] The paramount question is whether the U.S. economy is capable of *sustained* growth at this level. Can we sustain, for example, 3 percent average growth into the foreseeable future? As we noted in Chapter 1, this would cumulate over time so that we would enjoy literally trillions of dollars of additional output over the next decade, compared with what the old consensus forecast of only 2.3 percent would give us.

Recall the equation we introduced in the previous chapter: the overall economic growth rate equals the growth rate in productivity plus the growth rate in labor supply. The consensus forecast was based on the belief that productivity will grow at no better than 1.2 percent per year well into the next century and that the total hours of work in the economy will grow by only 1.1. percent.[63]

How much better might we do on both of these? As we have already suggested, we believe the productivity drought is over. Based on the turn-around we have already seen, we believe it is possible for productivity to grow somewhere in the 1.5–1.7 percent range at least through the first decade of the new millennium. This assumes continued strength in the manufacturing sector and the spread of higher productivity growth to an increasing share of the service sector.

But what about labor supply? Is there any chance that we might get more output from more input? The mainstream consensus is pretty pessimistic about this as well. Few demographers see much hope that labor supply will increase. We have a fairly accurate forecast of the number of *potential* workers between now and, say, the year 2006. After all, those who will be working adults by then have already been born. Only an unexpected change in death rates or in immigration can alter this number.

Otherwise, between now and 2006 — as well as into the foreseeable future — the population is projected to grow at 1 percent a year, give or take a few hundredths of a percentage point.

The question, therefore, is whether we can expect any more labor supply despite slow population growth. The answer is yes, and the reason is that labor supply growth depends on more than just an expanding population. The most appropriate and complete measure of labor supply growth is the *annual change in the total number of hours actually worked by the employed labor force.* This number can be obtained by taking into consideration all of its components — population growth being only one of them. The others are (1) changes in labor force participation, (2) fluctuations in unemployment, and (3) variations in annual work hours per worker. The historical impact of these factors on total hours worked in the postwar economy is summarized in Table 3.5.

A casual examination of the Total Hours Growth column appears to provide some powerful ammunition for the growth pessimists. Recall that the official forecast of 2.3 percent annual GDP growth into the next century is based on labor supply expanding at 1.2 percent per year. Only during the baby boom cycles of 1973–79 and 1979–89 have we experienced faster growth in total hours worked. Otherwise, we were lucky to have labor supply growth even as strong as the current forecast. Indeed, labor supply will have to grow 25 percent faster than during the first half of the 1990s if we are to meet the official forecast.

Fortunately, a more sanguine view of potential work hours is found by examining the remaining columns in the table. Since World War II, each business cycle's annual hours growth has been fostered by a different set of factors. For example, in the 1950s the anemic growth in total work hours was due to unusually small increases in the nation's adult population, combined with a decline in men's labor force participation and an increase in the unemployment rate. Only the entrance of a greater number of women into the labor force kept hours growth from being zero or even negative. In the following decade (1959–69), overall growth in hours recovered. It grew by a healthy 1.2 percent per year as the first contingent of baby boomers entered the labor market, women surged into paid work, and the jobless rate plummeted to postwar lows. This was the heyday of postwar economic growth — an economic boom fueled in

Table 3.5. The Sources of Employment Growth,* 1949–1995

Years	Total Hours Growth (%)	Population Growth (Age 16+) (%)	Labor Force Participation (LFP) Growth (All) (%)	Labor Force Participation Growth (Men) (%)	Labor Force Participation Growth (Women) (%)	Average Unemployment Rate†	Average Annual Hours per Worker (%)
1949–59	0.2	1.0	0.07	−0.3	1.2	+1.6	n.a.
1959–69	1.2	1.5	0.13	−0.5	1.4	−2.0	n.a.
1969–73	1.1	2.3	0.29	−0.3	1.2	+1.4	0.23
1973–79	1.8	1.9	0.78	−0.2	2.2	+0.9	−0.57
1979–89	1.6	1.2	0.43	−0.2	1.2	−0.5	0.42
1989–95	0.9	1.1	0.03	−0.3	0.4	+0.3	0.32

Sources: *Economic Report of the President,* 1987, 1996; authors' analysis of CPS data on hours of work.

*Annual growth rate.

†Change in rate.

part, we can now see, by the coming of age of the baby boomers and the strong recovery in employment growth.

During the business cycle that began in 1969 and ended in 1973, overall hours growth remained reasonably strong at 1.1 percent per year. This growth too was mostly due to baby boomers reaching their prime working years. Many who had been in college through 1969 had graduated and were now entering the labor force on a full-time basis.

But by far the heftiest postwar growth in work hours came during the 1973–79 period. Growth in the adult population continued at a healthy pace, but more important, a wave of women flooded into the labor market. On average, during each year of this period, women's labor force participation increased by better than 2 percent. In 1973, a little less than 45 percent of women over age 16 participated in the labor force; six years later, 51 percent of all adult women were working or seeking work. Without this surge, overall GDP growth would have fallen well below 3 percent per year as productivity growth slackened. Instead, growth remained at a strong 3.2 percent for the entire decade. America continued to enjoy the last remnants of the high-growth glory days, but now the growth was getting harder to come by.*

Strong employment growth continued throughout the 1980s. But this time the key factor was neither population growth nor an extraordinary surge in labor force participation. Instead, the growth in total hours worked in the economy was due almost exclusively to a factor that has given rise to the concept of the "overworked American."[64] Facing falling average wage rates, families did everything they could to hold on to their middle-class living standards. For most, this meant taking on extra paid work. The average work year expanded by nearly 74 hours during the course of the decade — the equivalent of workers adding nearly two full-time workweeks to their previous yearly schedules. Prime-age men (ages 25–54), who had reduced their average hours almost steadily during the 1970s, now reversed course, increasing their annual work time by more than 25 hours, or 1.2 percent. Prime-age women increased their annual work time by a staggering 128 hours during the decade. This 8.9 percent increase in annual hours was equivalent to each woman already in the workforce putting in more than three additional full-time workweeks per year.[65] What was traditionally a part-time job for women was turning into full-time work.

All this additional work permitted business output to grow at nearly 3 percent a year, despite a total collapse in the rate of productivity improvement. As before, we were producing more to satisfy our continuing appetite for more consumption, but we were now doing so only by sacrificing leisure time. For most Americans, working longer hours did no more than compensate for shrinking wages. Seven out of ten dual-earner families were caught in an *Alice in Wonderland* world where they had to run faster and faster just to stay in the same place. Total hours were up by 17 percent for the typical dual-earner family; total earnings were up by less than 4 percent.[66] Thus, the baby boomers began to prop up employment growth in the 1960s. Women kept the boom going during the 1970s through their extraordinary entry into the labor market, and we all

---

*Note that during the 1973–79 period, the length of the working year as found in the eighth column of Table 3.5 declined. This is largely due to the extraordinarily large contingent of women who entered the labor force during this period and took part-time and seasonal jobs. This helped reduce the average work year for the labor force as a whole, but the total number of work hours increased sharply.

kept employment growth from slowing during the 1980s by becoming workaholics.

Then, in the first half of the 1990s, the growth in labor supply all but collapsed. The baby boom generation was replaced by the smaller cohort of Generation X, driving the civilian population growth rate to the lowest level since the end of World War II. Even more important, growth in labor force participation all but ceased after decades of increase. And the unemployment rate crept up, also reducing overall hours. Only a continued increase in individual work hours kept total hours growth from shrinking to less than 0.9 percent per year — still the lowest growth rate since the 1950s. This slow growth in hours worked plus dismal productivity performance gave us the first sustained period of GDP growth below 3 percent since the Great Depression.

Given this recent trend, is there anything now on the horizon suggesting that we could once again see an increase in labor supply sufficient to boost GDP growth back to the 3 percent range or higher? Let's take a look at some reasonable forecasts for the individual components of labor supply.

Population Growth. As we noted earlier, the chance of procuring additional labor supply out of faster population growth is quite low. Even with continued immigration, the Census Bureau forecasts a slight slowing of the growth rate for the civilian noninstitutional population.[67] What that means is that by the end of the first decade of the next century, we will have 3.8 million fewer potential workers than we would have had if the population growth rate of the 1980s had been sustained into the future. Since there is little we can do about this, short of allowing greater immigration (or making a big breakthrough in the treatment of disease or a reduction in life-ending accidents), there is little room here for higher growth. Even a new baby boom would not help, since the new children would not enter the labor market until at least the year 2015.

Labor Force Participation. If we cannot count on population growth, is there any chance that we could see an increase in the proportion of the population entering the workforce? After hovering in the narrow range of 66.2 to 66.6 percent throughout the first half of the 1990s, the labor force participation rate actually began to rise in early 1996. A year later the rate was up to 67.3 percent. It is possible, of course, that this is a temporary blip that will disappear in another year or two. But there is fresh evidence that this renewed increase in labor force participation has a solid foundation. It is located in the retirement decisions of older workers.

For decades, the labor force participation rate of men over age 60 had been falling, as private pension prospects improved and Social Security benefits increased. In 1968, 80 percent of men aged 60–65 participated in the labor force. Twenty years later, participation was down to 56 percent.[68] One presumed that, over time, this rate would continue to decline, and this expected decline is built into many forecasts of future labor supply. Yet the data show that labor force participation among older workers has leveled off and is perched to rise a bit.[69]

This new trend is driven by public policies that encourage Americans to spend a longer period of their life span at work than they did in the past. Beginning in 1986, mandatory retirement was outlawed for most American workers. It is now illegal for employers to jettison workers simply because they are over the age of 65. Even more important, workers now have a greater economic incentive to take advantage of their newly won right. Recent changes in federal tax laws permit older workers to keep more of their Social Security checks if they continue to work. The amount of earnings permitted before Social Security benefits are reduced is now indexed to wage growth, so that as average wages increase, the exempt portion of Social Security rises as well.[70] Also, more of Social Security income is being taxed today, so that the after-tax benefits of the public pension system are lower. For high-income recipients (couples with income over $44,000, singles over $34,000), 85 percent of Social Security benefits are now considered taxable income. Added to this, the age of "normal" retirement — when a retiree can receive full Social Security benefits — is scheduled to increase from 65 to 66 by the year 2005.[71] Together with the improved health and life expectancy of older workers, these policy changes add to the incentive to work longer and provide disincentives to retiring early. In turn, they suggest that the labor force participation of older workers — those 55 and over — is likely to increase in the future, reversing the long-term trend that still dominates most forecasts of labor force participation rates. If the recent rise in labor force participation continues, we will get a little bit of added growth out of this factor alone.

Unemployment Rate. The official government forecast of 2.3 percent GDP growth through 2007 is predicated on maintaining an unemployment rate of 5.7 percent. We now know from experience that we can do much better than that, reaching jobless rates at least a point lower without igniting inflation. A general rule of thumb concerning the "welfare cost" of unemployment was first formulated nearly forty years ago by Arthur Okun, chairman of President Johnson's Council of Economic Advisers. According to "Okun's law," (in its original form), a temporary increase in the unemployment rate of 1 percentage point reduces real national output by about 3 percent.[72] This is the price that society pays for keeping workers unemployed. Conversely, Okun's law provides an estimate of the growth dividend we enjoy when we put people to work. Today, the ratio is about 1 to 2.[73] Hence, if we could move the long-term unemployment rate down to, say, the 4.8 percent level we enjoyed during the 1960s, we could boost GDP by 2 to 3 percent above forecasted levels. Driving the long-term unemployment rate below 5.7 percent would initially raise the GDP growth *rate*. Keeping it below 5.7 percent would boost the *level* of GDP each year thereafter above what it would be at higher jobless rates.[74] Simply by running the economy so that we can maintain unemployment below 5 percent, rather than the higher levels in official projections, yields higher GDP all by itself.

Hours per Worker. The real kicker, however, is a factor overlooked by the official labor supply growth forecasts: Americans are working longer hours, and there is no sign that this will reverse in the near future. A 1 percent increase in the number of hours worked per worker for a fixed labor force is mathematically equivalent, in terms of labor supply, to a 1 percent increase in the number of workers. Hence, as we saw in past decades, a decline in the rate of population growth or in labor force participation can be offset by a sufficient increase in hours worked by those who are already counted in the workforce, that is, experienced or incumbent workers. Such an increase does double duty for growth, adding to labor supply *and* productivity, since experienced workers are generally more productive than new workers just entering the workforce.

How important will this factor be in the future? We know that the nature of working time is continuing to change dramatically. An ever larger proportion of the American workforce deviates from working a standard work week and standard work year. One in six workers now report working part-time schedules, with one-quarter of these doing so involuntarily — a sign of underemployment and shorter average work time. At the same time, however, over 6 percent of workers now report working at two or more jobs, while many seek as much overtime as is offered them. More and more workers are also self-employed as "consultants" or are working in nonprofit institutions. The U.S. General Accounting Office reports that the number of individuals who are self-employed or working under personal contract has been growing at over 13 percent a year.[75] One out of nine American workers is now self-employed. As this number climbs, the total hours of work by the American workforce should rise — since many of the newly self-employed are already working full-time for an employer and putting in extra hours on their own.

All of these trends are having an enormous impact on the working time of Americans. In 1991, Juliet Schor's seminal book, *The Overworked American,* provided the first glimpse of how many hours Americans were now putting in at the workplace. She estimated that Americans worked an average of 163 more hours a year in 1990 than they had in 1970 — the equivalent of nearly an extra month of full-time work.[76] Men were working two and a half more weeks per year; women an average of seven and a half more weeks. This increase reversed a trend more than a century long of declining working time. American workers were now putting in more work on a yearly basis than workers in any other advanced economy.[77] Others have found comparable trends.[78]

Recent research by Bluestone and Rose has updated and confirmed Schor's findings.[79] Focusing on prime-age workers (ages 25–54), in order to study what was happening to those no longer in school and not yet contemplating retirement, they found that we were undergoing a U-turn in working time (see Figure 3.8). Between 1967 and 1982, average annual hours per worker fell by nearly 140 hours. Women were increasing their working time as more of them moved from part-time to full-time work. But this was more than offset by a massive decline in men's hours. During this period, men's average annual work time declined by nearly 330 hours — the equivalent of a year-round worker reducing his weekly hours from over 45 to only 39. If this trend had continued, labor supply surely would have declined in the 1980s and 1990s. American men

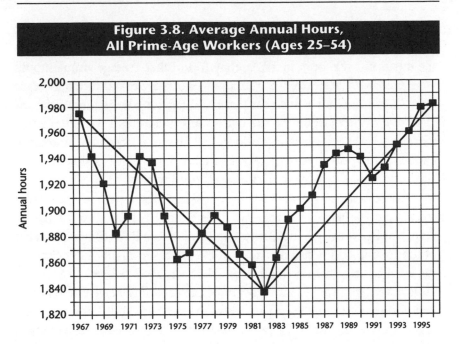

Figure 3.8. Average Annual Hours, All Prime-Age Workers (Ages 25–54)

Sources: Bluestone and Rose, "The Unmeasured Labor Force," Figure 5, p. 32.

would have been enjoying a lot more leisure, but the nation's material growth rate would have suffered even more than it did.

As it turned out, the trend did not continue. Instead, right after the 1981–82 recession, men stopped taking more leisure and went back to work. Between 1982 and 1995, prime-age men's annual hours increased by 140 hours. In combination with continued increases in women's working time, we experienced a total recovery of incumbent worker labor supply by 1995. Indeed, average annual hours in 1995 were higher than in 1967 — before the enormous decline in men's working time. Nothing in the data suggests that this new trend toward more working time among experienced workers will slow down appreciably in the near future.

Bluestone and Rose replicated their analysis for *all workers* (ages 16 and above) for the period 1975 through 1995. By studying all workers, they dealt with the criticism that early retirement decisions by older workers and longer schooling among younger workers were actually reducing labor supply despite the increase in working time among prime-age men and women. Again they found a sharp upward trend in hours of work after 1975. All told, the average work year increased from 1,680 hours to 1,820 hours twenty years later. Comparing hours in 1995 with the business cycle peak in 1979, they found that average annual hours were increasing at nearly 6.8 hours per year per worker. If this increase were to continue for a five-year period, the extra labor supply from incumbent workers would be the equivalent of adding 2.5 million additional workers to the civilian workforce.[80] That is a substantial amount of extra labor supply *beyond* increases in labor force participation and any short-term increases due to declining unemployment.

The reasons why Americans are working such long hours are quite interesting in their own right. Part of the story is related to stagnating wages and growing job insecurity. Real (inflation-adjusted) hourly wages of production and nonsupervisory workers peaked in 1973. Since then, the average wage has declined from $8.55 (in 1982 dollars) to $7.43 in 1996. Even with the recent recovery of the economy, wage rates continued to stagnate for the most part. Between 1991 and 1997, the real average wage rose by just $0.02 per hour. In such a long-term wage climate, workers *need* to work longer simply to pay the bills.

Similarly, there is evidence that feelings of job insecurity are on the rise. Alan Greenspan cites, for example, a time series survey of workers carried out at 444 large companies by the International Survey Research Company. In 1986, only 20 percent of respondents were "frequently concerned about being laid off." Even during the deep recessions of the 1980s, no more than 24 percent of those working for these companies were worried about job loss. By 1996, however, the number was 46 percent.[81] Faced with such insecurity, it is not unlikely that workers will feel greater pressure to take on added work when it is available — and will be willing to do so even at their current wage rate.

But there is another reason as well, which has to do with increasing education. In general, the more educated the worker, the longer the workweek. College-educated workers averaged 41.6 hours per week in 1995, compared to only 35.2 hours for high school dropouts. High school graduates and those with one to three years of college fell near the middle of these two extremes. These results help explain the overall upward trend in average weekly hours. As the labor force has become better educated, a larger proportion of the workforce falls into schooling categories that normally work longer hours. By 1995, 25 percent of the workforce had a college degree. By contrast, in 1975 only 16.1 percent was this well educated. If the level of education had not increased over these twenty years, average work time per week would have increased by only about nine minutes (from 38.16 to 38.31 hours) between 1975 and 1995.[82] The actual increase was forty-eight minutes. Hence, more than 80 percent of the long-run increase in average weekly hours over the past twenty years can be associated with the increased educational level of the workforce. Schooling contributes to faster economic growth not only by improving labor productivity but also by adding to the overall level of labor supply. As the labor force becomes better educated, as it inevitably will, average hours of work will continue to rise.

How Much Will Increased Labor Supply Enhance Future Economic Growth?

What does all this tell us, then, about the prospects for economic growth based on increases in labor supply? If we have to rely on increased population growth alone, then there is not much hope. But, as we have seen, the trends in labor force participation, hours worked, and unemployment are not set in stone. If the first two increase and the third is kept low, the economic growth dividend could be sizable. The CEA projections for 1995 through 2002 assume a 1 percent annual increase in population, a 0.1 percent annual increase in labor force participation, a 0.1 percent increase in employment resulting from slightly lower joblessness than in 1993–94, and no change in average individual hours worked per year. That comes out to the predicted 1.2 percent annual increase in total hours of work per year — half of the contribution to overall economic growth in the private business sector.

This overall labor supply forecast may be in line with recent experience since 1989, as Table 3.5 indicated. But the official forecast for each of the *components* of labor supply is well below the growth rates for most of the postwar period. The 1.2 percent official projection is based on a continued collapse in *all* of labor supply's components. If we simply returned to *half* of the labor force participation growth rate of the 1980s, we could boost growth in total hours of work by 0.1 percentage points to 1.3 percent per year. If, in addition, annual hours per worker increased by just 0.1 percent per year — one-fifth the rate of increase during the

1980s — growth in total hours would rise to 1.4 percent. This would hardly be extraordinary. Such an annual growth rate in employment would still be 0.2 percentage points below the average growth for 1981 through 1995. Yet this would be a good down payment toward a realistic goal of 3 percent real GDP growth through much of the next decade.

To prepare a more concrete forecast of labor supply, we have taken the information we gathered about trends in population, labor force participation, and hours of work and have combined them to produce an overall prediction about the likely increase in total hours worked for the period 1996–2006. Our best guess is a 1.5 percent annual growth rate, 0.3 percentage points higher than the official government estimate. This scenario is presented in Table 3.6.[83]

To put this forecast in context, the table includes data for two previous periods: 1979–89 and 1989–95.* According to this analysis, from 1979 through 1989, total hours of work increased by 1.8 percent per year.[84] Simple population growth was responsible for about 70 percent of the growth in total hours during this period. Growing labor force participation, particularly due to the entry of women into the workforce, accounted for most of the rest. Only 5 percent of the annual growth rate was due to increased hours of incumbent workers.

In the subsequent period, 1989–95, growth in total hours of work slowed to 1.2 percent per year. This was overwhelmingly due to the plateauing of labor force participation and slower population growth. Increases in the weekly hours growth rate offset only a small portion of this general decline.

If we were to assume that the future would look identical to the 1989–95 period, we would obtain a forecast through 2006 virtually identical to the official forecast: total hours growth of 1.2 percent per year. But

---

*The astute reader will note that the growth rates in total hours shown here are higher than the growth rates found in Table 3.5. This is due to the fact that in Table 3.5, the data refer to the "private business sector" — the government's key category for measuring productivity and output — while the estimates in Table 3.6 refer to the entire economy. The private business sector, as defined by the Bureau of Labor Statistics, excludes general government, nonprofit institutions, paid employees of private households, and the rental value of owner-occupied dwellings. As such, the output in the private business sector accounts for only 76 percent of GDP.

	Table 3.6. Forecasting Labor Supply to 2006			
Years	Population Growth Rate (%) Age 16+	Labor Force Participation Growth Rate (%)	Growth Rate of Weekly Hours Per Worker (%)	Growth Rate of Total Hours of Work (%)
1979–1989	1.24	0.43	0.09	1.8
1989–1995	1.06	0.03	0.14	1.2
1996–2006	1.00	0.28	0.23	1.5

Sources: U.S. Census Bureau population projections; *Economic Report of the President,* 1997; *Economic Indicators,* July 1997; Bluestone and Rose, "Overworked and Underemployed."

based on everything we have presented in this chapter, we have several reasons to believe the number will be higher than this, even accepting the official Census "middle series" projection for population growth of 1.00 percent through 2006.

For one, labor force participation is on the rise again. Between the first quarter of 1996 and the first quarter of 1997, the participation rate grew at an annual rate of nearly 0.75 percent. While we do not expect labor force participation to continue to rise at this torrid pace, it seems likely that it could rise at some rate between what we experienced in 1979–89 and the almost complete lack of growth during the first half of the 1990s. This seems reasonable, based on what we now know about the incentives facing older workers and the fact that if we maintain low unemployment rates, more prime-age individuals will take advantage of the bounty of job offers available in the market. We therefore project growth in labor force participation of 0.28 percent per year, the trend rate for the entire 1979–95 period. At this rate, the labor force participation rate will reach .688 by 2006, up from .672 in 1997. This does not seem at all far-fetched.

As for our forecast of weekly hours worked, we rely on an estimate of what increased education alone will do to average work time.[85] Accordingly, weekly hours will increase by 0.23 percent per year. This may end up being an underestimate. Only about four-fifths of the increase in overall weekly hours is due to improved education. If the residual increase we have experienced since 1975 continues into the future, then the annual growth in weekly hours will be closer to 0.28 percent. Add the expected growth rates for population, labor force participation, and average weekly hours together and you get 1.5 percent growth in projected labor supply.

Is this estimate pie in the sky? Given what we now know about the American labor market, this kind of improvement in labor supply represents only a tiny fraction of our underutilized workforce. As MIT economist Lester Thurow has written, "The great untold story of the American economy in the 1990s is the disguised high rate of unemployment."[86] Thurow attempts to calculate the "real unemployment rate" from official, but rarely reported, statistics of the U.S. Department of Labor. He notes that in the fall of 1995, the official unemployment rate hovered around 5.7 percent, representing about 7.3 million unemployed workers. But given the way we measure unemployment, this number does not take account of anywhere near the total amount of underutilized labor. Between 5 and 6 million people who are not disabled, not in poor health, not in school, not retired, nor needed at home to take care of other family members show up as out of the labor force because they were not at work and not actively seeking work. It is hard to believe that all of these people are so independently wealthy that they need not work in order to enjoy a reasonable standard of living. Many of these workers are discouraged by their job prospects and have dropped out of the official labor force. In part, the historical decline in the male labor force participation rate reflects these potential workers. Another 4.5 million workers in 1995 were working, but only at part-time jobs, when they desired full-time work.[87] A buoyant economy will provide the opportunity for many of these workers to get the hours of work they wish. As a result, faster growth and low unemployment will beget even more growth.

Even then, we have only scratched the surface of the underutilized workforce in America. Today 8.1 million workers are found in temporary jobs. Many of these people are working full-time but can only find work for 30 or 40 weeks of the year. Not all of these are counted as unemployed between jobs. Another 2 million work "on call" and are not fully recognized in the official unemployment statistics. Still another 8.3 million are self-employed "independent contractors," many of whom can find only temporary employment or part-time employment after losing regular full-time jobs as employees in downsized private business establishments or government agencies. Again, maintaining a strong economy will provide the opportunities for many of these workers to spend more weeks of the year at work, leading to higher overall growth in annual hours worked.

Do we have any evidence that the pool of underutilized workers could be anywhere near this big? The answer is yes. Normally, we would expect that as the official unemployment rate fell much below 6 percent and stayed there for a time — as it has since mid-1994 — we would begin to see upward pressure on nominal wages. Spot shortages of workers would spread from market to market, and employers would begin to bid up wages to attract workers. Instead, we have had little or no upward pressure on wages, despite low official jobless rates. The most plausible explanation for this lack of upward wage pressure is hidden unemployment. There is still so much slack in the labor market because of those not working but not counted as unemployed and because of already employed workers seeking more work that employers have generally been able to find sufficient numbers of qualified recruits without having to offer higher compensation.

Underutilized workers, numbering in the millions, represent a vast untapped resource for faster economic growth. For the most part, these are workers who are "job-ready." What is lacking is sufficient aggregate demand to put them to work. The real question, then, turns to the demand side. How can we keep aggregate demand rising fast enough to provide enough work for all those who would like to earn a living — or to earn more by working more?

Of course, beyond the job-ready are millions of potential workers who are not in the labor force because they never had, or no longer have, the skills that the new economy requires. In some cases they lack technical skills. Illiteracy or "innumeracy" (a lack of math skills) makes them too costly for employers to hire. In other cases the problem is social skills or a prison record. In a service economy, where the "producer" meets face to face with the consumer, businesses seek employees who present well to the public and who are well socialized in middle-class mores and courtesies. In both cases, investments in education and training can unleash additional resources for future economic growth. Even today, more than half the U.S. workforce has no more than a high school degree and less than a quarter of all workers have completed college.[88]

All in all, contrary to the growth pessimists, there is much we can do to lift the level of economic output by a fuller and better utilization of the potential labor force. Even if we did nothing to provide jobs for those who are out of the labor force now, we have the potential for much more labor supply coming from experienced workers wanting more hours and from the elderly who now have the incentive to work later in life. Supply of labor is not the key barrier to faster growth. The bottleneck turns out to be demand.

Growth at 3 Percent Is a Feasible Goal for America

Official growth forecasts therefore sell America short. We can do much better than 2.3 percent economic growth without much of a stretch. In the short run, we can expect to get more labor supply and more productivity. Each could contribute at least 1.5 percentage points to the growth rate, giving us the potential for 3 percent growth over the next few years. After that, with American families feeling both richer and more secure, we may see a slight falloff in labor supply growth as more workers decide to cut back their overtime hours and perhaps take a bit more vacation. But by then we can expect productivity growth rates to be back in the 1.6 to 1.8 percent range or better, as more firms and industries reach the higher stages of the learning and diffusion curves for the new information technologies. This will mean that we really can sustain 3 percent growth for a long time into the twenty-first century.

Yet all of these rosier forecasts are premised on economic policies that promote productivity growth and maintain aggregate demand at levels that signal the private sector to maintain high investment rates in both physical capital and new technology. Here is where we become much more pessimistic. The potential for faster growth is in the economy. It is not clear that it is in our economic institutions and public policies.

To understand why we may end up, despite the economy's potential, with sluggish growth (and persistent economic inequality), we need to turn our attention to what we have called the Wall Street model. This relatively new approach to guiding the economy has been in the making for several decades, but only in the 1990s has it actually been put fully into practice. With the roaring success of the economy in the last half of the decade, the model has quickly gained widespread credence in Washington and is being looked upon with some envy by our European competitors, whose economies seem to be stuck in a lower gear. In short order, the Wall Street model has displaced the earlier Main Street model that had served the economy so well in the first quarter century following World War II.

Indeed, the new model is elegant and quite compelling, as we shall see in the next chapter. And its proponents have done an extraordinary job of convincing policy makers of its worth. But as we shall soon discover, the logic of the model is fatally flawed, the virtuous growth cycle it promises is highly unstable, and the public policies it promotes will do more to sabotage long-term growth and exacerbate inequality than stimulate a new era of economic prosperity. Thus, we have the potential and the promise for greater growth more equally shared. The question is whether we have the right set of public policies.

Chapter 4

The Wall Street Model

WITH THE HOT summer days of 1998 about to descend on Washington, the chairman of the Federal Reserve System, Alan Greenspan, was summoned to Capitol Hill to present his semiannual assessment of the nation's economy. More than a dozen members of the Joint Economic Committee of Congress sat in rapt attention while TV cameras whirred. The Fed chairman began his testimony by voicing a cautionary note about the mounting Asian financial crisis, but he was soon reveling in the stunning performance of the U.S. economy. With undisguised contentment, he told the committee that the current economic performance, with its combination of strong growth and low inflation, "is as impressive as any I have witnessed in my near half-century of daily observation of the American economy."[1] Indeed, it seemed that Greenspan had much to crow about. America was enjoying the fruit of an economy the likes of which we had not experienced since the glory days of the quarter century following World War II.

The growth rate for the first three months of the year had just been announced by the Department of Commerce, and it exceeded all expectations. On an annual basis, the economy was expanding at a breakneck clip of 5.5 percent — more than double the average for much of the 1990s.[2] Greenspan could now point to an economy that had grown at better than 3 percent for eight of the previous nine quarters. Profits continued to boom, with before-tax corporate earnings exceeding $750 billion for the first time in history. The Dow Jones industrial average had broken through the 9,000 mark and was now double the level of just three years earlier. Total civilian employment was also at an all-time high of 131 million. The official unemployment rate was only 4.5 percent and it had been as low as 4.3 percent during the previous two months. The tight labor market was finally generating higher real wages after nearly a quarter century of stagnating or declining individual earnings. Strong productivity growth, rising labor force participation, and longer working hours were keeping inflation at bay. In the two years leading up to Greenspan's testimony, real weekly earnings were up 6 percent — the largest two-year earnings leap in decades — yet consumer prices were rising at a paltry 1.7 percent per year, and producer prices for such things as capital equipment were actually falling. Median family income was rising and poverty rates were coming down.

If this were not enough, the prospects for future growth seemed rosier than ever. Business investment in new equipment surged at a 34.2 percent annual rate in the first quarter of the year and continued at almost 18 percent in the second — the fastest two-quarter pace in fourteen years.[3] That new investment would surely add to businesses' ability to turn out more and presumably better products and services in the years to come.

Greenspan was clearly proud of the role the Fed had played in bringing about what nearly everyone now saw as a public policy miracle. On Pennsylvania Avenue, an embattled Democratic president worn down by scandal and a controversial Republican House speaker were grateful for such good economic news, each taking credit for it. In the halls of academe, economists gloated in the knowledge that their theories were being proven in practice. Few questioned either the strength of the economy or the factors that had brought it about. By all appearances, the nation was following a path to prosperity that had been proffered by the high priests of the economics profession for generations and was now being put into practice by President Clinton, a Republican-dominated Congress, and Greenspan's central bank.

In the succeeding chapters of this book, we will critique this grand mainstream consensus and offer a very different recipe for achieving sustained growth with equity. But first, it is useful to take a look at the new conventional economic wisdom that seems, by all appearances, to have worked so wondrously in practice. Why, after decades of anemic growth, did American policymakers finally buy an elixir that economists had been hawking for decades? How does the conventional wisdom explain the newfound success of the American economy, particularly at a time when

Europe is struggling with double-digit unemployment rates and the Asian "tigers" are trying to claw their way out of a deep financial crisis? To answer these questions, we need to describe what we have called the Wall Street model and show how public policies crafted at both ends of Pennsylvania Avenue have put this model into play. The story begins more than forty years ago.

A Primer on the Conventional Theory of Growth

The MIT economist Robert Solow developed the first complete rendering of what was to become neoclassical growth theory in the 1950s.[4] Today this body of work nearly monopolizes economists' thinking about the sources of national prosperity. Its simple elegance justifiably earned Solow the Nobel prize in 1987. Hundreds of economists have followed in Solow's footsteps, using his theoretical work to expand our knowledge of the sources of growth.

In this pioneering work, Solow called attention to both capital formation and "spillovers" from technological innovation as the main forces driving labor productivity — the level of output per worker — the major source of increased economic growth. According to the model, a nation's output will increase as long as two things take place: First, workers must be continually equipped with additional physical capital. Second, improvements in technology must be introduced constantly to make those workers more efficient. This (according to the model) is why bigger and better steam engines eventually led to dramatic increases in factory output in the nineteenth century and why the introduction of the electric motor was such a boon almost a century later.

To the casual observer this formulation must seem patently obvious and may provoke wonder as to why such a "discovery" would be worthy of the Nobel prize. The reason is that Solow worked out a mathematical model for growth that revealed not only the ultimate sources of economic prosperity, but also the conditions under which growth would be stymied or enhanced.

In this formulation, the capital stock of a nation can be estimated by adding up all of its investment in plant and equipment and then properly discounting the total to account for depreciation. As the measured stock of capital per worker increases, it is possible to assess the increase in labor productivity and, with it, the rate of overall economic growth. Technological improvement is absolutely critical in the model as well, but unlike the stock of physical capital and the level of employment, improvements are assumed to be *exogenous*. That is, scientific progress, or advances in knowledge — which entrepreneurs can use to improve productivity in their enterprises — are seen as a series of serendipitous events that somehow pop out of laboratories and think tanks almost randomly to influence growth. Reflecting economists' ignorance about what determines the rate of such technological and organizational advance, Solow "solved" the tricky problem of technology by making the flow of inventions and innovations a function of time in his original mathematical model. He then measured technology's impact as a residual after taking explicit account of the concrete, measurable things in his model: the value of machines and the number of workers who operate them. Presumably, geniuses such as Leonardo, Edison, Ford, and Bill Gates contribute mightily to social and economic advancement, but we have no idea when one of these geniuses is going to come along and provide the revolutionary inventions and innovations that contribute to a surge in economic growth. Therefore, the value of these discoveries — and those of countless other scientists, inventors, and tinkerers — simply ends up in a residual term called "technological progress," a black box if ever there was one.

Even if it could not be measured directly, Solow did stress the central importance of technological progress in the neoclassical model. He demonstrated mathematically that in the absence of technological improvements, there is a powerful tendency for growth to slow down and eventually cease altogether. As the ratio of capital to labor increases, the productivity of labor goes up. But just the opposite happens to the productivity of capital: its value, or *marginal product,* declines. Each additional unit of capital, other things equal, yields a smaller increment in output. As a result, the incentive for further investment declines and finally disappears. Economists Gene Grossman and Elhanan Helpman note, "At this point the economy enters a stationary state with an unchanging standard of living."[5] Growth — at least growth in output per capita — stops.

It is of historical interest to note that Karl Marx, using a very different theory about capitalism, came to virtually the same conclusion more than a century earlier. Underestimating the crucial role of technological progress, Marx argued that capitalism was ultimately doomed not simply or conclusively because of alienated or immiserated labor, or because exploited workers mount the barricades in revolt. In his most trenchant analysis of competitive capitalism, Marx foresaw a tendency for capitalists to add more and more physical capital to the production process, driving the rate of profit toward zero. At some point, the profit incentive disappears, entrepreneurs stop investing, and capitalism implodes. When the father of communism declared that capitalism contained the "seeds of its own destruction," this is exactly what he meant.[6]

Marx predicted that the first countries to abandon capitalism would be those whose economic systems were the most advanced — Germany, England, and the United States. After all, these were the countries that were "overinvesting" the most. Clearly, this has not come to pass. Capital-labor ratios have risen sharply in all developed countries, yet there is still enough profit incentive to keep investment dollars flowing and stock market prices rising. If Marx had lived another half century or so, he would have had to try to explain (paraphrasing Mark Twain) why news of capitalism's death was so greatly exaggerated.[7]

Solow's answer was that advances in technology augment labor productivity, producing the equivalent of increased labor supply. Growth rates have a tendency to fall because of declining returns to capital, but we are periodically saved by those serendipitous innovations that stimulate growth by increasing the effective amount of labor used in production. Technological improvements in machinery and equipment raise capital's marginal product and therefore raise the incentive for new investment. Similarly, human capital improvements in the form of education and training boost labor's marginal product, and innovations in the organization of the entire system of production increase the level of output of the whole shebang.

This explanation seems tidy enough, but it begs several critically important questions: From a pure accounting perspective, how much of growth is due simply to accumulations of more capital and labor, and how much to scientific, technological, and organizational improvements? If technology stopped advancing, but we continued to equip workers with more and more machines of the existing vintage, how much growth would we actually get?

Extending the Neoclassical Approach: The Accounting Model

Dale Jorgenson has spent much of his professional career trying to answer these questions, and his answers provide the most fully developed expression of what has come to be known as the *accounting model* of growth. According to Jorgenson, investment in tangible assets — factories, offices, commercial buildings, machinery, and other forms of equipment — is paramount. You can pretty much forget about technological progress as a separate, independent source of growth. "Growth in capital input," according to Jorgenson, "is the most important source of growth in output, growth in labor input is the next most important source, and productivity growth [associated with technological progress] is least important."[8] In lay terms, this means that the amassing of machines and equipment and investment in human capital are much more important than the state of technology, the organization of production, or the quality of labor-management relations.

The accounting model dispenses with the concept of labor productivity altogether. Any change in labor's output is seen as largely due to the accumulation of nonlabor inputs — particularly physical capital — elsewhere in the production function. The farmhand in the Wheat Belt is now more productive, not mainly because of anything he has done himself, but because he has been equipped by his employer with a more powerful harvester. According to Jorgenson's bookkeeping, any "productivity" improvement in a given factor that results from investment *somewhere else in the production function* should rightly be attributed to the new asset, not the factor of production that uses it. Proper accounting requires carefully measuring the amount of investment in each factor. The cost of new technology embodied in plant and equipment should be counted in the value of the stock of physical capital. The cost of educating and training workers should be counted as part of the value of the labor input. Only the residual growth — growth that cannot be traced and specifically assigned to a physical or human asset — counts as a productivity improvement in this model.

This residual is called *total factor productivity* (TFP), a term drawn from the work of Moses Abramovitz, who in 1962 defined it as "the effect of 'costless' advances in applied technology, managerial efficiency, and industrial organization."[9] The operative word is *costless*. In Jorgenson's model, almost any technological improvement has a direct cost attached to it and does not improve output until it is embedded in capital or labor. Properly accounted for, most of the mysterious "advances in knowledge" (TFP) encased in the production function should rightfully be attributed to either capital or to labor. Hence, the main thrust of the empirical work by Jorgenson and his colleagues has been aimed at taking as much of the growth that might have earlier been attributed to the technological residual and redistributing it within the production function to physical and human capital.

An example will help to clarify this. A worker equipped with a powerful mechanical backhoe digs a lot more drainage ditch in a given period than the same worker toiling with pick and shovel. Under standard accounting, his "labor productivity" has increased enormously. To Jorgenson, however, the extra ditch digging should be attributed not to increased productivity but to the increase in capital input — the backhoe — and perhaps a little to increased labor input for the investment in human capital the worker needed to learn how to operate the new machine. After appropriately accounting for these investments and incorporating them as augmented tangible capital and augmented labor, society is not getting more output per unit of input (productivity), but more output because of *more* input (factor accumulation). Hence, the case of the enhanced-technology ditchdigger does not constitute a case of productivity or efficiency gain in TFP terms. It is simply a case of getting more output from more inputs, something like the workaholic who produces more by working longer (more input) rather than by working smarter (higher productivity per hour of input). After taking full account of the additional cost of the mechanized backhoe, the total factor productivity gain of the man + machine over the man + shovel may be slightly positive, close to zero, or perhaps even negative.

Jorgenson's evidence for the contention that investments in physical and human capital are the dominant sources of growth comes from meticulous studies of fifty-two industry sectors spanning the entire U.S. economy, painstakingly carried out with his colleagues Frank Gollop and Barbara Fraumeni.[10] Combining the industry results into a model of the entire economy, the three conclude that from 1948 through 1979 capital input was responsible for 46 percent of growth in output, labor input for 31 percent, and productivity growth (more output per unit of capital *and* labor), the remaining 24 percent.[11] In subsequent work with Zvi Griliches, Jorgenson got total factor productivity to explain no more than 4 percent of economic growth by correcting for various errors in model specification and measurement.[12]

This conclusion — that most of growth in total output may be explained by growth in total input — is, in Jorgenson's own words, "just the reverse of the conclusion drawn from the great body of past research on total factor productivity."[13] Indeed, in the type of empirical research that Jorgenson criticizes, Robert Solow had concluded that capital accumulation explained only 12.5 percent of per capital output growth, with all the rest being attributed to autonomous changes in productivity due to technology.[14] In the new order of priority, with both physical and human capital given star billing in the growth drama, Jorgenson concludes, the single most important thing we can do to boost output is simply increase the dollar value of total investment. Equipping workers with more and bigger machines and investing more in education and training are seen as the most significant ways — indeed, just about the only ways — to boost national output.

This does not mean that improved technology is irrelevant to explaining growth. But technology must be seen as just another input in the production process, not something special in form and influence or in how it is produced. "Our conclusion," Jorgenson and Griliches explain, "is not that advances in knowledge are negligible, but that the accumulation of knowledge is governed by the same economic laws as any other process of capital accumulation. Costs must be incurred if benefits are to be received."[15] In other words, there is no such thing as a free lunch.

This all seems reasonable enough. Yet the implications of this accounting model are enormous. The "same economic laws" that Jorgenson and Griliches refer to include the all-important assumption of diminishing returns to investment. That means if technology is just like a piece of machinery, additional increments of technological progress over time will yield ever smaller increments to output. Ultimately, this places a damper on the prospects for growth, just as mounting investments in physical capital hobbled growth in Solow's model. Technology's a good thing, but according to the accounting model, not a panacea.

Moreover, since true scientific advance is seen as marching mysteriously to its own drummer, it is difficult to predict and thus nearly incapable of being influenced by public policy. Like the 'man who searches under the lamppost for his keys, regardless of where he lost them, most economists, following Jorgenson, have naturally turned their attention to *measurable* capital and labor as the levers that can be used to steer the growth process. If we want to grow faster, in this view, then we as a nation have to find a way to encourage more investment, pure and simple. If we devote more of today's resources to accumulating capital, we can have faster growth and greater prosperity tomorrow. If we don't, then we had better get used to living in an age of diminished expectations.

The Crucial Roles of National Savings and Interest Rates

It is precisely here that the neoclassical model of growth moves from pure theory to policy prescription. The emphasis on capital accumulation as the surest path to faster growth yields a very specific approach to policy.

Mathematically, a nation's gross investment ultimately equals the level of its gross savings. Equivalently, gross investment is the part of gross domestic product (GDP) that is not consumed by households, businesses, and government.[16] Hence, if we want to invest more, we must consume less and save more. If investment in physical (and human) capital is ultimately the most critical input in the growth process, as the accounting model asserts, then increased savings is the only route to faster growth.

America's growth problem, according to this wisdom, can be traced directly to the fact that we as a nation have done a very poor job of building up savings. Instead, families have gone on a consumption binge, saving little and piling up debt — the equivalent of dissaving. The federal government has done the same. Instead of building up public savings by running government surpluses, we ran large and growing federal deficits from the early 1970s through the early 1990s. By 1992 the annual federal deficit was nearly $300 billion and the accumulated federal debt exceeded $4 *trillion.*[17]

We can see this alleged double tragedy in the making in Figure 4.1, which charts the household savings rate from the end of World War II to the present. It is clear that during the postwar glory days, personal saving as a proportion of disposable income was high and rising. Since the 1970s, savings rates have trended downward, reaching a postwar low in

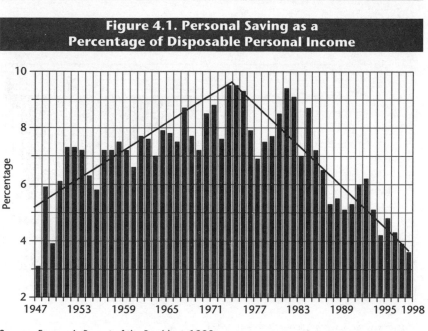

Figure 4.1. Personal Saving as a Percentage of Disposable Personal Income

Source: *Economic Report of the President,* 1999.

the 1990s. The correlation between these personal savings rates and the growth rates we presented back in Chapter 2 is quite high.

Similarly, as Figure 4.2 demonstrates, federal government deficits began to pile up after the mid-1970s and exploded in the 1980s, producing another high correlation, this time between the federal budget balance and national economic growth. Because public deficits are covered by borrowing from the private sector, deficits (say Jorgenson and most mainstream economists) sop up savings that could have gone into private sector investment.

Based on such data, the conventional wisdom has a forthright explanation of why U.S. growth rates were high during the glory days and then began falling in the 1970s and continuing through the early 1990s: the blame lies squarely with profligate families and a government addicted to deficit finance.

According to this logic, low savings rates depress economic growth by forcing up interest rates, thereby discouraging investment.[18] If households save little, they put away little in bank accounts, credit unions, or other forms of financial deposits. With a smaller supply of savings, other

Figure 4.2. Federal Surplus/Deficit, 1947–1998

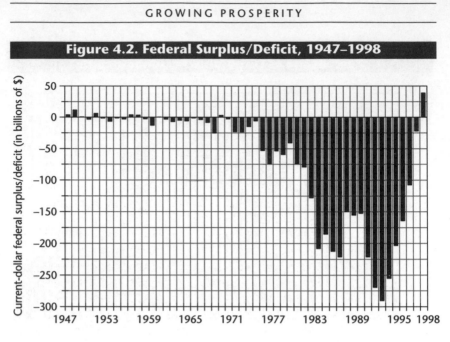

Source: *Economic Report of the President,* 1999.

things equal, financial institutions will essentially ration their loans by charging higher interest rates to borrowers. The federal government is a culprit here too. To cover a deficit, the government must borrow. When it competes for loans with the private sector, interest rates presumably rise. The combination of low household savings rates and high public deficits is therefore lethal when it comes to interest rates, the former reducing the supply of loanable funds, the latter increasing the demand. The result is moribund economic growth as investment in plant and equipment shrinks.

This is precisely why balancing the federal budget or, better yet, running surpluses has been received with such acclaim. While there was still not much good news on the personal savings front as late as 1998, the seemingly miraculous disappearance of the federal deficit is being credited as the key factor responsible for the recent surge in the economy. Cut the deficit, counseled economists for decades, and the economy will grow faster. The medicine seems to have worked. In just six years, the United States moved from a $290 billion deficit to a nearly $40 billion surplus. The alleged result by early 1998 was an economy hitting on all cylinders, growing much faster than anyone could have imagined.

The worry now is that the exemplary behavior of the federal government will be offset by the continued extravagant consumption of private households. With wealth piling up in household portfolios as a result of the stock market surge, families have apparently become less concerned about meeting savings goals for retirement and college educations. Savings rates during the booming mid-1990s were even lower than during the slow-growth 1980s and were plummeting toward zero by early 1998.[19]

This has made for a good deal of pessimism about growth among conventional theorists, with the blame for expected lackluster future growth shifting from big government to the American family. Unless personal savings rates can be improved, economists say, it is not only possible but nearly certain that growth will slow. Expecting little in the way of increased private savings, an increasing number of influential policymakers, including Fed Chairman Greenspan, have suggested the need to run ever larger federal budget surpluses, since the private sector apparently will not do the responsible thing.[20]

The Central Role of Inflation in the Wall Street Model

There is one more very important and related piece to this neoclassical growth story. It has to do with what the model's advocates see as the central role of inflation. As we have seen, the very interest rates that are viewed as so critical for capital investment are determined by the supply and demand for loanable funds. In turn, this supply and demand is influenced by the expected rate of inflation. If price hikes are anticipated, bank depositors will insist on higher interest rates as compensation for keeping their money in savings rather than spending it.

There is a simple reason for this. To get individuals to lend money, they must be assured that they will receive in return at least enough to cover any possible price increases while their money is out on loan. After all, it would be foolish to lend someone $100 for one year at 7 percent if one believed that the prices of goods would increase during the year by 10 percent. The purchasing power of that $100 would be less a year from now than if the money were spent today. Generalizing from this insight, the higher the expected rate of inflation, the higher interest rates will be. Hence, anticipated inflation discourages investment by raising interest rates.

Even if we do not face actual inflation, the new conventional wisdom suggests that uncertainty over prices can be just as destructive to capital accumulation. If future prices are unknown, business managers find it tricky to plan future production levels. An unexpected spurt in inflation could increase costs, making a particular new investment unprofitable. Building a new office or factory and equipping it with new equipment does not guarantee that people will come to buy the additional products you produce, and a rise in prices can chase away customers. An unanticipated dive in prices can erase sales margins, leaving the company just as unprofitable. In a world with price uncertainty, there is a strong incentive to limit investment in long-term projects for fear of building too much costly capacity in relation to what the market will bear. Uncertainty about inflation shortens time horizons. Managers desire long-run price stability so that they have some firm economic expectations on which to base their investment plans. Controlling inflation thus becomes a critical factor, in addition to boosting savings rates, in the standard normative model of growth.

The Neoclassical Growth Syllogism

We now have in place most of the pieces needed to understand what promotes faster growth according to the tenets of the neoclassical economic model. These can be neatly summarized in a syllogism:

1. Faster economic growth will occur only if there is increased investment in physical capital.
2. Increased investment in physical capital will occur only if interest rates are kept low.
3. Low interest rates will occur only in an environment of stable prices and enhanced savings.
4. *Therefore,* increased economic growth will occur only if inflation is kept firmly under control and high savings rates are achieved.

Essentially, to grow the economy faster requires strict adherence to a policy of stable prices and promotion of a high level of personal and public saving. Only then will there be enough investment to make labor and capital more productive. Put as simply as possible, in the standard model of growth, about the only things anyone should worry about are inflation rates and savings rates.

In the past, mild inflation in the range of 3 to 4 percent per year was considered a nuisance, since it eroded the value of household savings and made it more difficult for businesses to plan. Still, a little inflation could be tolerated because it was generally believed to signal an economy operating close to its potential capacity.

According to the neoclassical growth syllogism, however, even mild inflation is considered a deadly curse, guilty of sabotaging long-term economic growth. Indeed, anything much above zero inflation has been criticized as too high. It is now argued that slow but persistent inflation produces an inflationary psychology. Expecting inflation to be the rule, workers demand compensating wage increases, and firms oblige their workers in the belief that they can pass their higher labor costs on to customers in the form of price increases. The result is a self-fulfilling prophecy. A little bit of inflation presumably leads to a whole lot more. However, if this psychology is broken by forcing price stability, then a reverse cycle can take hold. As the *Wall Street Journal* notes, "if enough executives, suppliers, consumers, and workers *believe* [low inflation] will last, they will act in ways that help make it last."[21]

By itself, however, the syllogism begs a critical question. It offers the means by which we augment the *supply* of output, but it is silent about the *demand* side of the economy. If higher production is made possible by higher investment, but there is insufficient demand for the additional output, increased productivity will simply result in unemployed workers, underutilized plant and equipment, and, ultimately, even slower growth.

The Wall Street Virtuous Cycle

Here is where the Wall Street virtuous cycle presumably comes to the rescue. Using the neoclassical growth syllogism as the basis for the supply side of economic growth, the new conventional wisdom has added a demand side based on the same motivating factor — stable prices. Alan Greenspan presented just such a model before the Joint Economic Committee in his triumphal testimony in the summer of 1998.

We first introduced the Wall Street virtuous cycle in Chapter 1. There we briefly explained how, at least hypothetically, keeping inflation under control raises the GDP growth rate through a complicated cycle that ties price stability to falling interest rates, rising stock prices, and finally increased personal wealth, consumer spending, capital investment, productivity, and corporate profits. Figure 4.3 reproduces the diagram we presented in Chapter 1, but segments the virtuous cycle into its demand- and supply-side components. Here we see how the neoclassical growth syllogism is improved upon by adding a mechanism to ensure that de-

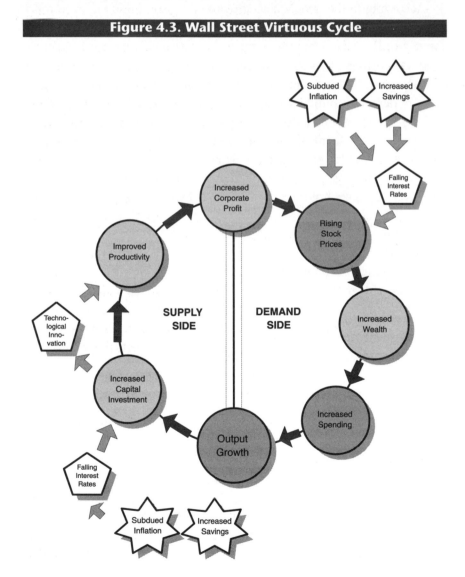

Figure 4.3. Wall Street Virtuous Cycle

mand will be sufficient to absorb the added supply of output that comes from the encouragement of capital investment and enhanced productivity.

Take the supply side first. Subdued inflation leads to falling interest rates, which in turn boost capital investment. The increased investment boosts productivity directly by adding more physical capital to the production process and indirectly by contributing to technological innovation. This presumably gives us the potential for accelerated growth.

That potential is realized, according to this view, if we add the demand side to the virtuous cycle. Subdued inflation not only boosts investment but also provides a sense of financial market stability that contributes to higher stock prices. Those stock prices in turn augment household wealth, encouraging consumers to spend more, buying up the additional output produced with the new investment. And so the virtuous cycle goes on its merry way.

Beginning in the mid-1990s, this cycle seemed to work like a charm. With the Dow Jones industrial average rising from less than 3,800 in 1994 to over 10,000 by early 1999 and the S&P's 500-stock index up by more than 130 percent, more than $12 trillion was added to the value of household assets in the span of just five years.[22] Only a tiny fraction of these capital gains was actually transformed into the purchase of goods and services. But even if the fraction were no greater than 4 percent, this *wealth effect* could conceivably have increased annual consumer spending by some $120 billion.[23] In this case, we could say that the Wall Street virtuous cycle boosted consumption about 2.1 percent per year — or equivalently, added about 1.4 percentage points to the annual GDP growth rate.[24] As Greenspan put it, "Our economy is still enjoying a virtuous cycle, in which, in the context of subdued inflation and generally supportive credit conditions, rising equity values are providing impetus for spending and, in turn, the expansion of output, employment, and productivity-enhancing capital investment."[25]

Most of the increased spending out of equity values is done by the wealthy. The top 1 percent of wealth holders in the United States owned 47 percent of total net financial assets in 1995; the top 10 percent of wealth holders owned 83 percent.[26] Still, if the wealthy feel confident enough in their enhanced financial position to treat themselves to a new Lincoln or an extra vacation trip to Hilton Head, some of that added spending trickles down to those who helped make the steel and glass that goes into Ford products, and to the clerks and chambermaids in resort hotels. It may be only trickle-down, admit the proponents of the Wall Street model, but it does promote growth.

The Wall Street–Pennsylvania Avenue Accord

Acceptance of the Wall Street model has fundamental — even revolutionary — implications for public policy. Since at least the Great Depression, the public sector has tried to encourage growth through general tax incentives, various corporate welfare policies (such as direct subsidies to particular industries), export promotion, and public spending to maintain aggregate demand. Until the election of Ronald Reagan, every U.S. president since Franklin Roosevelt explicitly or implicitly followed a Keynesian economic policy. The federal government was seen as having a legitimate role in encouraging growth by manipulating tax rates and government spending, by setting industry regulations, and by investing in public sector infrastructure, research and development, and education and training. Congress, particularly in the hands of so-called tax-and-spend liberal Democrats, bought into the model with few reservations.

In the new Wall Street model, government has a much more limited role. The control of inflation and the promotion of savings become the most important objectives of the federal government. Indeed, according to the new conventional wisdom, all other government policies play second fiddle to inflation control and are irrelevant to growth or even downright counterproductive. Acceptance of the neoclassical growth syllogism therefore establishes the central constraint on all government policy: Any policy that contributes to stable prices, boosts personal savings, or reduces government deficits is considered sacrosanct. Any policy that threatens any one of these must be assiduously avoided.

By 1993–94 there was a new consensus in Washington, shared by both Clinton Democrats and Newt Gingrich Republicans, that growth depended on adhering to the logic of the Wall Street model. Implicitly, a new accord was being forged between Wall Street and Pennsylvania Avenue. If Washington would oblige with policies to control inflation and boost savings, financial markets would do their part to boost economic growth.

Balancing the Federal Budget

What *are* the specific public policies that the federal government brings to this accord between Wall Street and Pennsylvania Avenue? First and foremost is the commitment to balanced federal budgets — or better yet, federal surpluses.

During the Reagan era, conservative Republicans had as their number one priority shrinking the public sector. In the end, however, the strategy backfired. In his book *The Triumph of Politics,* David Stockman, Reagan's White House budget director, frankly admitted that the massive Kemp-Roth tax cut of 1981 was intended to deprive the government of the resources that advocates of social spending needed to finance the social programs they coveted.[27] By depriving the government of tax revenue, it was thought that social welfare spending would have to shrink. Instead, as a result of Democratic control of Congress and Reagan's opulent spending on defense, the tax cuts were not met with equal spending cuts. The annual federal deficit ballooned from $75 billion in 1980 to nearly $225 billion in 1986. On President George Bush's watch, the deficit swelled even further.

By the 1992 presidential election, there were attempts to turn the budget deficit into a salient political issue, but with little immediate success. During his well-financed presidential campaign, the billionaire businessman Ross Perot repeatedly pointed to dozens of charts that he said showed the devastating impact of a federal government running so deeply in the red. He went so far as to advocate a balanced-budget amendment to the Constitution to force the government to live within its means. But with the deficit approaching $300 billion under his own administration, George Bush, running hard for reelection, could hardly jump on the deficit reduction bandwagon without being pummeled by Perot. Meanwhile, the young Democratic challenger, Bill Clinton, spent at least as much time laying out his plans for new public investment programs — on health care, highways, railroads, technology, and education — and for new labor market regulations to help struggling working families, as he spent on deficit reduction. These priorities were clearly stated in *Putting People First,* Clinton's official campaign platform statement. Costed out by his staff in the weeks after his election, the full-blown package of investments carried a price tag of nearly $90 billion.[28]

Clinton won the contest with Bush and Perot, in no small measure because even among Perot voters only one-fourth cited the deficit as the first or second most important problem facing the country. Far more of those interviewed noted the economy, unemployment, and health care.[29]

Before the end of his first six months in office, however, Clinton was already radically shifting his position, both because the federal deficit was seen as careening further out of control and because of strong pressure from one faction within his own cabinet. On the liberal side, Secretary of Labor Robert Reich and the chairwoman of his Council of Economic Advisers, Laura Tyson, continued to support a variant of the public investment stimulus package Clinton had adopted for the campaign. On the other side were Secretary of the Treasury Lloyd Bentsen and the former cochairman of Goldman Sachs Robert Rubin, then the Deputy Treasury Secretary. Already firm believers in the Wall Street model, they counseled the president to come out strongly for deficit reduction. If a presumed liberal like Clinton made balancing the budget his top priority, they argued, the news would be so refreshing to bankers and securities traders that confidence in financial markets would rise and interest rates would fall. If the government actually moved toward a balanced budget, its borrowing needs would decrease sharply, reducing the competition between the public and private sectors for loanable funds. With reduced demand, interest rates would have to fall. The result, Bentsen and Rubin promised, would be an investment boom and faster growth. This would go a long way toward accomplishing the president's stated goal of bringing down unemployment and reversing the erosion in wages.

With his public investment strategy in trouble in Congress, his early bumbling of such social issues as gays in the military, and his national health policy under attack, Clinton decided to give the advice from his Treasury Department a try. He publicly announced a commitment to cut government spending with the explicit goal of lowering the deficit. In preparing the 1993 federal budget, the administration backed away from a "middle-class" tax cut and instead included gas and general tax increases. On the spending side, there were cuts in projected budgets for most government agencies. The objective of the new budget was explicit: first and foremost, cut the deficit.[30] Wall Street was used to hearing such things from Republican presidents, but it was stunned to hear them from a Democrat. Leading Congressional Democrats swallowed hard, bit the bullet, and followed their president. Despite misgivings about the economics of the model and the possible electoral fallout from reversing course on taxes and spending, they joined the Republicans in voting for the package.[31]

In the next few months, interest rates did fall and the economy began to grow faster. Real private fixed investment in plant and equipment jumped by 7.5 percent in 1993 and by 8 percent the following year. Four million new jobs were generated in less than twenty-four months. Unemployment was coming down, from 7.5 to 6.1 percent, and the president's popularity was going up.

Skeptical at first, Clinton became a born-again deficit cutter and a convert to the Wall Street model. According to the journalist Bob Woodward, after just a few months in office, Clinton had

> reached some core conclusions about economics, Washington, and Wall Street. There was no question in his mind that interest rates had been too high for too long, that the middle class could not improve its lot until interest rates came down so people could refinance their homes, businesspeople could expand and feel free to hire again. Clinton believed he could get more overall economic growth from a drop in interest rates than suggested in conservative estimates by what he considered conservative economists.
>
> "All the folks that I ran to help would be more hurt by a slow economy than they would be helped by a marginal extra investment program," he said later. He was not trying just to help the bond market, he claimed. The bond market was just the vehicle for helping the middle class.[32]

When the Republicans seized control of Congress in 1994, they redoubled their efforts at deficit reduction, passing a budget-balancing Constitutional amendment in the House that failed by just one vote in the Senate. Taunted by Newt Gingrich and Trent Lott, Clinton announced plans to produce federal budgets that would cut the deficit to zero by 2002. Thereafter, even while continuing to seek modest gains for workers (through small increases in the minimum wage, expansion of the Earned Income Tax Credit, passage of the Family Leave Act, and somewhat more extensive health insurance coverage under Medicare and Medicaid), the Clinton administration and the Republican-led Congress devoted most of their attention to passing and implementing policies that fully accorded with the neoclassical growth syllogism.

Once again, the market responded favorably. The Dow Jones industrial average went on a rampage, rising by more than 20 percent a year in 1995, 1996, and 1997 and by another 16 percent in 1998. Investment in plant and equipment continued to rise, increasing by an astounding 48 percent between 1994 and 1998. Real GDP grew by an average of better than 2.8 percent per year. Altogether, 8.4 million new jobs were created (see Table 4.1). Well before this four-year spurt in the economy was in the record books, Clinton and the Republicans needed no more evidence to convince themselves that the Wall Street model worked and that public policies following the model's prescription were worth implementing.

To all appearances, moving swiftly toward balancing the budget seemed to work as it was supposed to. Ten-year Treasury bond yields had been as high as 8.85 percent in 1988. By 1997 they were down to 6.35 percent. Over the same period, Moody's corporate Aaa bonds, initially trading at 9.71 percent, had fallen to 7.27 percent.[33] The stock market surged and personal wealth increased by trillions of dollars. On the supply side, capital investment was soaring and productivity growth was finally beginning to pick up speed. According to its advocates, the Wall Street model and the Wall Street–Pennsylvania Avenue accord were working exactly as promised.

Table 4.1. The Renaissance Economy, 1994–1998 (1992 Dollars)				
Year	Real GDP ($ billions)	Real Fixed Nonresidential Investment ($ billions)	Dow Jones Industrial Average	Civilian Employment (millions)	Civilian Unemployment Rate (%)
1994	6,610.7	648.4	3,793	123.1	6.1
1995	6,761.7	710.6	4,494	124.9	5.6
1996	6,994.8	776.6	5,742	126.7	5.4
1997	7,269.8	859.4	7,441	129.6	4.9
1998	7,551.9	960.7	8,626	131.5	4.5

Sources: *Economic Indicators,* March 1999, and *Economic Report of the President,* 1998.

Free Trade

The commitment to balancing the federal budget was not the only policy aimed at revving up the economy. In 1997 foreign imports into the United States exceeded $1 trillion for the first time in history. Goods and services coming from abroad now equaled 13 percent of GDP, up from 11 percent in 1990 and just 5 percent in 1970.[34] While exports had been growing, they hardly kept pace with imports. The trade deficit, which had been close to zero for nearly a century up to the early 1980s, rose as sharply as the federal budget deficit. Unlike the federal deficit, however, the trade deficit kept rising right on through the 1990s with no sign of reversal. By 1997 imports of goods and services exceeded exports by $110 billion. With the Asian crisis deepening and the dollar strengthening, annual trade deficits of more than $200 billion were being forecast for the foreseeable future.[35]

While estimates vary, every additional billion dollars in the trade deficit means roughly 10,000 jobs foregone due to lost export sales or displaced domestic production.[36] It is not surprising, then, that strong political forces within the country have demanded protection from the flood of foreign-produced goods and services. The AFL-CIO, whose member unions contributed millions of dollars to the Clinton-Gore campaigns in 1992 and 1996, has consistently been a leading voice in this movement. The populist branch of the Republican Party led by Pat Buchanan has taken a similar position, as has Ross Perot.[37] All lobbied heavily against extending free trade to Mexico under the North American Free Trade Agreement (NAFTA) and opposed virtually all other proposed treaties aimed at lowering barriers to international trade and capital mobility. While these organizations and political leaders have routinely been accused of being out of touch with new global realities, they have apparently not been out of touch with the American people. According to a Business Week–Harris poll taken in the fall of 1997, only 42 percent of Americans favored NAFTA, and a clear majority (54 percent) opposed giving the president greater authority to negotiate new trade agreements with other countries.[38]

Nonetheless, the leaders at both ends of Pennsylvania Avenue have repeatedly pledged themselves to extending free trade and have opposed adding provisions to the body of trade agreements that would mandate international labor standards, labor rights, and transnational environmental standards.[39] They have done this at what appears to be substantial political cost. For the Democratic White House, endorsement of trade liberalization has alienated its most loyal constituency, organized labor, as well as party leaders in Congress. For the Republicans, support has produced a deep rift between the free-traders and the so-called populists. So why is there such ardent government support for what appears to be a politically unpopular stance?

The economic argument for free trade is rooted in the 150-year-old theory of *comparative advantage*. According to this theory, nations differ in their natural endowments. Some have climates and skills most suitable to producing one set of products and services; others are particularly adept at producing others. The original example from the nineteenth century economist David Ricardo involved the benefits of Spain trading wine for English wool and vice versa. Free trade benefits all trading partners by permitting each nation to specialize in the things it does best and not waste labor and capital on those things it does less well. Through trade, the global pie is enlarged, and each country is more prosperous than it otherwise would be.

In the real world, matters do not necessarily accord with theory. Many countries produce the same or similar goods, with developing countries adding to the duplication. The issue then becomes which countries will dominate in this kind of global market. Liberalized trade is presented as good for our economy because it permits U.S. companies easier entry into foreign markets. Opening up closed foreign markets to our goods and services by lowering tariff and nontariff barriers abroad will supposedly pave the way for export-led growth. With foreign tariffs generally higher than ours, the push for free trade can be seen as helping U.S. producers by "leveling the playing field." This is the good-news part of the story.

The problem is that as more trade agreements were signed during the 1980s and 1990s, and as the World Trade Organization (WTO) came into being with the United States as key author and signatory, exports trailed imports rather than the reverse. NAFTA provides a good example. Before NAFTA, the United States actually ran a small trade surplus with Mexico.

Soon after its passage in 1994, Mexico was forced to devalue the peso, Mexican exports immediately became cheaper, and the small U.S. surplus turned into a bilateral trade deficit in excess of $14 billion a year by 1997.[40] In practice, freeing up trade seems to have worsened America's balance of trade, not improved it. Nevertheless, advocacy for expanding trade agreements remains robust in the Clinton White House and among Republican leaders in the House and Senate, even with an exploding trade deficit. Why?

The answer to this apparent political paradox is that free trade has a second, but less often recognized, function: it helps mightily to contain domestic inflation.[41] Given the parameters of the Wall Street growth model, encouraging the very imports that swell the trade deficit is seen as healthy for the economy. Increased international competition undermines the ability of domestic firms to raise prices. In the old days, for example, before foreign-made automobiles gained widespread access to the U.S. market, General Motors, Ford, and Chrysler could implicitly collude to raise prices with the intent of meeting prearranged profit targets. Oligopolies — markets with few sellers — dominated large segments of the American economy. As a result, it was fairly easy for producers to raise prices without fear of retaliation or competition. When prices rise in a few key industries, inflationary pressure begins to build. If enough sectors are characterized by limited competition, inflation can take off.

The key point, made by most advocates of free trade, is that nothing so undermines domestic oligopoly as the elimination of tariffs, quotas, and other barriers to the global exchange of goods and services. When borders are permeable, General Motors, Ford, and Chrysler can try to boost their prices at home, but if Toyota, Nissan, and BMW do not follow suit, U.S. producers will eventually see their market shares erode as Americans buy the comparatively less expensive foreign brands. The recent entry of cars from South Korea now helps to hold down prices among even the cheapest domestic models on the market.[42] The more competitors there are — foreign and domestic — the harder it is for industries to engage in collusive pricing and the greater the potential for excess capacity, which forces all companies to raise productivity, cut costs, and pass these cost reductions onto the consumer in the form of lower prices — or go out of business.[43] The Organization of Petroleum Exporting

Countries (OPEC) provides a prime example. In 1973 and again in 1979, OPEC was able to get its member states to voluntarily limit oil supplies and thereby drive up prices. But with the successful exploitation of oil and gas in the North Sea by Britain and Norway and increased production from countries like Mexico, the cartel shattered. Today gasoline sells for less than bottled water.

Thus, free trade has become a key component of the anti-inflationary thrust of the Wall Street growth model. Its heralded role in export promotion is actually less important than the downward pressure it puts on prices. In 1997, with the Asian financial crisis developing at the end of the year, the impact on prices was particularly significant. Prices for all foreign goods *fell* by 6.1 percent in the year ending in January 1998.[44] Now that one-seventh of U.S. consumption is satisfied by imports, it is not surprising that such a dramatic decline in import prices would bring overall domestic inflation to record-setting low levels — exactly in line with the growth syllogism and the Wall Street virtuous cycle.[45]

Flexible Labor Markets

Balancing the federal budget reduces pressure on interest rates; expanding free trade reduces inflationary pressure on prices. What more could the Wall Street model ask for? The answer is quiescent labor markets. Oligopoly pricing power is one source of inflationary pressure. Organized labor markets are potentially another. In what economists call *perfectly competitive* labor markets, employers compete for workers and workers compete for jobs. The result, analogous to the market for winter wheat no. 2 or any other commodity, is that wage levels are determined by supply and demand. If there is sufficient supply, workers have no bargaining power and must settle for whatever wages the market will bear.

It is precisely with the objective of taking wages out of competition that trade unions have been formed and that government regulations of the labor market have been formulated. Traditionally, unions have striven to place a floor under wages in the industries where they have large memberships. They have also attempted to create job security by demanding seniority-based systems governing layoffs and promotions, grievance machinery to limit management's right to fire workers, and even explicit no-layoff language in some contracts. By limiting competition from potential employees, unions have created islands of wage protection for their members in a sea of income insecurity.

In the past, this has helped unionized workers gain wage advantages that a free labor market would not permit. As long as these wage increases did not exceed productivity growth, firms could afford to pay them without raising prices to cover their higher labor costs. There have been times, however, when powerful unions have been able to extract wage and benefit increases that exceeded productivity growth, and these almost inevitably led company managers to raise prices in order to maintain profit margins. In the mid-1970s, for example, when productivity was shrinking in the primary metals industry, the United Steelworkers union was successful in winning nominal wage increases of 7.5 to 9.7 percent. This proved counterproductive for workers as well as for the companies they worked for. As prices of domestic steel products were raised by management in an attempt to maintain profit margins, foreign producers with lower costs and lower prices began to take market share from domestic producers. Between 1974 and 1986, almost 340,000 steel jobs in America disappeared.[46] If unions are strong enough and widespread, the fear has always been that their actions could lead to a national wage-price spiral, where wages push up prices and then cost-of-living clauses in union contracts lead to successive rounds of escalating wages and prices.[47]

Little wonder then that there has been little support in the White House — and none from the Republican leadership in the House and Senate — for strengthening labor laws that would make it easier for unions to organize workers and easier to obtain first contracts once they have signed them up. A union-free environment is seen as more "flexible," with fewer regulations, meaning less prone to wage-push inflation. Again, this is crucial to the Wall Street model. The initial reluctance within the White House to raise the minimum wage was at least partly due to this same concern.

Spot shortages in the labor market also spell potential trouble on the inflation front. This is one reason why the White House has emphasized job training. Providing a ready supply of entry-level workers can prevent bottlenecks from arising as the economy speeds up. Meeting the need for technical workers through community colleges and vocational training programs helps as well. Support for lifting immigration quotas, particularly for foreign workers with high-tech skills, has not been fully embraced by either end of Pennsylvania Avenue, but it is under consideration whenever the labor market tightens.

While most workers on Main Street see stagnating wages and job insecurity as the scourge of the labor market, the Wall Street model depicts them as quite useful, contributing to stable prices and, therefore, the potential for faster growth. In what may seem like a topsy-turvy new world to workers, rising imports, stagnant wages, and job insecurity are said to be peculiarly good for the economy, according to the mainstream growth model.

The Role of the Fed

Backstopping all of these anti-inflation policies is the Federal Reserve Board, which stands ready to step in with higher interest rates to cool the economy whenever inflation threatens.[48] Under the firm hand of Alan Greenspan, the Fed has recently shown remarkable restraint in keeping interest rates stable, despite unemployment rates well below what was considered prudent just a year or two ago.

This was not always the case. In 1988, when the economy had accelerated to a 3.8 percent growth rate from 2.9 percent the year before and unemployment was trending downward to 5.5 percent from 6.2, Greenspan and the Fed decided the economy was overheating. Over the course of a year, the Fed imposed a dozen small increases in the federal funds rate, which, combined, raised short-term interest rates from 6.5 to over 9 percent. In retrospect, this was overkill. During the next three years, the economy slowed continuously until it dropped off into a full-scale recession in 1991. Unemployment surged back to 7.5 percent as nearly 3 million workers were added to the jobless rolls.[49] One of these was President Bush, who after enjoying such widespread popularity during the Gulf War, was unable to maintain his political support in the face of a sputtering economy.

The Fed was back at it again in 1994, even though the unemployment rate was still in the 6 percent range. In early February, Greenspan announced the first small increase in the federal funds rate in five years, described as a "preemptive strike" against inflation.[50] Six weeks later the

Fed raised rates again, and it followed with a third increase in April. The hope was that tapping on the monetary brakes would reassure Wall Street that the Fed was serious about preventing inflation. This would bring long-term interest rates down and sustain the growth already underway. Unfortunately, Wall Street did not oblige, and the benchmark long-term rate rose to 7.4 percent, higher than at any time in Clinton's presidency.[51] Within twelve months, the economy forfeited nearly half its growth rate and unemployment rose.

However painful to those whose jobs were sacrificed, the belt-tightening in the late 1980s and again in 1994 raised the Fed's credibility on Wall Street. Although the Humphrey-Hawkins Full Employment Act of 1978 instructs the Fed to conduct monetary policy so as "to promote effectively the goals of maximum employment, stable prices, and moderate long-term interest rates," it was clear that the Fed had taken as its number one mission keeping inflation at bay. Anything else was secondary.[52] The nation had come a long way from the original Federal Reserve Act of 1913, which established the modern Federal Reserve System, and the Employment Act of 1946, which made responsibility for the nation's economic success a federal government priority. Controlling inflation was not even mentioned in either of these pieces of legislation![53]

In the end, with Greenspan's anti-inflation credentials well established, the Fed and Pennsylvania Avenue could come to a new understanding. As long as the president and Congress fulfilled their pledge to attack the budget deficit and expand free trade, the Fed could cut the economy a little slack. Instead of having to offset an implicitly expansionary fiscal policy of more public spending and higher federal deficits, the Fed could now wait a little longer before tightening up monetary policy to counter the potential inflationary bias of faster growth and lower unemployment.

Thus, in the current boom, even as the unemployment rate fell below what was formerly considered a safe level and remained there, the Fed this time did not instantly react with higher interest rates. Instead, it waited, its foot poised over both the accelerator and the brake, touching neither. When the Asian and Russian financial crises deepened and Brazil looked as though it were next, the Fed wisely lowered interest rates a tad in hopes of keeping the global financial crisis at bay. Still, if prices begin to creep up again, one fully expects that the Fed will not hesitate to jack up interest rates to keep price increases from spiraling upward — even if there is little evidence of real inflation.

Global Capital Mobility and the Wall Street Model

The Wall Street–Pennsylvania Avenue accord is structured to promote capital accumulation by keeping inflation under control and interest rates low. But, assuring that vast pools of capital will be available is, of course, not all that is necessary to assure America a reasonable growth rate. Firms must gain access to these funds and must also be motivated to use what capital they acquire effectively. If domestic firms cannot access capital resources from wherever they might be available worldwide, the law of supply and demand suggests they will have to pay more for credit. On the other hand, if American firms are guaranteed credit by restrictions on capital flows, they may not use what they have efficiently. Companies may be profitable because capital is cheap, but they would have less incentive to pay careful attention to productivity. We could end up then with profits but little economic progress. For both reasons, the Wall Street model rests on the concept of unlimited global mobility of capital in addition to global free trade in goods and services. Economists call this making global markets "perfect."

The perfecting of markets for finance capital means reducing, and ultimately eliminating, laws, regulations, and even customs, expectations, and norms that in any way hamper the free flow of financial investments from one firm, sector, locale, or country to another. The stakes get bigger every day. The pace and extent of what, many years ago, we originally termed the "hypermobility" of capital is unprecedented.[54] In his primer on the subject, published in 1992, geographer Peter Dicken (citing Peter Drucker) reports that "the London Eurodollar market, in which the world's financial institutions borrow from and lend to each other, turns over $300 billion each working day, or $75 trillion a year, a volume at least twenty-five times that of world trade. . . . Foreign exchange transactions [in 1992] run around $150 billion a day or about $35 trillion a year — twelve times the world-wide trade in goods and services."[55]

Such immense capital and currency flows, accomplished almost instantaneously through state-of-the-art, fully computerized stock, bond, and currency markets can mean that a firm — or for that matter, an entire country — can see its capital resources dry up almost completely in a matter of days or even hours, while another firm or country is the beneficiary of such shifts in global resources. The investment banker and former deputy secretary of the Treasury Roger Altman noted that as seamless worldwide twenty-four-hour capital markets have developed, the result has been like "an extraterrestrial force: gigantic flows of money, directed electronically, which dominate world finance and can change direction in an hour."[56]

Only a few years ago, it was not widely believed that such rapid capital movement was desirable. Quite the contrary, informed opinion in the academic community and even among many business leaders held that such instantaneous worldwide capital fluidity undermined investors' willingness to put their money into the kinds of long-term projects that contribute to long-run growth and development.

This viewpoint culminated in June 1992, when a private corporate research and lobbying organization, the Council on Competitiveness, issued some two dozen working papers by an all-star cast of economists, business finance specialists, industrial relations theorists, and historians of business, collected under the title *The Harvard Business School Time Horizons Project.* The renowned Harvard professor of business strategy Michael Porter wrote the comprehensive overview for this enormous undertaking.[57] The authors concluded that the Germans and Japanese had inherited from their own past, and then refined after World War II, a system of domestic financial controls that favored long-term over short-term private investment and growth. American institutions, they said, were too supportive of short-term profit seeking. This was seen as contributing to America's productivity drought. It was not surprising to this distinguished group that both Germany and Japan enjoyed faster economic growth than the United States and that their level of productivity now equaled or even surpassed ours. "Patient capital" was given much of the credit for their success; the lack of it was seen as the reason for our failure.

In one of the project's most important papers, Larry Summers — who as deputy secretary of the Treasury under Robert Rubin would later become one of the most ardent advocates for taking the Wall Street model global — and James Poterba reported on their interviews with CEOs from a sample of Fortune 1,000 corporations in the United States and the fifty largest firms in Japan, Germany, and the United Kingdom.[58] They confirmed that U.S. managers tend to require much higher and quicker returns on new investments than do their foreign counterparts for similar projects. This was found to be true especially for investments in basic research and development, where any short-term payoffs are elusive but where long-term payoffs can be enormous. With shorter time horizons, U.S. firms were leaning much more heavily toward spending on mergers and acquisitions, a practice that a number of economists, including Harvard's Frederick Scherer, had shown to be less profitable over the long run for the enterprises themselves and much less supportive of the country's long-term growth.

In 1992, when the Harvard report was released, there seemed to be a powerful ring of truth to the critique of capital markets and business practices that forced short-term planning horizons on American business. In a matter of just a very few years, however, the relative fortunes of the United States and its European and Asian competitors changed dramatically. As we have seen, the U.S. growth rate rebounded, productivity growth recovered, and unemployment plummeted. In Germany and much of the rest of Europe, meanwhile, unemployment reached double digits. In Japan, growth went negative. What had seemed a curse to our economy — high-speed capital mobility and short-term planning horizons — now seemed to be a blessing in disguise. Even such an outspoken advocate of the Asian model of patient capital as Jeffrey Garten, the dean of Yale's School of Management (and former assistant secretary of commerce), is now humbly eating crow, remarking that the American recovery is a "triumph of Wall Street" and admitting that he "certainly made some misjudgments about the Japanese system."[59] Wall Street, only recently reviled as the bane of American business, is now seen as its champion.

The apparent benefit of rapid and unrestricted capital movement is summed up quite compactly by MIT economist Peter Temin when he says that "One person's short-term focus is another person's market discipline."[60] With global capital markets, the financial system determines who gets capital and who does not. If a company fails even briefly to make the profits global investors expect, it will find it difficult to attract new investment to modernize or enter new markets. Thus, in a world where financial markets rule, managers must constantly strive to raise efficiency and improve the quality and innovation in their products or services. If they do not, they will see their stock prices tumble and their bond ratings downgraded. Obtaining capital will become difficult, if not impossible. It is discipline like this that boosts productivity and therefore also the chances for faster growth, according to the Wall Street model.

It is now widely agreed that there are two major characteristics that distinguish the U.S. financial system from systems in other countries: One is that stock and bond markets have displaced commercial banks as the main source of capital for American companies. The other is the shareholder activism that goes along with the rise of nonbank financial sources, particularly mutual funds and private pension funds. Why do they matter?

Even the most bottom line–oriented banks allow some time for projects to gestate. And once they make a loan, they tend to be passive observers of the company's use of their funds. By contrast, bond markets and, even more so, equity markets can invest in — and cash out — as quickly as they want, which means virtually instantaneously. They end up as active participants long after the financing is granted—on a day-to-day, even a minute-to-minute, basis.

Table 4.2 shows recent estimates by the World Bank of the relative magnitudes of bank and bond lending as shares of gross domestic product in the United States, Japan, and Germany. Total bond credit is now more than double the size of bank loans and investments in the United States. Elsewhere, bank lending is still far more important than the financial markets as a source of investment capital.

Table 4.2. Bank and Bond Lending as a Percentage of GDP, United States, Japan, and Germany		
Country	Bank Loans as % of GDP	Bond Credit as % of GDP
U.S.	50	110
Japan	150	75
Germany	170	90

Source: Murray, "Asia's Financial Foibles Make American Way Look Like a Winner," *Wall Street Journal,* Dec. 8, 1998.

The explosive growth of nonbank financial institutions, and particularly of the mutual fund industry, pioneered by firms like Massachusetts Financial Services, Putnam, and Fidelity, created an entirely new source of both equity and credit.[61] Instead of having to satisfy conservative bank officers, companies now have to do everything they can to convince mutual fund managers to rate their stocks as "best buys" and to make sure that the bond raters at Moody's and Standard & Poor's are likewise impressed. Displease these Wall Street operatives and even the largest corporation has a great deal of explaining to do to its stockholders. As just one example, in 1998, while automobile sales were brisk, General Motors (GM) refused to quickly settle a strike over work rules initiated by several hundred members of the United Automobile Workers (UAW) union in Flint, Michigan. GM took the strike to demonstrate to Wall Street and its own stockholders that it was finally serious about cutting costs and boosting productivity.[62] This ended up costing the company over $2 billion in foregone sales, as the work stoppage in one critical parts plant shut down most of the company's production nationwide. Whether it was successful in convincing the UAW to permit changes in work rules that would enhance long-term productivity remains an open question. But if GM's stock had been rising as fast as Chrysler's and Ford's, it is hard to believe that management would have picked such an inopportune time to try to bring the autoworkers' union to its knees. From the Wall Street model's perspective, this hard-headed approach is good for the economy because it forces management of even the largest corporations to mount a continuous campaign to weed out inefficiencies and costs.

The success of American-style financial institutions has led to broader support for a new international initiative to open up global financial markets in the same way that creation of the World Trade Organization (WTO) opened up global markets in goods and services by outlawing tariffs and other barriers to trade. The Multilateral Agreement on Investment (MAI), now being negotiated by the world's twenty-nine richest countries, is aimed at eliminating government regulations that inhibit the free flow of capital resources between nations.[63] Currently, in many countries, governments regulate the conditions under which foreign investors can buy domestic businesses, banks, television stations, and utilities. The accord would bar the U.S. Congress, state legislatures, and even city councils from using trade sanctions to punish nations for human rights abuses, violations of labor standards, or religious persecution. Other provisions could limit such investment incentives as enterprise zones and end minority set-asides and "Buy American" rules.

Why would such a treaty be in America's interest? The answer is that U.S. companies want stronger rules protecting their investments overseas and more incentives for luring foreign money into the United States. It turns out that other nations are even more protective of their own businesses and local economies than is America. Breaking down such deterrents to foreign investment will remove the final barrier to the market discipline of truly globalized financial markets. In anticipation of new opportunities worldwide, as well as the completion of the European Common Market with its new common currency, the euro, U.S. securities firms such as Merrill Lynch and Charles Schwab are setting up offices throughout Europe and branching out rapidly in Asia and Latin America.[64]

The same market discipline that now applies to prices through free trade is thereby reinforced in the Wall Street model by the free mobility of investment funds through global capital markets. The first keeps inflation directly in check, while the second does so indirectly, by pressuring firms to redouble their efforts at cost reduction to maintain their stock prices and bond ratings. Both are central to the neoclassical growth syllogism and the Wall Street model.

The Role of the IMF in Globalizing the Wall Street Model

The MAI is only the latest of many international developments aimed at making the world economy more like that of the United States. In the closing days of World War II, the Allied powers met in Bretton Woods, New Hampshire, to create a new economic world order. The innovative central institution in the new system was the International Monetary Fund (IMF). Back then, there was unanimous agreement that national governments had to be free to set their own goals for employment, taxation, and social services. It was also assumed that excessively rapid capital mobility across countries would be a destabilizing force, and therefore that mutually agreed upon regulations controlling capital flows (along with fixed exchange rates) would be a sine qua non for the postwar system. Indeed, Article VI of the Bretton Woods Articles of Agreement *required* members to institute such controls as would be deemed necessary to maintain global economic stability.[65]

But by the 1980s, the IMF — backed and financed principally by American taxpayers and encouraged by the global financiers to whom it was making itself increasingly accountable — was beginning to stand these original objectives on their heads. Instead of relieving foreign exchange crises at acceptable costs to borrowing countries, as it had done since the late 1940s, the IMF began to insist that borrowers follow the Wall Street model and open their capital markets and their industries to foreign investors and buyers. Attracting foreign equity investment was now to be the solution to global poverty. Free flows of capital would integrate (or "perfect") the markets of different countries, more accurately price capital assets, and reduce lenders' risks, thereby lowering the interest rates that borrowers would have to offer to attract capital. Increased global investment would in turn lead to faster economic and productivity growth for all countries, including the United States. Insecurity and instability, once viewed as the bane of international markets, were now seen as its boon.

In the 1990s, bolstered by the principles underlying the Wall Street model, the IMF has pursued these policies with a vengeance. Not only have borrowers in Asia, Latin America, and Eastern Europe been told to deregulate capital controls as a quid pro quo for receiving IMF assistance, they have been further challenged to privatize what had previously been state-owned enterprises, reduce social expenditures, liquidate many domestic banks, and reduce or eliminate altogether local content and other requirements that had been placed on foreign firms as a condition for producing locally. The theory — and the practice — are simply an extension of the Wall Street–Pennsylvania Avenue accord. The accord, like everything else, is going global.[66]

Conclusion

The globalization of the Wall Street model continues apace. Back in Chapter 1, we quoted Deputy Treasury Secretary Larry Summers's off-hand remark to the *Wall Street Journal:* "Financial markets don't just oil the wheels of economic growth; they are the wheels." This, ultimately, is what the architects of and advocates for the Wall Street model of economic growth are about. This is their deepest conviction.

The apparent success of the Wall Street model and the political accord that accompanies it marks a historic accomplishment for the economics profession and for the policymakers who have advocated balanced budgets, free trade, flexible labor markets, and a Federal Reserve that is vigilant in its efforts to stabilize prices. Indeed, all who have advocated a smaller, more limited role for the federal government in economic affairs seem vindicated by the renewed economic growth America has enjoyed in the middle of this decade.

It would seem hard to argue with such apparent success. But at this point we must ask some discomforting questions: Was it really the slaying of inflation that ignited the current surge in the economy? Was it the dramatic elimination of the federal government's deficit that brought price stability? Is the current period of growth really based on Wall Street confidence and the surging stock market? Is investment in physical capital, via the neoclassical growth syllogism, the key to economic success? Will extension of free capital markets throughout the world produce more rapid growth in the United States and other countries?

It turns out that each one of the links in the growth syllogism has a crack in it, the Wall Street model is precariously unstable, and the Wall Street–Pennsylvania Avenue accord — in both its domestic and international aspects — has a lot less to do with current growth than first impressions suggest. The new conventional wisdom seems to have worked wonders, but what seems obvious can be deceiving. In the next chapter we begin to explain why.

Chapter 5

The Wall Street Model:
Too Little Long-Term Growth

THE CELEBRATION of an American economic resurgence began on Wall Street, spread to Pennsylvania Avenue, and by mid-decade could even be heard on Main Street. For the first time in decades, there was an inkling that the economy had turned the corner, and the future looked significantly brighter. What had changed? What had brought about such improvement in productivity, employment, and growth?

The answer seemed obvious. The return of economic growth coincided almost perfectly with the decade's progress toward defeating inflation, which all assumed had been achieved through balanced budgets, free trade, flexible labor markets, and Federal Reserve Board vigilance. Leaders in Washington, basking in the economy's success, took much of the credit. After all, in the days when budget deficits were rising, growth was moribund. Only after the White House and Congress formed an alliance to balance the federal budget did strong economic growth reemerge. Moreover, the passage of NAFTA, signaling a new era of free trade, had immediately preceded the economy's takeoff, suggesting that bringing down trade barriers played a role as well.

Also given credit for the new burst in economic growth was Washington's commitment to boosting labor market "flexibility." Both the White House and Congress refused to "coddle" organized labor with labor law reform, while their tough new approach to welfare centered on ending payments to recipients who refused to work. Workers were now sufficiently insecure that they were willing to work harder and longer, even without improvement in their pay. With little upward pressure on wages and intensified competition from foreign producers, firms had less reason to raise prices and little discretion to do so. All of this helped keep inflation in check. Finally, after years of running a tight monetary ship, the Fed had earned the full confidence of bankers and of financial leaders on Wall Street for its vigilance in keeping inflation at bay. So when the Fed did lower interest rates in late 1998 to keep the Asian and Russian financial crises from prolonging a sell-off in the U.S. stock market that might have triggered a domestic recession, investors reentered the market and quickly bid equity prices back up. Trust in the new growth model — and in those implementing it — remained high even as fears of global recession spread from one continent to another.

While only economists might use the formal jargon of the *neoclassical growth syllogism* and the *Wall Street virtuous cycle* to describe this new political-economic regime, there was widespread acknowledgment even on Main Street of the broad outlines of a paradigm shift. The activist fiscal policies associated with Keynes were now considered passé, if not discredited, in this new globalized economy. A new model of growth was ascendant. As a result, when the White House and Congress adopted the Wall Street view of the world and moved with amazing speed to put its prescribed policies in place, there was general acceptance of their actions. When the policies began to pay off in skyrocketing stock prices and plummeting unemployment, acceptance turned into exuberance. Even when the economy stumbled briefly in the second half of 1998, few questioned the essentials of the model. (Although some did begin to challenge the wisdom of permitting the unregulated short-term international capital mobility that had so terribly and swiftly destabilized Indonesia, Thailand, and South Korea, and threatened Brazil.) We were witnessing a triumph of economic theory and Washington resolve, the likes of which we had not seen since the 1930s. A stunning paradigm revolution had occurred. We now had a fresh model that could be used to guide American prosperity into the twenty-first century.

As we noted at the end of the previous chapter, it is difficult to argue with such apparent success. But before we blindly submit to the logic of the new growth model and its policy implications, it is appropriate to consider just how much credit we should give it. After all, correlation and causation are not the same thing. Good timing can be mere coincidence. Therefore, in this chapter, we subject the neoclassical growth syllogism and the Wall Street virtuous cycle to careful scrutiny. We dissect the syllogism piece by piece to see whether its internal logic holds water. We inspect both the demand and supply sides of the Wall Street virtuous cycle to see whether it really could have been responsible for the healthy U-turn the economy has taken. Finally, we consider the policies established in the Wall Street–Pennsylvania Avenue accord to see whether they deserve such high praise for the nation's apparent economic renaissance.

In the end, we believe the facts indicate that, regardless of the timing of events, neither the virtuous cycle and accord, nor the growth syllogism on which they are based, could have been responsible for much of the improvement the economy has experienced. We show that each argument in the syllogism is badly flawed, and that the virtuous cycle is dangerously unstable. Consequently, the policies of the Wall Street–Pennsylvania Avenue accord, far from contributing to economic growth and improved equity, cannot be given much credit for either. Worse yet, as we shall see, adherence to the Wall Street model and continued reliance on its policy implications could very well end up sabotaging the very prosperity that its proponents claim is the model's strength, while exacerbating inequality. Ironically, what the majority of economists and policymakers view as the salvation of the economy is likely to be its damnation.

At the very core of the neoclassical growth model is an obsession with inflation. Because virtually every national policy initiative is now subordinated to this obsessive — and, as we will show, overblown — fear of price instability, the Wall Street–Pennsylvania Avenue alliance is apprehensive of a truly sustained robust economy. Politicians may want to take credit for short spurts of rapid growth and declining unemployment, but the deeply ingrained fear of inflation imparts a built-in bias against anything more than modest economic expansion. Because the fear of breaking the 2.3 percent speed limit on growth is so great, those who now guide the economy never have their feet far removed from the brake pedal.

To show why this is so, we shall take another look — this time more critically — at each component in the Wall Street model. We begin with the neoclassical growth syllogism and go on from there.

Chinks in the Links: Weakness in the Growth Syllogism

Recall that at the root of the Wall Street model is a powerful piece of economic theory, which we expressed as a syllogism. In such a formulation, if each of the individual arguments is valid, then the conclusion follows as a matter of pure and incontrovertible logic. "If all A are B, and all B are C, then all A are C." Nothing more needs to be said. The only issue then is whether there is sufficient evidence to uphold each premise in the syllogism. One fundamental flaw in a single premise, and the model disintegrates. Alternatively, if every premise in the syllogism is only partially true, then there is likely to be a great deal of slippage between the syllogism's first premise and its conclusion. In the case of the neoclassical growth syllogism, we find there is a chink in *every* premise; therefore, the conclusion that growth is directly and inalterably tied to price stability must be taken with a large pinch of salt.

As stated in the previous chapter, the first argument in the neoclassical growth syllogism runs as follows: *Faster economic growth will occur only if there is increased investment in physical capital.* It would seem that we could take this premise at face value. If for some reason all new investment were to cease, or if there were just enough to make up for depreciation of worn-out equipment and no more, growth would obviously slow appreciably. Capital is a key ingredient in the growth process. But it is important to realize that even in this case, growth would not stall completely unless technological progress were to collapse as well. After all, as the father of modern growth theory, Robert Solow, demonstrated, both capital accumulation *and* technological progress contribute to increased labor productivity. If workers somehow found a way to use existing capital more efficiently, then output could increase even in a state of no net increase in physical capital. How much increase depends on the pace of technological innovation and the form it takes.

Here we need to make a distinction much remarked upon by Solow in his early formulation of the neoclassical growth model and later adopted as the centerpiece of Dale Jorgenson's contribution. Technological progress can be of two types: One is *embodied* in new capital. For example, the great post–World War II improvements in steelmaking productivity resulted not from equipping steelworkers with more and larger open hearth furnaces, but from switching to capital equipment incorporating new basic oxygen furnace technology and to the innovative electric furnace, which uses scrap steel as an input.[1] In a more modern context, increased computer throughput is due not to putting three 286-vintage PCs on each desk, but to substituting a high-speed Pentium III for an older 486, 386, or earlier-vintage machine. In both of these cases, technological progress occurred only as a result of investments embodied directly in new physical capital, in line with with the first premise in the growth syllogism.

The other form of technological progress is *disembodied*. This is what the growth accountant Edward Denison called "advances in knowledge" and the economist Moses Abramovitz referred to as "costless improvements" in the way production is carried out. Rearranging the way existing machines and tools are set up, learning how better to operate old equipment, or restructuring labor-management relations can make a significant difference in how well capital is utilized. One can get more productivity from the same capital stock if one is clever. Many studies have confirmed that companies adopting formal employee involvement systems, profit sharing, and worker ownership show improved productivity even when the physical plant and equipment of the enterprise remain unaltered.[2] In this case, we can obtain more growth without investments in new machinery.

This would seem to make the first premise a bit shaky. But following Jorgenson, one might argue in response that none of these disembodied improvements are truly costless, and therefore even these types of changes should be seen as equivalent to embodied technological progress, requiring new investment. If not mere window dressing, such changes in organizational structure and behavior entail real outlays of resources and therefore should be regarded as investments in capital assets, even if they are not carried on a company's books as such. Switching from the standard assembly line to the use of teams in auto production may not count as a capital outlay, but presumably it takes some investment to pull it off right. Following this line of argument, virtually all growth can be viewed as dependent on investment, fully in accord with the first premise in the syllogism.

There is a compelling reason, however, to discount this interpretation. The implicit assumption in Jorgenson's approach is that capital investment occurs in a competitive market and obeys the neoclassical law of diminishing returns. If that is true, an extra dollar spent on investment A yields the same return (marginal product) as the last dollar spent on investment B. Otherwise, rational investors would reallocate their capital budgets to the higher-productivity machine or technological advance. But as we shall see in Chapter 7, this does not hold when it comes to invention and innovation. A dollar spent on a new innovation may yield a bonanza, as did the introduction of the transistor, the integrated circuit, or for that matter, the introduction of employee involvement at the Magma Copper mine in San Manuel, Arizona.[3] While it may be true that all advances in knowledge cost something, as Jorgenson's theory implies, the return on innovation may be so high that the technological progress is essentially "costless" in relative terms. A large investment in physical capital could end up yielding a small improvement in labor productivity, while a low-cost innovation could bring enormous increases in efficiency and output.

The real productivity boosts embodied in the steam engine, the mechanical reaper, and the electric motor flowed not so much from the size of the capital investments in these new devices, but from the fact that a dollar spent on the new technology ultimately produced so much more output than a dollar spent on more of the old. Consequently, while there is clearly a positive link between the level of investment in physical capital and the rate of output, growth depends on a whole range of technological factors that are distinct from the normal form of investment associated with traditional capital assets. This certainly casts doubt on the universality of the initial premise in the growth syllogism, that faster growth is impossible without wholesale investments in physical capital.

For the moment, however, and for the sake of argument, let us agree that the first premise is still 80 percent true. That would mean only a 20 percent "chink" in the syllogism, certainly small enough to consider the syllogism a solid foundation for the Wall Street model and its related policy prescriptions.

But let us go on to the second premise: *Increased investment in physical capital will occur only if interest rates are kept low.* Again, the premise seems reasonable enough. After all, any firm would soon be out of business if it persisted in borrowing funds at 10 percent when the investment made possible by the borrowed funds yielded only 8 percent. The higher the interest rate, the smaller the number of investment projects worth pursuing. Conversely, projects that might have been unprofitable at higher interest rates become moneymakers at lower ones.

This is all true, but it tells only part of the investment story. Firms must, and generally do, pay careful attention to factors other than interest rates when planning the level of their capital outlays. Even more closely watched than the cost of credit is the expected demand for the products or services made possible by a potential new investment. The last thing a firm wants to do is purchase new or additional plant and equipment, only to see the production from this new capacity turn into unsold inventory. To those who design and build office complexes, for example, low interest rates suggest a good time to build. But if the low rates mainly reflect a softening of aggregate demand, taking advantage of low-cost credit can leave the investors with empty buildings and mortgages they cannot afford to service. The point is that low interest rates may encourage more investment, but their impact can easily be overshadowed by other factors.[4] This is undoubtedly the case for property developers, but it holds equally true for any business.

The individual firm's assessment of potential demand also has a great deal to do with whether the specific product or service in question made possible by new capital outlays will be greeted favorably by customers and whether there are competing goods that might capture the market. Hence, the price, quality, and uniqueness of the product are of paramount importance. Unless these are assured, investing in the product would be a questionable undertaking at any interest rate — including zero.

Yet even the best new product can face weak sales if the economy suddenly softens and aggregate demand declines. Millions of consumers may have a desire for the product, but if their pocketbooks are squeezed or they feel insecure about their near-term income prospects, actual demand — desire backed up by dollars — will fail to materialize. In this case, the firm's best-laid investment plans can go terribly awry. If enough firms fear that the economy will grow only slowly in the future, slow growth will become a self-fulling prophecy as companies rationally downsize their investment plans, reducing the *potential* for output as well as its current level.

During the Great Depression, interest rates fell to as little as half a percent, but looking out over the bleak economic landscape, few firms took advantage of them. Economists call this a *liquidity trap,* where no matter how low interest rates go, investment fails to follow. This is no mere theoretical construct; the Japanese seem to have fallen into just such a liquidity trap in the late 1990s, unable to rekindle their economy even with interest rates below 2 percent. High interest rates can certainly choke off an expansion, but low rates will not necessarily reignite one.

This is part of the reason why managing monetary policy is so challenging. Let us say that the Federal Reserve, fearing an outbreak of inflation, hikes short-term interest rates to deliberately cool down the economy. Such a preemptive strike against impending inflation is supposed to work like a vaccine. Until the medical profession wiped out the deadly smallpox virus so that no preventative was necessary, people were protected by injecting a small dose of cowpox, which deterred the more dreaded virus from attacking. In the Fed's case, the vaccination involves an attempt to prevent a serious infection (rising long-term interest rates) by subjecting the economy to a small dose of a minor disease (a calculated increase in short-term rates). Given just the right amount of the Fed's vaccine applied at just the right time, the result is a healthy, stable economy.

But if ill-timed or overzealous, the Fed's intervention can easily slow the economy to the point where aggregate demand falls sharply. In this case, the slowdown in the economy can turn existing capital outlay decisions into unprofitable ones and discourage firms from making new investments altogether. Trying to rectify such an overdose by subsequently lowering interest rates can prove very difficult. A worst-case scenario is supplied by the Fed's actions to contain inflation at the beginning of the 1980s. William Greider, who chronicled the internal workings of the Fed in his 1987 best-seller, *Secrets of the Temple,* explains what happened.[5] In anticipation of the deep 1981 Reagan tax cut, the Fed under Paul Volcker raised short-term interest rates to protect the economy against the inflationary potential of the expected increase in the federal deficit. Even though the inflation rate was already moving lower, the Fed maintained high short-term interest rates for months on end. Ultimately, this policy helped bring inflation under control more rapidly, but the damage to the economy of such a quick deceleration was staggering. Instead of tapping on the monetary brakes to bring the economy to a controlled stop, the Fed slammed on the brakes and the economy skidded off the road.

The engineered slowdown in the economy caused real GDP to fall by 2.1 percent in 1982, the biggest one-year decline in thirty-five years. Unemployment reached 10.8 percent by December 1982 with 12 million jobless, the worst unemployment since the Great Depression. Huge companies like General Motors bled red ink to the tune of billions; Ford nearly went bankrupt; Chrysler was saved from Chapter 11 only by a $2.5 billion federal loan guarantee. What happened to these industrial giants was typical of literally thousands, if not tens of thousands, of smaller firms. The prime rate fell from nearly 19 percent in 1981 to less than 11 percent two years later. But the damage to the economy was done. During the same period, real nonresidential net fixed investment in plant and equipment fell by more than half, from $106 billion to only $50.4 billion — just the opposite of what the second premise in the growth syllogism would suggest.[6]

In short, the link between interest rates and investment is anything but straightforward. Investment responds to many other factors besides interest rates, and interest rate manipulation to promote investment is anything but a sure thing. Still, to give the neoclassical model a fair shake, let us assume for the sake of further argument that the second premise is 50 percent true.

The last premise in the growth syllogism states: *Low interest rates will occur only in an environment of stable prices and enhanced savings.* Here, the link between prices and interest rates is clear-cut: higher expected inflation will invariably lead to higher interest rates. But the link between savings rates and interest rates is problematic. The premise implicitly suggests that low savings rates are bad for the economy because they inevitably drive up interest rates, which in turn discourages investment. Hence, anything that can be done to boost saving is presumably good for the economy.

The late Robert Eisner, eminent Northwestern University economist and past president of the American Economics Association, tirelessly campaigned against myopic thinking in this regard. The act of saving puts the saver in a position to consume more later, he noted. But in what amounts to a *paradox of thrift,* this does *not* imply that a higher savings rate for a nation necessarily increases the amount of investment, output, or consumption its households can enjoy in the future. Eisner explains:

> Let us suppose that an individual does decide to cut consumption in order to increase saving. Trips to the barber shop or hairdresser go by the board, as does eating out. Relaxation at home may replace going to a golf or tennis resort at vacation time. Our individual's

saving goes up, as we have noted. But what happens to the saving of the barber or hairdresser, the restaurant owner and workers, and the golf or tennis pro and other workers in the forsaken resort? Their incomes go down, perhaps by the full amount that an individual increases his saving. . . . Suppose the barber and the others cut their consumption in response to a loss of income. If they cut it dollar for dollar with the loss, their saving does not change. But then still others' incomes go down. And as *they* cut their consumption, new links are added to the income-loss chain.[7]

Trying to boost personal saving (or public saving) is therefore not necessarily good for economic growth at all. Too much saving can reduce consumption below the level needed to maintain aggregate demand. The result is lower investment, lower output, and, ironically, lower total savings.

Again, one need only look at Japan today in order to see the paradox of thrift in practice. For years, economists lauded the Japanese for their parsimony — their abstinence from consumption and consequently their high investment rates. Economists railed against the pitifully low savings rates in the United States, asserting that Japan outperformed hapless America because their people were willing to save and ours were not.[8] No doubt, in the 1970s and 1980s the saving behavior of the Japanese did contribute to their nation's extraordinary growth. But in the 1990s, the virtue of high savings has turned into a vice. When its Asian trading partners were moving from recession to depression in the wake of sudden short-term capital flight, Japan could no longer count on exports to buoy its economy. The parsimonious behavior of its own citizens now undermined the very consumption Japan needed to extricate itself from deepening recession. Meanwhile, the U.S. savings rate has fallen below 3 percent, yet its citizens are enjoying the highest growth rate in decades. Moreover, because of rapid growth, even a declining savings rate applied to a substantial increase in income can translate into reasonably stable *levels* of savings, which help to keep interest rates low.[9]

Regardless of the current economic boom, the conventional wisdom among American economists and policymakers still rues the opulent lifestyles of U.S. families and presses for higher savings rates. The argument offered is that although we are enjoying the good times now, a low savings rate will inevitably undermine future investment and, in turn, jeopardize economic growth.[10]

Assume then for the moment that despite the Japanese case, we still bought the premise that personal savings rates are absolutely critical for investment and growth. Would this mean that we should now do everything we can to encourage families to save more? As it turns out, the answer is no, and there is a simple reason for this: the true American savings rate is not nearly as low as feared, and indeed, it is already rising on its own. The problem is that the official data on savings are all wrong.

As William Nordhaus of Yale University has argued, the nation's official income and product accounts are extremely strict about what is counted as consumption and what as savings, but the categories are not particularly logical.[11] In the national accounts, savings exactly equals investment by construction.[12] Essentially, any dollar not consumed is assumed to be put aside for investment. Yet despite its contribution to future income streams, household spending on such items as education, medical care, and automobiles used for commuting to work are all counted as consumption, not investment. In 1993, for example, the national accounts record $105 billion of private, nonbusiness education and research spending.[13] Every last penny was counted as consumption rather than savings and investment. This makes for some curious outcomes. Whenever a family takes $500 from its savings account to spend on the education of a child, the official savings rate and, consequently, the investment rate go *down*. If we followed this twisted logic, one of the most powerful ways to improve the nation's official savings rate would be to ban all colleges and universities. Then, every time a family deposits the money that would have gone for tuition payments into its bank account, the nation's savings rate would actually go up a notch!

A corresponding argument can be made about health care. A good deal of medical spending goes for the care of the elderly who are no longer contributors to national income. This spending is properly considered consumption according to the economist's definition. But most health care spending pays for those who are currently productive or, in the case of children, potentially productive. Without these medical "investments" in human capital, our future growth rate would no doubt be lower. Yet we measure virtually all household spending on health insurance, doctors, hospitals, and drugs as consumption, not savings.[14]

Nordhaus has attempted to measure the missing components of savings in the household sector. This inevitably requires making some heroic assumptions about what is consumption and what is investment. He classifies all education and research expenditures as investment in his calculations of a revised savings rate, but he leaves all personal care expenditures in consumption.[15] Surely, some portion of schooling should be considered as consumption. For most of us, that English course on Shakespeare's sonnets that we took in college has done little to increase our market value, no matter how much joy it may have added to our lives. On the other hand, at least for fashion models, personal care expenditures can be a critical investment good. For the rest of us, how we appear at a job interview may be as important an "investment" as anything else. In any case, this is quibbling; Nordhaus's numbers are certainly more accurate than the official statistics, which count *all* household spending as consumption and *none* as investment.

Using this accounting framework, Nordhaus finds that capital spending by households as a share of total spending has actually *risen* over time, and the increase has accelerated since 1973 — regardless of whether interest rates were going up or down. An indication of the share of household spending that might best be assigned to investment rather than consumption is found in Table 5.1. The sharp increase in household "investment" over the past twenty years suggests that the official statistics on family savings are seriously misleading and that the call for boosting savings further may be badly misplaced.[16]

All of this leaves the third premise of the syllogism pretty much in tatters. Savings rates, properly accounted, may not be very highly correlated

Table 5.1. Household "Investment" as a Share of Total Household Spending	
Year	%
1929	28.3
1955	28.4
1973	31.9
1993	39.2

Source: Nordhaus, "Budget Deficits and National Saving," *Challenge,* March–April 1996, p. 47.

with interest rates, and if even more savings is encouraged, growth may be undermined rather than enhanced. At best, we might count the third premise as 30 percent right.

That finally brings us to the conclusion — and main policy implication — of the neoclassical growth syllogism: *Therefore, increased economic growth will occur only if inflation is kept firmly under control and high savings rates are achieved.* Since each of the syllogism's premises is, at best, only partially valid, the conclusion does not necessarily follow after all. Indeed, if our estimates of the percentage "correctness" of each premise are in the right ballpark, then there is a very weak relationship between inflation and savings rates on the one hand and economic growth on the other — on the order of about 12 percent, if you do the math (.80 × .50 × .30). Clearly there is some correlation and perhaps *some* causation, but it is not particularly strong.

This does not mean that we can stop worrying about inflation altogether. Nor does it suggest that families would do well to raid their savings accounts in order to take long, luxurious vacations. Price instability does impose real costs on the economy, and saving is necessary to ensure sufficient investment in productivity and growth-enhancing capital goods production. But undue obsession with inflation and official savings rates can actually hamper the economic growth that stable prices and high savings are supposed to generate.

What really counts in the growth game is a set of factors very different from those highlighted by the neoclassical syllogism:

1. Disembodied technological change is clearly as important to growth as investment in physical capital.

2. Expected aggregate demand is at least as important as interest rates in determining the level of capital investment.

3. Consumption is potentially more important than savings in setting in motion the dynamics of a growth economy.

The chinks in the syllogism suggest that our current preoccupation with slaying inflation and boosting savings rates may lead us to target the wrong variables for sustaining economic growth. Indeed, the syllogism may actually divert our attention from the growth phenomena that really matter.

Breaks in the Wall Street Virtuous Cycle

The unwavering acceptance of the neoclassical growth syllogism has lent the Wall Street virtuous cycle intellectual credibility and has made it easier to sell to policymakers at both ends of Pennsylvania Avenue. But given the flaws we have found in the syllogism, it follows that there are likely to be serious breaks in the virtuous cycle, as well.

Recall that the Wall Street model, as shown in Figure 4.3 of the previous chapter, has essentially two epicycles, or minor cycles, embedded within it. One of these we identified with the supply side, the other with demand. The supply-side epicycle derives directly from the growth syllogism: subdued inflation permits interest rates to fall, which in turn encourages capital investment, which, with its embodied technological change, raises productivity and growth. Simple and straightforward as it may be, it nevertheless suffers from the same flaws we found in the syllogism: capital investment is driven by things other than interest rates alone, the link between savings rates and interest rates is weak, and productivity improvement is driven by other factors in addition to capital investment.

The most serious problem with the Wall Street model, however, lies on the demand side. Here subdued inflation supposedly works its magic by boosting stock prices, which in turn increases household wealth and spending, leading to faster growth. Like the old complaint about the cheap restaurant where the food tastes bad and, adding insult to injury, the portions are small, this epicycle provides an unpalatable repast. If stock prices do not affect consumption much, we need another mechanism to uphold demand. If stock prices do matter a great deal, the economy is in a lot more trouble than generally feared.

The problem is that rising stock prices do not create an actual stream of income; they merely generate increased paper assets. Only when stockholders exercise the option to sell their shares do they have a palpable claim on output, but rarely do stockholders do this in order to purchase goods and services. Instead, rising stock prices operate on the real economy mainly through psychology. When stock prices rise, shareholders *feel* wealthier. If they are confident that stock prices will remain high or, better yet, continue to rise, that sense of greater wealth may induce them to buy things they might not have otherwise.

151

No doubt such a psychological boost induces some extra spending, but the overall impact on the economy will generally not be conse-
quential. First, unless increases in equity values are extraordinary, and
these increases are perceived as more or less permanent, they will have
little psychological impact and therefore induce very little additional
spending. Second, since stocks are held disproportionately by the very
richest households, which tend to have the very highest savings rates, the
propensity to consume out of additional income and wealth, whether realized or on paper, is exceptionally low.

In the previous chapter we suggested that increased spending from
the stock market boom in the early 1990s probably amounted to only
about 4 percent of the value of the increase in total stock market assets.
Only if the stock market rises sharply over an extended period and there
is little expectation of a major correction in stock values will the wealth
effect be very substantial or long lasting. No doubt it contributed something to the exceptional growth rates in the mid-1990s, but it could
hardly be responsible for most of the improvement we have seen.

Furthermore, over the long run stock prices cannot continue to rise
as fast as they did during the extended bull market of the late 1990s. Even
if Wall Street was responsible for a spurt in the growth rate, it can hardly
sustain growth indefinitely. Massive run-ups in stock values are a transitory phenomenon that we enjoy only briefly and periodically. It is hard to
base year-in and year-out growth on something so episodic.[17]

But the greater threat comes from the dynamic instability of the Wall
Street virtuous cycle. Few markets are as unstable, speculative, or influenced by random events as the stock market. After rising sharply during
the first six months of 1998, all major stock price indexes stalled and then
plummeted. The Dow Jones industrial average gave up over 1,800 points
in a matter of weeks. The panic selling was caused by the deepening
Asian crisis, which threatened the profitability of large multinational
firms, the devaluation of the Russian ruble, and a continuing sex scandal
in the White House. That the market recovered much of the lost ground
by the late fall — at least for the moment — does not alter the main
point. Is it wise to anchor our prospects for economic growth, employment, and income on such a precarious foundation? Simply asking the
question is sufficient to warn against placing this model at the center of
the nation's growth strategy.

Alan Greenspan has repeatedly voiced his concern about the stock market and its potential downside impact on the economy. Despite the vast differences between the economy of the late 1920s — which ended with the stock market crash, followed by the Great Depression — and that of the 1990s, the worry remains that if the wealth effect is large enough to have contributed to a spurt in growth, a sharp reversal in the stock market could throw the virtuous cycle into reverse.[18] Feeling poorer, households that have seen the values of their stock portfolios shrink would delay their purchases of new luxuries, triggering a downward spiral in output and employment. The conservative economist Milton Friedman added his voice to a growing chorus of liberal economists, admitting to *The New Yorker* magazine that he suspected we would have a recession when the bubble bursts, and only the Fed could keep it from being a serious one.[19] That a purge of stock market values could lead to a worldwide recession, with only the Fed around to put its finger in the dike, is a pretty unsettling thought. The Wall Street virtuous cycle turns out to be not so virtuous after all.

The Wall Street–Pennsylvania Avenue Accord Reassessed

It is not clear whether the Clinton White House and the Republican leaders on Capitol Hill recognized the chinks in the growth syllogism or the broken links and instability in the Wall Street virtuous cycle — at least until the Asian and Russian economic crises began to have a decidedly negative impact on the U.S. stock market. In any case, since at least 1992 nearly every new legislative initiative has been aimed, directly or indirectly, at the single objective of keeping inflation under control. Balancing the federal budget became the number-one domestic priority in Clinton's first term and remained the top economic priority in his second. The House of Representatives narrowly rejected the bill extending fast-track authority for the negotiation of new trade agreements, but the administration and the Republican leaders in Congress have vowed to reintroduce the legislation. They have also been contributing to the drafting of the Multilateral Agreement on Investment. On the labor front, Clinton and the Democratic congressional leadership were finally successful at passing minimum wage legislation, but refused to introduce any amendments to the National Labor Relations Act (NLRA) that would create a "level playing field" for labor organizing. This has been true despite the fact that such legislation was endorsed by a high-level commission appointed by President Clinton himself in 1993 and headed by former labor secretary John Dunlop.[20] At best, the Clinton administration rallied to oppose Republican legislation that would have undermined the NLRA's provisions against the establishment of company-dominated unions.

Meanwhile, with the president and Congress riveted on budget balance as their contribution to sound fiscal policy, stewardship of the economy shifted almost completely to the Federal Reserve. Essentially, the Fed has now been given, by default, sole responsibility for monitoring and reacting to perturbations in prices and employment.

The real question is this: Was it really this policy prescription that cured the American economy of its growth malaise and restored its health? Just how therapeutic has this new policy regime been in terms of the economic renaissance we have experienced so far, and what are its likely consequences for the future?

Contrary to both expert and popular belief, there is surprisingly little evidence connecting the Wall Street–Pennsylvania Avenue accord to the increase in economic growth after the 1991–92 recession. To be sure, economic growth has accelerated, but the accord, we will see, has had surprisingly little to do with it. Remember that economic growth requires improved productivity or increased labor supply on one side of the market and increased aggregate demand on the other. At best, the implementation of the accord has had a superficial impact on aggregate demand, while long-term historical factors — the ones we talked about in Chapter 3 — have been responsible for improved productivity. If the accord can be credited with anything, it is the increase in labor supply that has its roots in stagnating wages and rising job insecurity. It is hard to believe that the proponents of the accord would want to campaign on a platform claiming credit for faster growth because they made the rich richer and made workers more insecure. But that is how the virtuous cycle is supposed to work, and that is what the accord has essentially done.

There are three major reasons why we should retract the kudos that have been showered on the Wall Street model of growth. The first is that the model's policy prescriptions have had very little to do with the defeat of inflation — the very centerpiece of the model. The second is that the defeat of inflation was hardly the most important factor in reigniting growth. And the third, perhaps most important, is that given conventional thinking about inflation, keeping it near zero *requires* keeping growth modest. Hence, a policy model centered on inflation control is, almost by definition, a model for slow growth and thus diminishes any expectations for real prosperity.

But why the obsession with inflation in the first place? Why has so much economic attention and political effort been directed at this one target? These are important questions, and we need to know a little about inflation theory to answer them.

A Brief Primer on Inflation Theory

In the Keynesian conception that first came into its own during the Great Depression, inflation was seen as a problem mainly when the economy tried to grow at a faster clip than productive capacities allowed. When factories were fully utilized and everyone who wanted work was employed, shortages would become chronic, and prices of inputs and outputs would begin to rise. The idea of crudely estimating the wiggle room in the economy by measuring a *deflationary gap* between actual and potential output was a popular tool of the Keynesian macroeconomists of the 1960s. It first appeared in the Council of Economic Advisers' 1962 *Economic Report of the President,* and for many years was a staple of college economics textbooks, beginning with the grandfather of them all, Paul Samuelson's classic volume, *Economics.*

In fact, Samuelson had already recognized that this supply-constrained explanation for inflation was too narrow. The great innovation of Keynes's *General Theory* had been the recognition that a market economy could come to equilibrium — a balance between aggregate supply and demand — at levels insufficient to provide full employment. Symmetry would suggest that systematic inflationary pressures could also occur in an economy shy of full utilization of its productive capacity. Samuelson was therefore already prepared to be impressed by the empirical studies of the relationship between unemployment, wages, and prices in Britain then being conducted by the London School of Economics scholar A. W. Phillips. What Phillips had found, using nearly a century of British data, was an inverse relationship between changes in the level of wages and the level of unemployment. The lower the unemployment rate, the higher the rate of wage increase.[21] At the 1959 convention of the American Economic Association, Samuelson and his MIT colleague and protégé Robert Solow presented a model reflecting and accounting for Phillips's empirical regularities, assuming along the way that wage increases get passed along by firms to customers in the form of proportionately higher prices.[22] Samuelson and Solow's version of the *Phillips curve* — depicted here in Figure 5.1 — became the profession's principal pedagogical tool for training a generation of students (including the authors of this book) about the dynamics of inflation and growth.

What Phillips, Samuelson, and Solow thought they had rediscovered was that truly "full" employment is potentially dangerous to a market economy. The reasoning behind this conclusion is not hard to fathom. As more and more people go back to work, the ranks of the unutilized labor force become depleted, the bargaining power of labor is enhanced, and wages are forced up. That is fine, at least until labor cost increases begin to exceed improvements in labor productivity. Then firms must either raise prices or see their profits erode. Ultimately, if rising prices in a few sectors begin to lead to widespread inflation, interest rates begin to rise.

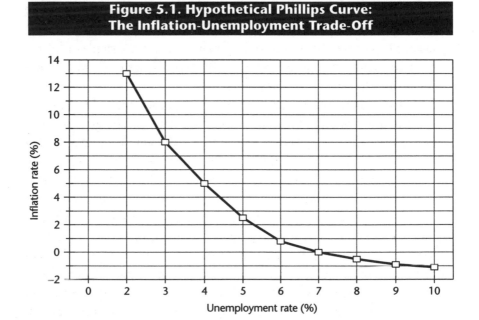

Figure 5.1. Hypothetical Phillips Curve: The Inflation-Unemployment Trade-Off

As the cost of credit increases, investment declines. And when that happens, growth ceases and the economy heads for recession. Essentially, an overly tight labor market generates its opposite: a new bout of high unemployment. Conversely, with rising unemployment resulting from slower growth, the "reserve army" of unemployed workers is replenished, workers with job offers take what they can get, and thus upward pressures on wages and prices recede. This is what drives the business cycle roller coaster, with its alternating bouts of painful inflation and painful unemployment.

Conservative successors built upon this Phillips curve idea and produced an even more potent model of inflation. In his own presidential address to the Economics Association in 1967, Milton Friedman argued that, at best, the Phillips curve trade-off might hold in the short run. But at unemployment rates below some particular level, inflation would not only rise but keep rising and accelerate explosively. Instead of the sloping shape of the relationship in Figure 5.1, Friedman's *long-run* Phillips curve becomes a *vertical* line whenever joblessness falls below a certain point, determined by the conditions of the economy and the qualities, skills, and inclinations of its workers. Instead of a ski jump, the Phillips curve follows the trajectory of a rocket ship. Inflation takes off through the stratosphere. Tight labor markets, according to Friedman, were therefore much more dangerous than previously thought.

Job training, the elimination of the legal minimum wage, and a variety of what would later be called "supply-side" policies, by making labor markets more flexible, could marginally lower the point in an economic expansion at which accelerating inflation might be set off, but Keynesian aggregate demand manipulation surely could not.[23] Friedman and others estimated that an explosion in inflation was inevitable if the unemployment rate remained at less than 6 percent for any length of time. Tighter labor markets would initiate round after round of rising inflationary expectations, which would ignite an upward and never ending wage-price spiral. The unemployment rate just sufficient to keep this from happening came to be dubbed, rather presumptuously, the *natural rate,* or, more precisely, the non–accelerating inflation rate of unemployment, since referred to by economists, policymakers, and journalists alike as the NAIRU (pronounced like "Nehru," the name of the former Indian prime minister).

The theory of the "natural" rate quickly gained currency within the economics profession. It became the underpinning of conservative reaction against the policy interventionism of the 1960s-style Keynesians, whose goal had been to get unemployment down to something like 4 percent — well below the conjectured natural rate.[24] The triumph of NAIRU thinking was so complete that by the late 1970s, the principle of discretionary demand management — the strategic deployment of deficit spending to achieve full employment — was practically obliterated within the economics profession. Even President Clinton's Council of Economic Advisers have adopted a NAIRU in the range of 5.5 to 5.7 percent for their calculations of potential long-term growth. Put less delicately, Clinton's own advisers have bought into a logic that suggests the United States needs to keep 7 to 8 million people unemployed in order to keep the economy healthy.

But *does* the NAIRU offer a sound, reliable basis for evaluating policy options? Is there really a tight natural speed limit on growth rates? Over the past several years, a host of impeccably credentialed mainstream economists have begun to wonder.[25] Now that we have had several years of less than 5 percent unemployment without inflation, it has become difficult for the NAIRU advocates to maintain this theoretical construct.

Economists Douglas Staiger and James Stock of Harvard and Mark Watson of Princeton have offered their own modification of the prevailing view.[26] They find that while both the level and rate of change in unemployment are certainly correlated with subsequent changes in inflation, estimates of just what threshold rate of unemployment would tip the scales — that is, just *where* the Phillips curve becomes vertical — are extremely imprecise. The 95 percent confidence interval for the current value of the NAIRU is 4.3 percent to 7.3 percent. In other words, we can be sure ninety-five times out of a hundred that inflation will start to accelerate when the unemployment rate reaches a certain point *somewhere* between 4.3 and 7.3 percent. At best then, the NAIRU is an incredibly imprecise, blunt policy instrument.[27] Others think it is totally useless. Thus, with the acerbic wit that apparently runs in his family, economist James Galbraith of the University of Texas remarks that not only is the exact location of the natural rate not actually observed, but "worse, the damn thing won't sit still. It is not only invisible, it moves!"[28]

Reconsidering NAIRU Historically

The architects of the original Phillips curve always acknowledged that the strength of the inflation-unemployment trade-off, reflected in the shape and position of the curve, was dependent on certain underlying institutional norms, regularities, and conditions. Sure enough, data on the past three business cycle expansions suggest that the terms of the trade-off have shifted over time.

Figure 5.2. Unemployment Rate/Inflation Trade-Off, Selected Economic Recovery Periods

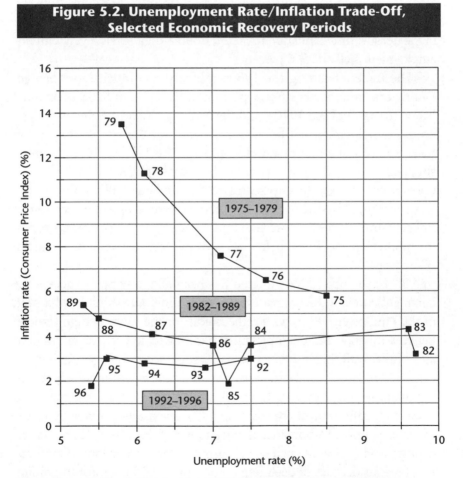

Source: *Economic Report of the President,* 1997; *Economic Indicators,* October 1997.
Note: Points refer to the inflation rate in a given year versus the unemployment rate in the previous one.

In Figure 5.2 we have plotted the inflation rate against the unemployment rate for the past three major economic recoveries. In each case, the data series begins in the year in which the unemployment rate reached a cyclical peak and is followed until it bottoms out. Clearly the trade-off between inflation and unemployment has improved remarkably since the 1970s. Back then, inflation was running in excess of 6 percent a year, even with 7.5 percent of the labor force unemployed. As the unemployment rate came down, the inflation rate rose sharply. Tightening labor markets on top of the release of pent-up price pressures from the abolition of Nixon era wage and price controls, plus the second oil shock of the decade, drove inflation to record double-digit levels, even with unemployment well above 6 percent.

The trade-off during the 1980s recovery was much more benign. During the entire expansionary portion of the cycle, inflation remained below the rates of the 1970s, and the Phillips "curve" became a plateau until unemployment fell below 6.5 percent. In the current expansion there is hardly any hint of a trade-off at all. This is what has economists stumped. History does not appear to be repeating itself, as the inflation-unemployment relationship seems to be fundamentally shifting. It *is* "time-varying," in the words of Northwestern University economist Robert Gordon, but we are not finding much price pressure even at unemployment rates well below his own particular estimated NAIRU of 5.7 percent.

Of course, official Washington has been all too happy to accept the commendation for the dramatic downward and inward shift in what's left of the Phillips curve. However, the credit for the more benign tradeoff between inflation and unemployment has little to do with the recent policies of the Wall Street–Pennsylvania Avenue accord per se. Rather, we can discern five critical factors that now limit the extent to which declining unemployment pushes up wages and prices: (1) the long-run trend toward globalization of the economy, (2) unexpected increases in the available supply of labor since the beginning of the 1980s, (3) a quarter-century legacy of weakened social supports for workers and their families, (4) four decades of declining union power, and (5) most important, the realization of technology's productivity premium.[29] All of these factors *predate* the commitment to balance the federal budget, the passage of

NAFTA, the refusal to consider labor law reform, the implementation of restrictive welfare legislation, and the early 1990s manipulation of interest rates.

Let's look briefly at each one of the causes of the new low-inflation regime.

Globalization and Heightened Competition. First and foremost as a systemic explanation of the benign shift in the Phillips curve is the dwindling discretion firms have to raise their prices at will. Whatever else it may mean, the decades-long trend toward globalization of economic life has profoundly increased the actual and potential price competition that more and more companies in every country face. Advances in transportation and communications technologies have dramatically shrunk the world of trade and investment. Technology has been at least as important as tariff reduction in making it economically feasible for firms to treat the world as their market.

There is little doubt that global competition is increasing. Developing countries' share of world manufacturing has been growing steadily since at least 1953, according to statistics from the United Nations Industrial Development Organization.[30] This means that U.S. manufacturers need to worry not only about exports from Europe and Japan, but increasingly from throughout Asia and Latin America as well. China and Korea, for example, have rapidly grown to become two of America's largest trading partners.

Moreover, whether produced by local firms, by the branch plants of multinational corporations, or by networks that link the two, manufactured exports from developing countries have become increasingly diverse, with a strong shift away from traditional low-value-added sectors. In 1964, reports Peter Dicken, "three sectors — apparel and clothing, miscellaneous manufactures, and textiles — constituted 65 percent of all [developing country–] manufactured imports into the developed market economies. By 1985 these same three sectors made up only 33 percent of the total."[31] The growth industries in low-wage developing countries were electrical machinery, telecommunications and sound recording equipment, office machines and data processing equipment, and motor vehicles. This enormous and increasingly diverse industrial base has surely increased global competition, thereby limiting the ability of firms in any particular country or region to casually pass on cost increases to their customers in the form of higher prices.[32]

Nor is global competition any longer the sole province of manufacturing. Once considered nontradable, all manner of services — from financial and banking services to engineering and architectural services — are increasingly being exchanged across national borders and produced by transnational corporations doing business all over the world. So while the thrust of the U.S. economy has shifted from manufacturing to services, the degree to which American firms are sheltered from international competition continues to decline.[33] In the words of the chief economist of Germany's powerful Deutsche Bank:

> The most important dimension in evaluating future wage pressure in the United States is regularly overlooked: the increased global outsourcing of services like data processing and computer programming. Computers let American companies tap into a labor pool without national borders — thus shattering old-school assumptions about tightness in domestic labor markets. . . . The global services labor pool, after all, is just a phone call or an e-mail message away.[34]

What is more, in a world of intense price competition, large firms — and, increasingly, middle-sized ones as well — have moved to protect themselves from being squeezed between downward price pressure and any possibility of rising wage demands. Having multiple locations, both within a country and across the globe, gives firms the power to keep wages and benefits down by threatening to move work from one site to another.[35] To be sure, NAFTA may have made this type of international capital mobility a bit easier to undertake, at least with respect to Mexico, but the trend toward global production and the outsourcing of production and services to foreign countries began well before the current Wall Street–Pennsylvania Avenue accord was sealed.

Thus, the trade-off between domestic unemployment and inflation has been enormously moderated as a result of globalization — precisely as we saw in Figure 5.2. And this has occurred not only through the trading of goods and services but also through the enhanced ability of investors and companies to shift capital out of the United States (or to threaten to do so) to obtain cheaper labor overseas. There is little doubt that what has hurt domestic workers on the wage front has provided some relief along the unemployment-inflation frontier.

Growing Labor Supply. A second critical factor that has flattened the Phillips curve has to do with the fundamental change in labor supply we first encountered in Chapter 3. Workers now toil as many hours as possible when jobs are plentiful, in anticipation of future downsizing and job loss, and they do this at existing wage rates. Moreover, *declining* hourly wage rates, even in the absence of job insecurity, have forced individuals and families to increase their hours of work simply to maintain their annual incomes. The magnitude of this shift in labor supply is anything but trivial and has made it possible for employers to meet their manpower needs even at very low unemployment rates. Instead of having to raise wages to attract more workers, firms have generally been able to fill their increased need for labor by giving their own workers longer hours or by offering second jobs to workers who are employed elsewhere. This is far different from the labor supply regime of the 1970s, when economic growth depended much more on coaxing additional workers into the labor force, often at the expense of increased wages.[36]

Weakened Social Protections. A third class of profound long-term institutional developments that has reshaped the inflation-unemployment trade-off affects people's willingness to accept a job at any particular wage. Over the course of the twentieth century, especially since the New Deal era, liberal unemployment insurance provisions have allowed displaced workers to hold out for new job assignments at wages closer to what they had previously been earning. Welfare payments and food stamps permitted the poor to stay out of the labor force altogether, depriving firms of the very "cheapest" employees. The legal minimum wage, periodically adjusted upward for inflation, constituted a floor to what people were entitled to earn, and thus to some extent also reduced the pressure on workers to accept extremely poorly paying jobs.

But the dismantling of social protections began well before the new Wall Street–Pennsylvania Avenue accord was ratified by the Clinton White House and the Republican-led Congress. The erosion in unemployment insurance, welfare programs, workplace benefits such as health insurance and pensions, and the real value of the national minimum wage is a legacy of the 1970s and 1980s. This may be regrettable from a social justice perspective, but there is no question that it further ameliorates upward pressure on market wages, flattens out the Phillips curve, and undermines the very idea of a "natural rate" of unemployment.

The Decline of Union Power. Added to this has been a profound erosion in the power of organized labor. Historically, unions have existed to organize and articulate the collective voice of workers and to bargain for more widely shared wage and benefit increases. As economic growth picks up and unemployment declines, a unionized company's desire to avoid a work stoppage increases. No company wants to shut down production when demand for its products or services is strong. In the past, when economic growth accelerated and unions exhibited solidarity, bargaining power shifted away from management in favor of labor. Unions could demand higher wages for their members and more often get them. Today, as the ranks of organized labor shrink, fewer and fewer workers have such an institutionalized voice to speak on their behalf. The weaker are unions, or the smaller the share of the workforce covered by collective bargaining, the less pressure there is on firms to concede wage increases in response to falling unemployment. In short, the strength of collective labor is also a parameter in the Phillips curve relationship.

Statistics on union membership make this clear: The proportion of the labor force covered by union contracts today has fallen to pre-1930s levels. From a peak of over one-third in the early 1950s, fewer than one in ten private sector employees in the United States now belong to unions (and only a slightly larger fraction are covered by collective bargaining agreements). Moreover, the growing heterogeneity of the work force, increasingly diversified by race, gender, ethnicity, and occupation, has been an obstacle to organizing. Add to this businesses' greatly enhanced willingness and ability to outsource work, hire replacement workers, or shut down a plant or store or warehouse altogether, and one begins to understand just how much labor's bargaining power has eroded. This decline of union power is still another development that contributes to an unambiguous inward and downward shift of Mr. Phillips's famous curve.

The Productivity Premium. But by far the most important factor responsible for the flattening of the Phillips curve, particularly in the late 1990s, has been the realization of high rates of productivity growth. With productivity rising rapidly, wages can increase without putting much pressure on prices. Higher productivity means that higher wages do not imply a higher cost per unit of output, since workers are producing more goods and services for each hour they put in at factories, offices, or retail shops. With productivity rising by better than 2 percent per year, real wages could increase by the same 2 percent without increasing companies' costs at all.

Even the Federal Reserve Board has finally recognized this critical point. As *Business Week* reported in May 1999, "Just within the past few weeks, a majority of Fed officials have rallied around a new consensus view: The nation is in the throes of a technology-driven productivity boom that is letting the economy grow faster than once thought possible without setting off growth-strangling price and wage hikes."[37] To his credit, Fed Chairman Alan Greenspan had been pushing his board to accept this new view for at least two years. Now the data on productivity growth seem incontrovertible, encouraging more of the Fed's governors to come over to this side in the Phillips curve debate.

It would appear, then, that most economic policy analysts, politicians, and journalists failed to recognize, at least for a decade, a set of institutional developments that are critical to assessing the country's anti-inflation policies.[38] Even if the NAIRU — the theoretical apparatus that most strongly argues for a speed limit on politically acceptable economic growth — offered a reliable, sound basis on which to forecast the likely impact of public policy, the structural conditions on which both it and its antecedent, the Phillips curve, are based have changed profoundly.

So while the Wall Street–Pennsylvania Avenue accord has bent virtually every national policy toward containing inflation, the real story is that inflation was already being contained by powerful long-term forces well beyond the tinkering of the White House, the Congress, or even the Fed. The recent, almost single-minded government obsession with inflation control is therefore largely redundant. NAIRU and the Phillips curve were on the way out well before Clinton announced a commitment to balancing the federal budget and before Congress passed NAFTA and welfare reform.

The Inherent Dangers of the
Wall Street–Pennsylvania Avenue Accord

If the government's obsession with anti-inflationary policies were super-fluous and nothing more, then we might conclude that embracing poli-cies consistent with the neoclassical growth syllogism and the Wall Street virtuous cycle does little to foster additional growth, but by the same token causes little harm. But just the opposite is the case. The specific policies of the accord almost certainly condemn America to slower growth over the long run. To begin with, consider the cost of the new-found bipartisan enthusiasm for federal budget balance and for the even grander goal of building up a prodigious fiscal surplus.

The High Cost of Budget Balance. Until the 1930s, economic analysis suggested that the government should always attempt to live within its means. If government tax revenues declined as a result of a slowdown in economic growth, the government was supposed to tighten its belt, cut-ting spending in line with reduced revenues. John Maynard Keynes showed the folly of this approach, demonstrating how the fiscal belt-tightening would actually exacerbate the economic downturn. The new theory suggested that the government would be wiser to deliberately run deficits to stimulate a slumping economy and then run surpluses when the economy was speeding ahead so much that further stimulation might cause inflation. The theory was first applied during the Great Depression in the form of Franklin Roosevelt's New Deal policies, and it continued to be used for the next fifty years with at least modest success.

When the economy is running well, mopping up past red ink and putting the federal government in the black is supposed to suppress in-flation, reduce interest rates, and maintain the economy's growth. With the U.S. economy surging ahead at nearly a 4 percent growth rate in the late 1990s and with unemployment near record-low levels, running a fed-eral government surplus makes good sense. The question is how large a surplus should be run, and how much surplus we should accumulate.

When this perfectly valid approach to managing the economy becomes an obsession with balancing the budget, or worse yet, accumu-lating the largest fiscal surplus possible, there can be several woe-fully negative consequences for the economy.[39] One is simply that the government is no longer in the business of stimulating faster growth through the sheer size of its own spending. A balanced budget is essentially neutral with respect to growth. A surplus actually slows the economy in the short run, and the larger the surplus, the more downward pressure on growth. Recall from Chapter 2 that during much of the postwar period up to 1973, the growth of government spending, in exceeding the rate of private business expansion, contributed to boosting GDP above what it otherwise would have been. As the growth of government spending slowed, it had a negative impact on overall growth.

This is not surprising, since the government acts as both a large-scale consumer and a giant investor. When families stay home from the mall, business suffers. When companies stop investing, growth slows down. The same is true of government, for precisely the same reason. Therefore, the immediate impact of smaller government is lower GDP. That the White House, the Council of Economic Advisers, and the Congressional Budget Office are all reluctant to project any more than 2.3 percent growth into the next century is based, in part, on the prospect of a smaller government — as President Clinton promised in his 1996 State of the Union message. Moving from the huge budget deficits of the late 1980s toward budget balance or even a small surplus is good for the economy when the economy is as strong as it was at the end of the 1990s, but we must take caution not to overdose on the prescription of fiscal surplus.

The reason for caution is that by focusing its efforts on generating a budget surplus, the government is forced to cut spending on public investments that are critical for future growth. As we shall see in Chapter 7, expenditures on infrastructure such as roads, bridges, ports, buildings, and communications networks have been found essential to both the productivity and profitability of the private sector. The same is true of investments in research and development, public health, education, and training.

Over the period 1965–93, federal investments in physical infrastructure, education, training, and civilian R&D taken together all display declining trends, measured as fractions of GDP.[40] Nor does the future look any better after the "historic" budget accord of 1997 between President Clinton and Congress. In the original plan to balance the budget by 2002 and at the same time provide some tax relief, spending on general science, space, and technology was cut by 18 percent below what would have been expected prior to the accord. Federal funds for energy development were cut by an additional 14 percent, and transportation by 7 percent. The 1999 budget agreed to between the White House and Congress does little to rectify the situation.

The two areas where funding was increased are education and health research. Clinton was able to win additional federal funds to pay for 100,000 new schoolteachers and begin to fix up dilapidated school buildings. Still, the total amount of additional funds pales in comparison to what many educators think is needed to improve our public schools. Congress has also seen fit to increase the budget for biomedical research. Between 1998 and 2003, the National Institutes of Health will see its budget double, rising by 15 percent a year.[41] At a projected $27 billion in 2003, this seems like a great deal of money for the federal government to spend on health care research. It is, until you realize that this amounts to less than 2 percent of what Americans will be paying for health care by then.

Even the conservative economist Gary Becker has argued for spending more of the government surplus on medical research. He notes that the federal government allocates only about $50 per person to such research, compared with total spending on all federal programs of about $5,000 per person. The potential benefits from reducing death rates from heart disease and cancer alone are so big, he writes, that "much higher expenditures on research would be justified even if they only yield small declines in death rates."[42] The enormous spending on AIDS research in the 1990s demonstrates that medical research can make remarkable progress in extending life. Putting the same kind of effort into defeating other diseases would likely pay off at least as handsomely.

The same is true for basic research in other fields. In the past we relied on the Pentagon to invest in radical new technologies as part of our defense strategy. Civilian applications of these technologies have provided a wealth of new products and services. But with the end of the cold war, spending on defense, including defense research, has slowed enormously. Spending less money for missiles and bombs is likely good for the economy, but the cutbacks in associated R&D are not.

The preoccupation with building up federal surpluses provides little room for such investment. Since peaking in the late 1970s, federal spending on all kinds of public investment, measured as a share of total economic output, has fallen by more than a third, according to Economic Policy Institute estimates. Given current projections, that share will decline by another 35 percent over the next ten years.[43] Such short-changing of public infrastructure, publicly sponsored R&D, education, and training will, in the end, make it more difficult to sustain prosperity.

The High Cost of a Free Trade Regime. The federal surplus is not the only sacred cow in the Wall Street–Pennsylvania Avenue accord. Free trade turns out to be another. To be sure, by building the global capacity of all countries to produce and consume, expanding trade *can* promote long-run U.S. economic growth. Clamping down hard on imports, as some economic nationalists and populists would have us do, would harm the economy, as it would no doubt lead to retaliation and loss of export markets and substantially reduce pressure on domestic businesses to enhance their productivity and competitiveness. But this still leaves open the question of what the *optimal* level of freedom in the international economic arena is. Already, over the past half century, trade barriers have fallen dramatically. Tariffs have been reduced or eliminated and nontariff barriers such as quotas have been outlawed by treaty. The Wall Street–Pennsylvania Avenue accord is based on the premise that if more free trade is good, totally unrestricted, unlimited free trade is even better.

But is this so? With the meltdown of the Asian economies and the shattering of the Russian economy, even a growing number of free-traders are wondering whether totally open borders are such a good idea. Without some basic rules and regulations, free trade and particularly unlimited capital mobility create enormous international instability and therefore can undermine growth rather than promote it. Current trade policies and the ways in which the institutions governing global financial expansion are being allowed to evolve are, in important respects, preju-dicial to widely shared, long-term economic growth and development around the world.

If the incomes of worker-consumers in other countries were growing sufficiently so they could purchase our exports in large volume, the U.S. trade balance — the difference between exports and imports — would not exhibit any particular trend. It would generally fluctuate around zero, as it did for the better part of the century leading up to the early 1980s.[44]

169

As Paul Krugman has pointed out, we need to be able to export in order to afford to purchase the imported goods and services that contribute to a rising domestic standard of living. But by any of several indicators — all merchandise trade, the non-oil, nonagricultural component of trade, or net foreign investment — the days of trade balance ended in the late 1970s, and America's trade deficit has continued to trend upward since then, both in absolute dollars and as a percent of GDP. Figure 5.3 shows the trajectory of merchandise trade. Few graphs in economics look like this — flat calm for decades and then, all of a sudden, calamity. This measure has displayed a generally worsening trend regardless of sizable swings in exchange rates and the cyclical expansions and contractions of the foreign economies that serve as our customers. Between 1991 and 1998 alone, the annual trade deficit exploded from $67 billion to over $230 billion.[45]

By definition, a chronic trade deficit reduces national GDP. If imports exceed exports, GDP is lower by exactly this amount. A dollar of trade deficit counts as a dollar of foregone output. Between 1989 and 1998, the cumulative trade deficit was nearly $1.4 trillion. Assuming trade balance, cumulative GDP would have been higher by this amount. Moreover, be-

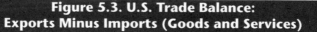

Figure 5.3. U.S. Trade Balance: Exports Minus Imports (Goods and Services)

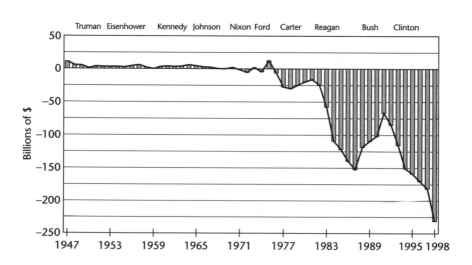

cause the trade deficit continued to balloon during this period, the deficit affected not only the level of GDP but also its growth rate. If our exports had matched our imports, annual growth in this period would have been more than 0.3 percentage points faster.[46] Hence, the stubborn trade deficits we have experienced since the early 1980s come at a substantial price in terms of economic growth.

Why has the U.S. trade deficit been so large for so long? There are a number of competing theories on this matter. One has it that high American wages have priced our workers out of their jobs. Lower-cost labor abroad means that lower-priced foreign goods and services can flood into the United States, while our higher-priced exports encounter little demand in foreign countries.

But data on international wage rates indicate that the rising trade deficit cannot be blamed on high U.S. wages, because the total compensation (wages plus benefits) of U.S. manufacturing workers — the people who produce most of the goods traded internationally — is actually quite competitive. In 1994, for example, hourly compensation in U.S. manufacturing was *below* that of German, Japanese, Dutch, and Danish workers, and almost identical to the level in France.[47]

Another explanation centers on the "twin-deficit" thesis of the eminent Harvard University economist Martin Feldstein. He has identified the proximate cause as the high federal budget deficits of the 1980s. In this view, large budget deficits require the government to borrow heavily in the bond markets, which drives up interest rates. This in turn makes dollars more attractive to foreigners, raising their demand for U.S. currency. But that demand strengthens the value of the dollar, making our exports more expensive in foreign currencies. With no other changes in the system, high budget deficits therefore lead to rising trade deficits. But if this explanation is correct, the Wall Street–Pennsylvania Avenue accord to balance the budget should have helped balance the trade deficit. Instead, as budget deficits came down and turned into surpluses, the trade deficit continued to mushroom.

The problem with Feldstein's popular thesis is that no one can find consistent empirical evidence that the correlation between the two deficits over time truly reflects any underlying causal relationship. Harvard economist Jeffrey Sachs estimates that even permanent elimination of the federal budget deficit would reduce the current trade account deficit by at most 50 percent, and that is a stretch.[48]

Our explanation — and the basis for our charge that the accord's pursuit of unlimited free trade may be sabotaging greater prosperity — goes well beyond the impersonal forces of the bond and currency markets, into the strategic behavior of policymakers themselves. Under the banner of free trade, the U.S. government, big business, and the financial markets are pursuing strategies that, perhaps not surprisingly, put short-run profits and corporate freedom to penetrate hitherto protected markets ahead of everything else. This often means failing to support (if not actually undermining) workers' rights to organize, especially in developing countries. And when international bankers effectively force currency devaluations on small countries as a quick fix to reduce their external deficits, wages and living standards are the big losers. Workers lose out abroad, but this also indirectly hurts American workers and the American economy because international wage competition becomes even more intense.

The recent checkered history of the North American Free Trade Agreement (NAFTA) with Mexico, ratified in 1994, provides a case in point. By reducing tariffs, abolishing quotas, and encouraging more trade and foreign investment across national boundaries, NAFTA was supposed to create jobs and profits on both sides of the border. But quite apart from the wildly unreliable estimates of job creation and losses in both countries, we know that wages along the Mexican side of the border have fallen, and what had earlier been a small U.S. trade surplus with Mexico had by 1996 already turned into a record $16 billion deficit. Side agreements to NAFTA regarding labor's right to organize and negotiate for better working conditions have generally been weakly enforced.

The policy stances of the two most powerful quasi-public international financial institutions, the International Monetary Fund (IMF) and the World Bank, have also undermined wage growth abroad. Since the mid-1970s their directors and senior staffs, dominated by American and British (and only recently Japanese) interests, have held more or less firmly to the standard growth and trade theories, convinced that giving free rein to market forces through deregulation, privatization, and general liberalization of the economy is the key to promoting long-run growth and development. Yet in practice, the freeing up of trade in the absence of basic labor standards and rights has led to downward wage pressure in all countries. Workers and their families in the countries we trade with have not seen their wages and incomes rise fast enough to allow them to purchase U.S.-made goods in sufficient quantity to reduce our chronic trade deficit. Hence, by opting for unlimited free trade and unlimited capital mobility, the Wall Street–Pennsylvania Avenue accord is undermining growth, not boosting it. Again, we find a case of overdosing on a policy prescription that could enhance growth and prosperity if it were taken in proper amounts.

Because the current global financial crisis originated in the relationship between the emerging nations and the Bretton Woods institutions, it seems useful to elaborate on how the Wall Street model is now influencing not only international trade policy, but foreign countries' domestic policies as well. New School economists Ute Pieper and Lance Taylor have documented how IMF stabilization and austerity measures and the World Bank's so-called structural adjustment policies have, in the interest of "perfecting" the labor, capital, and commodity markets of the countries of the world, systematically weakened local institutions of worker solidarity in the pursuit of a decidedly neoliberal political agenda.[49] Experts in the field, including staff at the IMF and the World Bank, now commonly refer to this strategy as the "Washington consensus" — clearly the global analogue to the Wall Street–Pennsylvania Avenue accord. This has effectively entailed forcing countries, through the threat of withholding credit, to privatize even their most successful public enterprises, to abandon or tone down expansionary macroeconomic initiatives, and to deregulate their domestic markets as a matter of principle. Ultimately, this strategy slows growth abroad in the same way that Federal Reserve monetary policy has tended until recently to constrain economic growth at home.

Under the twin banners of "conditionality" (do what your creditors say, as the price for gaining access to development finance) and "transparency" (substitute market forces for the "black box" of public management), the ostensible goals of the measures imposed on borrowers by the IMF and World Bank are to reduce chronic trade deficits and debt burdens, and to introduce market forces and competitive pressures. "Getting prices right" is how economists writing about the two organizations often put it. The belief is that these policies will eventually make even the poorest countries and their resident firms profitable and internationally viable. But as Pieper and Taylor document in case studies of Chile, Mexico, Turkey, postsocialist Eastern Europe, and sub-Saharan Africa, the IMF's and the World Bank's insistence on across-the-board privatization, deregulation, and currency devaluation have instead either caused or worsened stagnation, increased financial speculation, encouraged a new class of sometimes lawless entrepreneurs, and led to even more overvalued exchange rates, thereby inhibiting exports and growth. The economic benefits of free markets might seem obvious on paper, but on the ground, where it counts, the results do not always follow economists' predictions.

Obviously, *we* are deeply concerned about these developments. But perhaps the most surprising expression of concern has emerged from one of the economics profession's most ardent free-trade theorists, a former chief economic advisor to the General Agreement on Tariffs and Trade (GATT), Columbia University professor Jagdish Bhagwati. While continuing to be an unreconstructed free-trader, he makes a sharp distinction between free trade in goods and services and unlimited trade in financial instruments.

In a blistering critique of the rush to deregulate global capital markets, published in the journal *Foreign Affairs,* Bhagwati argues that those who equate finance capital with "widgets and insurance policies" are disingenuous.[50] They assert, rather than factually demonstrate, the magnitude of benefits from completely free flows of finance capital — benefits that he believes to be historically negligible. And they systematically ignore the demonstrated, visible downside of unrestrained capital mobility: the frequent creation of currency and debt crises that the smaller, poorer countries in particular simply cannot manage. Bhagwati certainly agrees that cronyism in the banking systems of a number of countries now in dire financial straits, including Japan, South Korea, and Russia, might have made the crisis worse. But crony capitalism did not create the crisis, he says, nor will IMF-imposed "reforms" cure it. Unregulated capital flows are, he insists, inherently unstable.

Then why, he asks, has global policy been moving in the direction of headlong deregulation of capital markets? Here, Bhagwati's criticism is especially sharp and explicitly political. He argues that the ideology of free trade has been "hijacked by the proponents of capital mobility. [These ideas] have been used to bamboozle us into celebrating the new world of trillions of dollars moving about daily in a borderless world, creating gigantic economic gains, rewarding virtue and punishing profligacy." And what special interest stands at the center of this bamboozling?

> Wall Street's financial firms have an obvious self-interest in a world of free capital mobility since it only enlarges the arena in which to make money. It is not surprising, therefore, that Wall Street has put its powerful oar into the turbulent waters of Washington political lobbying to steer in this direction. . . . There is, in the sense of a power elite à la C. Wright Mills, a definite network of like-minded luminaries among the powerful institutions — Wall Street, the Treasury Department, the State Department, the IMF, and the World Bank.

Bhagwati gives this network a name; he dubs it "the Wall Street–Treasury complex." This is not far from our notion of the Wall Street–Pennsylvania Avenue accord — and for the record, the Treasury building sits directly on Pennsylvania Avenue!

So the Wall Street–Pennsylvania Avenue accord's embrace of free trade — in goods, services, and financial capital — turns out to be very much a two-edged sword. Free trade in goods and services does play a significant role in keeping inflation under control, but it has also generated massive trade deficits that directly undermine growth. If adding further controls on inflation has only a weak and indirect positive effect on growth, and trade deficits have a powerful and direct negative effect, the weight of the evidence suggests that unlimited free trade, on balance, is not conducive to American prosperity. And if unhindered capital mobility leads to speculative crises abroad, if not at home, then growth can be stopped in its tracks when investment capital is diverted worldwide from constructive uses in new industry to the safety of Treasury bonds and other low-risk securities. In keeping their gaze fixed on the inflation bogeyman and ignoring almost everything else, the advocates of the Wall Street–Pennsylvania Avenue accord run the risk of ignoring the more debilitating aspects of unbridled global trade.

The High Cost of Making Labor Markets More "Flexible" at Home and Abroad. The Accord is equally myopic on the home front. Implicit in the accord is the conventional belief that trade unions, minimum wage laws, and other forms of government regulation of the labor market undermine the prospects for growth. They do this, supposedly, by discouraging firms from hiring workers and by generating inflationary pressures when companies are forced to capitulate to the wage and benefit demands made by government fiat or by unions at the bargaining table. Weakening these labor market institutions should therefore be good for growth.

Yet there is a good deal of evidence that unions, minimum wages, and labor market regulations actually contribute positively to growth rather than detract from it. They do so by encouraging the types of investments that promote faster productivity growth and by maintaining a high level of aggregate demand.

Recent empirical research, now generally well accepted, has found that the supposed negative employment effects of minimum wages are negligible. Contrary to popular opinion, raising statutory labor rates at least moderately does not cause much unemployment at all.[51] In the real world of fast-food restaurants and other low-wage employers, modest increases in minimum wages have been found to have virtually no negative impact whatsoever on employment levels, even among low-skilled teenagers.

But more important for the issue at hand, an increased minimum wage may actually lead to *higher* productivity in the economy and thus contribute to faster growth. At current wage levels, there is little incentive for low-wage employers to introduce new technology or find other ways to boost the output of their workers. Required to pay a higher wage, firms would have to find ways to use their workers more effectively.[52] One of the reasons why European countries have traditionally had higher service sector productivity than the same industries in the United States is that wage "solidarity" policies on the continent require wages in services to more closely approximate those in manufacturing. As just one example, European countries pioneered the credit card–activated gasoline pump, long before it was common in the United States, for the simple reason that higher wages for service workers in Europe encouraged oil companies to find ways to reduce the need for low-productivity service station attendants.

Unions play a similar role. No one denies that unions have won higher wages for their members. Most estimates place the average union premium somewhere between 15 and 20 percent above nonunion wages.[53] How could such a wage premium *not* have priced unionized companies out of the market? The answer is that unionized firms receive higher productivity in return for paying higher wages. One of the first studies to demonstrate this found that unionized establishments in the manufacturing sector were on average 24 percent more productive than equivalent nonunion firms.[54] Case studies of several industries, including cement, construction, hospital care, and mining, subsequently showed union productivity premiums ranging from 6 percent (cement) to 22 percent (construction).[55] As for productivity *growth* — changes in productivity over time — the data indicate that unions have generally not prevented improvements in operating efficiency. Productivity growth historically has been just as rapid in unionized shops as in union-free companies. Overall, then, unionized firms historically have had higher productivity levels, and the efficiency differential between the unionized and nonunionized sectors has remained roughly constant over time.[56]

Thus, the reluctance to increase federal wage floors very much and the refusal of the White House and Congress to change labor market regulations to help reverse the downward trend in union membership, far from encouraging faster economic growth, actually undermine the productivity growth that could lead to it.

The Social Cost of the Fed's Anti-Inflationary Bias. Rounding out the accord is the Federal Reserve's backstopping of the battle against inflation. Alan Greenspan has proven to be considerably more flexible than his predecessor, Paul Volcker, in managing monetary policy. Greenspan resisted raising interest rates in the mid-1990s even as the unemployment rate fell below what nearly everyone considered its natural rate. Then in late 1998, as the Asian and Russian financial crises threatened to undermine the global economy, the Fed moved to *cut* interest rates despite continuing tight labor markets at home. With productivity improving in the late 1990s, the Fed continued to resist raising interest rates even as unemployment remained below 5 percent. This is a refreshing approach to monetary policy, for which Greenspan richly deserves credit. Nevertheless, the Fed continues to watch warily for any spark of inflation. Dousing it before it could possibly ignite a greater conflagration is still its main mission.

As a result, any hope of maintaining the growth rate at 3 percent or better is likely to be defeated by Fed action. The Fed will permit short-term bursts of growth in this range but still considers the economy unable to absorb such growth on a permanent basis. The threat of inflation at such growth rates is considered simply too great to resist countering it before it becomes manifest.

What makes the Federal Reserve so powerful today is the demise of fiscal policy. Before the Wall Street growth model gained nearly hegemonic adherence, the Fed had to contend with the fact that political bodies at both ends of Pennsylvania Avenue played a role in accelerating or retarding growth as well. Through traditional discretionary fiscal policy — the setting of tax rates and federal spending levels — the President and Congress could attempt to influence the growth rate with a power at least equal to that of the central bank. Lowering taxes and increasing spending could speed up the economy and lower unemployment rates. Raising taxes and cutting government expenditures could slow the economy in order to squeeze inflation out of the system.

With their acceptance of the accord, the White House and Congress have abdicated their authority in this realm. The commitment to balancing the budget leaves little discretion for fiscal policy, and this surrender of economic responsibility carries a price. While both monetary policy and fiscal policy can, theoretically, be used to fight either inflation or recession, in practice these policies historically have had different inherent biases. Monetary policy, because of the influence of the banking system, has always taken its responsibility to fight inflation more seriously than its responsibility to maintain rapid growth and full employment. Fiscal policy has had the opposite bias. Because of political pressures, the president and Congress would always rather cut taxes than raise them, and until recently, both liked to spend money as well, especially if it put unemployed workers who vote back to work. Even liberals who rued the idea of building up a huge nuclear arsenal and a massive fleet of warships and planes voted regularly for defense appropriations because the Department of Defense took care to make sure that workers in nearly every single congressional district got a piece of the largesse. As a result, fiscal policy was always inclined toward a policy of faster growth.

Now, with fiscal policy in retreat and the more conservative monetary policy in ascendance, the pro-growth bias in fiscal policy no longer offsets the slow-growth bias in monetary policy. Under the Wall Street–

Pennsylvania Avenue accord, the nation's growth rate is now controlled exclusively by the Fed. That is the real legacy of adopting the neoclassical growth syllogism, buying into the Wall Street virtuous cycle, and agreeing to a Wall Street–Pennsylvania Avenue accord that shifts power away from the democratic control of elected representatives to bankers and the appointed leaders of the Federal Reserve.

In the end, Robert Eisner is surely right when he rhetorically paraphrases William Jennings Bryan's century-old dictum: "We must not crucify our country and its economy on the cross of misguided and misaddressed fears of inflation."[57] Yet that is exactly what the policy bias of the federal government has a tendency to do. It is as though the president, the leaders in Congress, and the officials at the Fed — at least until very recently — were behaving like old soldiers, still fighting the current war with the last war's weapons, rather than realistically considering contemporary conditions and the strategies needed to win this one.

What's Responsible for the Recent Spurt in Growth?

Certainly by this point, the astute reader might ask the following question: If the Wall Street model is so perverse, how did we attain the growth we have enjoyed beginning in the mid-1990s? If balancing the budget, freeing up trade, making labor more "flexible," and adding to the anti-inflation credentials of the Fed did not give us faster growth, what did? The answer, in brief, is technology — plus an unexpected boom in labor supply.

Potential growth was the product of the information revolution, which finally began to reach full bloom in the 1990s. The productivity premium became manifest only after a long lag, as we discussed in Chapter 3. The premium's debut occurred simultaneously with the rise of the Wall Street model, but the latter did *not cause* the former. Increasing labor supply, in good part from the extra hours of wage-starved, insecure workers, augmented higher productivity to further boost the potential for faster economic growth.

On the demand side, investment played a critical role. But this was the red-hot investment drive spurred by technological revolution, not by low interest rates. Whether or not there were immediate payoffs to the new information technologies that proliferated during the 1980s and early 1990s, company executives believed they could not afford to be left out of the stampede to be among the first to adopt new computers, new communication modes, new manufacturing technologies, and new software. They invested heavily in these technologies, generating in the process a whole new array of individual businesses and entire new industries. The stories of Microsoft, Intel, Cisco Systems, and Dell are hardly unique in this period. The massive employment generated in the information technology industries and the jobs created in other industries to take advantage of the new technologies drove the demand that turned the potential for faster growth into reality.

Along the way, consumers helped out by continuing to run up their credit cards. One estimate suggests that over half of all households — more than 50 million in all — carried credit card debt with an average balance of around $7,000 in 1998. This amount of indebtedness was double the average of just six years earlier.[58] By late 1998, in fact, consumption was outstripping income growth. The official savings rate for September of that year was *minus* 0.2 percent, the "worst" performance since 1959, when the government began tracking the rate on a monthly basis. On an annual basis, the rate has not been negative since the depression year of 1938.[59] From the perspective of the Wall Street model, this is calamitous. But on Main Street, the combination of debt-fueled household consumption and business investment in the latest information technologies offset the drag on growth caused by slowing government expenditures and chronic trade deficits. For this reason, the U.S. economy grew at 3.9 percent in both 1997 and 1998, an astonishing performance given the continuing global financial crisis and a periodically stumbling stock market.

Note how little of this resembles the story told in the neoclassical growth syllogism or the Wall Street virtuous cycle. The slaying of inflation was no doubt important, but it resulted from rising productivity and increased labor supply, *not* from balanced budgets or the liberalization of trade under NAFTA. Moreover, the run-up in equity prices was driven not so much by low inflation as by the wild expectations of investors who had as much faith in the new companies building hardware and software as did the businesses across the country that bought the hardware and software those new companies developed.

This growth spurt we have enjoyed is, therefore, driven by technology, workers, and consumers, and is not a product of Wall Street or Pennsylvania Avenue. In other words, our growth trajectory has a lot more to do with the likes of Bill Gates than Bill Clinton, and more to do with new technology than with Newt Gingrich.

The question for the twenty-first century is whether the Wall Street model will be allowed to undermine the prospects for sustaining this growth, or whether we will find a more constructive way for government policy to encourage it. Our prospects for growth may be a good sight better if we are willing to reject the current conventional wisdom and try something completely different. In Chapter 7 we will consider an alternative growth model, one which relies on a more positive role for government in the economy and places the needs of those who live on Main Street above the needs of Wall Street.

First, however, we must consider one more problem with the mainstream consensus. At the same time that the Wall Street model will, over the long term, generate too little growth, it also tends to create too much inequality. We discuss this issue in the next chapter to complete our investigation of the Wall Street model and to prepare the ground for examining an alternative "bridge to the twenty-first century," to borrow President Clinton's well-turned phrase.

Chapter 6

The Wall Street Model:
Too Much Long-Term Inequality

URING THE GLORY DAYS of the post–World War II era, Americans enjoyed a revolution in their living standards. Average wage rates for hourly and salaried employees, after controlling for inflation, rose by nearly 80 percent between 1947 and 1973. This, combined with an increase in the number of two-earner families, made it possible for the typical household in America to more than double its real income in a single generation.[1] The family that could afford a new automobile every six years in 1947 could afford to buy a new one every three years by 1973. It took seventy years for the telephone, introduced in 1876, to find its way into the homes of half of all American families. By contrast, more than half of all homes had a television only eight years after its introduction in 1946.[2] By 1970, 99 percent of American homes had refrigerators, electric irons, and radios; more than 90 percent had automatic clothes washers, vacuum cleaners, and toasters — a far cry from the equipment in the typical home before the war.[3]

And that prosperity was widely shared. In that first postwar generation, the poorest fifth of all families saw their real family incomes grow by 3 percent a year. The top fifth did not fare quite as well in percentage terms, their incomes rising at a 2.4 percent annual clip (see Figure 6.1). As a result, by 1973 inequality had actually declined a little and the proportion of families in poverty decreased by nearly 50 percent. This was truly an era of growth with equity. Sustained economic growth and the sometimes rocky but seemingly irreversible political commitment to broadening the social safety net and to raising labor standards joined to narrow the gap between those of us with the most income and those with

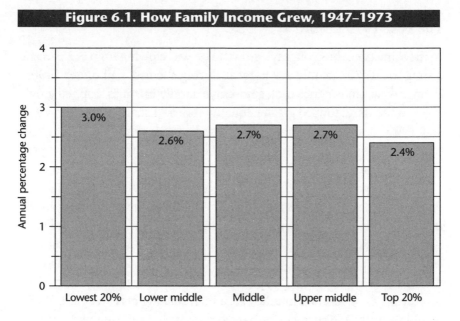

Figure 6.1. How Family Income Grew, 1947–1973

Source: U.S. Department of Labor.

the least. Gradually, even the gulf in economic conditions between the races began to narrow.

Unfortunately, the good times were not to last. As the economy faced increasing global competition, as new technologies made some old skills obsolete, and as the bargaining power of organized labor weakened, wages stopped growing and inequality surged. For twenty years following 1973, most of the trend lines were dismal. Except for those at the very top of the income ladder, incomes stagnated or actually fell.

The dramatic slowdown in productivity growth was much to blame for the troubled times. Now that productivity is on the rise again, incomes are increasing. But what is happening *on average* does not necessarily hold for those at the bottom of the heap — or even those in the middle. A rising tide once lifted all boats. But it is not clear that the Wall Street model works as well for the rowboats as it does for the yachts. Indeed, as we shall see, the Wall Street virtuous cycle and the Wall Street–Pennsylvania Avenue accord inherently exacerbate inequality.

The Post-1973 Record

At the same time the economy's growth rate was slowing from 3.2 percent during the 1970s to only 1.9 percent during the first half of the 1990s, average wages in America took a nosedive, family incomes stopped growing, and the trend toward greater equality reversed sharply. Between 1973 and 1995, real hourly wages *fell* by 10 percent, while median family income rose by a total of just 4 percent over the entire twenty-two year period — despite the continued influx of women into the labor force.

Life was particularly difficult for workers with limited schooling. The real average hourly wage of male high school dropouts plummeted by 28 percent, while even men with some college saw their wages drop by 15 percent. Women did slightly better, but only those with at least some college saw any improvement in their pay. Whereas the average young man during the glory days could expect to see his earnings rise by more than 50 percent as he reached middle age, a man starting his career after 1979 would see only a 20 percent gain — and even that increase was concentrated among the most highly educated.

The growing gap between the best-off and the worst-off among us has taken many forms. For example, in 1982 people in the top 10 percent of the work force earned 3.95 times as much in average hourly wages as those in the bottom 10 percent. By 1996, that ratio had grown to 4.72 times. If total compensation is counted instead — including the current cash value of such benefits as paid vacations, health insurance premiums, and pension contributions — the ratio rises from 4.56 in 1982 to 5.56 in 1996.[4]

Instead of growing together, incomes grew apart. The wealthiest fifth of all families continued to see their incomes rise by 1.3 percent a year, while the poorest two-fifths saw their incomes actually decline. Those in the middle went nowhere (see Figure 6.2).[5] Inroads against poverty ceased. America was undergoing a "Great U-Turn" in living standards by almost any relevant measure — hourly, weekly, and annual individual earnings; household income; the black-white income gap; the incidence of poverty; and the distribution of personal wealth.[6] No other market economy, not even in the newly developing world, and no socialist country underwent such a sudden and dramatic surge in inequality.[7]

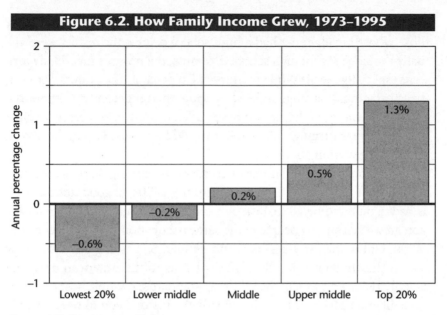

Figure 6.2. How Family Income Grew, 1973–1995

Source: U.S. Department of Labor.

That family incomes stopped growing and inequality started accelerating was by no means due to families deciding to take more leisure. In fact, the opposite was true. Bluestone and Rose, in extending their earlier research from individuals to households, have shown that between 1973 and 1988 the combined annual income for families in which both husband and wife worked rose by 18.5 percent.[8] But this increase in income was bought primarily by working more — 16.3 percent more hours. Thus, over the entire fifteen-year period, the combined average husband-wife *hourly* wage increased by only 1.8 percent — the equivalent of a real hourly wage increase of less than 30 cents over the entire period, or 2 cents each year.

These results are for all families combined. When households headed by someone with less than a college degree — two-thirds of all dual-earner families — were examined, Bluestone and Rose found that families were working longer hours just to stay in the same place economically. Prime-age dual-earner families headed by someone who had some college experience, but not a four-year degree, increased their combined working time by 17.4 percent between 1973 and 1988. But from this sizable

185

increase in hours, they derived only 3.8 percent more family income. For those whose breadwinner had a high school degree, the results were virtually the same. As for high school dropouts, the rewards for added work were especially bleak. While working 11.6 percent more hours per year, their real annual earnings *declined* by more than 8 percent.[9] Without the extra work, these families would have suffered nearly a 20 percent decline in their average earnings. Many more would have ended up in the official ranks of the working poor.

This worsening trend in the distribution of earnings and income proceeded right through the 1980s and into the 1990s, in good times as well as bad. Confounding all mainstream economic thinking, income dispersion grew even among people in the same occupation, with the same education, and of the same age, race and gender. Something genuinely new was in the air, something deeply pernicious to the American dream of steadily rising and widely shared living standards. A whole host of prestigious liberal economists concluded that the historic connection between faster economic growth and declining poverty and inequality was now permanently severed, leaving policymakers with even fewer effective levers for reducing inequality.[10]

Added to this was the story of rising wealth inequality. Whereas the lowest four-fifths of the population enjoyed substantial increases in wealth during the 1960s and early 1970s, especially in the form of home ownership, after 1983 the same group experienced absolutely no improvement in their wealth. An especially chilling way to express this surge in wealth inequality in the 1980s, using estimates from New York University economist Edward Wolff, is to ask: How many months could the average family survive on the basis of its total savings, should financial failure hit?[11] In 1989, the answer was that families in the highest quintile could survive for about nineteen months — a year and a half. Middle-class and upper-middle-class families could survive for far less than half a year. Families in the lower middle class had two weeks of savings between them and destitution. And for those in the bottom quintile, there was no safety net at all. If they had to subsist on their savings, they could not do so for even two minutes. These families are in such debt that they owe more than they have in monetary assets.

The especially dire condition of African-American families in terms of accumulated wealth and safety nets has been measured and reported in detail by the sociologists Melvin Oliver and Thomas Shapiro.[12] What they have taught us is that measuring income — whether individual earnings or family income from all sources — is insufficient to capture the continuing gap in wealth between black and white Americans. Even black families whose breadwinners have the same occupational and educational attainment as whites find themselves $43,000 behind in home equity and financial assets.[13] Over the course of the 1980s, the average black family's net worth did indeed grow, but the average for white families grew so much faster that the gap actually widened by another $40,000. If you exclude home ownership — the single most important asset for families of all races — the growth in net financial assets of even those black families whose breadwinners have the best jobs and have the most stable work histories amounts to an unbelievable mean of *zero* dollars.[14] Some black families have positive savings, but this is offset by the debt position of other black families.

Some experts speculated, or at least hoped, that while income and wealth were becoming more unequally shared, families and individuals might be experiencing increased mobility over time within the distribution, so that few would remain stuck within their income class for long. Now we know that, at least during the 1980s, this was not the case. The majority of families and workers, certainly those in the bottom two-fifths of the population, were still stuck in that condition up to five years later. And this degree of income class immobility was not improving over time.[15] On all these scores, the post-1973 era seemed to signal the end of the American dream.

An End to the Inequality Surge?

Following the mild recession in 1990–91, the national economy commenced what has turned out to be one of the longest expansions of the last half century — longer than the Reagan-Bush expansion of the 1980s. It is based on far better balanced growth, with less dependence on military spending and — at least until the recent Asian crisis — a strong revival of manufacturing exports to go along with the boom in business services. As shown in Chapter 3, aggregate economic growth and its principal components — productivity and labor supply — turned around sharply and exhibited surprising and unexpected improvements.

Thus, we have been growing again. But are we finally growing more equitably, as in the heyday of the post–World War II era? Have inequality and poverty really become more or less impervious to economic growth, or has the historical connection been restitched?

It is simply too soon to tell for certain. Even so, there are indications that a partial reconnection is indeed being made. Growth, if fast enough and sustained for years, eventually does appear to pull up the bottom of the income distribution and give a larger share to those who have been disadvantaged in the labor market. But — and this is critically important — this only seems to occur when the economy is being run red hot with unemployment rates well below what used to be considered the natural rate. Modest growth of the type forecast by the White House and Congress will not do. Nor are we likely to do much in the long run to reverse inequality if the Wall Street virtuous cycle remains the chosen engine of growth and the Wall Street–Pennsylvania Avenue accord is used to implement it. To understand why this is so, we need to get a better understanding of the relationship between growth and inequality.

How Do Economic Growth and Inequality Affect Each Other?

In conventional economics textbooks, inequality and growth are often treated as though there were no systematic relationship between the two. Any rate of growth in GDP, depending on your theory, is supposed to be consistent with any number of different distributions of income and wealth. What matters in the standard theory is the stage of development. It was the great economic historian Simon Kuznets who first posited a long-term relationship between the level of a nation's development and how equal or unequal its income distribution was.[16] As poor countries underwent development and industrialization, he wrote, their income distributions would become increasingly unequal during the transition. This would be caused by the emergence of a skilled working class and a propertied middle class, who would initially gain over the farmers and unskilled migrants who were moving to the cities and working in factories. Over time, however, as capitalism matured, more and more people would be incorporated into the "modern" economy, narrowing wage and income differentials across classes and between individuals.

Kuznets is so much a part of the teaching, not only of basic economics in the Anglo-American world, but of high school and college social science generally, that even young academics who have never encountered his writings regularly repeat his ideas. That is why so many economists were surprised — even alarmed — by the trend toward growing inequality over the past quarter century in the United States and United Kingdom, even during periods of economic expansion in highly developed countries. In a Kuznets world, this was not supposed to happen.

It could very well happen, however, in the world of Arthur Okun, the Keynesian economist and policy adviser to Presidents Kennedy and Johnson. Okun posited a "big trade-off" between equality and aggregate economic efficiency.[17] He argued that political decisions to distribute income more fairly, through social legislation, job creation schemes, and the like — interventions which, by the way, Okun personally endorsed — necessarily intrude into market relationships, detracting from private savings and investment and otherwise causing the society to forego private gains elsewhere. If the costs of the taxes and transfer payments needed to finance the redistribution were less than the value society placed on the distributive gains, then those losses in efficiency would be fully justified. But losses there certainly would be.[18]

More recently, some economists have begun to question Okun's "big trade-off," turning the logic of Okun's conjecture on its head. Suggesting that there is a positive relationship between public education spending on the one hand and productivity and growth on the other, they argue that greater equality stemming from education spending might promote growth rather than hinder it. Moreover, at the level of individual companies, productivity improvements may depend not just on internal capital improvements and the skills of their own employees but on the general capabilities of the whole industry, sector, or cluster, at least within their region. In short, everyone in a highly skilled region benefits from the mutual learning and exchange of talent, and this supports faster growth.[19] The more equally spread the talent, the greater the beneficial effect on growth. Urban economists call these *neighborhood effects*.[20]

Economists Alberto Alesina and Dani Rodrik have an even more general formulation. Examining countries around the world, they argue that social fragmentation is detrimental to economic performance. In particular, inequality impedes economic growth by promoting distributional conflicts that cost real resources to contain and get in the way of social and political agreements across classes to move forward on a growth agenda.[21] Countries with extreme income inequalities are likely to experience more crime, and it takes enormous resources to contain it. Beyond the costs of the entire criminal justice system (e.g., massive spending on police, courts, jails, and penitentiaries), individuals have to pay the price to secure their own persons and household possessions (e.g., locks and burglar alarm systems) and pay for theft insurance.

There will always be the old conservative notion that inequality is actually *good* for growth. By reinforcing work incentives among the less well paid, by reminding the better-off of the cost of failing to work hard, and by shifting income to the rich, who have the highest marginal propensity to save, growth is supposedly enhanced through more work and more savings.[22] Those with this slant on things are probably beyond being persuaded by the evidence.

But the evidence to the contrary is compelling. While the amount saved from every dollar of additional income received by a high-income person will surely be greater than the extra dollop of savings by someone at the bottom, what counts for growth is the *aggregate* volume of savings (if, indeed, savings matter that much, as we noted in the last chapter). The simple fact is that there are not enough people in the upper tier of the income distribution for their aggregate savings to be capable of fueling a wave of investment — even if such people did not place their savings in speculative stocks and bonds, real estate, and foreign currencies. The problem is that widening inequality so hurts the middle class and the poor that they are forced to live off their credit cards and past savings — in a word, to *dissave*. To the extent that neighbors and television idols offer role models of continuing high consumption, this gets even worse. Thus, inequality actually *impairs* the ability to save, and thereby hampers economic growth insomuch as savings can contribute to it.[23] This leaves Okun's trade-off between growth and inequality much in doubt.

The Multiple Sources Behind the Surge in Inequality

That growth and declining inequality can coexist was made clear during the post–World War II glory days. The conditions that made this possible are now fairly well understood. When sustained growth keeps labor markets tight, the wages of even the least-skilled, lowest-paid workers are eventually bid up. Foreign competition from low-wage countries, which was to become such a threat to American living standards later on, had not yet materialized. Union bargaining power was extended to a growing fraction of the work force, including millions of workers who, while not themselves union members, worked in factories, warehouses, or offices that were subject to collective bargaining agreements or in businesses that tried to convince their employees that they didn't need a union to enjoy better wages and benefits. Government was expanding during this golden era — as a source of aggregate spending, as a guarantor of the minimum wage floor, and as a relatively high-paying (and more equitable) employer. And of course, as we have already seen, productivity was rising rapidly, expanding the size of the pie over which managers and workers bargained and making it less costly for managers to buy labor peace. So growth and inroads against inequality came together.

But it was not to last. During the 1970s, all the conditions that had been so favorable to rising living standards and declining inequality were in the process of being reversed. Foreign competition from low-wage countries (often from the offshore operations of American companies) was on the rise. Productivity was trending downward. The growing influence of the Wall Street model was increasingly putting unions on the run. Even before Ronald Reagan came to the White House, and then with special vigor thereafter, government spending (except on weaponry) and public investment generally came under assault. Managers who had previously subscribed to the philosophy of sharing the wealth with their workers in order to buy labor peace and increased work effort were increasingly turning to what would eventually be called the "lean and mean" approach to corporate "restructuring."[24]

Would faster, sustained economic growth have prevented this surge in inequality in the 1980s? By itself it surely would not have done so. The sobering truth is that the surge in inequality has had many sources. For much of the twentieth century, race and gender discrimination created large earnings differences among workers, regardless of education, skill, or talent. Yet as more virulent expressions of prejudice became less common, and with the dramatic and measurable successes of affirmative action, the role of educational and skill differentials has been greatly magnified. The correlation between schooling and wages has increased significantly. This would suggest that we are moving toward something of a "meritocracy," where differences in income and wealth are mostly due to differences in skills, education, and motivation. With the payoff to education increasing in modern society, this would naturally lead to big bonuses for those with the most schooling and big penalties for those with the least. Thus, we would expect to see growing inequality closely related to education. Even if the schooling distribution remained fixed, higher returns to schooling would mean more income inequality.

In this case, it seems natural to attribute the growth in earnings inequality to advances in technology. After all, it would seem that those who have equipped themselves with the skills needed to operate the new information technologies would be the winners in this game, with nearly everyone else losing out. This conclusion seems obvious, but the sources of growing earnings inequality turn out to be more elusive than that. The more concurrence we find among the experts regarding the statistical *fact* of rising inequality, the more dispute there seems to be regarding the assignment of blame. Technology may have played a part, but it was hardly the sole cause of this phenomenon.

What, exactly, caused the meritocratic shift toward greater inequality? At latest count, there are no fewer than ten key suspects: technological change, deindustrialization, deunionization, industry deregulation, the declining real minimum wage, the "winner-take-all" phenomenon, expanded global trade, acceleration in transnational capital mobility, increased immigration, and the chronic U.S. trade deficit.[25]

Technology seems at first to be the obvious culprit. After all, high-tech capitals like Silicon Valley seem to demand a disproportionate number of skilled workers who command high salaries in return for their specialized knowledge, while there is little demand for those with limited schooling. *Skill-biased* technological change supposedly drives a growing wedge between the skilled and unskilled. But attempts to build a case regarding this suspect have not been compelling.

Part of the problem is that no one has any direct measure of the skill content of technology, and proof of this hypothesis requires not just skill-biased technological change but its acceleration during the period in which inequality expanded. Presumably, if technology is driving inequality, this would show up in a rapid shift in the skill mix of the labor force. But this does not seem to have occurred. After extensive research, New School economist David Howell concludes that there is no direct evidence whatsoever of a historically distinctive, much less accelerating, shift in the skill mix of employment since the early 1980s in the United States or in most other major developed countries. Indeed, the observed change in skill mix is far greater in the decade prior to the onset of computerization, in direct contradiction to the theory.[26]

The technological explanation for increased earnings inequality runs into an especially tricky problem when one looks at earnings growth between 1979 and 1995 across broad occupations. If technology is driving wage differentials, one would expect to find that those in science-related professions and technical specialties would have enjoyed the most wage growth. But according to a new study from the Educational Testing Service, this is not the case at all. Science-related professional men with at least a bachelor's degree saw their real earnings decline by 2 percent between 1979 and 1995 while "science technicians" with a completed college education enjoyed only a 6 percent increase. The real winners in the earnings derby were not those on the forefront of the new computerized technologies, but medical doctors (up 43 percent), lawyers (24 percent), sales representatives and brokers (24 percent), and managers (15 percent).[27]

On this subject, Alan Greenspan is in agreement. In his remarks to the 1998 meeting of the Fed governors at Jackson Hole, Wyoming, Greenspan observed that "the considerable diversity of experiences across countries as well as the finding that earnings inequality has also increased *within* groups of workers with similar measured skills and experience suggest that we may need to look deeper than skill-biased technological change if we are to fully understand widening wage dispersion."[28]

If technology didn't do it, then we need to open Pandora's box to see what might have. One obvious suspect is the shift from goods-producing sectors into services — deindustrialization. Between 1963 and 1987, the earnings ratio between college graduates and high school dropouts working in the goods-producing sector widened from 2.11 to 2.42 — an increase of 15 percent. At the same time, the school-related earnings ratio in services moved from 2.20 to 3.52 — a 60 percent increase.[29] That virtually all of the employment growth in the economy during the 1980s came in the service sector, where income disparities were growing four times faster than in manufacturing, could therefore explain at least part of the dramatic increase in earnings inequality.

Reinforcing this conclusion, some suggest, has been the decline in

193

unionization. Unions have historically negotiated wage packages that narrow earnings differentials. This is one of the reasons for the lower wage dispersion found in manufacturing. That unions have made only modest inroads into the service economy may explain in part why earnings inequality in this sector outstrips that elsewhere. Still, the proportion of workers in unions is so small, it is hard to imagine that declining unionization can explain more than a fraction of the rise in earnings inequality.

Government deregulation of the airlines, trucking, and telecommunications industries may have contributed a fraction as well. In each of these industries, intense competition from new nonunion, low-wage entrants, such as the short-lived People Express airline, forced existing firms to extract large wage concessions from their employees to keep from going bankrupt. This could explain a bit of the decline in real wages and perhaps a bit of the increase in earnings inequality.

Somewhat more important may have been the impact of government regulation of wages. The real (inflation-adjusted) value of the national minimum wage has fallen steadily since its high point all the way back in the late 1960s. The decline was especially steep during the 1980s — when inequality surged the most. Even with the legislated increases in 1996 and again in 1997, the real value of the minimum wage today is still 18 percent below what it was in 1979.[30] This would help explain why the bottom of the wage distribution fell so far behind everyone else, at least through the mid-1990s. To be sure, when they were rising on a fairly regular basis, federally imposed wage floors tended to offset the otherwise strong tendency toward growing inequality in wages emanating from other causes.[31]

At the other end of the income distribution is a phenomenon that has been dubbed the "winner-take-all society." As Robert Frank has explained, in winner-take-all markets, "a handful of top performers walk away with the lion's share of total rewards."[32] The difference between commercial success and failure in such markets may depend on just a few star performers — in movies, the director and leading actor or actress; in celebrated murder trials, the conduct of just one or two defense attorneys. Given the high stakes involved in a multimillion dollar movie project or a murder trial involving a rich client, investors are willing to pay a bundle to make sure they employ the "best in the business."

Today the fields of law, journalism, consulting, investment banking, corporate management, design, fashion, and even academia are generating pay structures that once were common only in the entertainment and professional sports industries. A mere handful of Alan Dershowitzes, Michael Milkins, and Michael Eisners can have a sizable impact on the dispersion of wages in each of their occupations. That inequality is not only rising across education groups but within them very likely reflects such winner-take-all dynamics. With minimum wages slipping at the bottom and bonanzas being made at the top, at least some of the growth in inequality can be explained by this twist in wage-setting institutions.

But even more fundamental to the recent restructuring of the labor market — and a likely cause of deindustrialization, deunionization, and the winner-take-all phenomenon — is the trend toward global free trade. In theory, free trade itself can generate skill-based inequality. According to *factor price equalization* theory, the simple fact of increased international trade — in an environment characterized by no tariffs or quotas, no significant differences across countries in consumer tastes or production techniques, and trivial cost barriers in transportation and communications — is sufficient by itself to equalize the price of each input factor (for example, the wages of unskilled workers) across trading countries. In a world of plentiful unskilled workers and a relative scarcity of well-educated labor, this translates into *inequality* between different factors (i.e., between skilled and unskilled workers).

Of course, textbook factor price equalization will not occur. The underlying assumptions are manifestly invalid. Trade is *not* literally "free." Nevertheless, the trend is definitely toward increasingly deregulated global commerce. Moreover, as we saw in earlier chapters, the movement of investment capital across borders inevitably speeds up this process. Modern transportation and communications technologies, combined with fewer government restrictions on foreign capital investment, have clearly led to increased multinational capital flows between countries. To the extent that companies move their facilities to take advantage of cheaper unskilled labor or outsource domestic production to cheaper offshore sites, transnational investment adds to the effective supply of low-skilled labor available to American firms, accelerating the entire disequalizing process.

Increased immigration potentially has the same effect, if a disproportionate share of new immigrants enter with limited skills and schooling.

At least among legal immigrants, we know this is true. In the United States, the typical legal immigrant today has nearly a year less schooling than native-born citizens. Undocumented immigrants, coming now from Mexico, the Philippines, Korea, Cuba, Vietnam, India, the Dominican Republic, China, Jamaica, and Iran, almost surely have less.

Finally, the continuing trade deficit in manufactured goods may be contributing to inequality to the extent that it has accelerated the decline in those sectors of the economy that have in the past helped to keep earnings inequality in check.

Quantitatively parsing out the relative impact of this array of forces on the wage distribution is fraught with enormous difficulty. Still, Richard Freeman and Lawrence Katz have attempted to do just that. Drawing on their research and that of others, including George Borjas, we can summarize their findings in Table 6.1.

If the Freeman and Katz estimates are anywhere in the ballpark, the answer to our "Who done it?" is not unlike the denouement in Agatha Christie's *Murder on the Orient Express:* They *all* did it! While it may provide a fascinating statistical phenomenon for econometricians, the most important fact about this mystery is that *every* major trend visible in the American economy portends the same fate for the distribution of earnings: greater inequality correlated with "merit."

Even into the early 1990s, none of these trends showed any sign of weakening. On the whole, companies seemed to be shifting toward greater reliance on highly skilled workers and new technology. The passage of the North American Free Trade Agreement, the formation of the European Union, the successful completion of the Uruguay Round of the General Agreement on Tariffs and Trade, and the creation of the World

Table 6.1 Sources of Inequality	
Source	Potential Contribution (%)
Technological change	7–25
Deindustrialization	25–33
Deunionization	20
Trade and immigration	15–20
Trade deficit	15

Source: Freeman and Katz, "Rising Wage Inequality," in *Working under Different Rules.*

Trade Organization all contributed to freer international trade and increased transnational capital investment. Immigration, both legal and illegal, had not slowed. Mass layoffs and plant closings in the manufacturing sector — now fashionable even among profitable firms — perpetuated the trend toward services and away from goods production. The ranks of organized labor continued to shrink. The merchandise trade deficit continued to swell. Under this set of conditions, it seemed almost inevitable that the high level of wage and income inequality of the 1980s and early 1990s would continue. A powerful force would be needed to reverse it.

Earnings, Incomes, Inequality and Poverty in the 1990s

Yet, as we more closely examine the current period of economic growth in the 1990s, especially since the middle of the decade, there is room to wonder whether red-hot growth can indeed raise wages and family incomes and offset all of these disequalizing factors.[33]

In the private sector, according to the Bureau of Labor Statistics' Employment Cost Index, overall compensation (including benefits as well as wages and salaries) increased by 3.4 percent in 1997 and 3.5 percent in 1998. Wages and salaries alone rose even faster, up 3.9 percent in both years. These were the largest annual increases in seven years.[34] By 1998 the average weekly wage had finally regained all the ground it had lost during the 1990–91 recession.[35] This has contributed to a favorable turnaround in family incomes. During the long economic expansion that began after 1992, household median annual income finally stopped falling and began rising again. The most recent census data we have (from the March 1998 *Current Population Survey*) show modest aggregate improvements between 1993 and 1995 and stronger improvement between 1995 and 1997 — four consecutive years of rising incomes.

What about the trajectory of inequality among individual wage earners? Inequality in hourly earnings began to shrink for the first time in 1996 with the initial rapid growth of the economy. According to statistics generated by the Economic Policy Institute, between 1996 and 1998 wages grew faster for the bottom tenth of the workforce than for any other group. As a result, the wage gap between the top and bottom of the wage distribution declined — sharply reversing the earlier trend.[36] James Galbraith has shown that very low unemployment rates produce large reductions in inequality in manufacturing wages, helping to explain these encouraging results.[37] As for inequality in annual household income, the Census Bureau reports that the *Gini coefficient* (which best measures inequality around the middle of a distribution) indicates no worsening since 1993, after an unbroken quarter century of rising inequality. An examination of the share of all household income going to the bottom 60 percent of the population shows the same thing: a sharp decline until 1993, and essentially no worsening since then.[38]

And what about the incidence of poverty? Among individuals, the rate of poverty has been falling throughout the expansion, from 15.1 percent in 1993 to 13.3 percent in 1997, the most recent year for which the Census Bureau provides information. For families, the levels of poverty are slightly different, but the trajectory is the same. As with other measures of income inequality, family and individual poverty rates appear to have finally leveled off and perhaps even started to trend downward during the sustained economic expansion of the 1990s.

Moreover, according to the Council of Economic Advisors, even the historic gap in poverty rates between whites and blacks narrowed somewhat during this period. In fact, in 1997, it was the poverty rates of blacks and Latinos that fell the most.[39] It begins to look as though aggregate economic growth matters to inequality after all. Perhaps the pessimistic pronouncements of the experts on this score were premature.

Poverty, Inequality, and Tight Labor Markets in the Big Cities

While poverty may finally have stopped rising for the country as a whole, it continued through at least the early 1990s to be disproportionately high in the nation's central cities. In 1970 one in seven residents of the typical big city was poor, and one-third of all poor Americans lived in central cities. By 1990 the incidence of concentrated urban poverty had risen to 20 percent, and 42 percent of all poor Americans lived inside cities.[40] The data to take this important comparison forward will not be available until we have access to the year 2000 population census sometime in the next century.

What we do know is that in 1993, the latest year for which the Census Bureau has estimated poverty for states and localities, the *level* of poverty continued to be dramatically higher in big cities than in the country as a whole. In that year, the individual poverty rate in the United States as a whole was 15.1 percent. In Los Angeles, however, it was 23.8 percent; in Boston, 19.4 percent; in Chicago, 17.6 percent; and in Miami, 25.4 percent.[41] And in New York City, the rates of poverty for the five boroughs were: the Bronx, 33.3 percent; Brooklyn, 31.6 percent; Manhattan, 22.3 percent; Queens, 15.3 percent; and Staten Island, 10.0 percent.

But even here we have evidence that rapid growth can make inroads into inequality and poverty. That evidence is based on *queuing theory* and recent data from New York's relatively prosperous neighbor to the northeast: Boston.[42] According to queuing theory, instead of competing against one another on the basis of the wages they are willing to accept, individuals compete against one another for job opportunities (or job slots) at more or less given wages. In jockeying for positions in the job queue, success for the individual worker rests on being able to signal to potential employers that he or she possesses a set of attributes (including credentials, behaviors, and attitudes) that firms find desirable. In Lester Thurow's conception of the queue, "One set of factors determines an individual's *relative* position in the labor queue; another set of factors, not mutually exclusive of the first, determines the actual distribution of job opportunities in the economy. Wages are paid based on the characteristics of the job in question, and workers are distributed across job opportunities based on their relative position in the labor queue. The most preferred workers get the best jobs."[43]

In this conception, the number of job slots available to be filled in any queue depends mainly on macroeconomic factors. As aggregate demand increases, employers must go deeper and deeper into the labor queue to fill vacancies. Only when aggregate demand is especially high do employers hire from the end of the queue — hiring those who ordinarily would be unemployed or out of the labor force altogether.

This model is at least implicitly behind research by William Julius Wilson and others who depict inner-city labor markets as being "jobless ghettos."[44] Blacks, particularly black men with limited schooling, who live in high-poverty neighborhoods have been found to have extremely high unemployment rates and low labor force participation. Commentators on the urban ghetto scene often speak of an "underclass" so far outside the mainstream of the American economy that their attachment to the regular economy is tenuous at best, if not nonexistent. Much of this research is based on urban areas that underwent extreme deindustrialization during the 1970s and 1980s, such as Chicago, where Wilson did much of his field work.

The queuing model suggests that we would not find the same tenuous labor market attachment among minority workers with limited education in cities where aggregate demand is strong. In labor markets where growth is rapid and the aggregate unemployment rate low, one would expect to find high jobless rates among inner-city residents only if this labor force were so devoid of technical and social skills that employers' training costs became prohibitively high or if employers practiced fairly blatant racial or ethnic discrimination.

The empirical question then is, How do racial and ethnic minorities with limited education fare in a labor market that has had low aggregate unemployment for some time? Since 1984, in contrast to Chicago and New York City, the unemployment rate for the Greater Boston region has averaged only 4.8 percent. Except for the 1991–92 recession, the rate has never been above 6 percent. Moreover, from 1984 until 1990 the rate never exceeded 4 percent and was as low as 2.7 percent in 1987. In the late 1990s it is just as low. In such a labor market, one would expect employers to reach deep into the workforce queue to come up with the labor supply they need. Indeed, a recent news story describes Boston-area employers' recruitment efforts as having reached even inside homeless shelters in inner-city neighborhoods.

In this tight labor market, the rates of labor force participation for black and Hispanic men turn out to be every bit as high as for white men — consistent with the queuing model. In addition, hourly wage differentials are reasonably modest. On the other hand, while black men in Boston are indeed working, those at the end of the labor market queue are much more likely to be cycling in and out of work, and are more likely to be in part-time and contingent jobs. The Boston "ghetto" is not "jobless," but the jobs are so unstable and intermittent, and the weekly hours so short, that black men end up earning only a little more than two-thirds of what non-college-educated white men earn on an annual basis, after controlling for education.

The lesson is clear: Aggregate demand growth *does* matter for creating employment and for reducing racial and ethnic inequality in urban economies.[45] The kind of growth we get matters too, as do the skills and job-finding social capital of workers, the enforcement of antidiscrimination laws and regulations (or lack thereof), and other institutional structures. These are all things which progressive, thoughtful, truly strategic public policy can promote — but a strong macroeconomic performance is a necessary condition for success.

Slowing Wealth Inequality in the 1990s

As we have noted, inequality in the distribution of wealth rose dramatically during the 1980s. Moreover, a principal driver of economic growth in the 1990s has been the amazing expansion of the financial sector generally, and of the bull market on Wall Street in particular, which lasted into the summer of 1998 and then picked up again in the late fall of that year. We might therefore expect that wealth inequality would, if anything, have increased during this decade.

If we thought that, we would be wrong. Using the Gini coefficient for nine categories of net worth, Edward Wolff finds that inequality in the holding of wealth actually *fell* somewhat between 1989 (the year prior to the last business cycle peak) and 1995, the most recent year for which data are available.[46] Make no mistake — the distribution of wealth in America remains scandalously uneven. The level of the Gini coefficient remains extremely high at .766 in 1995 (on a scale from 0, indicating perfect equality, to 1, if all the wealth in the country were owned by just one person). For all the talk about how widespread stock ownership has become through the growth of mutual funds (40 percent of all households today own at least one share of stock), the richest 10 percent of the populace still accounts for 82 percent of the total value of these assets.

Still, in the 1990s the share of all wealth going to the top 1 percent of wealth holders grew by only 1.1 percentage points between 1989 and 1995, whereas it had increased by 3.6 points between 1983 and 1989. To be sure, the bull market really took off *after* 1995, so perhaps more up-to-date figures will show that wealth inequality is rising again. That would likely be true for financial rather than real wealth holdings, which include real estate.

Inequality and the Wall Street Model

The evidence from the mid-1990s provides us with enough confidence to suggest that a fast growing economy is the sine qua non for reducing inequality. *If* we could keep running the economy at growth rates closer to those prevailing during the postwar glory days *and* keep unemployment down in the neighborhood of 4 percent, the recent improvement in real wages, family incomes, and income distribution would almost certainly continue. It might take a decade or more to regain the more equal income distribution that existed in the 1960s. But if we run fast enough, we can actually win the race. By the same token, more modest growth and higher unemployment rates will almost surely take us back to the wage, income, and distribution trajectories that we suffered from 1973 to 1995.

And here is the rub. The Wall Street model makes dealing with the inequality issue all that much more difficult. Whether the model contributes to growth or not, every last one of its policy prescriptions tends to exacerbate inequality. Hence, we need to continuously run the economy like a race car screaming around the track, its engine cranked up to redline, simply to offset the wind resistance.

To balance the budget and produce future surpluses, the White House and Congress have deliberately shrunk government programs. To the extent that this shrinkage is accomplished by moderating the budgets for transfer programs such as welfare and public housing and limiting the amount that can be spent on programs that financially empower those at the bottom of the income and wealth distribution, this central element in the Wall Street–Pennsylvania Avenue accord works directly at cross-purposes to redressing inequality.

If on top of cuts in government spending, there are cuts in taxes, these are likely to benefit the wealthy more than the poor. Similarly, as we found in our Agatha Christie mystery, the combination of trade liberalization, deindustrialization, and deunionization explained more than half the growth in the earnings gap between college-educated men and high school graduates in the 1970s and 1980s. Therefore, to the extent that the accord rests on extending free trade and making labor markets even more "flexible," two more factors are at work that exacerbate inequality. Add tight monetary policy to the list and you have the equivalent of the Four Horsemen of the Apocalypse arrayed against the trend toward greater wage and income equality. We need to superheat the economy simply to do battle with these warriors.

Of course, the Wall Street model also poses a serious distribution problem simply because it relies on wealth effects to carry the economy. Recall that the Wall Street virtuous cycle requires rising stock values to generate mountains of paper wealth in order to stimulate the consumption of wealth holders. Growth based on asset appreciation is an extreme form of trickle-down economics, where enormous wealth accumulation by the rich is required to provide the most modest improvements in the real incomes of everyone else. If you pour enough wealth into the funnel at the top, those at the bottom eventually receive a little of the benefits themselves. One might ask, what kind of decent society requires making the rich that much richer to prevent everyone else from getting poorer? Even as the spread of mutual funds and 401(k) pension plans gives more and more families a piece of the equity market, studies show that the spread of stock ownership and the rise in stock prices have not led to a rise in the share of stock and mutual fund assets owned by the bottom 90 percent of the wealth distribution.[47]

In the end, however, it is the very essence of the neoclassical growth model underlying the Wall Street virtuous cycle and the Wall Street–Pennsylvania Avenue accord that blocks the path to a sustained battle against growing income and wealth disparity. The obsession with keeping inflation under control necessitates running the economy at a speed well below redline. At 2.3 percent growth, inequality is almost surely encouraged, and running the economy at 3 percent for any more than short spurts will not be allowed.

Ironically, then, the Wall Street model imposes modest growth on the economy as a condition to keep inflation under control, while acceptance of the model requires red-hot growth if we are to deal with the inequality that it implicitly generates. This contradiction is at the heart of what is wrong with adopting the Wall Street model as the growth engine for the future.

Wall Street, the Private Sector, and the Low Road

Of course, no matter how benign or well-crafted, government policies alone cannot cure cancer, solve the urban crisis, or guarantee rising equality. While the tax revenues, surplus profits, and general good feeling that economic growth makes possible all contribute to the opportunity to make progressive structural change, they do not by themselves assure it. How the private sector operates is critical as well. Unfortunately, under the Wall Street model, firms are under continual, intense pressure to show strong bottom-line results. This has often induced businesses to follow what many call the "low road," in which employers emphasize downsizing, outsourcing, the shift from full-time to part-time work schedules, the movement of operations abroad, and cuts in wages, benefits, and job security.[48] These policies may please Wall Street, but they tend to increase income inequality. Hence, the dominance of financial markets at the center of the economy does not bode well for private sector behavior that could help redress the massive gap in living standards between America's wealthy and nearly everyone else.

The Wealthy Win No Matter What

In closing this chapter, we might ask why the modest growth objectives of the Wall Street model are not anathema even to those who make their money on Wall Street. After all, wouldn't faster growth make the wealthy even wealthier? Why aren't the rich clamoring for the fastest growth rate possible?

It turns out there is a compelling reason for this. While the slow-growth era after 1973 corresponded to little growth in family incomes for nearly everyone in America, there was one group that did not suffer. For the richest 5 percent of all families — the elite who make most of the key economic and political policy decisions in America, and who shape culture and public opinion — income after 1973 grew *just as rapidly* as it had during the glory days: about 2.3 percent per year. The pie grew slowly after 1973, but because the slice going to the top 5 percent expanded so much, the elite did not suffer at all from slower growth. Whether the economy grows at 3 percent or just 2.3 percent, the richest families make out just as well.

Hence, if there is going to be a movement for running the economy faster, it will have to begin on Main Street, not Wall Street. And this movement will need an alternative to the Wall Street model in order to make the case for faster growth, more equitably shared. There is such a model and we shall now turn to it.

Chapter 7

The Main Street Model for Growth with Equity

A S THE HISTORIAN Thomas Kuhn reminds us, the reigning conventional wisdom in any scientific discipline is invariably defended with great tenacity.[1] This is as true of the neoclassical growth model in the latter part of the twentieth century as it was of the Ptolemaic conception of the universe five centuries ago. Ptolemy's critic, Copernicus, was not accepted by his academic peers any more readily than by the church elders who considered his ideas about the solar system blasphemy. Similarly, a trusted icon like the neoclassical growth model, which has enjoyed the allegiance of so many economists and seems to explain so well the recent resurgence of the American economy, is not easily displaced. To mount a revolution against entrenched thought requires nothing less than constructing an alternative paradigm that explains the world better.

Is there, then, a different conception of how the economy grows than the one we have been examining in the last three chapters? Can that alternative be successfully wedded to a concern for promoting greater equity? Our answer is yes — on both counts.

Fortunately, a coterie of economists and historians of science and technology are already providing the elements for a very different model of what makes nations prosper. Empirical and historical evidence to support this alternative view is being unearthed — even if most of the mainstream assiduously avoids acknowledging it. This alternative has been dubbed the *New Growth theory* by its adherents and the few journalists who have followed their work. As we will see, it provides a refreshingly optimistic perspective on America's growth potential.

When all is said and done, however, we need more than a theory about potential. We need to join the New Growth theory, which is chiefly a story about the supply side of the economy, to a construct for the demand side if potential growth is to be translated into real improvements in national income. By constructing a demand side to go along with the New Growth theory's supply side, we believe we can keep actual growth close to its potential and directly address the desire for greater distributional equity. Instead of fashioning a policy that addresses the income side of the ledger mainly by stimulating new consumption out of enhanced personal wealth — which, as we saw, is the Wall Street conception of the modern economic universe — we propose an alternative: *wage-led growth* with a substantial role for *public sector investments* that promote technological advance. By working directly on wages, shoring up the bottom and the middle of the income distribution, this approach not only enhances growth but meets head-on the stubborn growth in income inequality that has been part of the nation's economic life for more than a quarter of a century.

What we have in mind is not simply a different way to slice up a pie of given size. What makes this demand-side approach feasible and affordable is the extra boost to productivity from following the policy implications of the New Growth theory. If done right, that productivity growth can pay for the increased wages out of which comes the additional demand that keeps the wheels in motion. Instead of a Wall Street virtuous cycle, we propose one based on Main Street. Our approach is straightforward: for growth with equity, we need to get the institutions right for both stimulating continuous innovation and raising wages. The old bumper sticker of the trade union movement, "America Needs a Raise," turns out to be a very good cathartic for growth.

Such a constellation of high-productivity, high-wage, institution-rich developments can be thought of as offering the possibility for a *high road to economic growth with equity.* What is encouraging is that the voices that have been calling for such an approach, based largely on qualitative and historical reasoning, are now being joined by the best mathematical economists of the younger generation, who have rigorously laid out the theoretical foundation for the successful pursuit of the high road. Adding our own thoughts to the discussion, we suggest the types of institutions and public policies needed to put this model into play. We suggest, for example, a broader role for government, in defiance of the knee-jerk obeisance to free-market ideology which undergirds the Wall Street model.

Here's how it might work.

The New Growth Theory

For his prodigious theoretical and empirical work, Dale Jorgenson, the chief theoretician of the neoclassical growth syllogism, is considered by many of his colleagues as an odds-on favorite to someday win the Nobel prize in economics. An equally likely, though younger, future contender for the prize is the Stanford University theorist Paul Romer. As a proponent of the New Growth theory, Romer and a small band of theorists, including Richard Nelson and Sidney Winter, have constructed sophisticated economic models that challenge the very essence of the old theory. This work is based on the earlier thinking of such giants in the profession as Joseph Schumpeter, Simon Kuznets, and even Adam Smith — economists who understood the critical role of technology in economic growth. The new theorists place technological progress at the very epicenter of growth dynamics, rather than capital investment per se. This shift in emphasis implicitly calls into question other aspects of the growth syllogism, including the power of low interest rates to stimulate investment and growth. In the new model, technology provides the engine for sustained growth in the face of the diminishing productivity associated with additions to the stocks of physical and human capital.

New Growth theory replaces the sobering prospect of diminishing returns that is so central to the old thinking, from Marx to Jorgenson, with a more expansive conception of economic processes. Such basically old ideas as technological spillovers, feedback loops, and increasing returns are put to clever new uses. Above all, advances in technology and interdependencies between new ideas and new investment ultimately save the day, yielding brighter prospects for long-run prosperity. In the eighteenth century, the avant-garde theories of Adam Smith concerning the wealth of nations provided a cheery alternative to the "dismal science" of Thomas Malthus. Today, the New Growth theory provides a more optimistic alternative to the conventional wisdom that counsels "diminished expectations" when it comes to future growth.

Recall that Robert Solow had, as such, no particular theory of technical progress. Innovations were simply assumed to unfold continuously over time. Jorgenson and his colleagues took the exogenous and almost mystical technology of Solow and embodied virtually all of it in physical and human capital. Like Solow, however, they proposed no theory of *how* technology evolves or how to speed it up.

Romer's contribution, and that of other new growth theorists, is to go the next step, "endogenizing" technology in their models by trying to explain how its evolution is linked to the institutions and dynamics of the economy. The New Growth theorists have peered into the "black box" of innovation and have tried to uncover how improvements in products, processes, and organizational structures actually come about. In doing this, the new theory shifts the focus to those important elements of technology that are *not* directly embodied in capital and labor. It stresses *complementarities* between capital accumulation and technical progress, between public and private investment, and between the factors of production and how that production is organized — on the shop floor, in the office, or anyplace else production occurs. Romer's model uses what Jorgenson had relegated to a trivial residual — disembodied technical change — and gives it top billing. In short, the new supersleuths of economics have taken on the enormous challenge of trying to understand what drives technology rather than taking it for granted, assuming it is serendipitous, or simply making it, like capital accumulation, a function of economic interest rates.

According to the new model, the process of invention, innovation, and diffusion is the result of *intentional* investment by profit-maximizing enterprises. As such, if invention and innovation are planned events (and, in contrast to Solow's conception, do not simply evolve through time at an unwavering lockstep rate of "t") and if they are the sine qua non of investment, then we should rightfully shift our attention from policies aimed merely at boosting capital accumulation to policies specifically directed at boosting the rate of technological and organizational innovation. This may sound like academics debating how many angels can fit on the head of a pin, but the implication for policy is profound.

The Essentials of New Growth Theory

The New Growth theory is based on four premises.[2] The first is that technological change — what Romer variously defines as "improvement in the instructions for mixing together raw materials," or the "recipe" for successfully combining capital and labor in the growth process — lies at the heart of economic growth. In particular, technological change provides the *incentive* for continued capital accumulation. This is a far cry from a growth model whose syllogism relies on low interest rates as the primary inducement to capital improvement.

The second premise is that technical progress is ultimately subject to various kinds of complementarities and feedback loops. Richard Nelson invokes the analogy of a well-made cake. He writes, "It is possible to list a number of inputs — flour, sugar, milk, and so on. It is even possible to analyze the effects upon the cake of having a little bit more or less of one ingredient, holding the other ingredients constant. But it makes no sense to try divide up the credit for a good cake to various inputs."[3] Without the flour or the sugar or the milk, you have no cake at all, not simply a less inviting dessert. As such, the complementarities among factors and processes make it impossible, or at least misleading, to try to add up their individual effects as though they represent marginal benefits to the whole. The old growth theory accounting scheme, which attempts to parcel out the specific contributions of physical capital, labor, and technology, cannot possibly work, because one cannot simply add up the impacts of individual factors to explain aggregate changes in output. Recall that Edward Denison tried to do this for years with little success. The New Growth theory explains why his search for the Holy Grail of economic growth was essentially doomed from the beginning.

Romer, in particular, emphasizes the complementarities between the rate of capital accumulation and the pace of innovation. Speeding up either one will likely speed up the other. But there is also a reciprocity between the rate of skill acquisition among workers and the growth dividend we obtain from new capital and new inventions. Improving technologies without equipping workers with the skills needed to adequately use the new tools and techniques or developing managers with the acumen needed to efficiently organize tasks and tools defeats the promise of innovation. As technologies change, what Richard Nelson and his longtime colleague Sidney Winter call "organizational routines" must change as well. The time horizons of business leaders, the orientation of labor-management relations, and government's commitment to the growth process all affect how the cake gets baked. For all intents and purposes, the old theory simply ignores these factors.

In this conception — and in dramatic contrast to the standard model's smooth production function — economic growth is likely to be a lumpy, discontinuous, nonlinear process. As such, the New Growth theory has no problem accounting for the productivity lags that accompanied the introduction of the steam engine and the electric motor. Indeed, adding a dollop of investment into a New Growth model may initially *reduce* the rate of growth because new technologies require a period of fitful adjustment before a firm's managers and employees can proceed up the learning curves and diffusion curves we encountered in Chapter 3. The learning curve itself may not be stable if the incessant introduction of updated technologies forces users to constantly relearn innovative systems. The old theory was largely at a loss to explain this. The New Growth theory recognizes and, indeed, predicts it.

The third premise undergirding this model is that technological change arises in large part because of *intentional* actions by people responding to market incentives. While the research scientist and the inventor may be motivated by the pure satisfaction of discovery or the more mundane goal of obtaining university tenure, the ultimate translation of new knowledge into real goods and services in a market economy is propelled by the pursuit of profit. Thus, a slowdown in expected growth becomes a self-fulfilling prophecy. Expecting a decline in demand to undermine future profits, firms curtail their investments in new research and development, and the pace of technological advance decelerates. In this case, *signals* about how the economy is expected to perform in the near future can change actual behavior. Expecting the economy to grow rapidly, firms invest in new capital and technologies, and the result is faster growth. Expecting the economy to slow down, companies cut back on their investments, and the economy responds by fulfilling expectations. Who gives these signals and how matters a lot.

Finally, and most fundamentally at odds with the old theory, is a fourth premise which states that technology is inherently different from other economic goods in one incredibly important respect. Once the fixed cost of creating a technology has been incurred, the recipe can be used over and over again at little or no cost. Indeed, this *spillover* property is taken to be the defining characteristic of technology. As Romer puts it, "The idea behind the transistor, the principles behind internal combustion, the organizational structure of a modern corporation, the concepts of double entry bookkeeping — all these pieces of information and many more like them have the property that it is technologically possible for everybody and every firm to make use of them at the same time without incurring additional costs."[4]

Software is a good example. It might require tens of millions of dollars to develop, test, and produce the first copy of a software package like the Corel WordPerfect 8.0 used in composing this chapter. But once the fixed costs are incurred, additional copies of the software can be produced for next to nothing. Everyone can use it for the small price of a few diskettes, a CD-ROM, and a site license, or they can (illegally but easily) obtain a copy of the software free by simply copying it from one machine to another. Indeed, now on the cutting edge of software development is the idea of object-oriented programming, which focuses specifically on the efficiency of writing interchangeable modules of code that become components of new programs. This is far different from the case of normal investment, where the increased output of steel, for example, requires building another monstrously expensive basic oxygen furnace, or the case of banking services, where increasing the number of transactions requires installing and servicing additional ATMs.

"Idea-based" inputs into the production process have another powerfully beneficial characteristic. New discoveries and inventions invariably accelerate the pace of discovery itself. While physical capital investment tends to be additive, essentially endowing the production process with one more machine after another, technology provides possibilities that tend to multiply.[5] That is, in practice ideas have a positive feedback mechanism of their own. The discovery of the transistor in Bell Labs ultimately led researchers to the integrated circuit and the personal computer. Ever faster microchips led to frustration with the size of storage devices, encouraging the development of ever smaller but more capacious hard disks and data compression techniques. The combination of faster processing speeds and high-density, low-cost data storage made it possible to create ever more powerful and elaborate computer software, which now provides whole new channels for multimedia discoveries by artists, architects, aerospace engineers, and a thousand other categories of inventor and innovator. The same virtuous cycle of discovery is now exploding in pharmaceuticals after the first breakthroughs in genetic engineering. They have been occurring for at least a generation in communications and medical diagnosis because of evolving imaging techniques, fiberoptic cable, and the original development of the laser. As a corollary, the original government investments in such newfangled ideas as the integrated circuit and the ARPANET led the way to exponential growth in a myriad of fields.

Technology thus has the extraordinary quality of providing increasing returns in the growth process and therefore the possibility of growth undiminished by the inherent limitations of finite physical or human capital. As one journalist who follows Romer's work has put it, this is a big deal. "In economics, saying you have found the way around diminishing returns is akin to saying you have discovered the Fountain of Youth."[6] With increasing returns, the potential for growth is limited only by human imagination and the resources needed to unleash it.

Along the way, the new theory had to break from the traditional assumption of perfect competition found in the old theory. Monopoly elements must exist for technology developers to earn a return on their discoveries, or the pace of technology will decline. Since discoveries, by definition, can be easily copied by anyone who learns of them, some proprietary means must be established for the discoverers to reap a reward for their efforts. Therefore, monopolistic competition rather than perfect competition is to be celebrated, not condemned. "Imperfections" in the competitive market in the form of temporary patents, licenses, and copyrights on intellectual property are indispensable for economic growth, as Joseph Schumpeter demonstrated as early as the 1930's.[7] These encourage growth without stifling it, for in a knowledge economy there are always new things to discover. In Schumpeter's tradition of "creative destruction," new innovators and inventors will attempt to circumvent patents and copyrights by making new discoveries that leapfrog the old. When this happens, a big jump in productivity and output normally occurs, leading to even more capital investment. There may be a long lag between initial discovery and full utilization of the new innovation, but in the end the innovation can unleash an enormous growth dividend.

The lesson is a simple one. Growth has always been initiated by improvements in technology, and technology, in turn, has always been encouraged by the promise of the profitable use of innovation. Putting these together, we arrive at a New Growth syllogism, which stresses the essential feedback loop in the growth process:

1. Growth is a function of technological innovation.

2. Technological innovation is a function of potential profit.

3. Potential profit is a function of *expected* growth in demand.

4. Thus, growth is a function of *expected* growth in demand.

We will soon see how this plays out in practice.

Lessons from the New Growth Theory

A host of fascinating associated conclusions flow from the premises of the new theory. Two are of particular significance. Since technology results from human inventiveness, the accumulation of human capital serves double duty. It augments the value of labor in the production of goods and services and, at the same time, promotes the discovery of new technology. Hence, there are potentially prodigious social returns to human capital that are not captured in the standard cost-benefit framework used for determining investment levels. We tend to underinvest in human capital because we ignore these particular social returns. Increased public investment in education and training will therefore more than pay for itself, since they will underwrite technological discovery, which will in turn raise national growth rates. These technological discoveries are not simply or even primarily the momentous scientific breakthroughs requiring an Einstein. The accumulation of small improvements in technology or in workplace organization can add up to immense changes in output. Hence, we need to train not just the Einsteins, the proverbial rocket scientists and brain surgeons, but everyone who potentially contributes to the productive enterprise.

A second implication of the New Growth theory is that given the fixed and finite costs of new discoveries, the larger the size of the market, the faster the rate of growth. Therefore, tapping into unexplored domestic markets and into foreign markets for trade can raise the rate of growth by boosting the incentive for technological discovery and thereby boost output itself. Deliberately slowing growth, for example, by deflationary monetary policy or through the austerity measures that international financial agencies impose on emerging nations, can actually lead to slower technological progress and thereby not only depress growth in the short term but undermine it in the long run as well.[8]

Historical Evidence for the New Growth Theory

We might ask at this point, is there any empirical verification for this radical new theory of growth? The answer is yes, and much of it comes from a careful reading of economic history. The standard neoclassical model with exogenous technology assumes that technology is the same in all countries, which leads to the conclusion that any observed differences in growth rates must be due to differences in savings rates and education.[9] But Romer points out that differences in savings and education do not explain, for example, why the United States grew so much faster than Britain around the turn of this century.[10] In 1870 per capita income in the United States was only three-quarters that of the British. In both countries, education per worker increased by about the same amount, and savings rates were roughly comparable. Yet by 1929, U.S. income levels surpassed those in Britain by 30 percent. What made for the difference in growth rates?

The answer lies in understanding the *incentives for investment* in both countries. British savers took their money and invested abroad, a good deal of it in the United States, where the market was so immense, where the technology of Edison and Ford was on the cutting edge, and where, consequently, the promise of growth was so great. Americans wisely invested at home. As Romer observes, "It is difficult to look at the data for these two countries without wondering whether the well-documented technological developments in the United States aren't at least part of the story" explaining the differential investment rates.[11]

Berkeley economist Gene Grossman comes to the same conclusion through a simple thought experiment. He tells us: "Imagine how the world economy would have evolved if none of the major inventions of the last 200 years had materialized — no steam engine, no electricity, no transistors, no computers, and so on. Would growth have proceeded nonetheless thanks to investments in ever more capital (more field animals and hand instruments?) and continued increases in levels of schooling?"[12] Merely asking the question explains why understanding technology, not simply capital accumulation, is essential for understanding the prospects for growth. Physical capital investment enters the model at the second or third remove. It is not that capital investment is unimportant, but that human capital investment and technological innovation become the true sine qua non of growth.

In the Dark Ages a millennium ago, this model would have had little or no applicability. Accumulating draft animals meant a nation could grow a little faster. But now, more than ever, we live in an information age where knowledge and technology are increasingly the primary factors separating rich nations from poor. And the good news is that unlike with physical commodities, there is no limit to knowledge. As Romer puts it, "One feature of knowledge can be summarized by Isaac Newton's statement that he could see far because he could stand on the shoulders of giants. . . . As we learn more, we get better and better at discovering new things . . . [so] there's no limit to the amount of things we can discover."[13] In the new theory, if ideas are the recipes we use to rearrange things to create more value, and wealth and ideas are potentially unlimited, then the more we can discover, the more we can grow. It is here where the New Growth theory and public policy meet.

Public Spending on R&D

No process is more central to the New Growth theory than investments in research and development. To be sure, most R&D spending in the United States is made by, or lodged within, private industry. To take one recent year (1995), approximately $102 billion of the roughly $171 billion spent on R&D, or 60 percent, came from industry; the federal government's contribution was some $61 billion.[14] But in the realm of technology, the question for policy is whether public investment stimulates private investment. For example, in the absence of Defense Department investment in chip designs emanating from Silicon Valley and the predecessor to the Internet, and National Institutes of Health investigations into the structure of genes, it is doubtful that private industry would today have the World Wide Web, distributed computer processing, or the high-productivity, high-wage, high-profit industry known as biotech.[15]

Actually, there are really *two* questions here. First, assuming that R&D does contribute to economic growth — and on that matter, the empirical evidence is overwhelmingly supportive[16] — are there technical properties of R&D that would lead us to expect that private firms would systematically *underinvest* in these activities in the absence of government sponsorship? Second, is there solid evidence that public sector investment in R&D, wherever it happens to be situated — in government laboratories, private or public universities operating with government grants, private companies making use of tax credits, or joint public-private consortia — stimulates subsequent private sector investment? The answer is yes to both questions. The conclusion, then, is that prosperity can be promoted, both directly and indirectly, by fiscal policies that expand public spending on R&D. The other side of that coin is that prosperity can be sabotaged if government ignores its subsidiary but crucial role in the R&D process.

A "yes" answer to the first question is based on the almost universal finding that the *social rate of return* to investment in R&D exceeds the private rate. That is, the total returns to all businesses and consumers combined — in other words, society at large — exceed the private returns to the individual firm (or laboratory, scientist, or manager) making the initial investment in new R&D. This may happen because, unlike investments in tangible capital such as machinery, the ideas flowing from R&D are, in the words of economists, nonrival and not fully appropriable. *Nonrival* means that my learning of a new innovation does not prevent you from using it. When returns are not fully appropriable, the original innovator cannot gain all of the profit that flows from the eventual application, especially the commercialization, of the new process or product.

A good example can be found in the development of the first spreadsheet software for personal computers. The idea of being able to manipulate a huge array of information by assigning every piece of data a specific cell address in a two-way table, identified only by a column letter and a row number, made it possible for millions of nonexpert users to keep records, make calculations, even model relatively complex phenomena to an unprecedented degree. But the originators of this wonderful tool, VisiCalc, could not keep other companies — notably Lotus and later Microsoft and Borland — from developing variants of the spreadsheet idea in the form of Lotus 1-2-3, Excel, and QuattroPro. VisiCalc eventually went out of business, but millions of users around the world had access to better and better spreadsheet programs as a result of the rapid diffusion of this nonrival, nonappropriable technology.

In many cases, however, the fact that the full profit from a new innovation is not fully appropriable by the innovator means that firms will often wait for others to do the innovating. Why spend your own resources on something if you can wait a little while, allow another company or lab to do the basic R&D, and then "free ride" on that effort? Because generic R&D has this quality, there is a natural tendency for everyone to wait for everyone else to make the first move. In such a situation, despite the *known* potential social gain from the innovative effort, the crucial original research is delayed, perhaps indefinitely. In this case, as a society there is a tendency to "produce" too little R&D — unless the public sector agrees to fund or perhaps even perform it. It is impossible to believe, for example, that the multibillion dollar Human Genome Project, which is in the process of mapping the entire human genetic code, could have been or would have been mounted by the private sector alone. Yet the future monetary gains to biotech firms resulting from this massive public sector R&D investment cannot easily be calculated. Put simply, whenever the social returns exceed the privately appropriable returns, there is likely to be private market underinvestment in new technology, reducing the overall potential for economic growth and prosperity.

On this question, the data are quite clear. Based on a wide variety of studies, it has been found that social rates of return exceed private rates by anywhere from 10 to an extraordinary 400 percent, depending on the sector studied and the data and method used to analyze the case.[17] Summarizing all of this research, the leading economist in this area, University of Pennsylvania economist Edwin Mansfield, suggests that the average social rate of return to R&D expenditures tends to exceed the private rate of return by a factor of two.

Public sector R&D spending, like human capital investment, also does double duty. It not only stimulates more economic growth directly but also encourages a second round of innovation, this time in the private sector. Research indicates there is a strong positive correlation between the trajectory of private R&D spending in a given year following public expenditures a year earlier.[18] This feedback effect was also powerfully confirmed in 1997 when a private research group released a study of private sector and university patent citations which the firm had been tracking for seventeen years. Among the researchers' findings: nearly *three-fourths* of the main science papers cited in American industrial patent applications between 1987/88 and 1993/94 were based on domestic and foreign research that had been financed by governments or by nonprofit agencies.[19] That is about as much proof of the importance of public R&D as anyone could wish for.

Yet despite all the evidence gathered, it is clear that the federal government has been neglecting its commitment to adequately support new R&D, especially outside the military sphere. Federal R&D expenditures as a percent of GDP reached their peak of 2 percent back in the early 1960s and then fell steadily thereafter to barely 1 percent by the end of the Carter administration. For a time, under the Reagan military buildup of the early 1980s, there was some recovery in this ratio. But since 1985 the trend has again been negative, with the current share now well below 1 percent.[20] According to the New Growth theory, a reversal in this trend is critical to accelerating economic growth.

The Role of Public Infrastructure Investment

R&D, however, is only one area in which the government has been ignoring its responsibilities. Another is the area of public infrastructure — roads, highways, ports, and other types of publicly provided physical construction. Jeff Faux, president of the Economic Policy Institute, observes that "America's history is studded with grand economic sectors opened up by government and profited on by business. Early in our republic's life, we built canals and highways and provided land for towns and schools in the territories. Government financed the first assembly lines, subsidized the railroads to settle the West, and developed long-range radio technologies. It created the suburbs after World War II and explored space."[21]

In a similar, if more modest vein, Bates College economist David Aschauer has made what one would think would be the common-sense observation that "good roads and safe skies are just as important as trucks and planes to the commercial viability of a company like UPS or Federal Express."[22] To back up this claim, Aschauer undertook a series of empirical studies to measure the social return on such infrastructure.

These early efforts to measure the rate of return on investment in government-owned capital stock were criticized by mainstream critics for being "implausibly" large.[23] But then Alicia Munnell, a former member of the Council of Economic Advisers and former senior vice president and research director of the Federal Reserve Bank of Boston, took on the task of reestimating Aschauer's equations, addressing a number of the criticisms that had been leveled at his work.[24] She found that Aschauer's precise estimates of the payoff to investing in infrastructure were indeed implausibly large but concluded that the impact was still positive, quite sizable, and statistically significant.[25]

Now Aschauer is back again, with new estimates. According to his latest findings on the effects of public investment spending at the *state* level over the period 1970–90, every one–standard deviation increase in public capital investment increases aggregate output growth by about 1.6 percentage points per year and employment growth by 0.5 percentage points per year. That means, other things equal, a state that spends roughly one-third more on public infrastructure enjoys aggregate growth about 1.6 percentage points faster than a state that does not.

In order to pay for that increased public investment, state governments have to raise taxes or incur debts by floating bonds. The costs of doing so must be subtracted from consumption and investment spending. In principle these taxes make it more expensive for private investors to borrow, which detracts from growth. The question is, what is the *net* effect of all this? Taking these costs fully into account, Aschauer estimates that the *net* impact of a one–standard deviation increase in the size of the public capital stock is still positive: about a 0.4 percentage point increase in economic growth per year and a 0.1 percentage point annual increment in the number of jobs. One should not be surprised by such numbers. Consider what would happen to economic growth if the interstate highway system were suddenly to disappear, or narrow down to one lane in each direction. Commerce would slow, workers would find it almost impossible to get to work, and entire industries linked to the auto industry would cut back investment and output. Now think about the chaos if airports disappeared — or the sewer system no longer worked!

Essentially, then, public infrastructure adds to economic growth by enhancing private sector productivity. Using sophisticated statistical techniques which tease out the direction of causality between public sector spending and private sector output, one well-respected researcher, Timothy Bartik of the W. E. Upjohn Institute, has shown that increasing public highway spending by 1 percent of a state's income would increase manufacturing output in the long run by 6.8 percent and boost productivity by

7.5 percent.[26] Public spending on elementary and secondary education, higher education, and health care all have similar impacts on output and boost productivity even more.[27]

That infrastructure investment is so important to the level of private output and productivity leads one to ask how much of the decline in economic growth suffered during the 1970s and 1980s might be attributed to the cutback in public goods spending after its heyday in the 1960s. Eastern Michigan University economist Sharon J. Erenberg has taken a crack at this question, examining U.S. Commerce Department data for the period 1947–90. Explicitly accounting for the fact that the taxes needed to pay for public goods might reduce private sector investment, Erenberg nonetheless concludes that over the long run, a 1.0 percent increase in public infrastructure investment leads eventually to as much as a 0.4 percent annual increment in private equipment investment. How much of a difference does this make to aggregate economic growth? If the average annual growth in the public stock of capital that characterized the long period 1947–66 had continued through 1990, instead of falling off as it did, she concludes that average annual GDP growth could have been 1.3 to 1.9 percentage points higher than it was. That alone would have made up for much of the slowdown in national economic growth after 1973.[28] Even cutting this estimate in half yields a sizable impact on economic growth. Obviously, to the extent that infrastructure investment facilitates private investment and growth, the New Growth theory implicitly has a much more benign view of government than does the Wall Street model.

Technical Progress and the Reorganization of Production and Work

Investing in "hard" stuff like roads and highways is one of the mechanisms to foster growth. But those who have thought about growth within this theoretical framework have identified another factor as no less important: the organization of the workplace. It has become almost commonplace, certainly in business schools, to emphasize how the transformation of management hierarchies into flatter, more decentralized organizational structures can promote productivity improvement in the firm and therefore faster growth in the economy.[29]

The aspect of workplace transformation that has probably received the greatest attention in recent years, and raised the greatest hopes and expectations for achieving productivity breakthroughs, is in the field of industrial relations. Scholars, management specialists, and business leaders have trumpeted the virtues, real and imagined, of the introduction of such organizational innovations as teams, pay-for-performance bonuses, worker ownership, profit sharing, and the like. These practices go under many names, from "employee involvement" to "high-performance work systems."[30] Economic Policy Institute economist Eileen Appelbaum offers a particular succinct definition: "The core characteristic of a *high performance work organization* is that front-line workers have the authority and the opportunity to make decisions that alter organizational routines."[31]

There are, of course, plenty of anecdotal examples of private companies (generally among the largest ones) that have made major commitments to greater labor-management cooperation. Motorola, Xerox, Corning, General Electric, Hewlett-Packard, Ford, Federal Express, AT&T, and Siemens are among the companies most frequently cited for their adoption of such innovations.[32] But whether these "success stories" add up to a *trend* toward restructuring corporate environments as high-performance workplaces is still contested. Even many of the early advocates, such as Appelbaum, Irving Bluestone, and Peter Cappelli, have become "cautiously pessimistic" about how many firms will be reorganized in any more than a cosmetic fashion. As University of Wisconsin economist Susan Parks puts it, "The types of practices discussed here are often applied piecemeal and are just as easily discarded when they fail to produce [instant] results. . . . Whether the implementation of these practices is determined by economic imperatives or is cyclical or random is not known."[33]

What we can say with some confidence is that when these practices *are* adopted and institutionalized, they more often than not pay off in higher productivity growth within the firm.[34] A careful review of nearly fifty statistical studies concerned with the productivity impact of employee participation done in the early 1990s came to the conclusion that over half demonstrated improved productivity directly as a result of employee involvement. Only two out of forty-seven reported negative effects.[35] In more recent research completed in 1997, former Labor Department chief economist Lisa Lynch and Federal Reserve Bank economist Sandra Black found that companies adopting major workplace reorganizations that permitted workers to be directly involved in regular decision making within the firm boosted productivity by an average of 11 percent where no union was present and 20 percent where it was.[36] The high-performance workplaces where productivity rose the most were those in which a high proportion of the workforce had access to computers, where more than half the workers met regularly to discuss workplace issues, where at least 30 percent of the workers were organized into self-managed teams, and where profit sharing was extended to ordinary workers as well as managers.[37]

Equally compelling evidence that such reorganization of work can indeed matter to productivity performance comes from studies of the information technology (IT) sector. Recall that back in Chapter 3 we had occasion to examine the work of organizational strategist Erik Brynjolfsson, who painstakingly assembled some of the first real evidence that the massive investment in IT by American business was in fact yielding measurable payoffs in productivity advance.

Following up on that research, Brynjolfsson and his colleague Lorin Hitt have gone even further in the direction of the New Growth theory's insights about the importance of complementarities. In this later work they investigate how much the relationship between IT investment and productivity is conditioned by changes in the industrial relations environment in the firm. Put more simply, to what extent do transformations in labor-management relations influence the size of the payoff to investments in IT hardware and software?

Brynjolfsson and Hitt look at data on 380 large U.S. corporations. Their conclusions strongly confirm the complementarity hypothesis: "We find greater demand for IT in firms with greater decentralization of decision rights (especially the use of self-managing teams), and greater investments in human capital, including training and screening by education. In addition, the output elasticity [i.e., the payoff] of IT is substantially higher in firms that adopt a more decentralized and human-capital-intensive work system."[38]

It certainly appears that how work is organized on the shop floor can matter to productivity growth as much as the simple accounting of how much labor and capital are being utilized in the production process. Encouraging workplace reorganization is therefore one of the best ways to encourage faster economic growth.

Investments in Education and Training

As might be surmised from what we have already mentioned, New Growth theorists are especially emphatic about the importance of maintaining social investments in education and training. Economists of all theoretical persuasions have always supported such a policy, but these investments play a special role in the new theory. Because of the principle of complementarity, investments in physical capital and technical innovations cannot achieve their full potential if the workers who must utilize these tools and techniques lack the skills to do so. Moreover, this is another case where increasing returns to investment based on complementarities seem to be present. The more well trained the work force, the greater the potential payoff to firms from investing in new technology, and higher payoffs induce increased investment beyond what would have been expected from a straight-line extrapolation of past trends.

Given the particular importance of investments in education and training, it is striking how both the public and private sectors have neglected this area in recent years. Federal government expenditures on education and training, which rose rapidly in the 1960s and 1970s, have dropped as a share of GDP by an astounding 50 percent since their peak in 1976. Even after adding in the modest education and training tax credits signed into law in 1998, planned federal government investment in human capital shows a steep downward trend well into the new century.[39] President Clinton's strong endorsement of education spending is refreshing in this respect, but fails to get the share of GDP devoted to federal investment in schooling and training back to anywhere near the necessary level.

And what of private sector investments in training? While precise estimates vary, the general conclusion that U.S. firms systematically underinvest in firm-specific training appears in study after study. Research also indicates that the U.S. private sector underinvests relative to private firms in Japan, Australia, France, Germany, the Netherlands, Norway, Sweden, and even the United Kingdom.[40]

Added to this problem is how the education and training dollar is distributed. There has been a particular bias in the private sector against spending on youth (and on low-skilled workers generally). At least two-thirds of the annual spending of all U.S. companies on education and training during the 1980s is reported to have been invested in their college-educated professional employees.[41] Since the early 1980s, only 4 percent of students aged 16–25 without a college education have received formal company-centered training of at least four weeks' duration.[42] Between 1983 and 1991, the average duration of formal training paid for and provided by employers for learning a new job declined substantially, especially for workers with less than 10 years seniority.[43] Moreover, while recent surveys show that the majority of private firms do make some investments in worker training, the American Society for Training and Development reports that a tiny handful are responsible for the vast majority of the total investment — 0.5 percent of all firms spend 90 percent of the total.[44]

The traditional explanation for this investment behavior on the part of private companies, in the context of American political institutions, is that workers here are more likely than those elsewhere to take whatever training they receive inside a particular firm and "jump ship" to another. At the level of high theory, Gary Becker many years ago drew a powerful distinction between firm-specific and more general training, predicting that private businesses would always underinvest in the latter since it could be used by footloose employees to ultimately benefit competitors. Cornell University's John Bishop confirms that over the past twenty years a smaller fraction of American workers had been on their current job for more than five years than almost anywhere else; the rates for Japan and Germany were half again as great.[45] Taken together, the evidence on seniority and the theory regarding general training forms the basis for economists' widely shared classification of general ("portable") training as a "public good," one which, if not subsidized by government — however and wherever it is actually provided — will be systematically underproduced.[46]

Of course, part of the explanation for the relatively limited level of private spending on employer-centered training is that most firms are small, and the incidence of spending on training declines dramatically, the smaller the establishment.[47] The reasons are apparent: small firms have smaller budgets, less organizational slack for managing such activities, and — because they also tend to pay lower wages and offer fewer job benefits — confront higher probabilities that employees will "job hop" sooner.

It is possible that in the late 1990s extremely tight labor markets and shortages of skilled workers have become so pressing that U.S. firms are changing their behavior. If so, this bodes well for the future. Periodically, the National Association of Manufacturers commissions the Grant Thornton consulting firm to survey the personnel and employment practices of its member firms. In the 1997 survey, nearly half of all respondents reported that they were investing 2 percent or more of their total payroll to train shop floor and other hourly workers. This contrasts dramatically with the estimate for 1991, which showed that the top half of respondents spent, on average, less than 0.5 percent. More companies than ever before are also turning to local community colleges to provide training for them, on contracts of varying length. And fully two-thirds of the responding firms said they thought that government-run programs for workforce training were "relevant" to their concerns.[48] Whether this apparent turnround will last beyond the momentarily tight labor markets of 1997–99 remains to be seen.[49] But it underscores another feedback loop, this time between rapid growth, low unemployment, and investments in training.

For all of these reasons, while the Wall Street model focuses on policies to keep prices stable, the New Growth theory suggests a very different agenda. One would expect that if the zeal of the Wall Street model's proponents for balanced budgets collided with the New Growth theory's call for more investment in R&D, public infrastructure, workplace reorganization, education, and training, the Wall Streeters would nix such expenditures. No matter how strong the evidence presented by those who have studied the growth benefits of public sector investments, the new conventional wisdom ranks balanced budgets, if not budget surpluses, as the higher priority. This clash between theories could not be greater.

But What about the Demand Side?

All of the factors we have been exploring so far are ones that expand the *potential* for growth. But the enhanced capacity of an economy to generate output is, as we have shown, not sufficient to assure or sustain it. If the resulting output cannot be sold, then all of the productivity advance will end up doing little more than adding to the stock of idle machines, plants, office buildings, and workers. This in itself can act as a negative signal to investors, producing a vicious cycle of falling investment, slower growth, and increasing unemployment. Hence, demand matters if the potential for growth is to be realized.

Furthermore, *how* that demand is generated will matter a great deal for social equity. In the Wall Street model, the critical boost in consumption is induced by the sense of increased wealth created by a rising stock market. This is a growth path that inevitably worsens income inequality. Investors and stock owners, after all, are not to be found in equal proportions among the wealthy, the middle class, and the poor.

In contrast, recall that the post–World War II virtuous growth cycle was based on a very different mechanism for generating incomes. Pent-up working-class demand, union and public sector wages that often served as benchmarks for nonunion sectors, and expansionary government fiscal policy joined to produce a historically unprecedented era of income growth and declining income inequality. Minimum wage laws were updated periodically. Social floors under income, such as the provision of unemployment insurance, were made more universal and generous. This could all be described as a period of *wage-led growth*.

Clearly, if we are to both realize the productive potential inherent in the precepts of the New Growth theory *and* return to a path of growing income equality, we are going to have to fashion some new version of the wage-led virtuous cycle. The specifics of what we need to do in this regard will be elaborated in the final chapter of this book.

In the balance of this chapter, however, we consider two additional issues that pertain to restoring sustained growth. Both emerge from the insights about "endogenous" growth contained in the New Growth theory. These concern, first, the relationship between innovation and the appropriate sectoral composition for promoting robust economic growth, and second, the point that public policy can powerfully influence whether the private sector chooses to pursue a high-wage, high-productivity, high-growth "high road" to expansion or a low-wage, low-productivity, slow-growth "low road" path.

Why the Mix of Sectors and Industries Matters

In a series of ingenious papers, most of them coauthored with her German colleague, Ronald Schettkat, Eileen Appelbaum has proposed an explanation for why, over the past two decades, a trade-off has appeared in most industrialized countries between the rate of job creation and the rate of productivity growth.[50] Most mainstream research on the productivity-growth nexus focuses on rigidities or inflexibilities in labor and capital markets. The story goes that unrealistically high wages imposed by unions or by minimum wage laws are responsible for unemployment. Appelbaum and Schettket pose a different story and get considerable mileage from systematically studying differences in income and price elasticities of product and service demand across various industries. The *elasticity of demand* refers to how a change in income or a change in price affects the level of consumption. A high elasticity of demand means that a given increase in income or reduction in price induces a large increase in consumption. A low elasticity means just the opposite: a given increase in income or reduction in price has hardly any impact on purchases at all. Two good examples are computers and potatoes. As the price of personal computers declined, demand exploded. But even if the price of potatoes were to decline by half, few families would make major changes in their diet. They would not all of a sudden have French fries with every meal. By exploring the elasticities for various goods and services, we can unearth some powerful information about whether increased productivity will lead to increased prosperity or to unfulfilled economic potential.

When economies first industrialize, the composition of demand generally shifts from agricultural products to manufactured goods. Initially, the demand for factory output is enormous, and the income and price elasticities are quite high. Thus, as productivity improvements make it possible to lower prices, sales of manufactured products soar. Millions of workers, including many who are displaced from farms, are needed to man the plants that produce these manufactured goods. As the market becomes saturated, however, income and price elasticities tend to decline. Now increased productivity means fewer jobs, not more.

Autos provide a case in point. Early in this century, when cars were just becoming popular, almost everyone wanted one. Thus, when Henry Ford introduced his cheap Model T, millions of Americans flocked to dealerships to buy their first cars. Today, however, the domestic demand for automobiles is practically exhausted. Those with rising incomes may buy more expensive cars, but they will not necessarily buy more of them or buy ones that require more workers to produce them. Not surprisingly, then, total sales of new cars and trucks in the United States, including imports, were roughly the same in 1979, 1989, and 1997, all years of peak production.[51] Increased productivity in this sector continues to create the potential for additional output, but the demand for that increased output is insufficient to maintain employment. As a result, between 1996 and 2006, the output of the U.S. auto industry is projected to grow at about 1.5 percent per year while the number of workers needed to produce it is expected to decline by 0.4 percent per year.[52] If the same phenomenon were to occur throughout most sectors of the economy, improved productivity would inevitably produce rising unemployment.

In mature economies the composition of demand tends to shift toward services. During the past twenty years, the demand for all kinds of services expanded rapidly while productivity hardly increased at all. The result was that many of those workers who were displaced from the manufacturing sector, where productivity growth was high, were only able to find jobs in the service sector, where advances in productivity were anemic. Low productivity in many of these service sectors meant a lot of jobs, but at low wages. Between 1988 and 1998, manufacturing employment *declined* from 19.3 to 18.8 million workers. Meanwhile, employment in services exploded by 12 million to 37.5 million, and wholesale and retail trade added another 4 million jobs to the 25 million that already existed.[53] The growth in trade and services, therefore, has been almost exclusively responsible for keeping unemployment from rising, and in recent years has driven it down to under five percent.

But most of this job growth came about when productivity growth in the service sector was effectively zero. If service sector productivity now begins to rise more rapidly, as we projected earlier in this book, what will happen to employment? Some, like the social activist and environmentalist Jeremy Rifkin, believe that we are on the verge of seeing *An End to Work* with an associated cataclysmic rise in joblessness.[54] Underlying this view is the implicit assumption that the income and price elasticities of services are so low that as we become more proficient at producing everything from communication and banking services to education and recreation, the demand will not be able to match supply. Productivity growth will, therefore, destroy jobs faster than new demand creates them.

Are we doomed, then, to more rapid growth as productivity improves, but only with immense unemployment? The answer, we believe, is no. For a host of reasons having to do with the exigencies of modern life, we think the income and price elasticities for a whole range of services will remain quite high and perhaps even rise. One important reason for this is related to the labor supply dynamics we mentioned in Chapter 3. American families are working so many hours that they need all the time-saving services and devices they can afford. As more and more families have two breadwinners and more of these breadwinners seek full-time jobs, there is an inevitable need to purchase all kinds of services to substitute for nonmarket work done in the home, simply to give families some free time to enjoy themselves. Time has become the most scarce resource in America.

That is why the use of ATMs has exploded and why so many Americans are now turning to the Internet to buy clothing, books, and all sorts of other things. These high-productivity services are facing consumer demand that is growing even faster than the pace of the efficiency gains these service industries are able to muster. L. L. Bean, Lands' End, and the bookseller Amazon.com are on the cutting edge of the new high-efficiency retail service, cashing in on consumers' demand to spend less time commuting back and forth to the mall.

The demand for another key service, education, is also likely to be quite income-elastic in the years to come. As income rises and the demand for skills increases, more and more adults have the desire and see the need to return to school. With long-distance university and college learning beginning to add to this sector's productivity, the demand for education is likely to increase along with the supply. Something of the same thing can be said of financial services. As incomes rise and families try to invest their savings wisely, the demand for mutual funds and other forms of financial assets is growing rapidly. This has spawned a huge increase in the ranks of portfolio account managers and other financial service workers. It is hard to believe that the demand for these services will not keep pace with improvements in productivity or perhaps even continue to exceed them.

The key to all of this, of course, is the assumption that family income will rise and that productivity improvements in services will help keep price increases under reasonable control. Obviously, if real income increases only slowly or if the prices of services rise rapidly, all bets are off. So the real question is, what might keep wages and incomes rising?

Labor Standards, Unions, and Wage-Led Growth

This same question faced the nation at the end of World War II, as we noted in Chapter 2. Back then, the pent-up supply of family savings from the war combined with four years of pent-up demand led to an unparalleled consumption boom that helped ignite the era of rapid postwar growth. Private investment followed, as did government spending on the civilian side of the economy. Exports also led to faster growth, as allies and former enemies alike took advantage of Marshall Plan loans and grants to buy American goods they desperately needed.

But this consumption-led boom might well have petered out in five to ten years had it not been for the expansion of the trade union movement and the creation of what has been called the "traditional workplace contract."[55] The broad outline of this new relationship between labor and management began to come into focus with the famous 1948 agreement between General Motors and the United Auto Workers. Its main provisions provided a guaranteed annual increase in real wages (through a productivity-related "annual improvement factor" and a cost-of-living allowance, or COLA, which indexed wages to inflation); a series of lucrative fringe benefits that provided for retirement and protected workers and their families in the case of ill health, accident, or death; and protection from layoff or arbitrary dismissal for workers who had built up some seniority. This traditional workplace contract spread like wildfire throughout the manufacturing sector of the economy and infiltrated other sectors as well.

While the traditional workplace contract was often criticized by management and conservative economists as undermining a free-market economy, it is clear in retrospect that the wage gains and job security it offered played a critical role in sustaining the postwar glory days for nearly two and a half decades. Higher wages fueled round after round of rising consumption. Fringe benefits and job security provided working families with the confidence that they could spend their wages rather than save as much as possible to cover any unforeseen tragedy. Moreover, the higher wages demanded and won by unions forced managers to do everything they could to boost labor productivity.

With the decline of trade unions and job security, the economy-wide benefits of the traditional workplace contract all but disappeared. In the

1970s and 1980s, this contributed to the downward trend in growth rates as workers' wages stagnated or declined and as job tenure became more precarious. Moreover, as wages remained relatively low in large segments of the burgeoning nonunion service sector, there was little impetus for managers in this sector to make large-scale investments in new technology to boost labor productivity. What productivity increases occurred were largely in unionized manufacturing, with service sector productivity lowering the overall level of efficiency gains in the economy to their lowest point in the twentieth century.

There is a lesson here. In order to sustain faster growth and boost productivity, we need to pursue a "high-road" strategy when it comes to wages and worker benefits. More than by any other single intervention, the federal government can promote the upgrading of productivity in the service sector by returning to the post–World War II commitment to gradually raising labor standards and by restoring the ability of labor unions to offer a viable collective voice to workers. This combination can boost economic growth while reducing economic inequality.

Workers' rights and public policies undergirding workers' living standards are commonly treated as subjects for politics, not economics, or at best for parenthetical debates over the fair distribution of income. This is appropriate — as far as it goes. But the level and coverage of the legal minimum wage, the extent of collective bargaining, the requirement that companies provide advance notice to workers before mass layoffs or outright closures, the extent of severance pay, the minimum fraction of a person's previous earnings replaced by government unemployment insurance, and laws and regulations regarding eligibility for paid vacations and sick leave — all of these factors have an impact as well on the economy's rate of growth.

On this point, economists Robert Buchele and Jens Christiansen have conducted an original and persuasive international cross-section analysis of the connection between labor standards and productivity.[56] They construct an index consisting of seven indicators of worker rights. The index turns out to be strongly correlated with the growth in labor productivity across the seven most industrialized countries (the G7) over the period 1972–88. This is true even after controlling across countries for the differential growth of capital-labor ratios — the amount of plant and equipment and software per worker, which figures so prominently in standard models of productivity growth among countries. In both comparisons, Germany looks best, scoring highest on the worker rights index and among the highest in total productivity growth. The United States is far and away the lowest-scoring country during this period on both labor rights and productivity.

The conventional wisdom in economic theory and policy analysis depicts wages, benefits, taxes, and regulations as straightforward costs of doing business — subtractions from the share of the surplus available for profit. This is what led such liberal economists as the late Arthur Okun to conclude that there was a trade-off between equality and efficiency.[57]

To be sure, in a static, short-run, textbook model of an economy, higher wages and benefits come at the expense of profits and therefore threaten the incentive to invest and, according to the old growth theory, retard the rate of economic growth. But if we take a more long-range, dynamic perspective, in line with the New Growth theory, investment in technical change, management innovation, and worker training are not independent of the level of wages. High wages will induce behaviors by both workers and managers that can lead to productivity increases, out of which those higher employee costs may be met *without* cutting into profits. Higher wages, in this dynamic model, are a stimulus to faster growth, not the other way around.

Drawing originally on the dissertation research of Louise Waldstein at MIT, Lester Thurow has carefully expanded on this alternative wage-productivity relationship, in effect arguing that higher wages lead to higher productivity, not the other way round as conventional theory assumes. He does so in the context of offering an explanation for why service sector productivity growth has been so lethargic for so long in this country, but *not* elsewhere.[58] To take but one case, European Union data show that in the 1970s and 1980s, service productivity grew seven times faster in Germany than in the United States.[59]

Why this discrepancy? Waldstein and Thurow answer that capital per worker had for years grown much more slowly in most corresponding service industries in the United States than in Europe or Japan:

> While the relative cost of labor to capital [went] up from 100 to 144 in the United States between 1964 and 1982, the relative cost of labor rose from 100 to 206 in West Germany and from 100 to 204 in

Japan. . . . Whereas private service workers in the U.S. are paid only 67 percent as much as those in manufacturing, in Japan they are paid 93 percent as much, and in Germany 85 percent as much. The pattern is even more dramatic in finance where American financial workers received only 84 percent as much as manufacturing workers, while financial workers in Japan receive 134 percent as much and those in West Germany 122 percent as much.[60]

Because wages in the United States grew so slowly in such industries as health care, recreation, and retail trade, managers were encouraged to economize on investment spending and forego organizational changes, choosing instead to produce services with more labor-intensive forms of work and production organization. When you can get enough labor at low cost, it makes sense to keep your production process labor-intensive. In Europe, where labor costs in services are much closer to those in manufacturing, it is simply too expensive to keep producing services in the old-fashioned, labor-intensive manner.

Public policies have a direct bearing on wage rates and the availability of benefits. The countries whose service sector productivity growth substantially exceeds ours are those in which labor laws support unionization, extend collective bargaining coverage to a broader and larger share of the workforce, and tend to rely on social solidarity in the process of wage setting. That means wage differentials between workers in different industries are not allowed to "fan out" to unacceptable levels, creating massive wage differentials between sectors of the economy. Moreover, the more generous social insurance systems in Europe and Japan reduce a worker's need to accept a low-wage job offer. European minimum wage laws have for many years mandated much higher levels than is the case in the United States — and they are enforced. It is well known that part-time and temporary workers in the United States are, on average, paid lower hourly wage rates than are full-time, regular employees.[61] And managers are encouraged to substitute such contingent labor for regular labor in part because social legislation tends to exempt contingent, especially contract, labor from the benefits and protections enjoyed by full-time workers. All of this encourages low-wage, low-productivity work.

In sum, higher wages can lead to faster productivity growth — in all sectors of the economy, but especially in the already expanding service sector. They do so by inducing greater worker effort and by encouraging managers to invest in capital, technology, training, and organizational innovation. Because unions promote and defend higher wages and benefits, more equally distributed, laws and regulations that promote the right to organize, whatever they may do to profits in the short run, clearly contribute to long-run productivity growth. This relationship was first established empirically in a now-classic study by Harvard's Richard Freeman and James Medoff.[63] In recent years, a host of other studies has further documented the positive effects of unionization on productivity.[63] Whatever government can do to encourage democratic unionization and improve job security is therefore a step toward faster growth, not a step toward stagnation as the common wisdom would have it.

The High Road or the Low Road?

Government has another role to play as well. In a highly abstract yet powerful formal model, Romer and several colleagues have now demonstrated mathematically the possibility that signals from the government regarding its fiscal and policy intentions can actually affect the investment decisions made by private sector firms. Government forecasts of economic growth can therefore turn into self-fulfilling prophecies. The model assigns a special place to the assumption that expectations about future growth shape current investment decisions, and it can go either way.[64] Expected future demand, up or down — not interest rates — are the key.

If, in response to signals from the government — say, a Fed announcement hinting at higher interest rates or a congressional decision to cut its own spending on infrastructure — actors in the rest of the economy expect growth to slow down, the expected payoff to additional private investment will be lower than it would have been otherwise. Consequently, less investment actually takes place. What happens next? Growth slows — fulfilling the prophecy. Only a concerted, collective effort by whole groups of firms to go against such signals has a chance of offsetting this outcome, and in a competitive economy, such concerted action is not just unlikely, it is usually illegal. Thus, slower actual growth dampens the private expectation of profitability from new investment, pushing the economy in the direction of a downhill trajectory.

234

Suppose, on the other hand, that actors come to expect faster growth — perhaps because the Fed has convinced them that it is committed to a regime of low interest rates or because federal budgets for R&D, infrastructure, and education have been given a fresh ten-year lease on life. Firms see this signal as raising the likelihood of greater profitability from further investment, and so they invest. In this case, the predicted additional growth actually occurs. The complementarities between augmented public investment and the new private investment that the signal induces lead to faster productivity growth. When workers are armed with suitable bargaining power, their wages rise. With higher incomes and greater job security, workers boost their consumption and the virtuous cycle of faster growth — this time based on government policy and higher wages — kicks into action.

What is particularly interesting about this model is that under certain conditions, *both* the high-growth and low-growth paths constitute what economists call "stable equilibria." That is, once set upon one course or the other, it is possible for the economy to continue in that direction indefinitely. But it is equally possible that growth can switch back and forth between the two trajectories, making for an uncertain, bumpy ride into the future.

Wall Street versus Main Street

What will we choose? Which path into the twenty-first century will the American government and the American economy take? It should be clear by now that as we enter the new millennium, we have not one model to guide economic policy but two. The conventional wisdom with its neoclassical growth syllogism, its Wall Street virtuous cycle, and the Wall Street–Pennsylvania Avenue policy accord provides one scenario for the economy. But as we demonstrated earlier, by no means does this road assure sustained rapid economic growth; on the contrary, it will, in all likelihood, exacerbate economic and social inequality.

The alternative involves following what might be called a Main Street model of growth that relies on assuring rapid technological progress based, in part, on a recommitment of government to substantial investments in R&D, public infrastructure, education, and training; fiscal and monetary policies tilted toward growth rather than inflation control;

public and private sector pressure to increase the pace at which we develop high-performance workplaces, and a renewed commitment to wage-led growth based on stronger unions, higher minimum wages, and measures that improve job security. Something like the Main Street model was responsible for the glory days we enjoyed during the first quarter century after World War II. The New Growth theory suggests that we could do it again. Because we have choices, this is not merely a matter of economics; it is a matter of politics as well.

Chapter 8

From Wall Street to Main Street:
Economic Policy for the Twenty-first Century

W
E CAN NOW consider a set of policy prescriptions for *sustaining* rapid economic growth and pursuing greater economic and social equity in America. These policies are based on what we have learned about the factors ultimately responsible for the growth spurt we have enjoyed since the early 1990s and which contributed to remarkable periods of rapid growth in the past.

We have argued that the recent growth spurt should *not* be credited to the Wall Street–Pennsylvania Avenue policy accord of balanced budgets, free trade, flexible labor markets, and vigilant monetary policy. Instead, it is due to a rebirth of productivity based on the maturing of the information revolution — a process well underway before the Wall Street model was embraced by the White House and Congress. The microprocessor, the personal computer, local area networks, the Internet, and enormous advances in software are finally paying off in a productivity premium, as businesses learn how to use these innovations in efficient ways, putting in place the organizational structures that can take full advantage of them. Productivity growth, already well under way in the manufacturing sector, is now spreading to a range of services, from gas and electric utilities, laundries, and cleaning establishments to apparel and home furnishing stores, commercial banks, and automotive repair shops. Almost inevitably, it will continue to diffuse to the entire range of service industries across the nation. Already, over the course of 1995–98, productivity in the private business sector as a whole was improving by 2.3 percent per year, more than doubling the performance turned in during the first half of the decade and substantially better than the efficiency growth rates of the 1970s or 1980s. All of these information technologies were the product of enormous investments initially begun in preceding decades, underwritten by both private enterprise and the public sector.

To sustain the heady growth we have recently enjoyed now requires adopting a set of public policies consistent with maximizing technological progress, improving the education and skills of the American workforce, and at the same time, maintaining a level of wage and salary growth that can continuously fuel aggregate demand. The recipe for growth with equity, we shall argue, calls for combining some of the old policies of the post–World War II glory days with a set of fresh prescriptions that emanate from the latest thinking of the New Growth theorists. Essentially, we must relearn the wisdom of *public-private partnership* as the surest means to sustain prosperity. In the present political climate of privatization and shrinking government, the suggestion of a significant role for the public sector may seem anachronistic. But this is only because so much energy has been put into selling the Wall Street model to a public long tired of rising insecurity and looking for any panacea that promises to reverse falling wages and stagnating incomes.

A return to robust long-run growth is going to require, first and foremost, abandoning the key provisions of the Wall Street–Pennsylvania Avenue policy accord. It will need to be replaced by a domestic policy regime that recognizes and reinforces the complementarities between physical and human capital, and between innovation and organizational change within firms. The new regime will have to acknowledge the indispensable role of government in underwriting basic research, public infrastructure, and public schools. Internationally, emphasis must be placed on raising the wages and working conditions in the labor markets of our trading partners, and global financial markets will have to be made subject to some regulation so that they do not periodically destabilize the entire world economic system.

Does rejection of the Wall Street–Pennsylvania Avenue accord mean we do not have to worry at all about inflation or interest rates? Of course not. But as important as low real interest rates are to encourage investment, we have found that they are less important for growth than nurturing an economic environment conducive to innovation. Moreover, low inflation is important as a precondition for maintaining low interest rates and a positive investment climate. But in the absence of price shocks in the energy market, which could undermine growth altogether, basic price stability will continue to follow mainly from existing global competition and rising productivity, not the largely redundant anti-inflation actions of government.

Let us explore this alternative policy agenda, item by item. We shall focus on three key policy areas: government budgets, labor policy, and market regulation.

Reasserting a Role for Government Spending

The very first step in disengaging from the stranglehold of the Wall Street model is to restore the principle that the balance between how much revenue the government takes in and how much it spends in any given year should not be held hostage to balanced budget zealotry or the argument that the bigger the budget surplus the better.

One need not be some kind of unreconstructed 1930s-style Keynesian to see plainly that the assault on federal government programs, once the province of conservative Republicans, has become the lingua franca of contemporary Washington. The conversion of President Clinton and Vice President Gore, first to balancing the budget and then to saving the bulk of the growing government surplus, was one of the major victories of the Wall Street faction within the government. It has unfortunately become an unexamined article of faith, mostly for political reasons rather than good economic ones. Genuflecting before the balanced budget icon needs to cease. As long as the budget deficit is declining as a share of GDP, we are on the right track. When the overarching goal of policy becomes the total elimination of the entire federal debt, we run the risk of turning a virtue into a vice.

Investments in R&D and Public Infrastructure. What those who favor saving the surplus fail to recognize is the need for adequate public sector investment in infrastructure, research and development, and human capital. As we have seen, the New Growth theory stresses the fundamental complementarities among public infrastructure, civilian R&D, investments in the education and training of the workforce, and private sector investment. That the federal government has been shortchanging these vital elements of fiscal policy since the late 1970s runs the risk of sabotaging long-run economic growth itself.

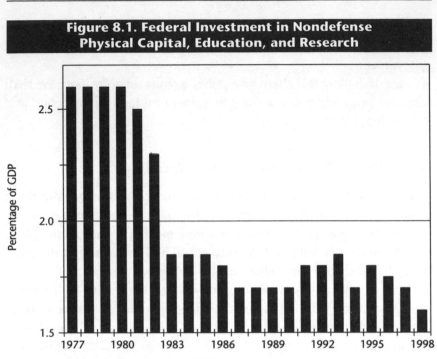

Figure 8.1. Federal Investment in Nondefense Physical Capital, Education, and Research

Source: *Wall Street Journal,* February 7, 1997, p A1.

As we documented in Chapter 7, one of the chief victims of deficit cutting and budget-balance mania has been the steady decline in public spending on infrastructure and research and development. The extent of the problem cannot be repeated often enough. Figure 8.1 reproduces a graph from the *Wall Street Journal* that tells the story in a nutshell.[1] Since 1979, the share of federal investment in public nondefense infrastructure, education, and research has fallen steadily. In the 1970s, when we were putting in place the investments that would eventually pay off in the 1990s, federal investment in these activities averaged better than 2.5 percent of GDP. The percentage shrank dramatically during the 1980s under the Reagan and Bush administrations, and, if anything, it has continued to decline under President Clinton and the Republican-dominated Congress. By 1998 it was down to only 1.5 percent of GDP.

Under current projections, the investment role of the federal government will continue to shrink in the future. As Figure 8.2 indicates, total discretionary federal spending (excluding Social Security, Medicare, Medicaid, and interest on the federal debt) was 13.6 percent of GDP in 1968.

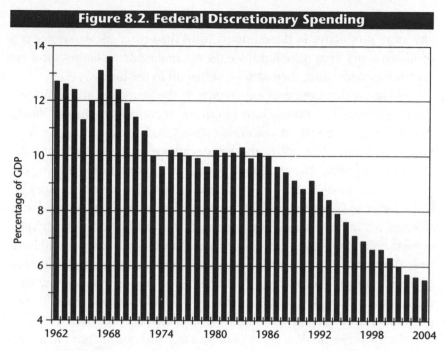

Figure 8.2. Federal Discretionary Spending

Source: U.S. Congressional Budget.

Even as late as 1986 it equaled 10 percent of GDP. Twelve years later it was down to 6.6 percent and is scheduled to fall to only 5.5 percent by 2004.[2] Thus, by midway into the next decade, the federal government's role in underwriting economic activity will have declined by almost half. Under these projected total budgets, fully 50 percent of *all* nondefense discretionary federal dollars would have to be allocated exclusively to R&D, physical infrastructure, and education programs if the share of GDP devoted to these activities were to return to 1970 levels. In this case, we would have to make draconian cuts in every other federal program, further weakening the federal commitment to aiding the poor, cleaning up the environment, and paying the wages and salaries of federal employees.

The impact of this decline in public investment effort is invisible in the short run because the payoff is always in the future, sometimes taking two decades or more. The long lag can fool us into believing that there is little relationship between what we invest in the public sector and what we reap in return. Putting more resources into medical research today will not show up in reduced cancer rates until well into the next century.

Pouring more dollars into public schools will not make second graders any more productive in the economy until they enter the workforce ten or fifteen years from now. But if we do not make adequate provision for such investments now, there will be no payoff in the future.

We know this from past experience. If the government had not invested enormous resources into electronic technologies during World War II, improvements in communications and television technology might have been delayed by another decade or so. If we had not built thousands of miles of interstate highways beginning in the 1950s, the growth of the post–World War II auto industry would have been stunted. If the Defense Department had not invested in technology for guidance systems on military aircraft and rockets, the introduction of personal computers and the myriad of devices based on the microchip would have been delayed or perhaps would never have occurred at all. Development of the panoply of hardware and software applications that we now take for granted would have been delayed as well. If it had not been for the government's development of the ARPANET, the predecessor to the Internet, the World Wide Web would still be a figment of someone's imagination. In sum, economic growth would have been slowed as invention and innovation were shortchanged.

The good news is that the current growth spurt is providing unexpectedly high levels of federal revenue. To use budget surpluses almost exclusively to reduce outstanding government debt is to ignore the lessons of both post–World War II history and the New Growth theory. Some portion of the revenue cornucopia should be devoted to public investment. Indeed, simply paying off the federal debt as fast as possible will do little on its own to "save Social Security first," as President Clinton would have it. Only faster growth can save Social Security, for only if the earnings of future workers are higher than currently projected will there be enough FICA tax revenues generated in the future to pay the benefits of the next generation of public pension and Medicare recipients.

Where some of that public investment could be best directed is not all that difficult to determine. Good candidates for increased R&D spending are medical research, biotechnology, and transportation technology (e.g., high-speed rail, safer aircraft, faster and safer highways, and fuel-efficient vehicles). We also need more public infrastructure investment aimed at rebuilding cities, redressing environmental hazards, constructing safer, "smart" highways, providing for high-speed railroad right-of-ways, and airport expansion. A national debate on how best to invest a portion of the budget surplus is sorely needed. Scientists and engineers should be part of this debate, as should corporate leaders, who must constantly peer into the future, scanning the horizon for the next technological breakthrough.

Investing in Education and Training. We bemoan the fact that American students seem to be failing, the further along in school they go. But we have not invested sufficiently in children when they are very young. By kindergarten, many children already have learning deficits that the public schools cannot redress. Having the federal government underwrite one or even two years of preschool for all children would likely have a massive impact on both long-term growth and equity. The federal government has never been responsible for more than 5 percent of total elementary and secondary education spending in the nation.[3] It could certainly afford more. Indeed, many of our major competitors, including Switzerland, Sweden, Norway, Japan, Denmark, Austria, West Germany, and Canada, spend more per student (through grade 12) than the United States; all of those countries, as well as Belgium, France, the Netherlands, England, and Italy, spend a higher percentage of per capita income on their schools.[4]

The federal government could also do more to help bring college education within the reach of more Americans. In 1997 only 26 percent of the workforce had at least a four-year college degree, while 65 percent had no more than a high school degree. Part of the reason more adults do not pursue college is the extraordinary cost and the often punishing debt burden students face after leaving school. On average, public university students graduate $12,000 in debt; private university students face more than $14,000 in loan repayments on average, and the number can go much higher than that.[5]

One very good application of the projected federal budget surplus would be to use it to capitalize an income-contingent postsecondary school loan program. Students would borrow money from the program and then repay the government through additional remittances to the IRS, with annual repayments pegged to current earnings. Students just coming out of school would have lower loan payments. As a borrower's earnings rose, the rate of repayment would remain the same, but the size of the annual repayment would increase in line with income. This would eliminate the often onerous payments that young workers face. At the same time, it would provide a form of loan repayment insurance, since in any year when a worker suffered an interruption in income, the required payment that year would fall accordingly. In so doing, this program would alleviate the fear of borrowing for college and thus would encourage a higher college attendance rate.

With more young people continuing their education beyond high school, and more adults investing in "lifelong learning," the nation's economic growth rate would increase. Indeed, if the income-contingent loan repayments were placed into the Social Security Trust Fund, this would end the fund's insolvency problem more surely than putting part of the federal surplus into the stock market, as the White House has urged. Such a loan program would create an intergenerational alliance between young people and retirees.

To be sure, there are some small positive blips on the screen regarding government investment. For example, a consortium of private corporations, universities, and state and local government agencies in Southern California has been laboring for years to develop a cost-effective and efficient electric vehicle, in order to reduce dependence on petroleum and improve air quality in the region. Both the Bush and Clinton administrations have supported this effort particularly through the consortium CAL-START.[6] In his 1998 budget request to Congress, President Clinton called for a five-year, $6.3 billion package of tax incentives and R&D expenditures devoted to developing fuel-efficient automobiles, including, but not limited to, the electric car and the associated fuel cell technology.[7] This is an exciting and sensible use of public revenues, especially as it realistically acknowledges that success or failure will ultimately depend on how committed the *private* sector becomes to these new technologies.

In the field of education, President Clinton has called for the construction of 100,000 new classrooms and for tax credits so that more Americans could afford community college. Vice President Gore has led the movement to wire every classroom to the Internet. Alas, for every bright prospect such as these, there are far too many examples of the government turning its back on its responsibilities. Consider the country's sad record of systematic underinvestment in the Head Start program —

arguably the most cost-effective program for early childhood education ever conceived. As for elementary and secondary school reform, we really do know quite a lot about what is needed, from retrofitting classrooms for year-round use (for example, with air conditioning) to making schools more easily available for late afternoon and evening programs. The White House has argued for more money for such programs, but the political commitment to saving the surplus is so strong that the administration's rhetoric remains very much ahead of its action.

How much of what government spends in these and other areas should be considered consumption and how much counted as public investment is admittedly fuzzy, and open to seemingly endless ideological, as well as technical, debate. The reason is that the federal government has no capital budget, unlike virtually all businesses, most households, nearly all U.S. states, and most foreign governments. As such, the federal government counts a mile of new road or an investment in medical research — both of which have long-term payoffs — as though they were equivalent to current expenditures for running tours of the White House or for operating the printing presses at the Treasury Department. This must be changed. The introduction of a federal capital budget is an organizational reform whose time has come. Most important, we should fund that capital budget at levels closer to what we did when growth was much slower and government spending was, in reality, considerably less affordable. This is the surest way for government to play its appropriate role in maintaining high levels of private sector productivity growth.

Republicans in Congress have been even less helpful than the White House in this regard. They not only favor running enormous surpluses, but would also give back a large share of future revenues in the form of tax cuts. This despite the fact that effective tax rates are lower than they have been in decades, even after taking into account the rise in payroll taxes to pay for Social Security and Medicare.[8]

The Labor Market and Economic Growth

Future economic growth depends on high levels of productivity growth, but it also depends on a sufficient supply of labor. In our alternative account of how economic growth accelerated in the 1990s and why — with appropriate policies — it can continue, we paid a lot of attention to the unexpected increase in labor effort. Many already employed people worked longer hours, and more people entered the workforce than anyone had predicted. But that cannot go on forever, say the critics. According to some projections, labor force growth will continue to slow in the new century and could reach zero by 2013, as baby boomers begin to retire faster than the baby bust generation replaces them in the workplace.[9] At this point, all growth would be based on productivity improvement alone.

What are the chances that this demographic transition will be less dramatic, and how might government help to ensure an adequate supply of labor? We know that labor force participation rates and hours of work are related to education level. If we invested more in education and raised the proportion of the workforce with postsecondary schooling, the amount of labor supply would increase almost automatically. Moreover, in 1996 there were 18 million Americans aged 65 to 74 who were neither in hospitals nor in nursing homes. Of these, only 3 million worked.[10] Do we expect this number to decline even further? Clearly, those who wish to retire fully should have this right after a lifetime of work. But many now see 65 as just another birthday. For them, continued involvement in the labor force is something to be desired.

Boosting Labor Supply. The fact is, the pace of economic growth itself affects labor force participation. We noted in an earlier chapter that as the GDP growth rate picked up in the late 1990s and unemployment plunged into the low 4 percent range, economic commentators kept worrying that we would soon run out of workers, and the result would be an explosion in wage inflation. What kept this from happening is that as wages rose and jobs became more plentiful, huge numbers of people were drawn into the labor force, and experienced workers decided to take on added work for added pay. Thus, demand created its own supply. Economic growth itself brings forth the labor force to produce the added output that faster economic growth implies.

Slower growth throws this benign growth cycle into reverse. In a slow-growth economy, seniors compete directly with younger workers for available jobs — and often lose out. Discouraged by their prospects, they drop out of the labor force. That is what happened in the 1980s and 1990s. In 1970 nearly four out of ten persons aged 55 and above were actively working or looking for work. By 1990 the proportion had fallen to under three in ten.[11] But with the right education and training policies — and a real commitment to more rapid, sustained economic growth — labor force participation can still rise further. Continued reductions in the Social Security penalty imposed on those working beyond 65 can help reduce the disincentive to work for seniors who wish to maintain their attachment to the labor force.

Boosting Wages and Benefits. The Wall Street model has a strong preference for wage restraint. After all, if employers are forced to raise their wages and benefits, they might pass along their higher costs to consumers in the form of higher prices. If enough employers do this, the result is inflation, and this, according to the model, undermines economic growth.

The Main Street model sees wage growth in a very different light. Rising wages actually have a positive impact on growth, benefiting both the supply side and the demand side of the market. On the supply side, higher wages give managers an incentive to work harder at improving productivity. This is at least part of the reason why productivity increases have been fastest in the manufacturing sector, where wages tend to be higher. Productivity growth has been slowest in the low-skill service and retail trade sectors, where wages are notoriously low. As we noted in an earlier chapter, this dichotomy in productivity growth rates is not nearly as prominent in Europe, where wage differentials between sectors of the economy tend to be much smaller. So rising wages can boost growth by increasing economic efficiency.

On the demand side, improved wages and greater job security permit families to consume more, which helps generate the aggregate demand that turns potential growth into actual output. Moreover, the very expectation of faster growth generates incentives for additional rounds of business investment and technological innovation. So higher wages are actually good for business. Indeed, most business leaders would like to see higher wages — at every company save their own. In such a world, there would be increased demand for their products without an increase in their cost of production.

Recall that during the postwar glory days, wages rose rapidly to a great extent because of the spread of trade unionism. Collective bargaining agreements did more than boost earnings; the spread of such job benefits as health insurance and company-paid pensions also created a tangible sense of income security, reinforced by union seniority rules and grievance machinery. What followed was a sustained consumer boom and the self-fulfilling dynamic of faster growth. As unions became weaker in the 1970s, wage growth virtually stopped, and the economy slowed down. It was not rising wages that killed off prosperity, but falling wages.

The Main Street model recognizes this lesson. Chief among its policy prescriptions are the strengthening of unions, increases in the minimum wage, the expansion of the Earned Income Tax Credit, and the rejection of those elements of welfare reform that force single parents into the job market with little regard for their skill levels or the state of the local economy. Proponents of the Wall Street model either reject the lessons of this history outright or, more usually, argue that what might have worked in the 1950s and 1960s is dangerously out of date in the twenty-first century. Not so, according to the Main Street model.

To reverse the decline in trade union membership will take a new approach to organizing and representing workers in the new millennium. Professional and technical workers do not want to be hemmed in by the bureaucratic rules that unions often insist upon in traditional workplace contracts, nor do they usually want to work in an adversarial environment. What they want is a greater say in how their firms are managed. If unions are to succeed in gaining adherents within the booming ranks of high-skilled workers, they will have to adopt wholly new approaches to addressing these needs.[12]

Government has a role to play as well. Under the complex rules of engagement between labor and management, first codified in the Wagner Act of 1935, companies have been able to disrupt union organizing drives by stringing out the process of union certification elections and then refusing to negotiate first contracts with the unions that prove successful in organizing their workers. Many businesses employ batteries of lawyers to turn the procedures outlined in the generally pro-union Wagner Act against the very workers the act was designed to help.

Labor law reform could help level the playing field between unions and companies. When it comes to union recognition elections, the government could amend the Wagner Act to sharply restrict the length of time between when a union begins an organizing drive and when the National Labor Relations Board (NLRB) holds a representation election. According to labor law experts, this would reduce "the time and temptation for employers to use illegitimate tactics to intimidate their employees."[13] Permitting interim injunctions in claims of unfair labor practices would also help, since delays in NLRB adjudication sometimes add years to an organizing drive. By the time the case is legally resolved, the union has often had to give up its drive for lack of resources. The company may lose in court and still win what it set out to achieve, remaining union-free. Whatever fines it must face — or the forced rehiring of fired union organizers — are usually considered by management a small price to pay.

Regularly increasing the federal minimum wage was another way that the government helped encourage faster economic growth and greater equity during the post–World War II boom years. Between 1950 and 1991, Congress raised the wage floor fourteen times. The real value of the minimum wage reached its peak in 1968, when, at $1.60 per hour, it represented, on a full-year, full-time basis, 118 percent of the poverty wage for a family of three. Since then, the real value of the wage floor has fallen, even after the statutory increase to $5.15 in 1996.[14]

To maintain the value of the minimum wage, the federal government could index it, tying its level to increases in the average hourly wage in the economy as a whole. That way, workers in minimum-wage jobs would be assured at least a modest increase in pay every year.

Along with indexing the minimum wage, the government should continue to increase the value of the Earned Income Tax Credit (EITC). First enacted in 1975, the EITC is a refundable wage subsidy tax credit aimed directly at helping poor working families with children. Being refundable, it has aspects of a negative income tax. If the credit due a family is greater than its federal tax liability, the IRS remits the balance to the family. Today, this program adds over $29 billion of spending power to low-wage workers or those with intermittent work throughout the year. This is $29 billion with a big multiplier. Since low-wage workers are unlikely to save much of their earnings, nearly every dollar finds its way back into the income stream almost immediately, helping to maintain aggregate demand.[15] Expanding the EITC to cover working couples and individuals without children would enhance the ability of the EITC to prop up the spending power of low-wage workers. Through such measures, we could begin to create the kind of earnings and income security at the bottom of the labor market that has eluded these workers for so long. This would help not only the workers affected, but also the economy as a whole.

Redressing some of the injury caused by recent welfare reforms would also help move the economy forward. Under the Personal Responsibility and Work Opportunity Reconciliation Act of 1996, initiated by President Clinton, the welfare system was restructured to impose stiff work requirements on aid recipients, including a five-year limit on the length of time that families can receive assistance. The intent may have been noble, and in an era of extremely tight labor markets, the results may have been generally benign. But when the economy periodically slows down, the added labor supply at the low end of the labor market will likely result in even lower wages. Increasing the minimum wage could offset this, but even more useful would be an injection of substantial funds to increase the skill level of welfare recipients so that they could bid for higher-wage jobs. Welfare recipients need more than just an injection of skills when they set out to work; they need ongoing "lifelong" training to upgrade their skills and earning potential.

The Wall Street model naturally looks askance at all of these policy initiatives, for they put upward pressure on wages. According to the Main Street model, however, these are precisely the kinds of measures that can maintain aggregate demand and feed the growth cycle. At the same time, since they are targeted to the least well-off in the labor force, they would exert a counterforce against income inequality.

Growth-Minded Federal Regulation at Home

In an era of free-market ideology, even some otherwise progressive politicians speak of across-the-board deregulation as a sine qua non for unleashing growth. In fact, the underlying forces that contribute to growth, especially innovative private investments and more productive workers, depend crucially on the right mix of government regulation. Richard Nelson and Paul Romer, two of the most important of the New Growth theorists, have carefully made the nuanced point that economic growth *requires* regulation — and getting the regulations right.[16]

Economists think conceptually about goods and services — including information and ideas — as falling into four possible categories, according to whether they can be characterized as *excludable* or not, and *rival* or not. A purely *private good* has two important qualities: In the short run, my consumption of such an inherently scarce good reduces the amount left for you to consume — the good is rival. Moreover, the good's producer owns the rights to making that good — it is excludable. I can, by law, prevent others from making exactly the same good through patent and copyright law. The Sony Trinitron computer monitor or the Hewlett-Packard inkjet printer are two of but millions of such examples.

The opposite case is called a *public good*. Nelson and Romer offer as an example the mathematical equations used to solve standard programming problems, such as recursive loops that perform repetitive operations like counting and adding. These rules can be copied by anyone out of a standard textbook or manual. They are *not* a scarce resource — my using them does not use them up, so they are nonrival. And the law does not allow either of us to exclude the other from using them, so they are nonexcludable.

Now consider a mixed case: Property laws sometimes allow many, or perhaps all possible, users to have access to the same resource, even when my consumption of that resource *does* reduce the amount left for you to enjoy. The good is rival, but because of a policy decision — or more often the lack of one — nonexcludable. The results can be disastrous. When government abandons its responsibility to regulate essentially rival goods like clean water, air, and urban space, we get pollution, resource exhaustion, overbuilding, and congestion. This is the world of "free riders." This is the "tragedy of the commons." In such cases, the government needs to regulate the production of such *negative externalities* by forbidding companies to unleash them on the environment or taxing the company that produces them so that the resources exist to clean them up. All but a handful of extreme free-market economists agree that the government has an important role to play in regulating the use of such rival but nonexcludable goods.

But there are also nonrival goods that need some protection from unauthorized use by others. Making an inherently nonexcludable good into an excludable good depends solely on government policy. Consider, as a prime example, genuinely new software — not just a repetitive routine but, say, an entire concept for making spreadsheets. Once the code is written, the routine can be used over and over again by anyone, making it essentially nonrival. But if that were how the intellectual property laws were written, it would never pay anyone to invest in the design and development of such innovative software. Some degree of regulation is necessary to protect the incentive for firms, research laboratories, and universities to invest in the production of what is essentially a nonrival good.

Exactly how much regulation is needed has become the major battleground for a domestic and international debate over intellectual property rights. Too much regulation can slow the diffusion of an innovation and thus retard the rate of economic growth. Not enough judicious regulation diminishes the incentive to invest in innovative activity in the first place. What to do?

The only practical answer is to think carefully when writing regulations in this slippery area. Generally, the more basic the concept, the weaker the property rights should probably be, in order to promote diffusion. The more concrete, commercial, and close to the customer the product — as in the case of software that one can buy off the shelf in a shrink-wrapped box — the stronger property rights should be. Only in this way can we ensure private profitability and thus encourage new investment in R&D.[17] The bottom line is that innovation actually *requires* a degree of regulation. This is not something one hears much of in Washington these days, anywhere along Pennsylvania Avenue.

Coping with the Globalization of Labor and Capital

In a global economy, we need more than just domestic regulation. The international movement of enterprise from one nation to another and the hypermobility of finance capital have become a universal source of anxiety. The Multilateral Agreement on Investment now being negotiated would further weaken countries' control over their domestic development plans, giving ever greater power to multinational corporations. What is needed is the creation of a *fair trade* regime and a new global economic architecture analogous to what the leading nations of the world developed at the end of World War II. Instead, we are getting a further devolution of power from individual governments to the private sector and growing international economic chaos. There are ways to counter this.

Taking Labor Rights and Standards Global. Economists never tire of debating whether or to what extent free trade affects the wages and labor standards of workers in one or another of the trading countries. Most mainstream economists have rather cavalierly concluded that globalization (in both trade and investment) has not brought much downward pressure on the wages of lower-skilled American workers. One noteworthy exception is Harvard's Dani Rodrik, otherwise very much the orthodox economist, who surprised his colleagues with the publication in 1997 of an argument that more open trade, regardless of whether the trading partners are rich or poor countries, reduces the domestic bargaining power of labor, possibly leading to lower wages or slower growth in wages.[18]

But even before Rodrik added theoretical rigor to their movement, workers' representatives in nearly all developed countries sought to establish international labor rights and labor standards, especially in poorer countries. The goal is to "bring up the bottom," raising the standards of living among workers in developing countries, while forestalling a race to the bottom in their own countries.

Unions have for years lobbied international organizations to enact labor rights and standards. In December 1996, 123 of the world's trading countries convened in Singapore for the first annual meeting of the new World Trade Organization (WTO). This was the new entity that was to continue the work of the General Agreement on Tariffs and Trade. Despite efforts by the French government and the Clinton administration, under pressure from the labor wing of the Democratic Party, the WTO delegates soundly defeated a proposal to include labor standards in the next round of negotiations. Everyone agreed that the International Labor Organization (ILO) was already doing a good job of worrying about labor standards and should be allowed to continue its work — even though the ILO has absolutely no enforcement power whatsoever.[19]

Principal opposition came from the delegates of the developing countries, led by Pakistan, India, and Malaysia. They feared that the developed countries were only trying to protect the relatively higher wages and workplace standards enjoyed by their own citizens. They saw the proposal to legislate global labor standards as a thinly veiled attempt to institutionalize protection against the exports of goods made in low-income countries — helping the workers in developed countries at the expense of those in the developing world.

The real question is whether the WTO could adopt something

stronger than existing protections (against slavery, forced labor, the suppression of unions, and the exploitation of child labor) without undermining the incentive for multinationals to invest in developing nations. Is it possible to institute some form of international labor rights and some minimum form of international standards regarding minimum wages, hours of work, health and safety, and benefits, without doing harm to poor countries?[20]

Answering this question involves making two distinctions: one between rights and standards, the other over different methods for setting standards. Many would agree that establishing enforceable international labor *rights* is a necessary condition for these rights to exist in any single country. In the new global economy with its enormous capital flows, there are no economic islands. If some countries permit the unregulated use of child labor or allow companies to unilaterally and brazenly shut out unions, then it becomes more difficult for other countries to enforce their own child labor laws or encourage union organization. The same is true when it comes to environmental standards. Private companies can punish progressive countries by threatening to move their capital and their operations elsewhere. This will be true particularly in lower-wage manufacturing industries, but it increasingly applies also to a range of services, including low-level computer programming now done quite cheaply in countries like India and Pakistan. Developing ways to impose trade sanctions on countries that refuse to enforce regulations against child labor, prison labor, and slave labor, or that deny workers the basic democratic right to join trade unions, is one direction such policy might take.[21]

The question of labor *standards* is much tougher. For example, setting a fixed minimum wage applicable to all countries clearly has the problem that countries are at very different levels of development. The $5.15 minimum wage in the United States is arguably too low; such a level in Thailand would bankrupt most businesses. One way to avoid this problem is to have the WTO set minimums for wages, health and safety standards, and employee benefits tied to the level of per capita income in each country. As per capita income grows, the standards increase. Another approach is to tie minimum wage increases, not to an absolute level, but to improvements in the measured productivity of a nation. For example, as U.S. companies have placed modern factories in Mexico, the productivity of Mexican workers in those factories has soared. Their wages, however, have not kept pace with increases in productivity. Setting a standard that imposed no sanctions on the *level* of wages, but only when wages failed to rise with productivity, could solve this problem. Future trade agreements could also be drawn up so that the speed of tariff reduction was tied not to a fixed timetable spread over many years, as is the case for NAFTA, but conditioned on the rate at which wage growth converged with productivity growth. There is, of course, always the problem of measurement, but presumably WTO investigators and the ILO could produce statistics reliable enough to stand up in international court.

Short of getting new multilateral agreements through the WTO, some labor leaders continue to push for labor rights and standards language in new bilateral and regional trade compacts. Union veteran Lance Compa, now teaching at Cornell University, acknowledges the weakness of the original side agreements to NAFTA (formally, the North American Agreement on Labor Cooperation). Still, he argues that they can be looked upon more optimistically as a kind of "first draft," to be gradually redrawn in successive rounds of negotiation, first with other Latin American countries, then with the European Union, and eventually (and one hopes more successfully) back in the WTO. Such drafts build knowledge and experience in coalition-forming and can serve as instruments for focusing international scrutiny, public pressure, and embarrassment against blatant offenders. In this way, we would evolve over time a new international regime for enforcing labor rights in trade. "Such a succession of incremental advances," he writes, "is exactly what brought the European Union's social dimension to a reasonably high level over the past 40 years."[22]

Moral suasion using well-aimed disclosures of especially egregious violations of basic labor rights, at home and abroad, can be helpful. In the closing days of his stint as President Clinton's labor secretary, Robert Reich led a series of well-publicized exposés of sweatshops in Los Angeles and exposed the sweatshop contractors of such brand-name companies as Wal-Mart, Disney, and The Gap. This led to the "voluntary" creation of the Apparel Industry Partnership, in which codes of conduct, modeled on those adopted by companies doing business with the former apartheid regime in South Africa, are written by the companies themselves and imposed on their offshore suppliers.[23]

Negotiated arrangements of this sort do not, of course, preclude more traditional labor organizing. In Mexico, for example, auto companies from around the world have built assembly plants and are now encouraging their first-tier domestic suppliers to build branches on the Mexican border too. As more and more of the continent's auto production gravitates to Mexico, it will become increasingly imperative for unions to organize these *maquiladora* workers to bring their pay scale closer to U.S. levels. Such cross-border organizing drives are already underway, with Mexican and American unions cooperating to an unprecedented degree.[24]

Civilizing the Globalization of Capital. One of the central tenets of the Wall Street model is that America's economic rebound is premised on the development of financial institutions that permit the accumulation of huge stocks of capital and the totally unlimited free flow of this vital resource between industries, regions, and nations. Recall Deputy Treasury Secretary Larry Summers's insight that finance capital now represents the very wheels of the international economy, not merely the oil that keeps the wheels turning.

To be sure, the raising of huge sums of investment capital and the ability to direct these resources to new business ventures is crucial to economic growth. But we have learned that when capital flows turn "hypermobile," constructive financial institutions can turn destructive. Virtually instantaneous capital inflows into an enterprise can help it grow quickly, as we have seen with the almost overnight creation of enormous enterprises like America Online, Netscape, and Amazon.com. Yet the same institutions that direct huge amounts of capital to a new start-up venture can just as instantaneously lead a retreat of funds, creating enormous economic instability. We see this when it comes to individual companies. If Wall Street decides a firm has not met its profit targets, it can punish that company's stock in a matter of minutes on the New York Stock Exchange or Nasdaq, forcing the company to take extreme measures to get back in the good graces of investors. Many a company has announced huge layoffs of employees, simply to signal to Wall Street that it is willing to take draconian action to become "lean and mean" to meet the Street's profit expectations.

What is true for individual firms is equally true for entire nations, as we saw with the meltdown of Southeast Asian economies in 1998. When bankers and global currency speculators began to sour on the economic prospects of Indonesia, currency speculators bet against the country's currency and finance capital fled the area. While the political domino theory tragically led the United States deeper and deeper into the Vietnam War in the 1960s, its economic variant in the 1990s has proven more reliable. Within days speculators not only punished Indonesia but also attacked Thailand and South Korea before turning their attention to Latin America. As William Greider writes, "The Robespierre of this [speculative] revolution is finance capital. Its principles are transparent and pure: maximizing the return on capital without regard to national identity or political and social consequences. Global finance collectively acts as the disinterested enforcer of these imperatives, like a Committee of Public Safety presiding over the Terror."[25]

By the fall of 1998, all but the most die-hard free-traders were acknowledging that unregulated cross-border finance — the globalization of the Wall Street model — was a dangerous menace to world economic stability and growth. While the experts disagreed on the relative merits and political feasibility of debt forgiveness, limited exchange rate controls, taxes on speculative transactions, and the creation of international bankruptcy procedures, there was widespread agreement that capital hypermobility was *not* necessarily leading to higher standards of living or rewarding good productivity performance. Instead, it was threatening to bring the entire world economic system crashing in upon itself.[26]

To rein in the hypermobility of finance capital, we must reregulate capital markets. To be sure, part of such a program of "civilizing" globalization will entail reforming and redirecting the key Bretton Woods organizations: the World Bank and especially the IMF. But literally returning to the old Bretton Woods system is neither possible nor desirable. After all, as Cambridge University economist John Eatwell reminds us, the Bretton Woods system was implicitly erected on the principle of the United States as global hegemon. It was governed by a system of fixed exchange rates, not by policy coordination among governments. It was never a multilateral system in the first place (which is why it broke down when the key currency — the dollar — was battered by speculators toward the end of the Vietnam War as the U.S. government attempted to enjoy both "guns and butter" without raising taxes to pay for them).[27] A "new Bretton Woods" will have to be, as Eatwell suggests, a genuine multilateral arrangement . . . dominated by the leaders of the world's three main currency blocks: Germany, Japan, and the United States. At the core of that new system should be a renewed commitment to securing the currency stability that is necessary to underwrite the coordinated international expansion needed to avert worldwide recession. The present largely ceremonial summits of the G7 would need to be replaced with meetings that actually deal with substantive issues. A permanent secretariat should be created with the skills and authority to manage the international payments system.[28]

Contrary to much casual observation, the power of nations to make policy has *not* been completely undone by globalization. Thus, believes Eatwell, "while the speculators may be able to borrow very large sums for short periods of time, the central banks, as the creators of currency, can, collectively, provide indefinitely large sums for just as long." Moreover, the very technological developments that have made finance hypermobile — the computer, the fax, the cell phone, and the Internet — actually facilitate monitoring speculative currency flows in the public interest. The fact that trading today is typically done by electronic transfer makes effective monitoring easier than ever before. Hence, with a set of international agreements, it would not be too difficult to link the legal right to trade to the requirement to accept appropriate monitoring. In this way, effective monitoring could be the starting point for more effective management of the global finance system.[29]

One of the specific ways to manage the global system more effectively would be to impose a "Tobin tax" on financial transactions.[30] Initially proposed by the Nobel economist James Tobin in his 1972 Janeway Lectures at Princeton, a small and presumably variable levy (Tobin originally suggested 0.2 percent) would be imposed on each individual international financial transaction in stock, bond, and foreign exchange markets. By raising transaction costs in this way, speculative excesses would be dampened. Those who trade most frequently would be penalized most heavily, which should make investments somewhat more "patient." The tax would accrue to the U.S. Treasury, which could put it to any number of uses (including assisting developing countries to restructure their outstanding debt.) Those who trade infrequently would hardly notice such a tax. Estimated revenues would depend on the extent to which any particular level of the tax limited short-term financial trade, in the same way that the size of tax revenues from new tobacco levies will be lower, the more effective the levy is at reducing smoking. But the chief purpose of the tax is not to generate revenues; it is to reduce the volume of speculative transactions.[31] The Tobin tax was never popular with the mainstream economics and policy communities, but it has become of increasing general interest in the context of the current wave of globalization.

In sum, there are policy designs and tools available to deal with the antigrowth aspects of globalized, hypermobile finance capital. It will take great leadership from the big powers, especially the United States, and an unprecedented degree of multilateral coordination and cooperation. What could emerge over time would be a new regime — a new system of governance — made up of elements of the Bretton Woods system plus a set of well-tuned taxes and regulations. It is fruitless and fanciful to imagine stopping globalization. We need and want continually expanding trade. But we also want to civilize the process.

Getting Private Business to Address the Main Street Agenda

Government, of course, cannot assure growth with equity all by itself. Most of the agenda must be carried out by private sector firms, where investments in technology are made and where productivity is enhanced. But government is not without some ability to encourage "high-road" behavior on the part of private enterprise.

One possibility for such encouragement was summarized in a 1996 proposal developed by Senator Jeff Bingaman of New Mexico.[32] The goal of the proposal was to provide incentives for corporate behavior consistent with boosting worker training and employment security, all in the name of increasing the nation's growth potential. Firms that demonstrated their understanding and commitment to these objectives would self-qualify for status as a "Business Allied With America's Working Families" — the so-called A-Corp firms.

A-Corp companies would be those that contribute more generously than others to a portable pension plan, that devote at least 2 percent of their payroll costs to investing in the education and training of their employees, and that subscribe to some sort of health plan covering all employees who had been with the firm at least three months. Such companies would also offer profit sharing, employee stock ownership, or some other form of gain sharing to encourage productivity enhancement, and would have a proven record of compliance with safety and health standards. In addition, they would agree to participate in national apprenticeship and school-to-work programs and demonstrate that at least half of their net R&D expenditures over some past period had been placed domestically rather than abroad.

The Bingaman plan would eliminate the existing corporate income tax entirely and replace it with a new business tax code with built-in incentives for "A-Corp" behavior. The proposed tax plan would also take some pressure off the payroll tax, reducing the current built-in bias to expand overtime hours rather than hire new workers. Whether or not Bingaman has the right public finance mechanism to accomplish these goals, it seems certain that if a critical mass of firms truly did follow such guidelines, we would be well on our way back to the high road. Rewarding such "best-practice" behavior is something the government can do — and in the process encourage higher private sector productivity and economic growth. Indeed, building a better partnership between the private and public sectors in all respects is critical to attaining the twin goals of faster growth more equitably shared.

Summing Up

All of these policy recommendations are put forward to initiate a debate over America's future. In this book, we hope we have given some reason for optimism about the long-term potential for faster growth and greater equity in America, while at the same time exploring how our own federal government (as well as foreign ones) may be following short-term policies that sabotage this potential. Overly cautious monetary policies; fiscal policies that shortchange R&D, infrastructure investment, education, and training; and the neglect or active undermining of laws and regulations that could improve wages and labor standards have been at the center of the new Wall Street model. Rather than equipping people with the means and the institutional supports for coping with a world of hypermobile capital and chronic uncertainty about the future, government has been promoting the low road of ever more brutishly competitive capital and labor markets. The notion that this has contributed to prosperity rather than threatened its sustainability needs to be recognized for the illusion it is.

In considering these issues, we begin to understand the all-important role of expectations and how they are formed. In order for private business to continually invest in new capital, new technologies, and the training of its employees, and to be prepared to undertake major (and risky) reforms of management practices with respect to the organization of work and production, managers and stockholders must believe that the output created by the new equipment will actually be sold and that the costs of investing in the reforms will be recouped. Expectations matter. The prospect of more demand for its products produces the supply of investment and innovation needed to make that prospect come true. If government officials continue to signal that 2.3 percent growth is the most we can achieve, then that is what we are more than likely to get. That is, in forecasting a future of slow growth and "diminished expectations," the government could very well be creating a self-fulfilling prophecy.

In Paul Romer's view, when all agents are trained to expect slow growth, they will begin to act accordingly. Expecting low returns on investment, less investment will actually take place and future growth will thereby be compromised. If, on the other hand, businesses are encouraged to expect faster growth and believe that fiscal and monetary authorities will put in place policies to encourage it, investment will be higher and growth actually will be more rapid.[33] In this sense, growth is *path dependent*. If we choose to take the high road, we will get faster growth and more equality. If we settle for the low road, we doom ourselves to slower growth with greater inequality.

As for policy, the differences between the Wall Street model and the Main Street model could not be sharper, as Table 8.1 suggests.

Everything we have seen in this book suggests that faster growth is now within the realm of possibility, and that *only* with faster growth can we hope to reduce income inequality. The maturing of the information age is providing the key ingredient to a new era of faster growth. Changes in the labor supply regime are providing another. Now, if we can make sure that fiscal, monetary, and trade policies and labor regulation do not sabotage growth, we may be on the path back to the high road to long-term prosperity. If we choose wisely how to use that growth dividend, it

| Table 8.1. Wall Street Policies versus Main Street Policies ||
Wall Street Model	Main Street Model
Balance federal budget/build up surpluses.	Invest in R&D, infrastructure, and human capital.
Encourage unlimited free trade.	Establish fair trade based on labor rights and standards.
Maintain downward pressure on wages.	Foster rising wages.
Encourage employment insecurity.	Improve employment security.
Deregulate domestic markets.	Create incentives for corporate best-practice policies.
Impose conservative Federal Reserve policy.	Allow expansionary Federal Reserve policy.
Deregulate global markets.	Regulate global speculation.

will mean that we can raise living standards, reduce the gap between rich and poor, and help solve some of our most pressing social problems.

One final word. Who is the active agent, the "we" to whom these last paragraphs refer? Obviously the authors of this book plead for a more enlightened public policy. But history shows that policies are ultimately driven and shaped by mass movements of ordinary people and local activists. This pertains every bit as much to getting growth with equity back on the national agenda as it does to any other subject.

In an interview with *Washington Post* writer Steven Pearlstein, conducted back in the mid-1990s, Harvard economic historian Claudia Goldin reminds us that cycles of growth and stagnation are not new in the United States: "Like today, the 1890s were a time of relatively slow growth, as the economy went through the expensive and messy transition from the old to the new. By the outbreak of World War I, however, the economy had finally reached a new, more favorable equilibrium. Millions of Americans ascended to the middle class and inequality began a 50-year decline. Business competition was brisk and there was a burst of economic activity." But Goldin goes on to note that the early turn toward growth and equality occurred only *after* unions had forced the mines and railroads to share some of their profits, and government moved to regulate monopolies, child labor, worker safety, and the prices charged by natural monopolies. History shows, Goldin notes, that the imbalances are corrected only after people intervene to tame the market's worst excesses.[34]

So while economists and political leaders have embraced the private market as the answer to all our troubles and have put their faith in un-regulated financial institutions to bring us a new era of prosperity, our analysis points to the need to resurrect many of the "liberal" policies that have been discredited since the 1960s. Hard as it may be to win the political battles for a better balance between the private and public sectors, hard as it may be to redirect the White House and Congress to take more positive steps to speed up the growth process, hard as it may be to reject a model that seems to have worked, these are the things that need to be done. We need a new era of liberal political economy if we are to regain true prosperity, equitably shared.

Notes

1. Growth with Equity

1. See, for example, Stephen D. Oliner and William L. Wascher, "Is a Productivity Revolution under Way in the United States?" *Challenge*, November–December 1995.

2. Herman Kahn, *The Coming Boom* (New York: Simon & Schuster, 1982), p. 65.

3. The data on real gross domestic product (GDP) come from the Council of Economic Advisers, *Economic Report of the President* (Washington, D.C.: GPO, 1999) and Council of Economic Advisers, *Economic Indicators* (Washington, D.C.: GPO, April 1999).

4. The employment/population ratio in early 1998 was 64.2 percent, up from 58 percent in 1969 and 55 percent in 1949. See *Economic Report of the President* (Washington, D.C.: GPO, 1987), Table B-34, p. 284 and *Economic Indicators* (Washington, D.C.: GPO, April 1998), p. 11.

5. See Jared Bernstein, "Real Median Wages Finally Recover 1989 Level," *Quarterly Wage and Employment Series* (Economic Policy Institute), vol. 1, no. 1 (First Quarter 1999).

6. See Alejandro Bodipo-Memba, "Consumer Confidence Hits 32-Year High," *Wall Street Journal*, February 24, 1999, p. A2.

7. As John Kenneth Galbraith tells us, even Ronald Reagan was a great Keynesian, spending hundreds of billions of dollars on defense and in the process raising the nation's growth rate. See John Kenneth Galbraith, *Name-Dropping* (Boston: Houghton Mifflin, 1999).

8. The iconoclastic conservative commentator Kevin Phillips recounts the conversion of President Clinton to the new model of growth. In *Arrogant Capital* (Boston: Back Bay Books, 1994), pp. 120–121, he writes, "Clinton had won the White House in 1992 as an outsider running on a relatively populist platform, including campaign speeches that used Wall Street and the University of Pennsylvania's Wharton School of Finance as backdrops for criticism of the financial elites for the greed and speculation of the 1980s. No one can be sure how much of it he meant. But even before the man from Arkansas was inaugurated, it was clear that strategists from the financial sector, more than most other Washington lobbyists, had managed the Bush-to-Clinton transition without missing a stroke. Well-connected Democratic financiers stepped easily into the alligator loafers of departing Republicans. The accusatory rhetoric of the campaign dried up. The head of Clinton's new National Economic Council, Robert Rubin, turned out to have spent the 1980s as an arbitrageur for Goldman Sachs. The unpurgable Washington

was now being joined by part of what was beginning to look like an equally unpurgable Wall Street."

9. Quoted in Alan Murray, "Asia's Financial Foibles Make American Way Look Like a Winner," *Wall Street Journal,* December 8, 1997, p. A1.

10. On Jack Kemp's ambitions for the U.S. economy, see David E. Sanger, "New Analysis: Stressing the Differences — Economy and Diagnoses," *New York Times,* October 11, 1996, p. A1.

11. See Jerry J. Jasinowski, "The Case for Higher Growth: Technology, Disinflation and New Economic Policies," Manufacturing Institute, National Association of Manufacturing, Washington, D.C., July 1996.

12. The young economics editor of *Business Week,* Michael Mandel, has been responsible for the *Business Week* "line" on growth. The first cover story in a long string of such articles asked "Why Are We So Afraid of Growth?" It appeared in May 1994. The key point of this article was that faster growth was not only possible but in the immediate offing because of a wave of productivity-enhancing innovations and the role that global competition was playing in keeping prices down. The latest article in this series appearing before our book went into production focused on "The 21st-Century Economy." It suggested that market volatility is here to stay, but technology and globalization will spur robust growth. See Christopher Farrell and Michael Mandel, "Why Are We So Afraid of Growth?" *Business Week,* May 16, 1994, and Michael Mandel, "The 21st-Century Economy," *Business Week,* August 24–31, 1998. See also Christopher Farrell and Michael Mandel, "Productivity to the Rescue," *Business Week,* October 9, 1995; Stephen B. Shepard, "The New Economy: What It Really Means," *Business Week,* November 17, 1997; and Michael Mandel, *The High-Risk Society* (New York: Times Business Books, 1996).

13. See Bob Davis and David Wessel, *Prosperity: The Coming 20-Year Boom and What It Means to You* (New York: Times Business Books, 1998).

14. *Economic Report of the President* (1999), Table 2.3, p. 85.

15. See Alan Blinder, "Can We Grow Faster?" *Challenge,* November–December 1996, p. 8.

16. The Social Security Administration forecasters continued to predict economic calamity for the public pension system based on an even more pessimistic forecast of less than 2.0 percent growth rates during the first decade of the new millennium and even lower rates thereafter. See Social Security Trustees, OASHDI, *Annual Report of the Board of Trustees of the Old-Age and Survivors Insurance and Disabilities Insurance Trust Funds* (Washington, D.C.: GPO, 1995). According to the trustees, the U.S. economy will grow at an average GDP growth rate of only 1.49 percent between 1997 and 2070.

17. These growth rates are based on a combination of data sources. The data for 1800–1840 are found in Paul David, "The Growth of Real Product in the United States before 1840: New Evidence, Controlled Conjectures," *Journal of Economic History,* vol. 27, no. 2 (June 1967), Table 8, p. 184. The data for 1840–1870 are derived from decennial rates of growth of GNP as reported in Robert E. Gallman, "Gross Na-

tional Product in the United States, 1834–1909," in *Output, Employment, and Productivity in the United States after 1800*, ed. Dorothy S. Brady, *Studies in Income and Wealth*, vol. 30 (New York: National Bureau of Economic Research, 1966), Table 2, p. 9. The data for 1870–1929 are derived from Angus Maddison, "Growth and Slowdown in Advanced Capitalist Economies," *Journal of Economic Literature*, vol. 25, no. 2 (June 1987): Table A-1, p. 682. The data for 1929–1959 are calculated from *Economic Report of the President* (1987), Table B-2, p. 246. Finally, the data for after 1959 are calculated from *Economic Report of the President* (1996), Table B-2, p. 282.

18. Stanford University's Paul Romer provides an interesting example of the power of compound growth rates. He notes what would happen if a banker placed one penny on the first square of a chess board, two pennies on the second square, four on the third, etc. "If the banker had asked that only the white squares be used, the initial penny would double in value thirty-one times, leaving $21.5 million on the last square. Using both the black and white squares makes the penny grow to $92,000,000 billion." See Paul Romer, "Economic Growth," in *The Fortune Encyclopedia of Economics*, ed. David R. Henderson (New York: Warner Books, 1996.)

19. It is noteworthy that just one additional year of 3.9 percent GDP growth (in 1998) caused the actuaries at the Social Security Administration to extend the date of Medicare trust fund bankruptcy by seven years, to 2015, and postpone the likely bankruptcy of the Social Security Trust Fund by an estimated two years, to 2034. See Joanne Keene, "Social Security, Medicare Bankruptcy Delayed," Reuters News Service, March 30, 1999.

20. For a good summary of this issue, see Barry Bluestone, "The Inequality Express," *American Prospect*, November 1994.

21. On the other hand, if we look only at the median annual earnings from longest job held of those who worked year-round and full-time — what we (and the BLS) have on other occasions called the "elite" of the work force — we see that, for men, they continued to fall through 1996 and yet are still well below their post–World War II peak back in 1973. For YRFT women, their steady growth in earnings going back to the 1950s hit a ceiling in 1990, and earnings have bounced along that ceiling throughout the 1990s. It appears, then, that improvements in income from working have resulted mainly from people working more hours (or more jobs), rather than from rising hourly rates of pay per se.

22. Bernstein, "Real Median Wages."

23. Taking into account the cash value of such income transfers as food stamps and employer contributions to health insurance, and of the net effect of taxes on household incomes, in 1996 a "fully adjusted" definition of income shows less absolute inequality (as measured by the Gini) — fully 11 percent less — than is indicated with a pretax, pretransfer definition of income. Noncash benefits account for most of the improvement — as they were intended by past Congresses and presidents to do. But there is no indication that such adjustments have affected the *trend* in inequality over time, which is our major concern here.

24. A recent study of the Boston economy is relevant to this story. Boston has for

years had one of the fastest growing local economies and one of the tightest labor markets in the country. Under these conditions, the rates of labor force participation for black and Hispanic men turn out to be every bit as high as for white men — something that is not true in cities with weaker economies. Even hourly wage differentials by race and ethnicity are reasonably modest. In other words, when the economy runs red-hot, the "ghetto" need not be "jobless," as it is often portrayed. See Barry Bluestone and Mary Stevenson, *Greater Boston in Transition: Race and Ethnicity in a Renaissance Region* (New York: Russell Sage, forthcoming). See especially chapter 8, "The Greater Boston Labor Market: How Workers with Limited Schooling are Faring in Boston."

25. Alan Greenspan, Testimony before the Joint Economic Committee, U.S. Congress, June 10, 1998.

26. According to Robert Reich, the Third Way has no formal statement of principles, but several common ideas lie at its core. These include: privatization of public enterprises, the fostering of unbridled global trade and investment, "flexible" labor markets, the necessity of trimming social safety nets, and the requirement of slashing budget deficits. See Robert Reich, "We Are All Third Wayers Now," *American Prospect,* March–April 1999. For a British interpretation of the Third Way, see "Goldilocks Politics," *Economist,* December 19, 1998, pp. 73–75.

27. We might add that another link in the Wall Street model's virtuous cycle might also be questioned. According to the model, low interest rates — the legacy of price stability — are responsible for the explosion in stock market valuations. But new research suggests that the stock market might have reached new highs for a very different reason: simple demographics. With the baby boom generation reaching prime age in the 1990s, one would expect a torrent of investment in the stock market, and that is what we got. Boomers are behind the massive expansion in pension fund assets, which doubled to $5.2 trillion in 1999 from its 1992 level. Over the next five years, boomers are expected to account for $9 trillion of the $10 trillion growth in total investment funds. See Kimberly Blanton, "Baby Boomers Index," *Boston Globe,* April 23, 1999, p. E1.

28. See Richard Nelson, *The Sources of Economic Growth* (Cambridge, Mass.: Harvard University Press, 1996); and Nathan Rosenberg and L. E. Birdzell, Jr., *How the West Grew Rich: The Economic Transformation of the Industrial World* (New York: Basic Books, 1986).

29. See Barry Bluestone, Peter Jordan, and Mark Sullivan, *Aircraft Industry Dynamics: An Analysis of Competition, Capital, and Labor* (Boston: Auburn House, 1981); and Randy Barber and Robert E. Scott, *Jobs on the Wing: Trading Away the Future of the U.S. Aerospace Industry* (Washington, D.C.: Economic Policy Institute, 1995).

30. See Andrei Cherny, "A 21st-Century Growth Agenda," *New Democrat Blueprint,* vol. 2 (Winter 1998), p. 30.

31. Paul Romer, "The Origins of Endogenous Growth," *Journal of Economic Perspectives,* vol. 8 (Winter 1994), pp. 20–21.

32. A good example of this dynamic is found in the steel industry. By late 1998,

the demand for steel for highway construction exceeded supply. But steel fabricators were loath to invest in more capacity for fear that they were facing just a short-term peak demand problem. In this case, new investments were delayed and new innovative equipment was not introduced. Steel executives reported that they would be happy to invest in new capacity if there were some way to assure them of continued high demand for their products. See Kristen Hays, "Too Many Projects, Not Enough Steel," Associated Press, March 14, 1999.

33. Burton G. Malkiel, "Wall Street Moves Main Street," *Wall Street Journal*, June 23, 1998, p. A20.

34. Louis Uchitelle, "Why America Won't Boom," *New York Times*, June 12, 1994, p. E1.

35. On this point, it is useful to heed the recent work of James K. Galbraith, *Created Unequal: The Crisis in American Pay* (New York: Century Fund, 1998).

36. See Barry Bluestone, "Who's Sabotaging Prosperity?" (paper prepared for the Conference on the Social Dimensions of Globalization, Instituto Europeo Di Studi Sociali, Rome, Italy, October 4–5, 1998).

37. See Alan Murray, "Clinton Plays to Aging Boomers," *Wall Street Journal*, March 29, 1999, p. A1.

38. See David Espo, "Congress Approves 2000 Budget Plan," Associated Press, May 25, 1999. Indeed, in pitching their budgets to the press, the Republicans and Democrats vied with each other over which party would set aside more money for Social Security and Medicare over the next fifteen years.

39. See John Carey, "U.S. Innovation Ain't What It Used to Be," *Business Week*, March 22, 1999, p. 6.

40. Stanley B. Greenberg, "Private Heroism and Public Purpose," *American Prospect*, September–October 1996.

41. See Mandel, *High-Risk Society*.

2. A History of American Growth

1. The 1996 projections are found in *Economic Report of the President* (1996), Table 2-2, p. 58. The 1998 projections are found in *Economic Report of the President* (1998), Table 2.5, p. 82.

2. The 1999 projections are found in *Economic Report of the President* (1999), Table 2.3, p. 85.

3. "Budget Aide Named by GOP Won't Stay On," *Boston Globe*, October 29, 1998, p. A11.

4. See Social Security Trustees, *Annual Report* (1995), and Dean Baker, "Saving Social Security with Stocks: The Promises Don't Add Up," in *Social Security Reform*, ed. Richard C. Leone and Greg Anrig, Jr., (New York: Century Fund Press, 1999), Table 1, p. 209.

5. According to Peter Dreier and Richard Rothstein, the January 1994 Southern California earthquake destroyed more than $15 billion in property, including 21,000 housing units. Damage to public schools in Los Angeles was valued at between $500

million and $700 million alone. In the months following the disaster, employment grew rapidly in the region. In the first three months, nearly 30,000 new jobs — most related to damage repair — were created. A conservative estimate by the Business Forecasting Project of UCLA's School of Management put employment gains at 20,000 new jobs in each quarter of the year following the quake. See Peter Dreier and Richard Rothstein, "Seismic Stimulus: The California Quake's Creative Destruction," *American Prospect,* Summer 1994.

6. The data for Figures 2.1 and 2.2 come from the sources listed in note 17, Chapter 1.

7. See Michael Elliott, *The Day Before Yesterday: Reconsidering America's Past, Recovering the Present* (New York: Simon & Schuster, 1996). See also Robert Samuelson, *The Good Life and Its Discontents* (Vancouver, Wash.: Vintage, 1996).

8. Rosenberg and Birdzell, *How the West Grew Rich,* p. 20.

9. Computed from *Economic Report of the President* (1989), Table B-2, p. 310.

10. For a well-documented account of the GI Bill and its economic impact, see Congressional Research Service, *Veterans' Education Assistance Programs,* Report no. 86-32 EPW (Washington, D.C.: Library of Congress, January 31, 1986).

11. The figures for highways and education were computed from *Economic Report of the President* (1989), Table B-83, p. 405.

12. For an enlightened discussion of this era, see Robert Kuttner, *The End of Laissez-Faire: Economics and National Purpose after the Cold War* (New York: Simon & Schuster, 1990).

13. The role of organized labor in the postwar boom is treated more extensively in Barry Bluestone and Irving Bluestone, *Negotiating the Future: A Labor Perspective on American Business* (New York: Basic Books, 1992).

14. *Economic Report of the President* (1987), Tables B-32 and B-34, pps. 282, 284.

15. Calculated from *Economic Report of the President* (1998), Table B-46, p. 335. Contrary to what many believe, state and local government has been responsible for almost 95 percent of the total growth in government employment since the end of World War II. Indeed, the number of federal government employees in 1996 was almost exactly identical to the number in 1969: 2.76 million.

16. The same calculus does not apply to government output because the accounting procedures used to measure it do not permit an estimate of public sector productivity growth. Since there is no market price for government services, there is no independent way to measure the monetary value of public sector productivity and therefore no way to measure its growth. All growth in the value of output is simply captured in the wages and salaries paid to public sector employees. Thus, while it might be possible to measure the increased efficiency of, say, garbage collection in terms of tons of trash collected per sanitation worker, there is no way to measure productivity across jobs or services. Public output is therefore simply measured as total hours of work by public sector employees multiplied by their average hourly cost.

17. Between 1949 and 1959, the overall civilian labor force participation rate rose by only 0.6 percentage points as labor force participation among men declined from 86.4 percent to 83.7 percent while female participation increased from 33.1 to 37.1 percent. At the same time, average weekly hours declined from 39.4 to 39.0. See *Economic Report of the President* (1987), Table B-34, p. 284.

18. We can represent this presentation mathematically. A simple production function can be expressed as $Y = f(K, L, N)$, where Y is the size of the wheat harvest, K refers to the amount of capital equipment used, L refers to the number of farm workers, and N is a measure of the land under cultivation. The little "f" out front can be translated as "is a function of", suggesting something about the nature of the technology and organizational form that combines the capital, labor, and land to yield wheat. Such a functional form makes *changes* in labor productivity (i.e., output per worker or Y/L) dependent on *changes* in the capital/labor ratio or K/L.

We can both simplify and at the same time complicate the basic model in order to take into account a number of key factors that go into the production function. First, for simplicity's sake, we can drop land as an input and only consider physical capital and labor. With the exception of commodities like the winter wheat we have been considering, this does not do too much damage to our overall analysis.

Next, consider that the quality of the labor used in production is not uniform and can be improved over time. Normally a skilled tool and die worker makes a larger contribution per hour to the total output of a manufacturing firm than an unskilled worker. Training unskilled workers therefore can raise labor's overall productivity. We can note this by adding the subscript hc to the labor term, allowing for improvements in the level of *human capital* embodied in the workforce. In the same way, the more technology embedded in a piece of capital equipment, the more productive it presumably can be. The steel output of a basic oxygen furnace (BOF) equipped with modern computer controls exceeds that of a similar BOF that relies on older-generation mechanical monitoring. We can denote the rate of *technological improvements* in physical capital by adding the subscript x to the K in the aggregate production function.

Finally, there is one more element we must add to our basic model. It has to do with what economists have called *disembodied technical change*. This is a catch-all term referring to any changes in technology that improve the overall efficiency of the firm through reorganization of existing inputs or the introduction of added knowledge to production that is not directly incorporated in either plant and equipment or the workforce. At one time this disembodied technical change was seen as costless, like manna from heaven. By convention, it is normally represented in production functions by the letter A with the subscript t referring to time. As we will see, a significant part of the growth controversy turns on this little term A_t.

Putting all of this together, and adding terms for the shares of capital and labor in the production process [ß and $(1-ß)$], yields the following expression:

$$Y = A_t \, (K_X{}^\beta L_{hc}{}^{(1-\beta)}).$$

While this concoction may look rather daunting to the nonmathematician, it is really quite straightforward given the preceding explanation for each term. Output (Y) is a function of capital as augmented by embodied technical change (K_X), labor as improved through human capital (L_{hc}), and a measure of disembodied technical change or organizational restructuring (A_t), where the shares of capital and labor in the production process are represented by β and $(1-\beta)$ respectively.

Measuring the labor input as we did before in terms of hours of work (H), this expression begins to provide a taxonomy for the critical variables we are after for constructing a reasonable explanation of economic growth. With the same mathematics we referred to in the simple formulation of growth near the beginning of this chapter (% ΔY = % $\Delta (Y/H)$ + % ΔH), we can explain all changes in output in a given industry or an entire nation in terms of (1) changes in the amount of basic labor used in production [ΔH] plus (2) changes in the productivity of those workers [$\Delta(Y/H)$], where labor productivity is now itself a function of available physical capital (K), embodied technical progress in that capital (x), improvements in human capital (hc), and the overall level of organizational or technical change that cannot be directly attributable to either capital or labor (At).

19. These books on growth accounting by Edward F. Denison include *The Sources of Economic Growth in the U.S.* (New York: Committee for Economic Development, 1962); *Accounting for Slower Economic Growth: The United States in the 1970s* (Washington, D.C.: Brookings Institution, 1979); and *Trends in American Economic Growth, 1929–1982* (Washington, D.C.: Brookings Institution, 1985).

20. Denison, *Accounting for Slower Economic Growth.*

21. In a separate table, Denison provides data on aggregate potential national income in the nonresidential business sector. These statistics take into account the contribution to growth of additional employment. According to his calculations, between 1948 and 1973, 15 percent of growth was due to "more work done" — a measure of the combined effects of the increased number of employees, a decline in hours worked per employee, and changes in the age and sex composition of the employed workforce. See Denison, *Trends in American Economic Growth,* p. 96.

22. These figures are calculated from Table 2.2 in Denison, *Accounting for Slower Economic Growth,* p. 9.

23. For the contributions of private fixed investment and government spending to GDP growth from 1954 to the present, see *Economic Report of the President* (1998), Chart 1.1., p. 20.

3. America's New Growth Potential

1. Maddison compares GDP growth for 1973–84 with 1950–73. For the United States, he calculates that growth rose 1.4 percent slower per year in the later period. Of this total decline in the growth rate, he could explain only 41 percent using fourteen variables ranging from labor and capital quantity to foreign-trade effects, the

OPEC-induced energy crisis, and increased regulation and crime. Thus, 59 percent was left to the residual, nearly identical to Denison's 60 percent. See Angus Maddison, "Growth and Slowdown in Advanced Capitalist Economies: Techniques of Quantitative Assessment," *Journal of Economic Literature*, vol. 25, no. 2 (June 1987), Table 22, p. 680.

2. According to Jorgenson, for the period 1948–79, the annual growth rate averaged 3.42 percent. During the subperiod 1973–79, the average growth rate was only 2.83 percent, a decline of 0.59 percent. By his own account, the contribution of capital input declined by only .12 percentage points per year between the two periods and the contribution of labor inputs was unchanged. By contrast, the decline in the rate of growth in total factor productivity was 0.47 percent or four-fifths of the decline in the growth rate of output. See Dale W. Jorgenson, "Productivity and Postwar U.S. Economic Growth," in *Productivity*, vol. 1, ed. Dale W. Jorgenson (Cambridge, Mass.: MIT Press, 1996), p. 11.

3. See, for example, John W. Kendrick, ed., *International Comparisons of Productivity and Causes of the Slowdown* (Washington, D.C.: American Enterprise Institute, 1984); John W. Kendrick, *The Formation and Stocks of Total Capital* (New York: National Bureau of Economic Research, 1976); Edwin Mansfield, "Social and Private Rates of Return from Industrial Innovations," *Quarterly Journal of Economics,* vol. 91 (May 1977); and Edwin Mansfield, "Technological Change and Market Structure: An Empirical Study," *American Economic Review,* vol. 73 (May 1983). Also, see Zvi Griliches, "R&D and the Productivity Slowdown," *American Economic Review,* vol. 70 (May 1980).

4. Denison, *Accounting for Slower Economic Growth*, p. 125.

5. See F. M. Scherer, "Technological Maturity and Waning Economic Growth," *Arts and Sciences* (Northwestern University) Fall 1978, pp. 7–11.

6. This rough estimate of the compliance time for dealing with government red tape was prepared by Denison based on Office of Management and the Budget, *Paperwork and Red Tape: New Perspectives — New Directions,* report to the president and Congress (Washington, D.C.: GPO, 1978).

7. The comments of Beryl W. Sprinkel are found in House Committee on Ways and Means, 95th Cong., 2d sess., *Tax Reductions — Economists, Comments on H.R. 8333 and S. 1860* (Washington, D.C.: GPO, 1978), p. 85.

8. See, for example, Seymour Melman, *The Permanent War Economy* (New York: Simon & Schuster, 1985) and Ann Markusen, "The Militarized Economy," *World Policy Journal,* vol. 3, no. 3 (Summer 1986).

9. See *Economic Report of the President* (1987), Table B-1, p. 244–45 and *Economic Report of the President* (1988), Table B-1, pp. 280–81.

10. See Herbert Stein, "Spending and Getting," in *Contemporary Economic Problems, 1977,* ed. William Fellner (Washington, D.C.: American Enterprise Institute, 1977).

11. In his own empirical work, Dale Jorgenson found that higher energy prices

were associated with the post-1973 decline in productivity in 29 of the 35 industries he studied. From this he concluded that the slowdown in sectoral productivity was "sufficient to explain the decline in U.S. economic growth." See Jorgenson, "Productivity and Postwar U.S. Economic Growth," p. 14.

12. See William J. Baumol, "Macroeconomics of Unbalanced Growth: The Anatomy of Urban Crisis," *American Economic Review*, vol. 57, no. 3 (June 1967).

13. For a good discussion of the possible impact of interindustry shifts on productivity, see Martin Neil Baily, *The Productivity Growth Slowdown by Industry*, Brookings Papers on Economic Activity no. 2 (1982): pp. 445–54; and Frank M. Gollop, "Analysis of the Productivity Slowdown: Evidence for a Sector-Biased or Sector-Neutral Industrial Strategy," in *Productivity Growth and U.S. Competitiveness*, ed. William J. Baumol and Kenneth McLennan (New York: Oxford University Press, 1985). This is not to say that the shift to services has not affected the level of median earnings or the distribution of income. Indeed, that case is made in Barry Bluestone, "The Great U-Turn Revisited: Economic Restructuring, Jobs, and the Redistribution of Earnings," in *Jobs, Earnings, and Employment Growth Policies in the United States*, ed. John D. Kasarda (Boston: Kluwer Academic Publishers, 1990).

14. Denison, *Accounting for Slower Economic Growth*, p. 145.

15. Ibid., p. 4.

16. Michael L. Dertouzos, Richard K. Lester, and Robert M. Solow, *Made in America* (Cambridge, Mass.: MIT Press, 1989).

17. Mancur Olson, *The Rise and Decline of Nations* (New Haven: Yale University Press, 1982), p. 4.

18. Mancur Olson, *The Logic of Collective Action* (Cambridge, Mass.: Harvard University Press, 1965).

19. The building trades are hardly alone in using government action to support the interests of its members. The state licensing of professionals — limiting competition among every one from doctors and dentists to hairdressers, embalmers, psychotherapists, and lawyers — is no different. The same can be said of corporate subsidies — sometimes dubbed "corporate welfare" — which can amount to nothing more than a thinly disguised income transfer to industry through tax breaks or regulation. The way political campaigns are financed, representatives are trapped supporting special-interest groups even when they know the general public is harmed. Moreover, the smaller the special-interest group, the larger the payoff to each member and the smaller the cost to every citizen — so even small special interest groups get their way.

20. So does a portion of the empirical work of Harvard economist Robert J. Barro, whose recent research also crosses over the line from economics to sociology and political science (see Robert J. Barro, "Determinants of Economic Growth: A Cross-Country Empirical Study," working paper no. 5698, National Bureau of Economic Research, August 1996.) An important question in growth theory is whether over time the growth rates in less developed countries "catch up" with the more developed countries. Using a panel of 100 nations followed over various periods be-

tween 1960 and 1990, Barro finds evidence to support the general notion of conditional convergence. Countries with a lower initial level of real per capital GDP tend, on average, to grow faster than countries that start out much richer. Part of this turns on the fact that the statistical relationship between economic growth and democracy appears to be "nonlinear." At low levels of political rights (as measured by an international index consisting of the extent to which adults have the right to vote, elected representatives have a decisive vote on public policies, and minority parties have influence on policy) all compiled by a team headed by Raymond Gastil of the Committees for a Community of Democracies, faster economic growth is associated with an expansion of these rights. However, once a moderate amount of democracy has been attained, a further expansion seems to retard growth (see Raymond D. Gastil, *Progress* [New York: Praeger, 1993]). Barro suggests a possible interpretation of this empirical result. "In extreme dictatorships," he writes, "an increase in political rights tends to raise growth rates because the limitation on governmental authority is critical. However, in places that have already achieved some political rights, further democratization may retard growth because of the heightened concern with social programs and income distribution." This is not unrelated to the concept of a "big trade-off" between efficiency and equity as developed in the work of liberal economist, Arthur Okun in the 1970s. See Arthur Okun, *Equality and Efficiency: The Big Trade-Off* (Washington, D.C.: Brookings Institution, 1975).

21. See Zvi Griliches, "Productivity, R&D, and the Data Constraint," *American Economic Review,* vol. 84 (March 1994), p.11.

22. Robert Gordon of Northwestern University comes to the same conclusion for different reasons. His argument is based on the idea that we have underestimated real productivity and real growth because we have overestimated the rate of inflation that we use to deflate nominal growth in order to come up with estimates of real growth. Until quite recently, for example, the official National Income and Product Accounts used fixed-weight bundles to measure price increases. Changes in consumption patterns (as when families substitute chicken for beef when beef prices rise) were ignored. This can lead to an overstatement of inflation and therefore an underestimate of real output. In addition, Gordon notes that it is widely recognized that the consumer price index (CPI) used for converting nominal output into real output fails to adjust adequately for improved quality in new products and new models — especially in services. For example, the CPI has missed such quality improvements as the higher resolution and flicker-free images in new color TVs, the longer lifetimes of many consumer products as the result of the use of corrosion-proof plastic in place of metal, and the reduced passenger discomfort of air travel once jet aircraft replaced the slower, noisier, more vibration-prone planes powered by piston-driven propellers. Added to these measurement problems, Gordon identifies a number of other issues that especially affect individual industries, including insurance, banking, and real estate, because of the difficulty in determining what to measure as output.

All told, Gordon concludes, there is good reason to believe we have enjoyed somewhat higher productivity growth than the officials statistics suggest. But this does not solve the productivity paradox or explain the slowdown in productivity after 1973, because these measurement problems affect the pre-1973 productivity statistics as well as the more recent ones. The productivity gap between the pre- and post-1973 periods still exists. See Robert J. Gordon, "Problems in the Measurement and Performance of Service-Sector Productivity in the United States," working paper no. 5519, National Bureau of Economic Research, Cambridge, Mass. March 1996.

We might also note that there are economists who believe we may now be *underestimating* the decline in productivity growth. Because of an erroneous downward adjustment made in the national output series in 1973, having to do with the way improvements in computers are counted, Larry Mishel has shown that productivity in manufacturing has probably been overstated in recent years, offsetting mismeasurement in the other direction. See Lawrence Mishel, *Manufacturing Numbers: How Inaccurate Statistics Conceal U.S. Industrial Decline* (Washington, D.C.: Economic Policy Institute, 1988).

23. According to Michael J. Mandel's analysis of data from the Bureau of Economic Analysis, the Federal Reserve, and the Mortgage Bankers Association, the official contribution of banks and nondepository institutions to real GDP was almost constant at $240 billion between 1990 and 1998. At the same time, outstanding consumer debt mushroomed from $875 billion to $1.2 trillion, the number of annual ATM transactions doubled from 5 to 10 billion, and the number of mortgage applications went up by a factor of five. See Michael J. Mandel, "Financial Services: The Silent Engine," *Business Week*, December 21, 1998, p. 76.

24. Mandel, "Financial Services."

25. In reworking the official Bureau of Labor Statistics productivity data, two Federal Reserve Board economists, L. Slifman and C. Corrado, have located what they believe is the source of the dismal productivity record in services. By arraying the data according to the *legal form* that enterprises take, they find that one particular sector of the economy is responsible for a disproportionate amount of the overall decline in labor productivity. This sector, which they call the nonfarm, noncorporate sector, consists primarily of sole proprietorships and partnerships. These are responsible for about a quarter of nonfarm business output in the United States.

While the nonfarm *corporate* sector has had reasonably steady productivity growth since the early 1960s — averaging between 1.6 percent and 1.8 percent per year — the nonfarm *noncorporate* sector has recorded *negative* productivity growth since 1973 (after a healthy 4.8 percent growth rate in the period 1960–73). When added to the corporate sector, the average productivity rate for the entire nonfarm business sector drops to the 0.9 percent we show in Figure 3.1.

Slifman and Corrado are highly skeptical of the noncorporate sector statistics. How can it be, they ask, that this sector could have remained so profitable (as proxied by proprietors' income plus rental income as a share of sector output) if it were undergoing a continuous decline in its productivity? They conclude the productivity data must be faulty. Measured output in these small nonincorporated enterprises may be badly underestimated by the Commerce Department. Alternatively, the data may reflect problems in measuring the prices of output used to obtain "real" estimates of productivity growth. Underestimated output and overinflated price indices could account for at least part of the apparent underwhelming productivity performance turned in by this sector. On such a basis, Fed Chairman Alan Greenspan feels confident that he can turn negative productivity numbers to zeros and come closer to the truth about overall productivity. Just doing this raises productivity growth for the 1990–96 period from 0.9 percent per year to 1.5 percent per year. See L. Slifman and C. Corrado, "Decomposition of Productivity and Unit Costs," *Occasional Staff Studies* (Federal Reserve Board), November 18, 1996.

26. The data on the speed of Intel microprocessors are reported in Otis Port, "The Silicon Age? It's Just the Beginning," *Business Week,* December 9, 1996, p. 150.

27. See Gary Loveman, "An Assessment of the Productivity Impact of Information Technologies," in *Information Technology and the Corporation of the 1990s: Research Studies,* ed. T. J. Allen and Scott Morton (Cambridge, Mass.: MIT Press, 1994).

28. See A. Barua, C. Kriebel, and T. Mukhopadhyay, "Information Technology and Business Value: An Analytic and Empirical Investigation," working paper, University of Texas at Austin, May 1991.

29. See C. J. Morrison and E. R. Berndt, "Assessing the Productivity of Information Technology Equipment in U.S. Manufacturing Industries," working paper, no. 3582, National Bureau of Economic Research, January 1990.

30. See Paul Attewell, "Information Technology and the Productivity Paradox," in *Organizational Linkages: Understanding the Productivity Paradox,* ed. Douglas H. Harris (Washington, D.C.: National Academy Press, 1994).

31. Stephen Roach, "Stop the Dice Rolling on Technology Spending," *Computerworld Extra,* June 20, 1988, p. 6, as quoted in Attewell, "Information Technology."

32. See Robert Franke, *Technology Revolution and Productivity Decline: The Case of U.S. Banks* (Cambridge, Mass.: MIT Press, 1989).

33. In one study, researchers found that writers composing on a word processor made five times as many modifications and corrections as those writing by hand. See S. K. Card, J. M. Robert, and L. N. Keenan, "On-Line Composition of Text" (Xerox Palo Alto Research Center, Stanford, Calif.), as noted in Attewell, "Information Technology").

34. See Paul Attewell, "Technology Diffusion and Organizational Learning," *Organization Science,* vol. 2, no. 4, (1992).

35. See Nathan Rosenberg, *Technology and American Economic Growth* (New York: Harper & Row, 1972), pp. 127–42.

36. The diffusion of hybrid seed corn gives an indication of the long lags that often accompany the introduction of a new technology. According to work by Harvard economist Zvi Griliches, hybrid seed corn was first planted in Iowa in 1933. Five years later, half of the total acreage in corn production in that state used the new seed varieties. It took another ten years for half of Kentucky farms to adopt the

new techniques and still another decade until half of the corn acreage in Alabama was planted with the new varieties. The delay in introducing the hybrid varieties accounts for some of the lag in farm productivity. See Zvi Griliches, "Hybrid Corn and the Economics of Innovation," *Science,* vol. 132, July 29, 1960.

37. See Paul David, "The Mechanization of Reaping in the Ante-Bellum Midwest," in *Industrialization in Two Systems: Essays in Honor of Alexander Gerschenkron,* ed. Henry Rosovsky (New York: John Wiley, 1966).

38. See A. Olmstead, "The Mechanization of Reaping and Mowing in American Agriculture, 1833–1870," *Journal of Economic History,* vol. 35 (June 1975).

39. The data on electric motor diffusion in manufacturing is found in Hans H. Landsberg and Sam H. Schurr, *Energy in the United States* (New York: Random House, 1968), pp. 52–53.

40. The study of the diffusion of electric motors in manufacturing is found in Paul A. David, "Computer and Dynamo: The Modern Productivity Paradox in a Not-too-Distant Mirror," *Technology and Productivity: The Challenge for Economic Policy* (Paris: OECD, 1991).

41. See Joel Mokyr, *The Lever of Riches: Technological Creativity and Economic Progress* (New York: Oxford University Press, 1990), p. 83.

42. The classic historical study of the steam engine is by David Landes, *The Unbound Prometheus: Technological Change and Industrial Development in Western Europe from 1750 to the Present* (London: Cambridge University Press, 1969).

43. See Rosenberg, *Technology and American Economic Growth,* pp. 85–86.

44. See Jeremy Greenwood, "The Third Industrial Revolution," (paper prepared for the American Enterprise Institute, October 25, 1996). For a more technical description of this work, see Jeremy Greenwood and Mehmet Yorukoglu, "1974," working paper no. 429, Rochester Center for Economic Research, University of Rochester, September 1996.

45. These data as reported in Greenwood appear in C. Knick Harley, "Reassessing the Industrial Revolution: A Macro View," in *The British Industrial Revolution: An Economic Perspective,* ed. Joel Mokyr (Boulder, Colo.: Westview Press, 1993), Table 3.5.

46. Greenwood obtained his U.S. antebellum productivity data from Moses Abramovitz and Paul David, "Reinterpreting Economic Growth: Parables and Realities," *American Economic Review,* vol. 63 (June 1973).

47. Greenwood's estimates of the U.S. antebellum skill premium come from J. G. Williamson and P. H. Lindert, *American Inequality: A Macroeconomic History* (New York: Academic Press, 1980).

48. See Kenneth Arrow, "The Economic Implications of Learning by Doing," *Review of Economic Studies,* June 1962.

49. Nathan Rosenberg mentions a number of such studies, including A. Alchian, "Reliability of Progress Curves in Airframe Production," *Econometrica,* vol. 24 (April 1956); Leonard Rapping, "Learning and World War II Production Functions," *Review of Economics and Statistics,* vol. 47 (February 1965); and Paul David, "Learning by

Doing and Tariff Protection," *Journal of Economic History,* vol. 30 (September 1970). See Nathan Rosenberg, *Inside the Black Box: Technology and Economics* (Cambridge: Cambridge University Press, 1982).

50. See Nathan Rosenberg, *Inside the Black Box: Technology and Economics* (Cambridge: Cambridge University Press, 1982), especially Chapter 6; and Nathan Rosenberg, "Technological Interdependence in the American Economy," *Technology and Culture,* January 1979.

51. Rosenberg, *Inside the Black Box,* p. 122.

52. See H. W. Bode, *Synergy: Technical Integration and Technological Innovation in the Bell System* (Murray Hill, N.J.: Bell Telephone Laboratories, 1971), p. 46, as noted in Rosenberg, *Inside the Black Box,* p. 138.

53. There have been some attempts at estimating the size of learning effects on productivity, and they turn out to be quite large. Paul David's study of the Lawrence no. 2 cotton mill is a classic example. Based on detailed inventory records of the Lowell, Massachusetts textile firm, no new machinery was added during the thirty-year period between 1836 and 1856. Yet output per hour increased by an average of 2.3 percent per year. Some of this increase was due to "speed-up" as mill owners forced employees to work faster and required each operator to monitor more and more looms. But it is hard to believe that workers who were already forced to work at a breakneck pace in 1836 were working twice as fast in 1856. Clearly, they were working not only faster, but in today's vernacular, "smarter." See Paul A. David, "The 'Horndal Effect' in Lowell, 1834–56: A Short-Run Learning Curve for Integrated Cotton Textile Mills," in *Technical Choice, Innovation, and Economic Growth: Essays on American and British Economic Experience,* ed. Paul A. David (London: Cambridge University Press, 1975).

Greenwood has reviewed studies of learning curves in more modern applications. What David found true in Lowell, Massachusetts textiles in the nineteenth century is apparently just as true when it comes to angioplasty surgery, flight control simulation, munitions manufacture, and steel finishing in the late twentieth. Greenwood cites B. Jovenovic and S. Lach, "Product Innovation and the Business Cycle," *International Economic Review* (forthcoming) for learning curve estimates in these fields. Such learning effects were found to be particularly strong in a recent study of information technologies in a sample of nearly 300 firms studied over the 1987–91 period. See Mehmet Yorukoglu, "The Information Technology Productivity Paradox," Department of Economics, University of Chicago, 1996.

54. See Jovenovic and Lach, "Product Innovation and the Business Cycle."

55. The statistics on steam and diesel locomotives are found in the *Historical Statistics of the U.S.,* as reported in Rosenberg, *Technology and American Economic Growth,* p. 160.

56. The recent work of Erik Brynjolfsson and Lorin M. Hitt can be found in "Paradox Lost? Firm-Level Evidence on the Returns to Information Systems Spending," *Management Science,* vol. 42, no. 4 (April 1996); "Information Technology as a

Factor of Production: The Role of Differences among Firms," *Economics of Innovation and New Technology,* vol. 3., no. 4 (1995); "Computers and Productivity Growth: Firm-Level Evidence," MIT Sloan School of Management, January 1997; and "Information Technology and Internal Firm Organization: An Exploratory Analysis," MIT Sloan School of Management, March 1997.

57. Lester Thurow, "Are Investments in Information Systems Paying Off?" *MIT Management Review,* Spring 1990; as quoted in Brynjolfsson and Hitt, "Paradox Lost?" p. 556.

58. See, for example, Richard Nelson and Sidney Winter, *An Evolutionary Theory of Economic Change* (Cambridge, Mass.: Harvard University Press, 1982); and Richard Nelson, "Capitalism as an Engine of Progress," in *The Sources of Economic Growth,* ed. Richard Nelson (Cambridge, Mass.: Harvard University Press, 1996). See also Maryellen Kelley's papers on technological diffusion and external learning, e.g., "Productivity and Information Technology: The Elusive Connection," *Management Science,* vol. 40 (November 1994); "New Process Technology, Job Design, and Work Organization," *American Sociological Review,* vol. 55 (April 1990); and Maryellen Kelley and Harvey Brooks, "External Learning Opportunities and the Diffusion of Process Innovations to Small Firms," *Technological Forecasting and Social Change,* vol. 39 (April 1991).

59. See Brynjolfsson and Hitt, "Information Technology and Internal Firm Organization," and Kelley, "Productivity and Information Technology."

60. The early work of Brynjolfsson and Hitt was criticized for failing to differentiate between the impact of IT on productivity and other activities of firms adopting the new technologies. Obviously, if those firms adopting new computer systems are also more likely to adopt other innovations, but these are not explicitly modeled, then the estimates of the unique contribution of computers will likely be overestimated. In later work, the two researchers take care to control for these other firm-level effects and conclude that their original results still stand up. In these latest estimates, they find that investments in computers in their sample of firms add between .25 and .50 percentage points to annual output and productivity. See Brynjolfsson and Hitt, "Computers and Productivity Growth."

61. See U.S. Department of Labor, Bureau of Labor Statistics, *Industry Productivity Statistics,* April 22, 1997, Table 1, Selected Industries: Employment and Annual Rates of Change in Output per Hour, Selected Periods.

62. See Council of Economic Advisers, *Economic Indicators* (Washington, D.C.: GPO, 1999), p. 3.

63. See *Economic Report of the President* (1998), Table 2-5, p. 82. More precisely, the official forecast for 1997: III through 2005 is based on a 1.1. percent annual increase in working hours plus a 1.3 percent increase in nonfarm business productivity minus 0.1 percent due to the fact that GDP also includes the farm and government sectors.

64. See Juliet Schor, *The Overworked American* (New York: Basic Books, 1991).

65. For more detail on hours worked, see Barry Bluestone and Stephen Rose,

"Overworked and Underemployed," *American Prospect,* March–April 1997. Bluestone and Rose's estimates appear to be quite robust. Using a different data source, Larry Mishel and Jared Bernstein of the Economic Policy Institute find almost exactly the same hours increase during the 1980s as Bluestone and Rose. For men and women combined, they report an increased annual work effort of 82 hours. See Lawrence Mishel and Jared Bernstein, *The State of Working America, 1994–95* (Armonk, N.Y.: M. E. Sharpe, 1994).

66. See Barry Bluestone and Stephen Rose, "The Unmeasured Labor Force," Public Policy Brief No. 39, Jerome Levy Economics Institute of Bard College, June 1998. Only those with a college degree or better made out well in this new world. Between 1973 and 1988, these dual-career families increased their annual work hours by 17 percent. In return, their already comfortable incomes rose by 32 percent. The highest-skilled workers in America opted for longer hours to enhance their careers and their incomes in an increasingly competitive labor market where the rewards flow disproportionately to the very few in any occupation who are truly outstanding or incredibly lucky. Economists Robert H. Frank and Philip J. Cook have described this new phenomenon as the "the winner-take-all society." See Robert H. Frank and Philip J. Cook, *The Winner-Take-All Society* (New York: Free Press, 1995).

67. From 1996 through 2000, this potential workforce population will grow by 1.08 percent per year compared with 1.13 percent during the 1980s. In the next century, our population will grow even slower, down to 1.01 percent per year from 2000 through 2005 and by only 0.88 percent for the five years ending in 2010. See U.S. Census Bureau, *Forecasts of the U.S. Population to 2050* (Washington, D.C.: GPO, 1997).

68. These participation rates are based on Current Population Survey (CPS) estimates and count as in the labor force anyone who participated at any time during the survey year. These numbers are slightly higher than conventionally measured labor force participation rates which measure participation for a single month (usually March or May) in each survey year.

69. Joseph F. Quinn and Richard V. Burkhauser, "Public Policy and the Plans and Preferences of Older Americans," *Journal of Aging and Social Policy,* 6, no. 3, (1994), p. 6.

70. For those aged 65–69, benefits are now reduced by only one-third of their earnings in excess of the exempt amount, rather than the one-half that applied before 1990.

71. See Scott A. Bass, Joseph F. Quinn, and Richard V. Burkhauser, "Toward Pro-Work Policies and Programs for Older Americans," in *Older and Active: How Americans over 55 Are Contributing to Society,* ed. Scott A. Bass (New Haven: Yale University Press, 1995).

72. For the simple definition of Okun's law, see *The MIT Dictionary of Modern Economics,* 4th edition, ed. David W. Pearce (Cambridge, Mass.: MIT Press, 1992).

73. While the inverse relationship between changes in output and the official unemployment rate still holds as Okun demonstrated, the value of the relation-

ship has declined since he first estimated it in the early 1960s. Reestimating the un-employment-output relationship with more recent data, we find a value closer to 2.0 than 3.0, suggesting that the welfare costs of an additional point in the unemployment rate is lower today than in the 1960s. When we use data on real GDP and the all-civilian unemployment rate for 1948–60 and apply Okun's statistical formulation $dLnGDP = a_0 + b_1 dUR.$, we obtain exactly the same result as Okun: 3.0. However, reestimating the relationship with more recent data suggests that Okun's "law" does not provide a fixed "speed limit" on how much growth we can get from additional labor. The value of Okun's law from 1948 to 1960 was 3.0; from 1948 to 1973, 2.7; from 1948 to 1978, 2.5; from 1948 to 1995, 2.2; from 1979 to 1995, 1.8. It is still costly to have people temporarily idle, but not nearly as much as forty years ago. Still, the cost of joblessness to the economy is hardly trivial. Using a value of 2, Okun's law suggests that in the recession of 1991–92, the unemployment rate of 7.5 percent reduced GDP by $250 billion compared with what it could have been if the jobless rate had been two points lower.

74. Recovery from the 1990–91 recession provides an Okun's-law hint of what the short-term impact of falling unemployment rates can do for growth. As the civilian unemployment rate fell from 7.5 percent in 1992 to 5.6 percent in 1995, annual GDP growth accelerated from −1.0 percent to +3.5 percent in 1994, before slowing to 2.0 percent in 1995.

75. The number of self-employed is reported in U.S. General Accounting Office, *Workers at Risk: Increased Number in Contingent Employment Lack Insurance, Other Benefits*, GAO Report HRD-91-56, March 1991.

76. See Schor, *Overworked American*.

77. According to a recent survey by the British news magazine, *The Economist*, Americans have now surpassed even the Japanese in annual work time and toil 15 percent longer than the typical German. See "Workaholics Anonymous: Why Do Americans Work So Hard?" *Economist*, October 22, 1994, p. 20.

78. Larry Mishel and Jared Bernstein carried out an analysis similar to Schor's and found that, while average annual hours had declined between 1967 and 1983, there had been a sharp turnaround in the 1980s. See Lawrence Mishel and Jared Bernstein, *The State of Working America, 1994–95* (Armonk, N.Y.: M. E. Sharpe, 1994), pp. 111–13. Mishel and Bernstein calculate that in 1973, the average workweek (for both employed and self-employed workers in the public as well as the private sector) was 38.4 hours. The average work year was 43.2 weeks, yielding an annual estimate of 1,659 hours of work. By 1992, the average workweek had climbed by 0.6 hours while the average work year had increased to 45.2 weeks. Hence, annual average hours had risen to 1,759, an increase of 100 hours, or 6 percent — 63 hours less than Schor's estimate. *Three-quarters* of the increase, they estimated, could be attributed to more weeks worked per year, one-quarter to increased hours per week. By 1989, workers were putting in an average of 110 more hours a year at the workplace than they had in 1983.

An alternative measure of working time is obtained from special studies that ask respondents to keep a twenty-four hour time diary of everything they do over a one-to two-week period. Such time diary surveys were first carried out by the University of Michigan Survey Research Center in 1965 and 1975 and then again by the University of Maryland in 1985. Similar time diary studies were carried out in the mid-1960s in a number of other countries as well. The accuracy of work time estimates derived from this survey approach is presumably better than CPS measures for three reasons: survey respondents are required to account for every minute of the time segment they are asked to audit, formal work time is not singled out for special attention, and the recall period is at most one or two days. Respondents do not have to think back to what they did a week ago or try to instantly calculate how many weeks they worked last year.

Based on a comparison of CPS-estimated hours of work and diary entries, John Robinson of the University of Maryland and Ann Bostrom of Georgia Tech University have found that the gap between hours reported using CPS-type questions and the hours reported in diaries increases as the number of reported hours of work rises. Among those reporting 20–44 weekly hours, the CPS-type estimates were only slightly higher than the diary entries. Among workers claiming to "usually" work more than 55 hours per week, the gap was found to be 10 hours or more per week. Values of the CPS-diary difference were generally found to be higher among women than men. Robinson and Bostrom conclude that "the diary data suggest that only rare individuals put in more than a 55–60 hour workweek, with those estimating 60 or more hours on the job averaging closer to 53-hour weeks."

These results imply that Americans are not as overworked as CPS estimates suggest. Moreover, using the diary studies for 1965, 1975, and 1985, Robinson and Bostrom find a systematic increase in the size of the CPS-diary hours gap over time. The gap rises from just one hour in 1965 to four hours in 1975 to 6 hours in 1985. This increase is more than enough to account for the alleged "overwork" that Schor and Mishel and Bernstein claim.

When the diaries for 1965, 1975, and 1985 are analyzed more carefully, Robinson and Bostrom find only small changes in hours worked among those who normally work 20 hours or more per week. Between 1965 and 1985, men's average hours declined by 0.7 hours per week from 47.1 to 46.4 hours. Working women's hours increased by the same amount (0.7) from 39.9 to 40.6 hours. This would seem to suggest that working hours have increased only modestly.

How can we reconcile the Schor and Mishel/Bernstein findings with Robinson and Bostrom? A large part of the answer lies in the fact that Schor and Mishel/Bernstein are looking at *annual* hours of work, and most of the increase in hours is due to increases in weeks worked, not hours worked per week — the focus of Robinson and Bostrom's diary studies. Indeed, according to Mishel and Bernstein, average hours per week increased by just 0.6 hours between 1967 and 1992. However, average weeks worked per year increased from 43.3 to 45.2 over this period. Hence, about three-fourths of the increase in annual hours of work is accounted for by increased weeks of work — the factor ignored in the diary studies. See John P. Robinson and Ann Bostrom, "The Overestimated Workweek? What Time Diary Measures Suggest," *Monthly Labor Review,* August 1994.

79. See Bluestone and Rose, "Overworked and Underemployed"; Bluestone and Rose, "The Unmeasured Workforce"; and Bluestone and Rose, "The Macroeconomics of Working Time," *Review of Social Economy,* vol. 56 (Winter 1998). Like Schor, as well as Mishel and Bernstein, Bluestone and Rose rely on Current Population Survey (CPS) data from the U.S. Bureau of Labor Statistics and the U.S. Census Bureau. However, they supplement this data series with independent information from the Panel Study of Income Dynamics (PSID), a longitudinal study of over 5,000 families which have been tracked for nearly thirty years by the University of Michigan's Survey Research Center. The two surveys use different questions to obtain information on hours worked, yet both surveys show amazingly comparable trends in hours worked, thus increasing our confidence in the estimated trends in working time.

80. The 6.8 more hours worked per year is equivalent to an increase of 0.39 percent per year. Over five years, this amounts to a 1.95 percent increase in annual hours. In May 1997, the U.S. civilian workforce was 129.6 million. Applying this percentage to this number yields the equivalent of 2.5 million additional workers.

81. Cited in *New York Times,* February 27, 1997, p. B6.

82. This value was calculated by weighting the 1995 weekly hours for each education group by the 1975 share of the workforce in each of these education groups. The difference between the actual 1995 weekly hours estimate and this 1975 education-weighted 1995 weekly hours estimate was then divided by the actual weekly hours increase between 1975 and 1995. This yields the percentage associated with increased education level (80.8 percent).

83. To produce this forecast, we rely on population data from the Census Bureau, labor force participation data from the U.S. Bureau of Labor Statistics, and weekly hours growth rates from Bluestone and Rose. We assume that the unemployment rate remains unchanged at the 1997 first-quarter rate of 4.9 percent.

84. To check this method against official Council of Economic Advisers (CEA) data, we also ran the analysis for the period 1982 through 1995, paralleling the reported CEA analysis for 1981:III through 1995:III. Based on our methodology, we estimate a total hours growth rate of 1.7 percent per year. This is nearly indistinguishable from the CEA's estimate of 1.6 percent for the almost comparable period. For the CEA's estimates, see Council of Economic Advisers, *Economic Report of the President, 1996* (Washington, D.C.: GPO, 1996), Table 2-2, p. 58.

85. To do this, we estimated the education distribution for the year 2006 and using the 1995 average hours estimates from Bluestone and Rose projected average weekly hours into the future based on these education "weights."

86. Lester Thurow, "The Crusade That's Killing Prosperity," *American Prospect,* March–April 1996.

87. Many of these discouraged and involuntarily part-time workers show up in the biennial U.S. Labor Department surveys of displaced workers. Since 1979, the surveys have shown that more than 43 million American workers have lost full-time jobs as a result of plant closings, plant relocations, and major layoffs. The number of workers displaced every year has more than doubled since the first survey and now exceeds 3 million per year. The latest survey conducted in January 1996 followed workers who lost full-time jobs in 1993 or 1994. Of these, only one-third had found new jobs with equal or higher pay by the time the survey was conducted. Nearly 10 percent of the displaced workers were unemployed and another 13.6 percent had dropped out of the labor force. Still another 9 percent were working, but could only find part-time work. Altogether then, of the more than 6.5 million workers displaced in 1993 and 1994, more than 1.5 million were still not back to work by 1996 and another half million were working, but in part-time jobs. The U.S. Department of Labor "Displaced Worker" survey is reported by Louis Uchitelle in *New York Times,* August 23, 1996, p. A1.

88. See Lawrence Mishel, Jared Bernstein, and John Schmitt, *The State of Working America 1996–97* (Armonk, N.Y.: M. E. Sharpe, 1997), Table 3.18, p. 169.

4. The Wall Street Model

1. Alan Greenspan, testimony before the Joint Economic Committee, U.S. Congress, June 10, 1998.

2. These statistics and the ones to follow are taken from the Council of Economic Advisers, *Economic Indicators,* (Washington, D.C.: GPO, June 1998).

3. James C. Cooper and Kathleen Madigan, "Business Outlook," *Business Week,* August 17, 1998, p. 28.

4. Robert M. Solow, "A Contribution to the Theory of Economic Growth," *Quarterly Journal of Economics,* vol. 70, no. 1 (February 1956).

5. Gene M. Grossman and Elhanan Helpman, "Endogenous Innovation in the Theory of Growth," *Journal of Economic Perspectives,* vol. 8, no. 1 (Winter 1994), p. 25.

6. Karl Marx, *Das Kapital* (New York: International Publishers, 1894), chapter 15.

7. Another, more subtle, aspect of Marx's critique of capitalism is not so easily dismissed. This is the tendency of the economic system to chronically overinvest in productive capacity in any sector, relative to the ability of workers (and firms) to consume all that the "productive forces" are capable of turning out. It is the system's "anarchy" — the absence of systematically planned investment — that Marx saw as the underlying problem. Eventually, chronic excess capacity would lead not just to falling profits in individual industrial sectors but to nationwide depression. That this idea is still alive and well in contemporary political economy is exemplified by William Greider's newest book, *One World, Ready or Not: The Manic Logic of Global Capitalism* (New York: Simon & Schuster, 1997).

8. Dale W. Jorgenson, ed. *Productivity,* vol. 1, *Postwar U.S. Economic Growth* (Cambridge, Mass.: MIT Press, 1996), p. 4.

9. See Moses Abramovitz, "Economic Growth in the United States," *American Economic Review,* vol. 52, no. 4 (September 1962).

10. See Dale W. Jorgenson, Frank M. Gollop, and Barbara M. Fraumeni, *Productivity and U.S. Economic Growth* (Cambridge, Mass.: Harvard University Press, 1987.)

11. These proportions are calculated from Jorgenson, *Productivity,* vol. 1, Table 1.1, p. 3.

12. Calculated from Dale W. Jorgenson and Zvi Griliches, "The Explanation of Productivity Change," in Dale W. Jorgenson, *Productivity* vol. 1, Table 3.9, p. 84.

13. Ibid., p. 85.

14. This point is emphasized in comments by Susanto Basu in response to a paper by Dale Jorgenson. See Susanto Basu, "Discussion," in *Technology and Growth,* ed. Jeffrey C. Fuhrer and Jane Sneddon Little, Conference Series No. 40 (Boston, Mass.: Federal Reserve Bank of Boston, June 1996), p. 78.

15. Jorgenson and Griliches, "Explanation of Productivity Change," p. 85.

16. Using the *Survey of Current Business* produced by the U.S. Department of Commerce, economist Robert Eisner provides a table that shows the precise relationship between gross investment and gross savings for 1992. See Robert Eisner, *The Misunderstood Economy: What Counts and How to Count It* (Boston: Harvard Business School Press, 1994), Table 3.1, p. 37.

17. Data on the federal deficit and national debt are from *Economic Report of the President* (1998), Table B-78, p. 373.

18. For a general discussion of the standard argument about low savings rates, see Martin and Kathleen Feldstein, "A Penny Saved? Hardly: Low Savings, High Spending Gum Up Economic Machinery," *Boston Globe,* August 18, 1998, p. D4.

19. In the first half of 1998, savings rates averaged just 0.2% while consumer spending surged at a 6% annual rate. See Howard Gleckman, Mike McNamee, and Ann Therese Palmer, "A Downturn Could Really Rock the Boat," *Business Week,* August 17, 1998, pp. 36–37.

20. See Alan Greenspan, statement before the Committee on the Budget, U.S. Senate, January 29, 1998.

21. See Jacob M. Schlesinger, "The Virtuous Circle of Low Inflation," *Wall Street Journal,* August 18, 1997, p. A1.

22. The $12 trillion figure is from Alan Greenspan, testimony before the Joint Economic Committee, U.S. Congress, June 10, 1998. If this amount of paper wealth had been divided equally, it would have amounted to about $120,000 per family. Of course, the lion's share went to the richest families in the country.

23. According to calculations by Sung Won Sohn, chief economist at Norwest Corp., about a quarter of consumer spending is due to wealth from the stock market. See Michael Siconolfi, E. S. Browning and Patrick McGeehan, "As Stock-Market Gains Dissipate, So Does a Bit of Economy's Froth, *Wall Street Journal,* September 2, 1998, p. A8.

24. The 4 percent figure is an estimate from economists as reported in Gleckman, McNamee, and Palmer, "Downturn Could Really Rock the Boat." The calculations presented here are based on the following numbers: Four percent of the $12 trillion runup in household financial wealth is $480 billion. Over four years, this amounts to $120 billion per year. In the first quarter of 1998, personal consumption spending was nearly $5.7 trillion. Hence, the $120 billion represents 2.1 percent of the total. Gross domestic product in 1998:I was about $8.3 trillion. That $120 billion in extra consumer spending represents about 1.4 percent of this total. The base figures are found in *Economic Indicators* (June 1998), p. 1.

25. Alan Greenspan, Testimony before the Joint Economic Committee, U.S. Congress, June 10, 1998.

26. These wealth figures are from Lawrence Mishel, Jared Bernstein, and John Schmitt, *The State of Working America, 1998–99* (Ithaca, N.Y.: Cornell University Press, 1999), and are based on statistics generated by Professor Edward Wolff of New York University.

27. David Stockman, *The Triumph of Politics* (New York: Harper & Row, 1986).

28. For an extensive and, indeed, thrilling account of the internal White House debate over budget matters, see Bob Woodward, *The Agenda* (New York: Simon & Schuster, 1994).

29. These polling results regarding Perot's supporters come from an opinion poll conducted by the centrist Democratic Leadership Council in April 1993 and reported in the *New York Times* on July 8, 1993, p. A4.

30. See Ruy Teixeira and Joel Rogers, *The New Politics of Prosperity* (New York: Century Fund, forthcoming).

31. Indeed, many Democrats now feel they lost control of the House and Senate in the 1994 election because they voted for an essentially Republican agenda.

32. Woodward, *The Agenda*, pp. 154–55.

33. *Economic Indicators* (June 1998), p. 30.

34. These figures are from *Economic Report of the President* (1998), Table B-2, pp. 282–83.

35. The trade deficit in goods already reached the $200 billion level on an annual basis in 1998. For all of 1997, the balance of trade in goods reached –$198 billion. By the middle of 1998, the *monthly* goods deficit exceeded $20 billion. For several decades now, a surplus in services has offset some of the deficit in goods. For example, in 1997 the balance of trade stood at –$110 billion. The $198 billion goods deficit was partially offset by an $88 billion surplus in services. However, with the Asian crisis deepening, the trade surplus in services was shrinking at the same time the goods deficit was rising. The combination has produced a rapidly worsening overall balance of trade. These statistics are found in *Economic Indicators* (June 1998), p. 35.

36. According to a statistical simulation of the increased U.S. trade deficit caused by the Asian financial crisis, a $100 billion increase in the deficit will reduce employment by nearly 1.1 million jobs, assuming no Federal Reserve policy to offset the

contractionary effects of the adverse increase in imports and reduced exports. That translates into roughly 10,000 jobs per billion dollars of additional deficit. According to their industry-by-industry, state-by-state analysis, 70 percent of the job losses will be concentrated in the manufacturing sector, with particularly large losses in industrial machinery, apparel and textiles, and transportation equipment. See Robert E. Scott and Jesse Rothstein, "American Jobs and the Asian Crisis: The Employment Impact of the Coming Rise in the U.S. Trade Deficit," Economic Policy Institute Briefing Paper, Summer 1998.

37. Patrick J. Buchanan's jeremiad on free trade can be found in his book, *The Great Betrayal: How American Sovereignty and Social Justice are being Sacrificed to the Gods of the Global Economy* (Boston: Little, Brown, 1998).

38. The Business Week–Harris poll also found that nearly 90 percent of those surveyed felt that any new free trade agreements should include language to protect the environment and nearly 75 percent favored the inclusion of labor standards. A clear majority (56 percent) felt that "cheap foreign labor" was the biggest threat to American jobs, not technological change, government regulation, or competition with imports. See "Freer Trade Gets an Unfriendly Reception," *Business Week,* September 22, 1997.

39. NAFTA passed the Congress and was signed into law by Bill Clinton over the strong objection of organized labor and the votes of Democratic Party leaders in the House of Representatives. Extension of NAFTA to other nations in Latin America was supported by the President and by the Senate in 1998. It failed only because the Republican leadership in the House of Representatives could not find five more votes in favor of "fast-track" authority, which would have allowed the White House to negotiate new trade agreements while denying Congress the right to amend them.

40. The 1997 U.S. trade deficit of $14.5 billion with Mexico was the fifth-largest bilateral deficit America had that year. Only the deficits with Japan (–$55.7 billion), China (–$49.7 billion), Germany (–$18.6 billion), and Canada (–$16.6 billion) were larger. See Associated Press report, Business News Center, American OnLine, February 18, 1998.

41. In a speech delivered in Dallas, Texas in early 1999, Alan Greenspan was particularly candid on this point. The reason for expanding trade is not to create new jobs, he told the audience of business executives and foreign ambassadors, but to force companies and workers to become more competitive by making it impossible to raise prices. See Richard W. Stevenson, "Greenspan Denounces Growing Protectionism," *New York Times,* April 17, 1999, p. B1.

42. One of the industries experiencing severe global overcapacity is the auto industry. By the year 2000, it is estimated that auto producers will have in place enough plant and equipment to produce 80 million vehicles a year. Total estimated worldwide demand is only about 53 million. Such overcapacity will require the shuttering of about a third of the physical capacity in this one industry. The big question is, in which countries will this downsizing take place. Figures on auto ca-

pacity come from Sean McAlinden, Office for the Study of Automotive Transportation, Transportation Research Institute, University of Michigan, Ann Arbor, Michigan, summer 1998.

43. See Lester Thurow, "Gazing into the Crystal Ball: Pressures of Globalization May Help Keep Boom Going," *Boston Globe,* May 14, 1998, p. D4.

44. See Elizabeth Daerr and Jacob B. Schlesinger, "Import Prices Declined 1.3% in January," *Wall Street Journal,* February 17, 1998, p. A2.

45. Trade has already had its impact on *domestic* prices in those industries most subject to import penetration. For example, according to the *Wall Street Journal,* in 1997, in the industry with the largest dollar value of imports, motor vehicles, the inflation rate was −0.6 percent. The inflation rate was negative in other import-sensitive industries, including jewelry (−2.7 percent), toys (−1.4 percent), televisions and VCRs (−4.6 percent), and household appliances (−3.5 percent. See G. Pascal Zachary, "Asian Exports Haven't Flooded the U.S., but American Consumers Still Benefit from Lower Prices," *Wall Street Journal,* April 14, 1998, p. A2.

46. For a discussion of this era, see Bluestone and Bluestone, *Negotiating the Future,* pp. 96–104.

47. In the 1970s, when unions represented nearly 25 percent of wage and salary workers in the U.S, nearly two-thirds were covered by automatic cost-of-living adjustment (COLA) clauses. Today, with a union density rate of less than 15 percent, only about 20 percent are covered by COLA. Hence, in the entire labor force, the proportion of workers covered by COLA has fallen from one in six to only about one in thirty-three. See Schlesinger, "Virtuous Circle of Low Inflation," p. A1.

48. For by far the best critical analysis of the role of the Federal Reserve, see William Grieder, *Secrets of the Temple: How the Federal Reserve Runs the Country* (New York: Simon & Schuster, 1987).

49. The account of Fed interest rate increases is found in Woodward, *The Agenda,* p. 378. The statistics are from the Council of Economic Advisers, *Economic Report of the President* Washington, D.C.: Government Printing Office, February 1998).

50. See Dean Foust, "Alan Greenspan's Brave New World," *Business Week,* July 14, 1997, pp. 45–50.

51. See Woodward, *The Agenda,* p. 378.

52. Indeed, the idea that the *only* objective of the Fed should be "stable money" has been advanced in legislation put forward by Florida Senator Connie Mack. In his proposed Economic Growth and Stability Act, he would amend the Humphrey-Hawkins Full Employment Act by exempting the Federal Reserve Board from any responsibility for pursuing any goal but zero inflation. In his opinion, price stability is such an important economic goal that the monetary authorities should never be under stricture to pursue anything less. For a critique of this legislation, see Paul Krugman, "Stable Prices and Fast Growth: Just Say No," *Economist,* August 31, 1996, p. 20.

53. See Alicia Munnell, "The Employment Act of 1946: 50 Years Later," in Con-

ference Proceedings of the Jerome Levy Institute at Bard College, April 25–26, 1996, p. 22.

54. In Barry Bluestone and Bennett Harrison, *The Deindustrialization of America* (New York: Basic Books, 1982), we first used the term "hypermobility" to refer to the accelerated movement of *physical* capital from one location to another as manufacturing firms, in particular, sought out new locations for production. In the current case, we are referring to the hypermobility of financial capital — the ability to move huge amounts of funds from one place and one use to another in literally seconds, via electronic transfer.

55. Peter Dicken, *Global Shift*, 2d ed. (New York: Guilford Press, 1992), p. 19.

56. Roger C. Altman, "The Nuke of the 90s," *New York Times Magazine,* March 1, 1998, p. 34.

57. Michael J. Porter, *Capital Choices: Changing the Way America Invests in Industry* (Washington, D.C.: Council on Competitiveness, June 1992). This report is reviewed in Bennett Harrison, "Where Private Investment Fails," *American Prospect,* September 1992, 906–14.

58. James Poterba and Lawrence H. Summers, "Time Horizons of American Firms: New Evidence From a Survey of CEOs," Council on Competitiveness and the Harvard Business School, October 1991.

59. Quoted in Alan Murray, "Asia's Financial Foibles Make American Way Look Like a Winner," *Wall Street Journal,* December 8, 1997, p. 1.

60. Quoted in Murray, "Asia's Financial Foibles," p. 1.

61. As David Hale, the chief economist at Zurich Kemper Investments, put it in 1996, "The U.S. is in the midst of creating a whole new financial system in which the mutual-fund sector is increasingly displacing commercial banks as the major repositories of household wealth, as well as suppliers of capital." All this makes the U.S. financial structure look quite different from that of other industrial nations. See John R. Wilke, "Surge in Investments Changes U.S. Economy," *Wall Street Journal,* June 10, 1996, p. A1.

62. See Kathleen Kerwin, "The Shutdown GM Needs?: It's a Chance to Clean House and Downsize," *Business Week,* July 13, 1998.

63. See Paul Magnusson and Stephen Baker, "The Explosive Trade Deal You've Never Heard Of," *Business Week,* February 9, 1998, and International Forum on Globalization, "Should Corporations Govern the World?" (advertisement), *New York Times,* February 13, 1998.

64. See Helene Cooper and Sara Calian, "With the Euro in View, U.S. Securities Firms Court the Europeans," *Wall Street Journal,* August 26, 1998, p. A1.

65. David Felix, "IMF Bailouts and Global Financial Flows," *Foreign Policy in Focus* (Interhemispheric Resource Center and Institute for Policy Studies), vol. 3, no. 5 (April 1998).

66. As just one example, to keep its once high-flying economy from sinking into depression, Brazil agreed in late 1998 to slash public spending and raise taxes as a condition for gaining IMF funding. The plan is so thorough that it even permeates

down to the state and municipal level, forcing local governments to reign in their spending. Sounding much like U.S. leaders at the time of the balanced budget accord, Brazil's finance minister explained the austerity plan to his nation's people, stressing that "the time has come for us to make government live within its limits — with clarity, conscience, and determination." Reported in Diana Jean Schemo, "Brazil Introduces $80 Billion Plan for Economic Ills," *New York Times*, October 29, 1998, p. A1.

5. What's Wrong with the Wall Street Model: Too Little Long-Term Growth

1. See James B. Sumrall, Jr., "Diffusion of the Basic Oxygen Furnace in the U.S. Steel Industry: A Vintage Capital Model," Ph.D. dissertation, Boston College, 1977.

2. The literature on the impact of employee participation, profit sharing, and worker ownership on productivity is now quite extensive. Much of it is reviewed in Alan S. Blinder, ed., *Paying for Productivity* (Washington, D.C.: Brookings Institution, 1990), and Bluestone and Bluestone, *Negotiating the Future*. A particularly good review of statistical studies is found in David I. Levine and Laura D'Andrea Tyson, "Participation, Productivity, and the Firm's Environment," in Blinder, ed., *Paying for Productivity*.

3. After adopting a revolutionary union-management agreement in 1989, Magma Copper Co. worked with its United Steelworkers' union members to raise productivity in its San Manuel mine. Without adding any substantial new capital, changes in work rules and the full engagement of the workforce in solving production problems led to a 61 percent increase in real productivity between 1988 and 1992. See "Magma Copper Company: A Cultural Revolution," Magma Copper Co., Spring 1992, and Magma Copper Company, Annual Report, 1992.

4. Robert Eisner reminds us that "the critical and crucial judgment of [John Maynard] Keynes, and one in which most business executives would concur, is that the rate of interest, while not without significance, is not of overwhelming importance to investment decisions. If the expected profitability of new investment is high, it will be undertaken in the face of high interest costs. If the expected profitabilty is low — and certainly if it is nil — the investment will not be undertaken, regardless of the interest rate." Eisner, *Misunderstood Economy*, p. 208.

5. See Greider, *Secrets of the Temple*, especially chapters 11 and 12.

6. Data are from *Economic Report of the President* (1987), Table B-68, p. 324 and Table B-16, p. 263.

7. Eisner, *Misunderstood Economy*, p. 35.

8. In 1993, gross domestic savings as a percent of GDP was 33 percent in Japan while only 15 percent in the United States. The Japanese rate was more than half again as large as the average savings rate for the entire high-income, developed world (20 percent). See World Bank, *World Development Report 1995* (New York: Oxford University Press, 1995), Table 9, p. 179.

9. In 1991, the personal savings rate in the United States was 6 percent. It gen-

erated nearly $260 billion in aggregate savings. In early 1997, the savings rate was down to 3.7 percent, but even at this much lower rate, total personal savings had declined by only about 17 percent (to $216 billion). See *Economic Report of the President* (1998), Table B-32, pp. 318–19.

10. We should note for the record that because there are limited ways to induce higher *private* savings rates, proponents of the conventional wisdom have been lobbying hard to have the federal government not just balance its budget but begin to amass large public surpluses to compensate for the shortfall in the private sector. We will come back to this later in this chapter.

11. See William D. Nordhaus, "Budget Deficits and National Saving," *Challenge*, March–April 1996.

12. Eisner reminds us of the mathematics of national savings and investment. Total gross national saving (GS) — except for a statistical discrepancy in the national accounts — is identically equal to the total of gross investment (GI). Put more completely: GS = PS + BS + FS + SLS (+ SD) = GI, where PS = personal saving, BS = business saving, FS = federal budget surplus, SLS = state and local government budget surpluses, and SD = statistical discrepancy. See Eisner, *Misunderstood Economy*.

13. Nordhaus, "Budget Deficits," p. 46.

14. Eisner provides a wonderful list of examples of the strange accounting procedures we use to define *investment* versus *consumption*. The purchase of an automobile by an individual is counted as consumption. That very same car, leased rather than purchased from the same car dealer is counted as a business investment by the leasing agent. Presto! Simply by choosing to lease rather than buy, an individual has increased national investment (and reduced consumption), according to official statistics. The value of a new dishwasher, stove, and refrigerator included in the purchase price of a new home is counted as investment. Buying the same durable goods a day after buying the house miraculously converts these purchases into consumption. Similarly, since all federal government spending is implicitly, if not explicitly, counted as consumption, a new mile of highway, computers for the IRS, or a new airport runway is not counted as investment, no matter how long its useful life or its contribution to future income. Eisner, *Misunderstood Economy*, p. 51.

15. For his calculation of revised savings rates, Nordhaus makes the following assumptions about the proportion of personal consumption expenditures which he treats as investment: food (0), housing (0), education and research (100), religious and welfare activities (100), housing operations (23), medical care (84), personal business (61), transportation (35), personal care (0), clothing (96), recreation (34), and foreign travel (0). See Nordhaus, "Budget Deficits," p. 49, n. 5.

16. Two research economists at the Boston Federal Reserve Bank have come to a similar conclusion about consumption and saving. According to Lynn Brown and Joshua Gleason, the share of household income spent on goods — mainly food, clothing, and gasoline — fell by 8 percentage points between 1975 and 1995. Conventionally measured saving fell by nearly 4 percentage points. Families shifted their spending to housing and transportation (up 1.5 percentage points), education and

recreation (up 1.8 percentage points), and medical services (up by a whopping 5.8 percentage points.) The Brown-Gleason study is reported in Gene Koretz, "Solving the Savings Riddle," *Business Week,* November 11, 1996, p. 26.

17. Of course, there is also a serious distribution problem if we are to rely on such wealth effects to carry the economy. We will touch upon these in the next chapter.

18. For an excellent treatment of the market and the economy in the 1920s and the 1990s, see John Cassidy, "Pricking the Bubble," *The New Yorker,* August 17, 1998. One should note that the Dow Jones industrial average (DJIA) has increased by an average of about 7.3 percent per year since 1955. However, this long-term trend is composed of three distinct periods. From 1955 through 1966, the DJIA rose at a 7.0 percent yearly rate before it went into a long drought. Between 1966 and 1982, the average annual growth rate was virtually zero (−0.2 percent per year). Since 1982, the Dow has surged at the dizzying rate of 16.4 percent per year, a rate more than double its long-term trend. This would suggest that the Dow will at some time soon settle down and essentially wait for the rest of the economy to catch up with it.

19. Quoted in Cassidy, "Pricking the Bubble," p. 41.

20. The findings of the Dunlop Commission are reported in the Commission on the Future of Worker-Management Relations, *Report and Recommendations,* U.S. Department of Labor and U.S. Department of Commerce, 1994.

21. A. W. Phillips, "The Relation Between Unemployment and the Rate of Change of Money Wage Rates in the United Kingdom, 1861–1957," *Economica,* vol. 25 (November 1958), pp. 283–99.

22. Paul A. Samuelson and Robert M. Solow, "Analytical Aspects of Anti-Inflation Policy," *American Economic Review Papers and Proceedings,* vol. 50 (May 1960), pp. 177–94.

23. Milton Friedman, "The Role of Monetary Policy," *American Economic Review,* vol. 58 (March 1968), pp. 1–17; Edmund Phelps, "Money-Wage Dynamics and Labor Market Equilibrium," *Journal of Political Economy,* vol. 76, part 2 (1968), pp. 678–711.

24. In the 1970s, even more conservative variations were erected atop the construct of the NAIRU, notably Robert Lucas's idea of "rational expectations." In what liberal MIT economist Lester Thurow has characterized as perhaps the "single most outrageous contribution to modern economic thought," Lucas (who subsequently won a Nobel prize for these ideas) and his colleague Thomas Sargent asserted that all participants in the economy — from world currency speculators to blue-collar assembly line workers to car parking attendants to day care providers — behave as if they were unceasing maximizers, making instant and continual computations of their "expected utility" while actively searching for and taking advantage of all available information. This caricature of worker behavior, with its extreme naivety about the limited choices that most workers face about, for example, when, where, and how much to work, became absorbed into inflation theory. More and more economists

simply assumed that workers more or less immediately internalize their expectation of future inflation based upon their current or recent experience with it, and so completely discount any temporary government-sponsored action to expand or contract the economy. In other words, the leads and lags and uncertainties and "money illusions" that Keynes understood to so confound ordinary people's perceptions of the workings of a complex economy were simply assumed out of existence, making any government effort at adjusting the economy literally useless. See Robert E. Lucas, Jr. and Thomas P. Sargent, "After Keynesian Macroeconomics," *Quarterly Review* (Federal Reserve Bank of Minneapolis), vol. 3 (Spring 1979), pp. 1–16, and Lester Thurow, *Dangerous Currents* (New York: Oxford University Press, 1983).

25. Mainstream economists are quite divided on this subject. See the special symposium issue on NAIRU in the *Journal of Economic Perspectives,* vol. 11 (Winter 1997). Here, we emphasize the nay-sayers. In fairness, other prominent mainstreamers such as Northwestern University's Robert J. Gordon and Princeton's Alan Blinder strongly believe that, for all the criticism, there is a theoretically grounded, statistically verifiable NAIRU, but that it has declined substantially since the 1980s, leaving the Federal Reserve more room to use monetary policy to permit an acceptably lower unemployment rate than before.

26. Douglas Staiger, James H. Stock, and Mark W. Watson, "The NAIRU, Unemployment, and Monetary Policy," *Journal of Economic Perspectives,* vol. 11 (Winter 1997), pp. 33–50.

27. The extreme sensitivity of NAIRU estimates is underscored by particular recent experiments with the assumptions about the *shape* of the relationship between inflation and unemployment. At the Brookings Institution, George Akerlof, William Dickens and George Perry reintroduce into the current discourse one of Keynes's old ideas, revived by James Tobin in still another (1971) AEA presidential address. Because of deeply held social norms and managers' reluctance to unleash employee resistance, outright wage cuts are actually relatively rare events; nominal wage rates tend to be "sticky downward." This might seem to be good for workers, but Tobin found that this wage rigidity acts as a brake on firms' willingness to raise wages, too, even in tight labor markets. A temporary boom might permit higher wages without inflation — or even require them, in order to attract a sufficient supply of workers. Nevertheless, firms will resist raising wages during the good times, knowing it will be difficult to lower them when the cycle goes bust. This means that even when the economy surges, wages are likely to trail behind — limiting the inflationary pressure from faster economic growth.

The Brookings economists also recognize the tremendous degree of heterogeneity among firms in a modern economy. This means both that the strength of the normative prohibition against cutting nominal wages will vary from one setting to another, and that wage setting decisions in any one company, sector, or place will transmit only imperfectly to other settings, with long lags, possibly petering out completely. This disrupts the unemployment-inflation nexus even further. See James

Tobin, "Inflation and Unemployment," *American Economic Review,* vol. 62 (March 1972), pp. 1–18.

28. James Galbraith, "The Surrender of Economic Policy," *American Prospect,* March–April 1996, p. 61.

29. Foreign political-economic developments matter, too. Most dramatic for the current period is the collapse of the Asian "economic miracle." With the yen, won, Hong Kong pound and other Asian currencies so battered by the run to the dollar by international speculators, the Fed is under tremendous pressure not to raise interest rates domestically to halt the current expansion, for fear of exacerbating these politically dangerous currency swings by making the U.S. dollar even more attractive.

30. Cited in Dicken, *Global Shift,* p. 20.

31. Ibid., p. 40.

32. For the record, there is not universal agreement among economists that heightened foreign competition restrains domestic price increases. The Boston Fed's Norman S. Fieleke, in particular, makes an argument that countries with particularly strong exposure to the global economy, as measured by the ratio of exports plus imports to GDP, do not systematically experience lower rates of domestic inflation over time. Moreover, given the sheer size of the U.S. economy with respect to its trading partners, surely domestic fiscal and monetary policy dwarf potential foreign competition as an influence over domestic price-setting. Why, then, the widespread belief that foreign competition does matter so much? Fieleke's answer: the complaints about foreign competition are coming mainly from those domestic industries (such as clothing, textiles, and steel) that are already in trouble, competitively, for other reasons. It is not clear to us that these arguments decisively disprove what just about every introductory textbook in international economics teaches: that potential competition *can* challenge oligopoly power. See Norman S. Fieleke, "Popular Myths about the World Economy," *New England Economic Review,* July–August 1997.

33. Data on the period 1986/87 through 1992/93, assembled by Norman Fieleke, vice president and economist at the Boston Federal Reserve Bank, suggests that nominal growth in world trade in services now substantially outpaces that in manufacturing, for both developed and developing countries. The relative importance of services to a country's overall trade vary widely, with Canada displaying the smallest share and France the largest. Travel is the United States' single largest traded service, on both the export (hosting foreign visitors) and import (Americans traveling abroad) sides of the ledger. Across the globe, foreign direct investment in services also increased more rapidly than investment in goods-producing industries. By 1990, services connected with finance and with trade accounted for almost half of the world's stock of foreign direct investment. This growing importance of services is reflected in the inclusion for the first time in 1993 of explicit language on trade in services in Uruguay Round of negotiations for the General Agreement on Tariffs and Trade. See Norman S. Fieleke, "The Soaring Trade in 'Nontradables,' " *New England Economic Review,* November–December, 1995, pp. 25–36.

34. Norbert Walter, "Deflating an Inflation Worry," *New York Times,* February 2, 1997, p. F14.

35. We have investigated and documented this process in great detail in two previous books. Bluestone and Harrison, *Deindustrialization of America;* and Bennett Harrison and Barry Bluestone, *The Great U-Turn* (New York: Basic Books, 1988).

36. The combined contribution of unemployed workers returning to work and incumbent workers putting in longer work weeks accounted for nearly *half* of the increased labor supply that sustained noninflationary economic growth in the first half of the 1990s. In the 1970s, these two factors accounted for only about a *fifth* of the total — the rest coming from new labor force participants. See Bluestone and Rose, "Unmeasured Labor Force."

37. Owen Ullmann, Laura Cohn, and Michael Mandel, "The Fed's New Rule Book," *Business Week,* May 3, 1999, p. 46.

38. It might be fair to ask why there has been such a long-standing policy of keeping a watchful eye out for inflation, and even of deliberately holding down economic growth in the name of price stability? Writing in the pages of the *Wall Street Journal,* Felix Rohatyn, managing director of Lazard Frères, attributed the "powerful anti-growth bias" in current policy to the financial markets' "theological commitment to the notion that higher growth inevitably *leads* to higher inflation." This is despite the fact that over the entire course of the twentieth century, the United States has never experienced German- or Brazilian-style hyperinflation. Neither the explosion of pent-up demand following World War II nor the huge deficits of the 1980s led to chronic inflation. As historians have shown, the growing rate of inflation at the end of the 1960s was a consequence of the political decision by Presidents Johnson and Nixon to minimize social disruption by both sustaining domestic spending and simultaneously funding the war in Vietnam without raising taxes. As the textbooks of the time said, to have *both* guns *and* butter, without adequately paying for either, overstimulated the economy. Even more important, the double-digit inflation of the late 1970s and early 1980s was a temporary consequence of the oil supply shocks created, first by the OPEC cartel in 1973 and then as a side-effect of the Iranian revolution in 1979. By the mid-1980s, these pressures had dissipated. Foreign and military policy have been devoted ever since to preventing their recurrence by providing continued support for oil-rich governments in the Middle East that are friendly to U.S. interests. This is, after all, what the American "liberation" of Kuwait in the Gulf War of 1991 was ultimately about. See Felix Rohatyn, "Clinton's Growth Agenda," *Wall Street Journal,* September 16, 1996, p. A18.

39. For more on this subject, see Robert A. Levine, "The Economic Consequences of Mr. Clinton," *Atlantic Monthly,* July 1996.

40. Dean Baker and Todd Schafer, "The Case for Public Investment," Economic Policy Institute, Washington, D.C., 1995, p. 8. While it has become customary to associate public infrastructure with the federal government, and while the financing does typically turn mainly on federal grants, in 1991 well over 80 percent of the stock of public infrastructure capital in the United States was owned by state and local gov-

ernments. David Alan Aschauer, "On Bridges to the Twenty-first Century: Figuratively *and* Literally," Report of the Jerome Levy Economics Institute of Bard College, vol. 7, no. 1, May 1997, pp. 12–13; Timothy J. Bartik, "Growing State Economies: How Taxes and Public Services Affect Private Sector Performance," Economic Policy Institute, Washington D.C., 1996. Edward Gramlich sensibly observes that spending on some categories, such as high school buildings and highways, should have been expected to decline at least somewhat, given demographic trends and the completion of the interstate highway system after a project lasting forty years. Edward M. Gramlich, "Infrastructure Investment: A Review Essay," *Journal of Economic Literature,* Vol. 32 (September 1994), p. 1180.

41. See Robert Pear, "Building Boom at Institutes of Health," *New York Times,* November 1, 1998, p. 26.

42. See Gary Becker, "Save Some of the Surplus for Medical Research," *Business Week,* April 19, 1999, p. 27.

43. See Dean Baker, "The Public Investment Deficit: Two Decades of Neglect Threatens Twenty-first Century Economy," Economic Policy Institute Briefing Paper, Washington, D.C., February 1998.

44. Actually, world growth needs to be substantial indeed if U.S. exports are to expand faster than imports. Under realistic assumptions about U.S. and foreign income and price elasticities of demand for imports and supply of exports, economist Candace Howes estimates that world output would have to grow more than twice as fast as U.S. GDP in order for our trade deficit to decline steadily. Candace Howes, "Long-Term Economic Strategy and Employment Growth in the U.S.: An Analysis of Clinton's Economic Policies," *Contributions to Political Economy,* vol. 14 (1995), pp. 9–10.

45. See *Economic Indicators* (March 1999), p. 35.

46. This assumes that nothing else in the economy would have been different as a result of trade balance. In particular, a smaller trade deficit would have meant that fewer investment dollars would have been available from foreign sources. To the extent that these dollars were needed to prop up capital spending in the United States, there might have been a small negative indirect effect on growth.

47. Edith Rasell, Barry Bluestone, Lawrence Mishel, and David Webster *The Prosperity Gap: Why Americans Are Falling Behind* (New York: New Press, 1999).

48. Jeffrey D. Sachs, "Global Adjustments to a Shrinking U.S. Trade Deficit," *Brookings Papers on Economic Activity,* no. 2 (1988), pp. 639–74.

49. Ute Pieper and Lance Taylor, "The Revival of the Liberal Creed: The IMF, the World Bank, and Inequality in the Globalized Economy," in *Globalization and Progressive Economic Policy,* ed. Dean Baker, Gerald Epstein, and Robert Pollin (New York: Cambridge University Press, 1998).

50. Jagdish Bhagwati, "The Capital Myth: The Difference between Trade in Widgets and Dollars," *Foreign Affairs,* vol. 77, no. 3 (May–June 1998), pp. 7–12.

51. See David Card and Alan Krueger, *Myth and Measurement: The New Economics of the Minimum Wage* (Princeton: Princeton University Press, 1995).

52. One of those who have commented on this possibility is economist Robert Gordon of Northwestern University. See Gordon, "Problems in the Measurement and Performance of Service-Sector Productivity in the United States."

53. For a review of the evidence of the union impact on wages and productivity, see Bluestone and Bluestone, *Negotiating the Future,* pp. 97–98.

54. Charles Brown and James Medoff, "Trade Unions in the Production Process," *Journal of Political Economy,* vol. 86, no. 3 (June 1978), pp. 355–78.

55. For productivity estimates in the cement industry, see Kim B. Clark, "The Impact of Unionization on Productivity: A Case Study," *Industrial and Labor Relations Review,* vol. 33, no. 4 (July 1980), pp. 451–69; in the construction industry, see Steven G. Allen, "Unionized Construction Workers Are More Productive," *Quarterly Journal of Economics,* May 1984; for the case of hospitals, see Charles A. Register, "Wages, Productivity, and Costs in Union and Nonunion Hospitals," *Journal of Labor Research,* vol. 9, no. 4 (Fall 1988); in the mining industry, see M. Connerton, R. B. Freeman, and J. L. Medoff, "Industrial Relations and Productivity: A Study of the U.S. Bituminous Coal Industry," Harvard University, Cambridge, Mass., 1983. In this last study, the authors found that during the 1960s, productivity was 30 percent higher in the union sector, but by the 1970s productivity had dropped 15 percent below that in nonunion mines.

56. Cross-section studies by Mansfield, Link, Hirsch and Link, and Terleckyi suggest that highly organized industries suffer an annual productivity growth rate deficit of at most 5 to 6 percent. Research by Sveikkaskaus and Sveikkaskaus, Freeman and Medoff, and by Allen concludes that there is no evidence to support any claim of a productivity growth effect. See Edward Mansfield, "Basic Research and Productivity Increase in Manufacturing," *American Economic Review,* December 1980; Albert N. Link, "Productivity Growth, Environmental Regulations, and the Composition of R&D," *Bell Journal of Economics,* Autumn 1982; Barry T. Hirsch and Albert N. Link, "Unions, Productivity, and Productivity Growth," *Journal of Labor Research,* vol. 5 (Winter 1984); Nestor Terleckyi, "What Do R&D Numbers Tell Us about Technological Change?" *American Economic Review,* May 1980; C. D. Sveikauskus and L. Sveikauskus, "Industry Characteristics and Productivity Growth," *Southern Journal of Economics,* January 1982; Richard B. Freeman and James L. Medoff, *What Do Unions Do?* (New York: Basic Books, 1984); and Steven G. Allen, "Declining Unionization in Construction: The Facts and the Reasons," *Industrial and Labor Relations Review,* April 1988.

57. Eisner, *Misunderstood Economy,* p. 194.

58. See Andrew Tobias, "Take Control of Your Credit Card," *Parade,* November 1, 1998, p. 4. The average cardholder in the U.S. has eleven credit cards.

59. See Dave Skidmore, "Americans Raid Savings in September," The Associated Press, November 2, 1998 (AP Web site).

6. What's Wrong with the Wall Street Model: Too Much Long-Term Inequality

1. Median family income more than doubled, from just around $19,100 in 1947 to $38,900 in 1973 (in 1995 dollars). For an excellent summary of data on trends in American living standards, see Rasell, Bluestone, Mishel, and Webster, *Prosperity Gap.*

2. See Bruce S. Glassman, ed., *The Macmillan Visual Almanac* (New York: Macmillan, 1996), p. 522.

3. See Charles Sabel, "The Re-Emergence of Regional Economies: Changes in the Scale of Production," in "Experimenting with Scale," Social Science Research Council, Western European Committee, August 1987, pp. 20–21.

4. Peter Passell, "Benefits Dwindle along with Wages for the Unskilled," *New York Times,* June 14, 1998, p. A1.

5. Rasell, Bluestone, Mishel, and Webster, *Prosperity Gap.* In addition, a recent study by the Washington-based Center on Budget and Policy Priorities reports that in New York State, where inequality is the highest among the fifty states, the typical family with children in the top fifth of the income distribution now receives *19.5 times* the income of the average family in the bottom fifth, up from 12.6 times in the mid-1980s (which was bad enough!). See Kathryn Larin and Elizabeth C. McNichol, *Pulling Apart: A State-by-State Analysis of Income Trends* (Washington, D.C.: Center on Budget and Policy Priorities, December 16, 1997), Table 2.

6. Harrison and Bluestone, *Great U-Turn.* Measuring inequality within the workforce was hard to do prior to the 1960s, until the U.S. Bureau of the Census and the U.S. Department of Labor launched the annual March Current Population Survey, in which some 55,000 households are interviewed. Harrison and Bluestone showed a sharp and steady drop in earnings inequality until the bottom of the 1975 recession, followed by an equally dramatic increase. This message has since been reproduced and reported by dozens of other scholars and journalists. Income inequality seems to decline when the economy grows for a sustained period.

7. Peter Gottschalk and Timothy Smeeding, "Cross-National Comparisons of Earnings and Income Inequality," *Journal of Economic Literature,* Vol. 35 (June 1997), pp. 633–87; World Bank, *World Development Report,* various issues.

8. Bluestone and Rose, "Unmeasured Labor Force."

9. The one group of dual-earner families that benefitted from working longer hours were those headed by someone with at least a college degree. Over the 1973–1985 period, these families increased their combined working hours by 16.6 percent and were remunerated handsomely for their efforts. They averaged a 32.5 percent increase in family earnings.

10. Sheldon Danziger and Peter Gottschalk, *America Unequal* (Cambridge, Mass.: Harvard University Press, 1996); Rebecca Blank, *It Takes a Nation* (New York: Russell Sage Foundation, 1997).

11. Edward N. Wolff, *Top Heavy: A Study of the Increasing Inequality of Wealth in America* (New York: Twentieth Century Fund, 1995).

12. Melvin L. Oliver and Thomas M. Shapiro, *Black Wealth/White Wealth* (New York: Routledge, 1995).

13. Ibid., p. 8.

14. Ibid., p. 117.

15. Annette Bernhardt et al., "Job Instability and Wage Inequality among Young Men: A Comparison of Two NLS Cohorts," Institute on Education and the Economy, Columbia University, January 1998; Richard V. Burkhauser, et al., *Income Mobility and the Middle Class* (Washington, D.C.: American Enterprise Institute, 1996); Steven Rose, "Declining Family Incomes in the 1980s: New Evidence from Longitudinal Data," *Challenge,* November–December 1993.

16. Simon Kuznets, *Economic Development, the Family and Income Distribution: Selected Essays* (Cambridge: Cambridge University Press, 1989).

17. Okun, *Equality and Efficiency.*

18. In two powerful books, the journalist Robert Kuttner has brilliantly refuted Okun's insistence on the inevitability of a trade-off between equality and growth. Even as he celebrates Okun's acknowledgment that unbridled market forces inevitably worsen inequality, Kuttner shows that whether and to what extent there is a trade-off ultimately depends on whether the economy is at or close to full employment. With unutilized or underutilized resources, we can have both growth and justice. Moreover, the more we give in to the market mentality, the stronger the vested interests in laissez-faire become, and the harder it gets in practice to legislate the lump sum transfer payments that Okun would enact to buy off the losers in the market game. See Robert Kuttner, *The Economic Illusion* (Boston: Houghton Mifflin, 1984); and Robert Kuttner, *Everything for Sale* (New York: Knopf, 1996).

19. For a review of this literature on so-called dynamic external economies, and an empirical test of the hypothesis for the machining sector, see Bennett Harrison, Maryellen Kelley, and Jon Gant, "Innovative Firm Behavior and Local Milieu: Exploring the Intersection of Agglomeration, Industrial Organization, and Technological Change," *Economic Geography,* vol. 72 (July 1996).

20. On all this, see Aaron Bernstein, "Inequality: How the Gap Between Rich and Poor Hurts the Economy," *Business Week,* August 15, 1994, pp. 78–83.

21. Alberto Alesina and Dani Rodrik, "Distributive Politics and Economic Growth," *Quarterly Journal of Economics,* vol. 109, no. 2 (May 1994), pp. 465–90; Rodrik, *Has Globalization Gone Too Far?* (Washington D.C.: Institute for International Economics, 1997). For yet another example, see Torsten Persson and Guido Tabellini, "Is Inequality Harmful for Growth?" *American Economic Review* vol. 84, no. 3 (June 1994), pp. 600–21.

22. For just one recent example of this kind of thinking, see Ernest Van Den Haag, "In Praise of the Wage Gap," *Wall Street Journal,* June 26, 1996, p. A18.

23. Robert Pollin, "Deeper in Debt: The Changing Financial Condition of U.S. Households," Economic Policy Institute, Washington, D.C., September 1990.

24. Bennett Harrison, *Lean and Mean: Why Large Corporations Will Continue to Dominate the Global Economy* (New York: Guilford Press, 1997).

25. The following builds upon a formulation originally published as Bluestone, "Inequality Express."

26. David R. Howell, Margaret Duncan, and Bennett Harrison, "Low Wages in the U.S. and High Unemployment in Europe: A Critical Assessment of the Conventional Wisdom," working paper no. 5, Center for Economic Policy Analysis, New School, New York, February 1998, p. 3. For a thorough history of this thesis, and a further demonstration of why it just cannot be that important, see Mishel, Bernstein, and Schmitt, *The State of Working America*, pp. 197–207.

27. See Anthony P. Carnevale and Stephen J. Rose, *Education for What? The New Office Economy: Technical Report* (Princeton: Educational Testing Service, 1998), Table 14, p. 45.

28. Alan Greenspan, "Remarks on Income Inequality," symposium sponsored by the Federal Reserve Bank of Kansas City, Jackson Hole, Wyo., August 28, 1998.

29. See Bluestone, "Great U-Turn Revisited."

30. Mishel, Bernstein, and Schmitt, *State of Working America*, pp. 189–95.

31. Ibid.; and Richard B. Freeman and Lawrence F. Katz, "Rising Wage Inequality: The United States vs. Other Advanced Countries," in *Working under Different Rules,* ed. Richard Freeman (New York: Russell Sage, 1994).

32. See Robert Frank, "Talent and the Winner-Take-All Society," *American Prospect,* Spring 1994.

33. The following data are drawn from the Census Bureau's Web site: http://www.census.gov/Press-Release/cb98-175.html.

34. See note 21 in Chapter 1.

35. Aaron Bernstein, "Why Wages Aren't Giving the Market Willies," *Business Week,* June 22, 1998, p. 37.

36. According to the EPI study, the bottom tenth of the workforce saw their real wages rise by 8.7 percent between 1996 and 1998, compared to 5.0 percent for the median worker and 4.3 percent for those in the top decile. This is in sharp contrast to the 1989–96 trend when wages at the bottom fell by 1.9 percent while wages at the top grew by 0.3 percent. See Jared Bernstein and Lawrence Mishel, "Wages Gain Ground," Economic Policy Institute Issue Brief no. 129, February 2, 1999.

37. See James K. Galbraith, "Inequality and Unemployment: Monthly Data for the United States," University of Texas Inequality Project, University of Texas at Austin, April 1999.

38. Taking into account the cash value of such income transfers as food stamps and employer contributions to health insurance, and the net effect of taxes on household incomes, in 1996 a "fully adjusted" definition of income shows less absolute inequality (as measured by the Gini) — fully 11 percent less — than is indicated with a pretax, pretransfer definition of income. Noncash benefits account for most of the improvement — as they were intended by past Congresses and presidents to do. But

there is no indication that such adjustments have affected the *trend* in inequality over time, which is our major concern here.

39. See *Economic Report of the President* (1998), Chapter 4, "Economic Inequality among Racial and Ethnic Groups," pp. 119–154.

40. Paul Jargowsky, *Poverty and Place: Ghettos, Barrios and the American City* (New York: Russell Sage Foundation, 1997).

41. These rates are actually for all of Cook County and all of Dade County, respectively. Undoubtedly the rates for the cities of Chicago and Miami, proper, were considerably higher.

42. The following is based on research conducted together with Mary Huff Stevenson.

43. Lester C. Thurow, *Generating Inequality: Mechanisms of Distribution in the U.S. Economy* (New York: Basic Books, 1975), p. 76. Also Barry Bluestone,, Michael Massagli, and Mary H. Stevenson, "A 'Job Competition' Model of Wage Determination: Applications to Blacks, Hispanics, and Whites in the Greater Boston Labor Market," Russell Sage Foundation Conference on the Multi-City Study of Urban Inequality (MCSUI), February 1996.

44. William Julius Wilson, *When Work Disappears: The World of the New Urban Poor* (New York: Vintage Books, 1996).

45. No less perceptive an economist than James Galbraith of the University of Texas has made a persuasive argument that economic growth is necessary (if not sufficient) for promoting a more equitable distribution of income. He writes that "strong and stable economic growth strengthens the weak and the poor while weak and unstable performance strengthens the powerful and the wealthy, in relative terms, for the simple reason that they can protect themselves more effectively." See James K. Galbraith, "Did Macro Policy Cause the Inequality Crisis?" Frank M. Engle Lecture, American College, Bryn Mawr, Pa., May 29, 1997, p. 3. For a full-length treatment of this story, see Galbraith, *Created Unequal.* In the same vein, at the 1998 annual Federal Reserve Bank Retreat in Jackson Hole, Wyoming, Harvard's Larry Katz told the central bankers gathered there that "strong macroeconomic performance is a necessary condition for economic improvements for the disadvantaged," although it would have to be complemented with policies promoting education, workforce preparation, and such income supplements as a strengthened Earned Income Tax Credit. See Larry Katz, "Commentary: The Distribution of Income in Industrialized Countries," paper prepared for the Symposium on Income Inequality: Issues and Policy Options, Federal Reserve Bank of Kansas City, Jackson Hole, Wyoming, August 27–29, 1998.

46. Edward N. Wolff, "Recent Trends in the Size Distribution of Household Wealth," *Journal of Economic Perspectives,* vol. 11 (Winter 1997). By a different measure, the shares of wealth accruing to the top and the bottom of the distribution, Wolff finds slower growth in inequality between 1989 and 1995.

47. On the spread of stock ownership, see Martha Starr-McClure, "Stock Market Wealth and Consumer Spending," *Finance and Economics Discussion Series,* 1998–20, Board of Governors of the Federal Reserve System, April 1998. On the distribution

of wealth after the dispersion of stock ownership to a greater proportion of American families, see Greenspan, "Remarks on Income Inequality."

48. Harrison, *Lean and Mean.*

7. The Main Street Model for Growth with Equity

1. Thomas Kuhn, *The Structure of Scientific Revolutions,* 3d ed., (Chicago: University of Chicago, 1996).

2. One of the best technical renditions of the New Growth theory is found in Paul Romer, "Endogenous Technological Change," *Journal of Political Economy,* vol. 98, no. 5, part 2 (1990). This article expands on his earlier research found in Paul Romer, "Increasing Returns and Long-Run Growth," *Journal of Political Economy,* vol. 94, no. 5 (1986). For a less technical rendition, see Paul Romer, "The Origins of Endogenous Growth," *Journal of Economic Perspectives,* vol. 8, no. 1 (Winter 1994).

3. See Nelson, *Sources of Economic Growth,* p. 42.

4. Romer, "Origins of Endogenous Growth," p. 12.

5. That the potential for new ideas is nearly unlimited and has a virtuous cycle of its own, see Romer, "Economic Growth."

6. See Bernard Wysocki, Jr., "Wealth of Notions: For This Economist, Long-Term Prosperity Hangs on Good Ideas," *Wall Street Journal,* January 21, 1997, p. A1.

7. Joseph A. Schumpeter, *The Theory of Economic Development* (Cambridge, Mass.: Harvard University Press, 1934.)

8. For a superb discussion of this mechanism, see George Evans, Seppo Honkapohja, and Paul Romer, "Growth Cycles," *American Economic Review,* vol. 88 (June 1998).

9. See, for example, Gregory N. Mankiw, "The Growth of Nations," *Brookings Papers on Economic Activity,* vol. 1 (1995).

10. See Paul Romer, "Why, Indeed, in America? Theory, History, and the Origins of Modern Economic Growth," working paper no. 5443, National Bureau of Economic Research, January 1996.

11. Romer, "Why, Indeed, in America?" p. 2.

12. Gene M. Grossman, "Discussion," in *Technology and Growth,* ed. Jeffrey C. Fuhrer and Jane Sneddon Little, Conference Series no. 40 (Boston, Mass.: Federal Reserve Bank of Boston, June 1996), p. 84.

13. See Joel Kurtzman, "An Interview with Paul M. Romer," *Thought Leader* (Booz, Allen & Hamilton, Inc.), first quarter, 1997, p. 2.

14. Martin Neil Baily, "Trends in Productivity Growth," in Fuhrer and Little, eds., *Technology and Growth,* p. 273.

15. Harrison, *Lean and Mean,* chapters 3 and 5.

16. Compare Edwin Mansfield, "Microeconomic Policy and Technological Change," in Fuhrer and Little, *Technology and Growth,* and the many references cited there.

17. Zui Griliches, "The Search for R&D Spillovers," *Scandinavian Journal of Economics,* vol. 94, Supplement (1992), pp. 541–42.

18. Baily, "Trends," p. 274.

19. Francis Narin, Kimberly S. Hamilton, and Dominic Olivastro, "The Increasing Linkage Between U.S. Technology and Public Science," *Research Policy*, no. 932 (July 1997).

20. Baily, "Trends," p. 274.

21. Jeff Faux, "Public Investment for a 21st-Century Economy," in *Restoring Broadly Shared Prosperity*, ed. Ray Marshall (Washington, D.C., and Austin: Economic Policy Institute and Lyndon B. Johnson School of Public Affairs, University of Texas, 1997), p. 149.

22. David Alan Aschauer, "On Bridges to the Twenty-first Century: Figuratively *and* Literally," Report of the Jerome Levy Economics Institute of Bard College, vol. 7, no. 1 (May 1997), p. 13.

23. Aschauer, "Is Public Expenditure Productive?" pp. 177–200.

24. Economists call this technique "pooling cross-section and time series data." Alicia H. Munnell, "Why Has Productivity Declined? Productivity and Public Investment," *New England Economic Review* (Federal Reserve Bank of Boston), January–February 1990, pp. 3–22; Munnell, with Leah M. Cook, "How Does Public Infrastructure Affect Regional Economic Performance?" *New England Economic Review,* September–October 1990, pp. 11–32.

25. Alicia H. Munnell, "Infrastructure Investment and Economic Growth," *Journal of Economic Perspectives,* vol. 6, no. 4 (Fall 1992): pp. 193–94. Earlier, two other economists had measured the contribution of public capital across metropolitan areas, and found the existence of a sizable class of places for which such public investment was indeed productive. Randall W. Eberts and Michael S. Fogarty, "Estimating the Relationship Between Local Public and Private Investment," working paper no. 8703, Federal Reserve Bank of Cleveland, May 1987.

26. See Timothy J. Bartik, *Who Benefits from State and Local Economic Development Policies?* (Kalamazoo, Mich.: W. E. Upjohn Institute for Employment Research, 1991), and Timothy J. Bartik, "Growing State Economies: How Taxes and Public Services Affect Private-Sector Performance," Economic Policy Institute, 1996.

27. Bartik, "Growing State Economies," figure 2, p. 18.

28. Sharon J. Erenburg, "Linking Public Capital to Economic Performance," Public Policy Brief No. 14, Jerome Levy Economics Institute of Bard College, 1994; Erenburg and Mark E. Wohar, "Public and Private Investment: Are There Causal Linkages?" *Journal of Macroeconomics,* vol. 17, no. 1 (Winter 1995), pp. 1–30.

29. There is a huge literature on this subject. For just one example, see John A. Byrne, "The Horizontal Corporation," *Business Week,* December 20, 1993.

30. The literature on the design and impact of employee participation, profit sharing, and worker ownership on productivity is now quite extensive. Much of it is reviewed in Blinder, *Paying for Productivity,* especially Levine and Tyson, "Participation, Productivity, and the Firm's Environment." See also Bluestone and Bluestone, *Negotiating the Future; What Works at Work,* ed. Casey Ichniowski et al., a special issue

of *Industrial Relations,* August 1995; Eileen Appelbaum and Rosemary Batt, *The New American Workplace* (Ithaca, N.Y.: ILR Press, 1994); and, most recently, Stephen A. Hertzenberg, John A. Alic, and Howard Wial, *New Rules for a New Economy* (Ithaca, N.Y.: ILR Press for the Twentieth Century Fund, 1998).

31. Eileen Appelbaum, "Reflections on the High Road Path: Work Organization, Knowledge Management, and Corporate Governance," Economic Policy Institute, June 1998, p. 4. In this discussion paper, based on her ongoing plant- and firm-level studies, Appelbaum also offers an insightful distinction between high performance work organization per se and innovations in the structure of corporate governance, e.g., the role of works council and union "voice" in deciding how to distribute profits or negotiate overtime rules — a theme we will return to in Chapter 8. She also notes that some workplace transformations may pay off in greater profitability *without* necessarily augmenting productivity, as when supplier firms secure longer-term contracts from customers as a reward for improved quality or timely delivery.

32. Ronald Henkoff, "Companies That Train Best," *Fortune,* March 22, 1993.

33. Susan Parks, "Improving Workplace Performance: Historical and Theoretical Contexts," *Monthly Labor Review,* May 1995, p. 26.

34. Ichniowski et al., *What Works at Work.*

35. See Levine and Tyson, "Participation, Productivity, and the Firm's Environment."

36. See Sandra E. Black and Lisa M. Lynch, "How to Compete: The Impact of Workplace Practices and Information Technology on Productivity," working paper no. 6120, National Bureau of Economic Research, August 1997.

37. Black and Lynch, "How to Compete," Table 2.

38. Erik Brynjolfsson and Lorin M. Hitt, "Information Technology and Organizational Design: Evidence from Micro Data," MIT Sloan School of Management, January 1998.

39. Dean Baker, "The Public Investment Deficit: Two Decades of Neglect Threaten the 21st-Century Economy," briefing paper, Economic Policy Institute, Washington, D.C., February 1998.

40. John Bishop, "The Impact of Previous Training on Productivity and Wages," in *Training and the Private Sector: The International Comparisons,* ed. Lisa M. Lynch (Chicago: University of Chicago Press, 1994). See also Bishop, "The Incidence of and Payoff to Employer Training," working paper no. 94-17, Center for Advanced Human Resource Studies, School of Industrial and Labor Relations, Cornell University, 1994; David Knocke and Arne L. Kalleberg, "Job Training in U.S. Organizations," *American Sociological Review,* vol. 59 (August 1994); and Paul Osterman and Rosemary Batt, "Employer-Centered Training Programs for International Competitiveness: Lessons from State Programs," *Journal of Policy Analysis and Management,* vol. 12 (Summer 1993). Bishop adds: "American employers appear to devote less time and resources to the training of entry-level blue-collar, clerical, and service employees than employers in Germany and Japan."

41. Ray Marshall and Marc Tucker, *Thinking for a Living: Education and the Wealth of Nations* (New York: Basic Books, 1992).

42. Lisa M. Lynch, "Payoffs to Alternative Training Strategies at Work," in *Working under Different Rules,* ed. Richard B. Freeman (New York: Russell Sage Foundation, 1993).

43. Peter Cappelli, "Rethinking Employment," *British Journal of Industrial Relations,* vol. 33, no. 4 (December 1995), pp. 563–602.

44. Cited in Henkoff, "Companies That Train Best," p. 62.

45. Bishop, "Incidence" p. 25.

46. American employers *do* contribute part of the social cost of general training, by forgoing the extra profits associated with putting up with generally less productive new workers. But then they are also partially recompensed, by being allowed — by social custom and by union contracts — to pay lower wage rates to apprentices and other novices.

47. Bishop, "Incidence," p. 8. The BLS confirmed this well-known relationship in a recent survey of formal training programs in the private sector; see Bureau of National Affairs, Inc., *Daily Labor Reporter,* Sept. 26, 1994, p. B-19. Of course, the proportion of private businesses that are small is much greater in Japan and Germany than in the United States; Harrison, *Lean and Mean,* chapter 2. Yet Japanese and German firms still manage to invest considerably more in worker training than do their American counterparts. Culture, social norms, and national public policy really do make a difference.

48. National Association of Manufacturers and Grant Thornton Co., "The Skilled Workforce Shortage," Washington D.C., 1997.

49. Unions have also (and traditionally) played an important role in negotiating to get employers to make investments in training that they would not otherwise have made. A good example is afforded by AT&T. Under a contract dating back to 1986, the firm, the Communications Workers of America, and the International Brotherhood of Electrical Workers established a joint labor-management training fund to support training of workers over and above what the company normally provided, targeted especially to help employees meet the entry-level requirements for changing jobs within the firm or for preparing them for new employment outside AT&T. Similar funds exist in the automobile industry, notably between General Motors and the United Auto Workers. But the durability of the AT&T commitment is presently being tested as never before, given the mass restructuring now underway in that company. The same can be said for the long-standing partnership between General Motors and the United Auto Workers, which collaborate in comanaging their famous Paid Educational Leave (PEL) program for union employees of the company, and for the training programs in the needleworks trades provided by UNITE in cooperation with the garment manufacturers in New York City, especially through the activities of the Garment Industries Training Corporation.

50. Compare Eileen Appelbaum and Ronald Schettkat, "Employment and Productivity in Industrialized Economies," *International Labour Review,* vol. 134, nos.

4–5, (1995); Appelbaum and Schettkat, "Product Demand, Productivity, and Labor Demand in a Structural Model," Economic Policy Institute, Washington D.C., November 1996; Richard B. Freeman, "Evaluating the European View That the United States Has No Unemployment Problem," *American Economic Review,* vol. 78, no. 2 (May 1988).

51. In each of these years, sales averaged between 14.5 and 14.9 million vehicles. See the U.S. Bureau of the Census, *Statistical Abstract of the United States* (Washington, D.C.: GPO, 1986, 1996).

52. See Eva E. Jacobs, ed., *Handbook of U.S. Labor Statistics* (Lanham, Md.: Bernan Press, 1998), p. 180.

53. See *Economic Indicators* (November 1998), p. 14.

54. See Jeremy Rifkin, *The End of Work: The Decline of the Global Labor Force and the Dawn of the Post-Market Era* (New York: Putnam, 1995).

55. For details on the traditional workplace contract, see Bluestone and Bluestone, *Negotiating the Future,:* chapter 2.

56. See Robert Buchele and Jens Christiansen, "Worker Rights Promote Productivity Growth," *Challenge,* September–October 1995, pp. 32–37.

57. Okun's now-classic statement is found in Arthur Okun, *Equality and Efficiency: The Big Tradeoff* (Washington D.C.: Brookings Institution, 1975). A fine criticism of this work is found in two of Robert Kuttner's books on the economy: *Economic Illusion* and *Everything for Sale.*

58. Louise Waldstein, "Service Sector Wages, Productivity and Job Creation in the U.S. and Other Countries," in *Toward a High-Wage, High-Productivity Service Sector* (Washington D.C.: Economic Policy Institute, 1989); Lester Thurow, "Wages and the Service Sector," in Marshall, ed., *Restoring Broadly Shared Prosperity.*

59. Cited in Thurow, "Wages and the Service Sector," p. 6.

60. *Ibid.,* p. 7.

61. See Harrison, *Lean and Mean,* chapter 9, for a detailed survey of the evidence.

62. Freeman and Medoff, *What Do Unions Do?*

63. See Bluestone and Bluestone, *Negotiating the Future;* Levine and Tyson, "Participation, Productivity, and the Firm's Environment,"; *Unions and Economic Competitiveness,* ed. Lawrence Mishel and Paula Voos (Armonk: M. E. Sharpe, 1992); Brown and Medoff, "Trade Unions in the Production Process," pp. 355–78; Register, "Wages, Productivity, and Costs."

64. Evans, Honkapohja, and Romer, "Growth Cycles." Romer et al. are not literally making the signals from government, per se, the initiating event; the signals in the pure theoretical model can come from many possible sources. Nor are they suggesting or endorsing the particular examples of government initiatives that we use here to set the machinery in motion. In other words, the particular exemplars in the text are ours, not theirs. But the underlying process is the same, based on the existence of what economists call models with multiple equilibria.

8. From Wall Street to Main Street: Economic Policy for the Twenty-First Century

1. See David Wessel, "Budget Seeks to Raise U.S. Living Standards and Reduce Inequality," *Wall Street Journal,* February 7, 1997, p. A1.

2. Robert Greenstein and Sam Elkin, "How Big Is the Federal Government — and Would the Administration's Budget Make It Bigger?" Center on Budget and Policy Priorities, February 2, 1999, Table 3.

3. In 1992, for example, the federal government provided state and local governments with $9.8 billion to assist local school districts. This represented only 4.3 percent of the $229 billion spent on elementary and secondary schools that year. Computed from U.S. Bureau of the Census, *Statistical Abstract of the United States, 1995* (Washington, D.C.: GPO, 1995), "Federal Aid to State and Local Governments 1970–1995," Table 479, p. 302 and "State and Local Governments–Summary of Finances: 1980–1992," Table 481, p. 304.

4. See M. Edith Rasell and Lawrence Mishel, *Shortchanging Education: How U.S. Spending on Grades K–12 Lags Behind Other Industrialized Nations* (Washington, D.C.: Economic Policy Institute, 1990).

5. See Tom Harkin, "The Intergenerational Growth Opportunity, Education, and Security Act (IGOES)," U.S. Senate Draft Report, March 1999. The IGOES Model is based on earlier research of Barry Bluestone et al., "Generational Alliance: Social Security as a Bank for Education and Training," *American Prospect,* Summer 1990.

6. For a comprehensive analysis of the history of the consortium, its intentions and activities, consult the writings of probably its most important scholarly advocate, UCLA geography professor and administrator, Allen J. Scott. Scott, "The Electric Vehicle Industry and Local Economic Development: Prospects and Policies for Southern California," *Environment and Planning A,* vol. 27 (1995), 863–75; Scott and D. Bergman, "Advanced Ground Transportation Equipment Manufacturing and Local Economic Development: Lessons for Southern California," WP-8, Lewis Center for Regional Policy Studies, UCLA, 1993; Scott, *Technopolis: High Technology Industry and Regional Development in Southern California* (Berkeley: University of California Press, 1993).

7. H. Josef Hebert, "Clinton Calls for $6.3 Billion Tax Package," Associated Press Web site, February 1, 1998.

8. George Hager, "Less Is More This Tax Year," *Washington Post,* National Weekly Edition, March 22, 1999, pp. 6–7.

9. See Wysocki, "Mixed Blessings of Low Unemployment," p. A1.

10. Glassman, "Lonely Unemployment Line."

11. The phenomenon is practically universal across the richest industrialized countries, and easily explained. Better health, more readily available pensions and social security, and the continued shift in the gender composition of seniors — more women living longer — all contributed to the decline in labor force participation. "Older Workers," Census Bureau Web site (www.census.gov/ipc/eurasia/ebisum97.pdf), figure 2.1.

12. For a discussion of these matters, see Bluestone and Bluestone, *Negotiating the Future.*

13. Paul Weiler, "Who Will Represent Labor Now?" *American Prospect,* Summer 1990, p. 83.

14. For more detail on the minimum wage, see Barry Bluestone and Teresa Ghilarducci, "Making Work Pay: Wage Insurance for the Working Poor," Public Policy Brief No. 28, Jerome Levy Economics Institute of Bard College, 1996.

15. Ibid.

16. The following section is drawn from Richard R. Nelson and Paul M. Romer, "Science, Economic Growth, and Public Policy," *Challenge,* March–April 1996, pp. 9–21; and from Kurtzman, "Interview With Paul M. Romer."

17. It is even more complicated, actually. By impeding the propensity to invest, misapplied property rights run the risk of reducing the *diversity* of innovations undertaken in an economy. Several economists have found diversity to be a crucial predictor of the ultimate rate of economic growth, on the principle that you have to have a lot of attempts in order to increase the odds that one or a few initiatives will "hit." On the other hand, weak property rights increase spillovers — externalities that reduce the private payoff to investment. Some of those externalities may be overcome by public spending — that, indeed, is the formal theoretical principle undergirding infrastructure spending. But failing to provide adequate incentives to investors cannot be good for growth in a market economy in the long run.

18. Dani Rodrik, *Has International Economic Integration Gone Too Far?* (Washington, D.C.: Institute for International Economics, 1997).

19. The ILO was created after World War I, together with the League of Nations. The League is of course long gone, while the ILO has become an important forum for discussion about labor issues, and a much-needed source of research and technical assistance, especially in and for emerging nations. Much of this would not be conducted, or even commissioned, if the ILO did not exist.

But as an adjudicator of international disputes on labor issues, the ILO is toothless. It is not a court and cannot impose penalties. It has been suggested that some kind of joint ILO-WTO monitoring and enforcement with respect to fair labor practices and mutually negotiated rights might be possible. Christopher L. Erickson and Daniel J. B. Mitchell, "Labor Standards and Trade Agreements: U.S. Experience," *Comparative Labor Law and Policy Journal* vol. 19, no. 2 (Winter 1998), pp. 145–83. See also *International Labour Standards and Economic Interdependence,* ed. Werner Sengenberger and Duncan Campbell (Geneva: International Institute for Labour Studies, ILO, 1994).

20. Robert B. Reich, "Keynote Address," in *International Labor Standards and Global Economic Integration: Proceedings of a Symposium* (Washington, D.C.: U.S. Department of Labor, July 1994).

21. Congressman Richard Gephardt has been a leading proponent of adding labor rights and labor standards to trade agreements such as NAFTA. His argument for such language in trade bills is well articulated in Richard Gephardt and Michael

Wessel, *An Even Better Place: America in the 21st Century* (New York: Public Affairs, 1999), especially pp. 89–107.

22. Lance Compa, "A Fast Track for Labor," *American Prospect*, September–October 1998, p. 61.

23. Erickson and Mitchell, "Labor Standards," p. 153.

24. Sam Dillon, "After Four Years of Nafta, Labor Is Forging Cross-Border Ties," *New York Times*, December 20, 1997, p. A1.

25. Greider, *One World, Ready or Not*, p. 25.

26. For a sample of mainstream opinions, see "Special Report: How to Reshape the World Financial System," *Business Week*, October 12, 1998. Harvard's Jeffrey Sachs — himself the original architect of the "shock treatment" to Eastern Europe that arguably profoundly hampered that region's ability to restructure patiently with the passing of communism — was calling for expansion of the G7 to a group that would include Russia and eight developing countries. A major feature of any new regime proposed by this "G16" would be widespread debt-forgiveness. Jeffrey Sachs, "Global Capitalism: Making it Work," *Economist*, September 12, 1998, p. 23.

27. John Eatwell, "Unemployment on a World Scale," in *Global Unemployment*, ed. Eatwell, (Armonk, N.Y.: M. E. Sharpe, 1996).

28. Ibid., p. 15.

29. Ibid., pp. 15–16.

30. For an excellent discussion of the Tobin Tax and other possible international regulations on capital flows, see Robert A. Blecker, *Taming Global Finance: A Better Architecture for Growth and Equity* (Washington, D.C.: Economic Policy Institute, 1999).

31. Mahbub Ul Haq, Inge Kaul, and Isabelle Grunberg, eds., *The Tobin Tax: Coping with Financial Volatility* (Oxford: Oxford University Press, 1997).

32. Jeff Bingaman, "Scrambling to Pay the Bills: Building Allies for America's Working Families," photocopy, February 28, 1996.

33. Evans, Honkapohja, and Romer, "Growth Cycles," p. 1.

34. Steven Pearlstein, "To Close a Widening Gap," *Washington Post*, November 19, 1995, p. H4.

Bibliography

Abramovitz, Moses. "Economic Growth in the United States." *American Economic Review,* vol. 52, no. 4 (September 1962).

Abramovitz, Moses, and Paul David. "Reinterpreting Economic Growth: Parables and Realities." *American Economic Review,* vol. 63 (June 1973).

Alchian, A. "Reliability of Progress Curves in Airframe Production." *Econometrica,* vol. 24 (April 1956).

Alesina, Alberto, and Dani Rodrik. "Distributive Politics and Economic Growth." *Quarterly Journal of Economics,* vol. 109, no. 2 (May 1994).

Allen, Steven G. "Declining Unionization in Construction: The Facts and the Reasons." *Industrial and Labor Relations Review,* April 1988.

———. "Unionized Construction Workers Are More Productive." *Quarterly Journal of Economics,* May 1984.

Altman, Roger C. "The Nuke of the 90s." *New York Times Magazine,* March 1, 1998.

Appelbaum, Eileen. "Reflections on the High Road Path: Work Organization, Knowledge Management, and Corporate Governance." Economic Policy Institute, June 1998.

Appelbaum, Eileen, and Rosemary Batt. *The New American Workplace.* Ithaca, N.Y.: ILR Press, 1994.

Appelbaum, Eileen, and Ronald Schettkat. "Employment and Productivity in Industrialized Economies." *International Labour Review,* vol. 134, nos. 4–5 (1995).

———. "Product Demand, Productivity, and Labor Demand in a Structural Model." Economic Policy Institute, Washington D.C., November 1996.

Arrow, Kenneth. "The Economic Implications of Learning by Doing." *Review of Economic Studies,* June 1962.

Aschauer, David Alan. "Is Public Expenditure Productive?" *Journal of Monetary Economics,* vol. 23 (1989).

———. "On Bridges to the Twenty-first Century: Figuratively *and* Literally." *Report of the Jerome Levy Economics Institute of Bard College,* vol. 7, no. 1 (May 1997).

Attewell, Paul. "Information Technology and the Productivity Paradox." In *Organizational Linkages: Understanding the Productivity Paradox,* edited by Douglas H. Harris. Washington, D.C.: National Academy Press, 1994.

———. "Technology Diffusion and Organizational Learning." *Organization Science,* vol. 2, no. 4 (1992).

Baily, Martin Neil. *The Productivity Growth Slowdown by Industry,* Brookings Papers on Economic Activity no. 2, 1982.

———. "Trends in Productivity Growth." In *Technology and Growth: Conference*

Proceedings, edited by Jeffrey C. Fuhrer and Jane Sneddon. Conference Series No. 40. Boston: Federal Reserve Bank of Boston, June 1996.

Baker, Dean. "The Public Investment Deficit: Two Decades of Neglect Threatens 21st-Century Economy." Briefing paper, Economic Policy Institute, Washington, D.C., February 1998.

———. "Saving Social Security with Stocks: The Promises Don't Add Up." In *Social Security Reform,* edited by Richard C. Leone and Greg Anrig, Jr. New York: Century Fund Press, 1999.

Baker, Dean, and Todd Schafer. "The Case for Public Investment." Economic Policy Institute, Washington, D.C., 1995.

Barber, Randy, and Robert E. Scott. *Jobs on the Wing: Trading Away the Future of the U.S. Aerospace Industry.* Washington, D.C.: Economic Policy Institute, 1995.

Barro, Robert J. "Determinants of Economic Policy Growth: A Cross-Country Empirical Study." Working paper no. 5698, National Bureau of Economic Research, August 1996.

Bartik, Timothy J. "Growing State Economies: How Taxes and Public Services Affect Private Sector Performance." Economic Policy Institute, Washington D.C., 1996.

———. "Who Benefits from State and Local Economic Development Policies?" Kalamazoo, Mich.: W. E. Upjohn Institute for Employment Research, 1991.

Barua, A., C. Kriebel, and T. Mukhopadhyay. "Information Technology and Business Value: An Analytic and Empirical Investigation." Working paper, University of Texas at Austin, May 1991.

Bass, Scott A., Joseph F. Quinn, and Richard V. Burkhauser. "Toward Pro-Work Policies and Programs for Older Americans." In *Older and Active: How Americans over 55 Are Contributing to Society,* edited by Scott A. Bass. New Haven: Yale University Press, 1995.

Basu, Susanto. "Discussion." In *Technology and Growth,* edited by Jeffrey C. Fuhrer and Jane Sneddon Little. Conference Series No. 40. Boston: Federal Reserve Bank of Boston, June 1996.

Baumol, William J. "Macroeconomics of Unbalanced Growth: The Anatomy of Urban Crisis." *American Economic Review,* vol. 57, no. 3 (June 1967).

Becker, Gary. "Save Some of the Surplus for Medical Research." *Business Week,* April 19, 1999.

Bernhardt, Annette, Martina Morris, Mark Handcock and Marc Scott. "Job Instability and Wage Inequality among Young Men: A Comparison of Two NLS Cohorts." Institute on Education and the Economy, Columbia University, January 1998.

Bernstein, Aaron. "Inequality: How the Gap Between Rich and Poor Hurts the Economy." *Business Week,* August 15, 1994.

———. "Why Wages Aren't Giving the Market Willies." *Business Week,* June 22, 1998, p. 37.

Bernstein, Jared. "Real Median Wages Finally Recover 1989 Level." *Quarterly Wage and Employment Series* (Economic Policy Institute), vol. 1, no. 1 (First Quarter 1999).

Bernstein, Jared, and Lawrence Mishel. "Wages Gain Ground." Economic Policy Institute, Issue Brief No. 129, February 2, 1999.

Bhagwati, Jagdish. "The Capital Myth: The Difference Between Trade in Widgets and Dollars." *Foreign Affairs,* vol. 77, no. 3 (May–June 1998), pp. 7–12.

Bingaman, Jeff. "Scrambling to Pay the Bills: Building Allies for America's Working Families," photocopy, February 28, 1996.

Bishop, John. "The Impact of Previous Training on Productivity and Wages." In *Training and the Private Sector: The International Comparisons,* edited by Lisa M. Lynch. Chicago: University of Chicago Press, 1994.

———. "The Incidence of and Payoff to Employer Training." Working paper no. 94-17, Center for Advanced Human Resource Studies, School of Industrial and Labor Relations, Cornell University, 1994.

Black, Sandra E., and Lisa M. Lynch. "How to Compete: The Impact of Workplace Practices and Information Technology on Productivity." Working paper no. 6120, National Bureau of Economic Research, August 1997.

Blank, Rebecca. *It Takes a Nation.* New York: Russell Sage Foundation, 1997.

Blanton, Kimberly. "Baby Boomers Index." *Boston Globe,* April 23, 1999.

Blecker, Robert A. *Taming Global Finance: A Better Architecture for Growth and Equity.* Washington, D.C.: Economic Policy Institute, 1999.

Blinder, Alan S. "Can We Grow Faster?" *Challenge,* November–December 1996.

Blinder, Alan S., ed. *Paying for Productivity.* Washington, D.C.: Brookings Institution, 1990.

Bluestone, Barry. "The Great U-Turn Revisited: Economic Restructuring, Jobs, and the Redistribution of Earnings." In *Jobs, Earnings, and Employment Growth Policies in the United States,* edited by John D. Kasarda. Boston: Kluwer Academic Publishers, 1990.

———. "The Inequality Express." *American Prospect,* November 1994.

———. "Who's Sabotaging Prosperity?" Paper prepared for the Conference on the Social Dimensions of Globalization, Instituto Europeo Di Studi Sociali, Rome, October 4–5, 1998.

Bluestone, Barry, and Irving Bluestone. *Negotiating the Future: A Labor Perspective on American Business.* New York: Basic Books, 1992.

Bluestone, Barry, and Teresa Ghilarducci. "Making Work Pay: Wage Insurance for the Working Poor." Public policy brief no. 28, Jerome Levy Economics Institute of Bard College, 1996.

Bluestone, Barry, and Bennett Harrison. *The Deindustrialization of America.* New York: Basic Books, 1982.

Bluestone, Barry, Peter Jordan, and Mark Sullivan. *Aircraft Industry Dynamics: An Analysis of Competition, Capital, and Labor.* Boston: Auburn House, 1981.

Bluestone, Barry, Michael Massagli, and Mary H. Stevenson. "A 'Job Competition' Model of Wage Determination: Applications to Blacks, Hispanics, and Whites in the Greater Boston Labor Market." Russell Sage Foundation Conference on the Multi-City Study of Urban Inequality (MCSUI), February 1996.

Bluestone, Barry, Alan Clayton Matthews, John Havens, and Howard Young. "Generational Alliance: Social Security as a Bank for Education and Training. *American Prospect,* Summer 1990.

Bluestone, Barry, and Stephen Rose. "The Macroeconomics of Working Time." *Review of Social Economy,* Winter 1998.

———. "Overworked and Underemployed." *American Prospect,* March–April 1997.

———. "The Unmeasured Labor Force." Public policy brief no. 39, Jerome Levy Economics Institute of Bard College, 1998.

Bluestone, Barry, and Mary Stevenson. *Greater Boston in Transition: Race and Ethnicity in a Renaissance Region.* New York: Russell Sage, forthcoming.

Bode, H. W. *Synergy: Technical Integration and Technological Innovation in the Bell System.* Murray Hill, N.J.: Bell Telephone Laboratories, 1971.

Bodipo-Memba, Alejandro. "Consumer Confidence Hits 32-Year High." *Wall Street Journal,* February 24, 1999.

Brown, Charles, and James Medoff. "Trade Unions in the Production Process." *Journal of Political Economy,* vol. 86, no. 3 (June 1978), pp. 355–78.

Brynjolfsson, Erik, and Lorin M. Hitt. "Computers and Productivity Growth: Firm-Level Evidence." MIT Sloan School of Management, January 1997.

———. "Information Technology as a Factor of Production: The Role of Differences among Firms." *Economics of Innovation and New Technology,* vol 3., no. 4 (1995).

———. "Information Technology and Internal Firm Organization: An Exploratory Analysis." MIT Sloan School of Management, March 1997.

———. "Information Technology and Organizational Design: Evidence from Micro Data." MIT Sloan School of Management, January 1998.

———. "Paradox Lost? Firm-Level Evidence on the Returns to Information Systems Spending." *Management Science,* vol. 42, no. 4 (April 1996).

Buchanan, Patrick J. *The Great Betrayal: How American Sovereignty and Social Justice Are Being Sacrificed to the Gods of the Global Economy.* Boston: Little, Brown, 1998.

Buchele, Robert, and Jens Christiansen. "Workers Rights Promote Productivity Growth." *Challenge,* September–October 1995.

"Budget Aide Named by GOP Won't Stay On." Associated Press/*Boston Globe,* October 29, 1998.

Bureau of National Affairs. *Daily Labor Reporter,* September 26, 1994.

Burkhauser, Richard V., Amy D. Creuz, Mary C. Daly, and Steven P. Jenskins. *Income Mobility and the Middle Class.* Washington, D.C.: American Enterprise Institute, 1996.

Byrne, John A. "The Horizontal Corporation." *Business Week,* December 20, 1993.

Cappelli, Peter. "Rethinking Employment." *British Journal of Industrial Relations,* vol. 33, no. 4 (December 1995).

Card, David, and Alan Krueger. *Myth and Measurement: The New Economics of the Minimum Wage.* Princeton: Princeton University Press, 1995.

Card, S. K., J. M. Robert, and L. N. Keenan. "On-Line Composition of Text." Xerox Palo Alto Research Center, Stanford, Calif.

Carey, John. "U.S. Innovation Ain't What It Used To Be." *Business Week,* March 22, 1999.

Carnevale, Anthony P., and Stephen J. Rose. "Education for What? The New Office Economy: Technical Report." Princeton: Educational Testing Service, 1998.

Cassidy, John. "Pricking the Bubble." *The New Yorker,* August 17, 1998.

Centrist Democratic Leadership Council. "Opinion Poll." *New York Times,* July 8, 1993.

Cherny, Andrei. "A 21st-Century Growth Agenda." *New Democrat Blueprint,* vol. 2 (Winter 1998).

Clark, Kim B. "The Impact of Unionization on Productivity: A Case Study." *Industrial and Labor Relations Review,* vol. 33, no. 4 (July 1980), pp. 451–69.

Commission on the Future of Worker-Management Relations. *Report and Recommendations.* U.S. Department of Labor and U.S. Department of Commerce, 1994.

Compa, Lance. "A Fast Track for Labor." *American Prospect,* September–October 1998.

Congressional Research Service. *Veterans' Education Assistance Programs.* Report no. 86-32 EPW. Washington, D.C.: Library of Congress, January 31, 1986.

Connerton, M., R. B. Freeman, and J. L. Medoff. "Industrial Relations and Productivity: A Study of the U.S. Bituminous Coal Industry." Cambridge, Mass.: Harvard University, 1983.

Cooper, Helene, and Sara Calian. "With the Euro in View, U.S. Securities Firms Court the Europeans." *Wall Street Journal,* August 26, 1998.

Cooper, James C., and Kathleen Madigan. "Business Outlook." *Business Week,* August 17, 1998.

Council of Economic Advisers. "Economic Indicators." Washington, D.C.: Government Printing Office, April 1998; June 1998; November 1998; February 1999, April 1999.

Council of Economic Advisers. *Economic Report of the President:* 1987; 1988; 1989; 1996; 1998; 1999. Washington, D.C.: Government Printing Office.

Daerr, Elizabeth, and Jacob B. Schlesinger. "Import Prices Declined 1.3% in January." *Wall Street Journal,* February 17, 1998.

Danziger, Sheldon, and Peter Gottschalk. *America Unequal.* Cambridge, Mass.: Harvard University Press, 1996.

David, Paul. "Computer and Dynamo: The Modern Productivity Paradox in a Not-too-Distant Mirror." *Technology and Productivity: The Challenge for Economic Policy.* Paris: OECD, 1991.

———. "The Growth of Real Product in the United States Before 1840: New Evidence, Controlled Conjectures." *Journal of Economic History,* vol. 27, no. 2 (June 1967).

———. "The 'Horndal Effect' in Lowell, 1934–56: A Short-Run Learning Curve for Integrated Cotton Textile Mills." In *Technical Choice, Innovation, and Economic Growth: Essays on American and British Economic Experience,* edited by Paul A. David. London: Cambridge University Press, 1975.

————. "Learning by Doing and Tariff Protection." *Journal of Economic History,* vol. 30 (September 1970).

————. "The Mechanization of Reaping in the Ante-Bellum Midwest." *Industrialization in Two Systems: Essays in Honor of Alexander Gerschenkron,* edited by Henry Rosovsky. New York: John Wiley, 1966.

Davis, Bob, and David Wessel. *Prosperity: The Coming 20-Year Boom and What It Means to You.* New York: Times Business Books, 1998.

Denison, Edward F. *Accounting for Slower Economic Growth: The United States in the 1970s.* Washington, D.C.: Brookings Institution, 1979.

————. *The Sources of Economic Growth in the U.S.* New York: Committee for Economic Development, 1962.

————. *Trends in American Economic Growth, 1929–1982.* Washington, D.C.: Brookings Institution, 1985.

Dertouzos, Michael L., Richard K. Lester, and Robert M. Solow. *Made in America.* Cambridge, Mass.: MIT Press, 1989.

Dicken, Peter. *Global Shift.* 2d edition. New York: Guilford Press, 1992.

Dillon, Sam. "After Four Years of Nafta, Labor Is Forging Cross-Border Ties." *New York Times,* December 20, 1997.

Dreier, Peter, and Richard Rothstein. "Seismic Stimulus: The California Quake's Creative Destruction." *American Prospect,* Summer 1994.

Eatwell, John. "Unemployment on a World Scale." In *Global Unemployment,* edited by John Eatwell. Armonk, N.Y.: M.E. Sharpe, 1996.

Eberts, Randall W., and Michael S. Fogarty. "Estimating the Relationship Between Local Public and Private Investment." Working paper no. 8703, Federal Reserve Bank of Cleveland, May 1987.

Eisner, Robert. *The Misunderstood Economy: What Counts and How to Count It.* Boston: Harvard Business School Press, 1994.

Elliott, Michael. *The Day Before Yesterday: Reconsidering America's Past, Recovering the Present.* New York: Simon & Schuster, 1996.

Erenburg, Sharon J. "Linking Public Capital to Economic Performance." Public policy brief no. 14, Jerome Levy Economics Institute of Bard College, 1994.

Erenburg, Sharon J., and Mark E. Wohar. "Public and Private Investment: Are There Causal Linkages?" *Journal of Macroeconomics,* vol. 17, no. 1 (Winter 1995).

Erickson, Christopher L., and Daniel J. B. Mitchell. "Labor Standards and Trade Agreements: U.S. Experience." *Comparative Labor Law and Policy Journal,* vol. 19, no. 2 (Winter 1998).

Espo, David. "Congress Approves 2000 Budget Plan." Associated Press, May 25, 1999.

Evans, George, Seppo Honkapohja, and Paul Romer. "Growth Cycles." *American Economic Review,* vol. 88 (June 1998).

Farrell, Christopher, and Michael Mandel. "Productivity to the Rescue." *Business Week,* October 9, 1995.

————. "Why Are We So Afraid of Growth?" *Business Week,* May 16, 1994.

Faux, Jeff. "Public Investment for a 21st-Century Economy." In *Restoring Broadly*

Shared Prosperity, edited by Ray Marshall. Washington, D.C. and Austin: Economic Policy Institute and Lyndon B. Johnson School of Public Affairs, University of Texas, 1997.

Feldstein, Martin, and Kathleen Feldstein. "A Penny Saved? Hardly: Low Savings, High Spending Gum Up Economic Machinery." *Boston Globe,* August 18, 1998.

Felix, David. "IMF Bailouts and Global Financial Flows." *Foreign Policy in Focus* (Interhemispheric Resource Center and Institute for Policy Studies), vol. 3, no. 5 (April 1998).

Fieleke, Norman S. "Popular Myths about the World Economy." *New England Economic Review,* July–August 1997.

———. "The Soaring Trade in 'Nontradables.' " *New England Economic Review,* November–December 1995, pp. 25–36.

Foust, Dean. "Alan Greenspan's Brave New World." *Business Week,* July 14, 1997.

Frank, Robert. "Talent and the Winner-Take-All Society." *American Prospect,* Spring 1994.

Frank, Robert H., and Philip J. Cook. *The Winner-Take-All Society.* New York: Free Press, 1995.

Franke, Robert. *Technology Revolution and Productivity Decline: The Case of U.S. Banks.* Cambridge, Mass.: MIT Press, 1989.

Freeman, Richard B. "Evaluating the European View That the United States Has No Unemployment Problem." *American Economic Review,* vol. 78, no. 2 (May 1988).

Freeman, Richard B., and Lawrence F. Katz. "Rising Wage Inequality: The United States vs. Other Advanced Countries." In *Working under Different Rules,* edited by Richard B. Freeman. New York: Russell Sage, 1994.

Freeman, Richard B. and James L. Medoff. *What Do Unions Do?* New York: Basic Books, 1984.

"Freer Trade Gets an Unfriendly Reception." *Business Week.* September 22, 1997.

Friedman, Milton. "The Role of Monetary Policy." *American Economic Review,* vol. 58 (March 1968).

Galbraith, James K. *Created Unequal: The Crisis in American Pay.* New York: Century Fund, 1998.

Galbraith, James K. "Did Macro Policy Cause the Inequality Crisis?" Frank M. Engle Lecture, American College, Bryn Mawr, Pa., May 29, 1997.

———. "Inequality and Unemployment: Monthly Data for the United States." University of Texas Inequality Project, University of Texas at Austin, April 1999.

———. "The Surrender of Economic Policy." *American Prospect,* March–April 1996.

Galbraith, John Kenneth. *Name-Dropping.* Boston: Houghton Mifflin, 1999.

Gallman, Robert E. "Gross National Product in the United States, 1834–1909." In *Output, Employment, and Productivity in the United States after 1800,* edited by Dorothy S. Brady. Studies in Income and Wealth, vol. 30. New York: National Bureau of Economic Research, 1966.

Gastil, Raymond D. *Progress.* New York: Praeger, 1993.

Gephardt, Richard, and Michael Wessel. *An Even Better Place: America in the 21st Century.* New York: Public Affairs, 1999.

Glassman, Bruce S., ed. *The Macmillan Visual Almanac.* New York: Macmillan, 1996, p. 522.

Glassman, James K. "Lonely Unemployment Line." *U.S. News and World Report,* December 22, 1997.

Gleckman, Howard, Mike McNamee, and Ann Therese Palmer. "A Downturn Could Really Rock the Boat." *Business Week,* August 17, 1998.

"Goldilocks Politics." *Economist,* December 19, 1998.

Gollop, Frank M. "Analysis of the Productivity Slowdown: Evidence for a Sector-Biased or Sector-Neutral Industrial Strategy." In *Productivity Growth and U.S. Competitiveness,* edited by William J. Baumol and Kenneth McLennan. New York: Oxford University Press, 1985.

Gordon, Robert J. "Problems in the Measurement and Performance of Service-Sector Productivity in the United States." Working paper no. 5519. National Bureau of Economic Research, Cambridge, Mass., March 1996.

Gottschalk, Peter, and Timothy Smeeding. "Cross-National Comparisons of Earnings and Income Inequality." *Journal of Economic Literature,* vol. 35 (June 1997), pp. 633–87.

Gramlich, Edward M. "Infrastructure Investment: A Review Essay." *Journal of Economic Literature,* vol. 32 (September 1994), p. 1180.

Greenberg, Stanley B. "Private Heroism and Public Purpose." *American Prospect,* September–October 1996.

Greenspan, Alan. "Remarks on Income Inequality." Symposium on Income Inequality: Issues and Policy Options, Federal Reserve Bank of Kansas City, Jackson Hole, Wyo., August 28, 1998.

———. Statement before the Committee on the Budget, United States Senate, Washington, D.C., January 29, 1998.

———. Testimony before the Joint Economic Committee. U.S. Congress, June 10, 1998.

Greenstein, Robert, and Sam Elkin. "How Big Is the Federal Government — and Would the Administration's Budget Make It Bigger?" Center on Budget and Policy Priorities, February 2, 1999.

Greenwood, Jeremy. "The Third Industrial Revolution." Paper prepared for the American Enterprise Institute, October 25, 1996.

Greenwood, Jeremy, and Mehmet Yorukoglu. "1974." Working paper no. 429, Rochester Center for Economic Research, University of Rochester, September 1996.

Greider, William. *One World, Ready or Not: The Manic Logic of Global Capitalism.* New York: Simon & Schuster, 1997.

———. *Secrets of the Temple: How the Federal Reserve Runs the Country.* New York: Simon & Schuster, 1987.

Griliches, Zvi. "Hybrid Corn and the Economics of Innovation." *Science,* vol. 132 (July 29, 1960).

―――. "Productivity, R&D, and the Data Constraint." *American Economic Review,* vol. 84 (March 1994).

―――. "R&D and the Productivity Slowdown." *American Economic Review,* vol. 70 (May 1980).

―――. "The Search for R&D Spillovers." *Scandinavian Journal of Economics,* vol. 94, supplement (1992).

Grossman, Gene M. "Discussion." In *Technology and Growth,* edited by Jeffrey C. Fuhrer and Jane Sneddon. Conference Series No. 40. Boston: Federal Reserve Bank of Boston, June 1996.

Grossman, Gene M., and Elhanan Helpman. "Endogenous Innovation in the Theory of Growth." *Journal of Economic Perspectives,* vol. 8, no. 1 (Winter 1994).

Hager, George. "Less Is More This Tax Year." *Washington Post,* National Weekly Edition, March 22, 1999, pp. 6–7.

Harkin, Tom. "The Intergenerational Growth Opportunity, Education, and Security Act (IGOES)." U.S. Senate Draft Report, March 1999.

Harley, C. Knick. "Reassessing the Industrial Revolution: A Macro View." In *The British Industrial Revolution: An Economic Perspective,* edited by Joel Mokyr. Boulder, Colo.: Westview Press, 1993.

Harrison, Bennett. *Lean and Mean: Why Large Corporations Will Continue to Dominate the Global Economy.* New York: Guilford Press, 1997.

―――. "Where Private Investment Fails." *American Prospect,* September 1992.

Harrison, Bennett, and Barry Bluestone. *The Great U-Turn: Corporate Restructuring and the Polarizing of America.* New York: Basic Books, 1988.

Harrison, Bennett, Maryellen Kelley, and Jon Gant. "Innovative Firm Behavior and Local Milieu: Exploring the Intersection of Agglomeration, Industrial Organization, and Technological Change." *Economic Geography,* vol. 72 (July 1996).

Hays, Kristen. "Too Many Projects, Not Enough Steel." Associated Press, March 14, 1999.

Hebert, H. Josef. "Clinton Calls for $6.3 Billion Tax Package." Associated Press Web Site, February 1, 1998.

Henkoff, Ronald. "Companies That Train Best." *Fortune,* March 22, 1993.

Hertzenberg, Stephen A., John A. Alic, and Howard Wial. *New Rules for a New Economy.* Ithaca, N.Y.: ILR Press for the Twentieth Century Fund, 1998.

Hirsch, Barry T., and Albert N. Link. "Unions, Productivity, and Productivity Growth." *Journal of Labor Research,* vol. 5 (Winter 1984).

House Committee on Ways and Means, 95th Cong., 2nd sess. *Tax Reductions — Economists' Comments on H.R. 8333 and S. 1860.* Washington, D.C.: Government Printing Office, 1978.

Howell, David R., Margaret Duncan, and Bennett Harrison, "Low Wages in the U.S. and High Unemployment in Europe: A Critical Assessment of the Conventional

Wisdom." Working paper no. 5, Center for Economic Policy Analysis, New School, New York, February 1998.

Howes, Candace. "Long-Term Economic Strategy and Employment Growth in the U.S.: An Analysis of Clinton's Economic Policies." *Contributions to Political Economy,* 1995.

Ichniowski, Casey, et. al., eds. *What Works at Work. Industrial Relations,* special issue, August 1995.

International Forum on Globalization. "Should Corporations Govern the World?" Advertisement, *New York Times,* February 13, 1998.

Jacobs, Eva E., ed. *Handbook of U.S. Labor Statistics.* Lanham, Md.: Bernan Press, 1998.

Jargowsky, Paul. *Poverty and Place: Ghettos, Barrios and the American City.* New York: Russell Sage Foundation, 1997.

Jasinowski, Jerry J. "The Case for Higher Growth: Technology, Disinflation, and New Economic Policies." Manufacturing Institute, National Association of Manufacturing, Washington, D.C., July 1996.

Jorgenson, Dale W. "Productivity and Postwar U.S. Economic Growth." In *Productivity,* vol. 1., edited by Dale W. Jorgenson. Cambridge, Mass.: MIT Press, 1996.

Jorgenson, Dale W., Frank M. Gollop, and Barbara M. Fraumeni. *Productivity and U.S. Economic Growth.* Cambridge, Mass.: Harvard University Press, 1987.

Jorgenson, Dale W., and Zvi Griliches. "The Explanation of Productivity Change." In *Productivity,* vol. 1: *Postwar U.S. Economic Growth,* edited by Dale W. Jorgenson. Cambridge, Mass.: MIT Press, 1996.

Jovenovic, B., and S. Lach. "Product Innovation and the Business Cycle." *International Economic Review,* forthcoming.

Kahn, Herman. *The Coming Boom.* New York: Simon & Schuster, 1982.

Katz, Larry. "Commentary: The Distribution of Income in Industrialized Countries." Paper prepared for the Symposium on Income Inequality: Issues and Policy Options, Federal Reserve Bank of Kansas City, Jackson Hole, Wyo., August 27–29, 1998.

Keene, Joanne. "Social Security, Medicare Bankruptcy Delayed." Reuters News Service, March 30, 1999.

Kelley, Maryellen. "New Process Technology, Job Design, and Work Organization." *American Sociological Review,* vol. 55 (April 1990).

———. "Productivity and Information Technology: The Elusive Connection." *Management Science,* vol. 40 (November 1994).

Kelley, Maryellen, and Harvey Brooks. "External Learning Opportunities and the Diffusion of Process Innovations to Small Firms." *Technological Forecasting and Social Change,* vol. 39 (April 1991).

Kendrick, John W. *The Formation and Stocks of Total Capital.* New York: National Bureau of Economic Research, 1976.

Kendrick, John W., ed. *International Comparisons of Productivity and Causes of the Slowdown.* Washington, D.C.: American Enterprise Institute, 1984.

Kerwin, Kathleen. "The Shutdown GM Needs?: It's a Chance to Clean House and Downsize." *Business Week,* July 13, 1998.

Knocke, David, and Arne L. Kalleberg. "Job Training in U.S. Organizations." *American Sociological Review,* vol. 59 (August 1994).

Koretz, Gene. "Solving the Savings Riddle." *Business Week,* November 11, 1996.

Krugman, Paul. *The Age of Diminished Expectations.* Cambridge, Mass.: MIT Press, 1990.

———. "Stable Prices and Fast Growth: Just Say No." *Economist,* August 31, 1996.

Kuhn, Thomas. *The Structure of Scientific Revolutions.* 3rd edition. Chicago: University of Chicago, 1996.

Kurtzman, Joel. "An Interview with Paul M. Romer." *Thought Leader* (Booz, Allen & Hamilton, Inc.), first quarter, 1997.

Kuttner, Robert. *The Economic Illusion: False Choices Between Prosperity and Social Justice.* Boston: Houghton Mifflin, 1984.

———. *The End of Laissez-Faire: Economics and National Purpose after the Cold War.* New York: Simon & Schuster, 1990.

———. *Everything for Sale: The Virtues and Limits of Markets.* New York: Knopf, 1997.

Kuznets, Simon. *Economic Development, the Family and Income Distribution: Selected Essays.* Cambridge: Cambridge University Press, 1989.

Landes, David. *The Unbound Prometheus: Technological Change and Industrial Development in Western Europe from 1750 to the Present.* London: Cambridge University Press, 1969.

Landsberg, Hans H., and Sam H. Schurr. *Energy in the United States.* New York: Random House, 1968.

Larin, Kathryn, and Elizabeth C. McNichol. *Pulling Apart: A State-by-State Analysis of Income Trends.* Washington, D.C.: Center on Budget and Policy Priorities, December 16, 1997.

Levine, David I., and Laura D'Andrea Tyson. "Participation, Productivity, and the Firm's Environment." in *Paying for Productivity,* edited by Alan S. Blinder. Washington, D.C.: Brookings Institution, 1990.

Levine, Robert A. "The Economic Consequences of Mr. Clinton." *Atlantic Monthly,* July 1996.

Link, Albert N. "Productivity Growth, Environmental Regulations, and the Composition of R&D." *Bell Journal of Economics,* Autumn 1982.

Loveman, Gary. "An Assessment of the Productivity Impact of Information Technologies." In *Information Technology and the Corporation of the 1990s: Research Studies,* edited by T.J. Allen and Scott Morton. Cambridge, Mass.: MIT Press, 1994.

Lucas, Jr., Robert E. and Thomas P. Sargent. "After Keynesian Macroeconomics." *Quarterly Review,* (Federal Reserve Bank of Minneapolis), vol. 3 (Spring 1979).

Lynch, Lisa M. "Payoffs to Alternative Training Strategies at Work." In *Working under Different Rules,* edited by Richard B. Freeman. New York: Russell Sage Foundation, 1993.

Maddison, Angus. "Growth and Slowdown in Advanced Capitalist Economies:

Techniques of Quantitative Assessment." *Journal of Economic Literature,* vol. 25, no. 2 (June 1987).

Madrick, Jeffrey. *The End of Affluence: The Causes and Consequences of America's Economic Dilemma.* New York: Random House, 1995.

Magma Copper Company. "Magma Copper Company — A Cultural Revolution," Spring 1992. Magma Copper Company, "Annual Report," 1992.

Magnusson, Paul, and Stephen Baker. "The Explosive Trade Deal You've Never Heard Of." *Business Week,* February 9, 1998.

Malkiel, Burton G. "Wall Street Moves Main Street." *Wall Street Journal,* June 23, 1998.

Mandel, Michael J. "Financial Services: The Silent Engine." *Business Week,* December 21, 1998.

———. *The High-Risk Society: Peril and Promise in the New Economy.* New York: Times Business Books, 1996.

———. "The 21st-Century Economy." *Business Week,* August 24, 1998.

Mankiw, Gregory N. "The Growth of Nations." *Brookings Papers on Economic Activity,* vol. 1 (1995).

Mansfield, Edwin. "Basic Research and Productivity Increase in Manufacturing." *American Economic Review,* December 1980.

———. "Microeconomic Policy and Technological Change." In *Technology and Growth,* edited by Jeffrey C. Fuhrer and Jane Sneddon Little. Conference series no. 40. Boston: Federal Reserve Bank of Boston, June.1996.

———. "Social and Private Rates of Return from Industrial Innovations." *Quarterly Journal of Economics,* vol. 91 (May 1977).

———. "Technological Change and Market Structure: An Empirical Study." *American Economic Review,* vol. 73 (May 1983).

Markusen, Ann. "The Militarized Economy." *World Policy Journal,* vol. 3, no. 3 (Summer 1986).

Marshall, Ray, and Marc Tucker. *Thinking for a Living: Education and the Wealth of Nations.* New York: Basic Books, 1992.

Marx, Karl. *Das Kapital.* New York: International Publishers, 1894.

Melman, Seymour. *The Permanent War Economy.* New York: Simon & Schuster, 1985.

Mishel, Lawrence. *Manufacturing Numbers: How Inaccurate Statistics Conceal U.S. Industrial Decline.* Washington, D.C.: Economic Policy Institute, 1988.

Mishel, Lawrence, and Jared Bernstein. *The State of Working America, 1994–95.* Armonk, N.Y: M. E. Sharpe, 1994.

Mishel, Lawrence, Jared Bernstein, and John Schmitt. *The State of Working America, 1996–97.* Armonk, N.Y.: M. E. Sharpe, 1997.

———. *The State of Working America, 1998–99.* Ithaca, N.Y.: Cornell University Press, 1999.

Mishel, Lawrence, and Paula Voos, eds. *Unions and Economic Competitiveness.* Armonk, N.Y.: M. E. Sharpe, 1992.

Mokyr, Joel. *The Lever of Riches: Technological Creativity and Economic Progress.* New York: Oxford University Press, 1990.

Morrison, C. J., and E. R. Berndt. "Assessing the Productivity of Information Technology Equipment in U.S. Manufacturing Industries." Working paper no. 3582, National Bureau of Economic Research, January 1990.

Munnell, Alicia H. "The Employment Act of 1946: 50 Years Later." In Conference Proceedings of the Jerome Levy Institute at Bard College, April 25–26, 1996.

———. "Infrastructure Investment and Economic Growth." *Journal of Economic Perspectives,* vol. 6, no. 4 (Fall 1992).

———. "Why Has Productivity Declined? Productivity and Public Investment." *New England Economic Review* (Federal Reserve Bank of Boston), January–February 1990.

Munnell, Alicia H., with Leah M. Cook. "How Does Public Infrastructure Affect Regional Economic Performance?" *New England Economic Review* (Federal Reserve Bank of Boston), September–October 1990.

Murray, Alan. "Asia's Financial Foibles Make American Way Look Like a Winner." *Wall Street Journal,* December 8, 1997.

———. "Clinton Plays to Aging Boomers." *Wall Street Journal,* March 29, 1999.

Narin, Francis, Kimberly S. Hamilton, and Dominic Olivastro. "The Increasing Linkage Between U.S. Technology and Public Science." *Research Policy,* no. 932 (July 1997).

National Association of Manufacturers and Grant Thornton Co., "The Skilled Workforce Shortage." Washington D.C., 1997.

Nelson, Richard. "Capitalism as an Engine of Progress." In *The Sources of Economic Growth,* edited by Richard Nelson. Cambridge, Mass.: Harvard University Press, 1996.

Nelson, Richard, ed. *The Sources of Economic Growth.* Cambridge, Mass.: Harvard University Press, 1996.

Nelson, Richard, and Paul M. Romer. "Science, Economic Growth, and Public Policy." *Challenge,* March–April 1996.

Nelson, Richard, and Sidney Winter. *An Evolutionary Theory of Economic Change.* Cambridge, Mass.: Harvard University Press, 1982.

Nordhaus, William D. "Budget Deficits and National Saving." *Challenge,* March–April 1996.

Office of Management and the Budget. *Paperwork and Red Tape: New Perspectives — New Directions.* A report to the President and Congress. Washington, D.C.: Government Printing Office, 1978.

Okun, Arthur. *Equality and Efficiency: The Big Trade-Off.* Washington, D.C.: Brookings Institution, 1975.

Oliner, Stephen D., and William L. Wascher. "Is a Productivity Revolution under Way in the United States?" *Challenge,* November–December 1995.

Oliver, Melvin L., and Thomas M. Shapiro, *Black Wealth/White Wealth.* New York: Routledge, 1995.

Olmstead, A. "The Mechanization of Reaping and Mowing in American Agriculture, 1833–1870." *Journal of Economic History,* vol. 35 (June 1975).

Olson, Mancur. *The Logic of Collective Action*. Cambridge, Mass.: Harvard University Press, 1965.

———. *The Rise and Decline of Nations*. New Haven: Yale University Press, 1982.

Osterman, Paul, and Rosemary Batt. "Employer-Centered Training Programs for International Competitiveness: Lessons from State Programs." *Journal of Policy Analysis and Management*, vol. 12 (Summer 1993).

Parks, Susan. "Improving Workplace Performance: Historical and Theoretical Contexts." *Monthly Labor Review*, May 1995.

Passell, Peter. "Benefits Dwindle along with Wages for the Unskilled." *New York Times*, June 14, 1998.

Pear, Robert. "Building Boom at Institutes of Health." *New York Times*, November 1, 1998, p. 26.

Pearce, David W., ed. *The MIT Dictionary of Modern Economics*, 4th edition. Cambridge, Mass.: MIT Press, 1992.

Pearlstein, Steven. "To Close a Widening Gap." *Washington Post*, November 19, 1995, p. H4.

Persson, Torsten, and Guido Tabellini. "Is Inequality Harmful for Growth?" *American Economic Review*, vol. 84, no. 3 (June 1994).

Phelps, Edmund. "Money-Wage Dynamics and Labor Market Equilibrium." *Journal of Political Economy*, vol. 76, part 2 (1968).

Phillips, A. W. "The Relation Between Unemployment and the Rate of Change of Money Wage Rates in the United Kingdom, 1861–1957." *Economica*, vol. 25 (November 1958).

Phillips, Kevin. *Arrogant Capital*. Boston: Back Bay Books, 1994.

Pieper, Ute, and Lance Taylor. "The Revival of the Liberal Creed: The IMF, the World Bank, and Inequality in the Globalized Economy." In *Globalization and Progressive Economic Policy*, edited by Dean Baker, Gerald Epstein, and Robert Pollin. New York: Cambridge University Press, 1998.

Pollin, Robert. "Deeper in Debt: The Changing Financial Condition of U.S. Households." Economic Policy Institute, Washington D.C., September 1990.

Port, Otis. "The Silicon Age? It's Just the Beginning." *Business Week*, December 9, 1996, p. 150.

Porter, Michael J. *Capital Choices: Changing the Way America Invests in Industry*. Washington, D.C.: Council on Competitiveness, June 1992.

Poterba, James, and Lawrence H. Summers. "Time Horizons of American Firms: New Evidence from a Survey of CEOs," Council on Competitiveness and the Harvard Business School, October 1991.

Quinn, Joseph F., and Richard V. Burkhauser. "Public Policy and the Plans and Preferences of Older Americans." *Journal of Aging and Social Policy*, vol. 6, no. 3 (1994).

Rapping, Leonard. "Learning and World War II Production Functions." *Review of Economics and Statistics*, vol. 47 (February 1965).

Rasell, M. Edith, Barry Bluestone, Lawrence Mishel, and David Webster. *The Prosperity Gap: Why Americans Are Falling Behind.* (New York: New Press, 1999).

Rasell, M. Edith, and Lawrence Mishel. *Shortchanging Education: How U.S. Spending on Grades K–12 Lags Behind Other Industrialized Nations.* Washington, D.C.: Economic Policy Institute, 1990.

Register, Charles A. "Wages, Productivity, and Costs in Union and Nonunion Hospitals." *Journal of Labor Research,* vol. 9, no. 4 (Fall 1988).

Reich, Robert B. "Keynote Address." In *International Labor Standards and Global Economic Integration: Proceedings of a Symposium.* Washington, D.C.: U.S. Department of Labor, July 1994.

———. "We Are All Third Wayers Now." *American Prospect,* March–April 1999.

Rifkin, Jeremy. *The End of Work: The Decline of the Global Labor Force and the Dawn of the Post-Market Era.* New York: Putnam, 1995.

Roach, Stephen. "Stop the Dice Rolling on Technology Spending." *Computerworld Extra,* June 20, 1988.

Robinson, John P., and Ann Bostrom. "The Overestimated Workweek? What Time Diary Measures Suggest." *Monthly Labor Review,* August 1994.

Rodrik, Dani. *Has Globalization Gone Too Far?* Washington, D.C.: Institute for International Economics, 1997.

———. *Has International Economic Integration Gone Too Far?* Washington, D.C.: Institute for International Economics, 1997.

Rohatyn, Felix. "Clinton's Growth Agenda." *Wall Street Journal,* September 16, 1996, p. A18.

Romer, Paul. "Economic Growth." In *The Fortune Encyclopedia of Economics,* edited by David R. Henderson. New York: Warner Books.

———. "Endogenous Technological Change." *Journal of Political Economy,* vol. 98, no. 5, part 2 (1990).

———. "Increasing Returns and Long-Run Growth." *Journal of Political Economy,* vol. 94, no. 5 (1986).

———. "The Origins of Endogenous Growth." *Journal of Economic Perspectives,* vol. 8, no. 1 (Winter 1994).

———. "Why, Indeed, in America? Theory, History, and the Origins of Modern Economic Growth." Working paper no. 5443, National Bureau of Economic Research, January 1996.

Rose, Steven. "Declining Family Incomes in the 1980s: New Evidence from Longitudinal Data." *Challenge,* November–December 1993.

Rosenberg, Nathan. *Inside the Black Box: Technology and Economics.* Cambridge: Cambridge University Press, 1982.

———. "Technological Interdependence in the American Economy." *Technology and Culture,* January 1979.

———. *Technology and American Economic Growth.* New York: Harper & Row, 1972.

Rosenberg, Nathan, and L. E. Birdzell, Jr. *How the West Grew Rich: The Economic Transformation of the Industrial World.* New York: Basic Books, 1986.

Sabel, Charles. "The Re-Emergence of Regional Economies: Changes in the Scale of Production." In "Experimenting with Scale," Social Science Research Council, Western European Committee, August 1987.

Sachs, Jeffrey D. "Global Adjustments to a Shrinking U.S. Trade Deficit." *Brookings Papers on Economic Activity,* no. 2 (1988).

————. "Global Capitalism: Making It Work." *Economist,* September 12, 1998.

Samuelson, Paul A., and Robert M. Solow. "Analytical Aspects of Anti-Inflation Policy." *American Economic Review Papers and Proceedings,* vol. 50 (May 1960).

Samuelson, Robert. *The Good Life and Its Discontents.* Vancouver, Wash.: Vintage, 1996.

Sanger, David E. "New Analysis: Stressing the Differences — Economy and Diagnoses." *New York Times,* October 11, 1996.

Schemo, Diana Jean. "Brazil Introduces $80 Billion Plan for Economic Ills." *New York Times,* October 29, 1998, p. A1.

Scherer, F. M. "Technological Maturity and Waning Economic Growth." *Arts and Sciences,* (Northwestern University), Fall 1978.

Schlesinger, Jacob M. "The Virtuous Circle of Low Inflation." *Wall Street Journal,* August 18, 1997, p. A1.

Schor, Juliet. *The Overworked American.* New York: Basic Books, 1991.

Schumpeter, Joseph A. *The Theory of Economic Development.* Cambridge, Mass.: Harvard University Press, 1934.

Scott, Allen J. "The Electric Vehicle Industry and Local Economic Development: Prospects and Policies for Southern California." *Environment and Planning A,* vol. 27 (1995).

————. *Technopolis: High Technology Industry and Regional Development in Southern California.* Berkeley: University of California Press, 1993.

Scott, Allen J., and D. Bergman. "Advanced Ground Transportation Equipment Manufacturing and Local Economic Development: Lessons for Southern California." WP-8, Lewis Center for Regional Policy Studies, UCLA, 1993.

Scott, Robert E., and Jesse Rothstein. "American Jobs and the Asian Crisis: The Employment Impact of the Coming Rise in the U.S. Trade Deficit." Economic Policy Institute Briefing Paper, Summer 1998.

Sengenberger, Werner, and Duncan Campbell, eds. *International Labour Standards and Economic Interdependence.* Geneva: International Institute for Labour Studies, ILO, 1994.

Shepard, Stephen B. "The New Economy: What It Really Means." *Business Week,* November 17, 1997.

Siconolfi, Michael, E. S. Browning, and Patrick McGeehan. "As Stock-Market Gains Dissipate, So Does a Bit of Economy's Froth." *Wall Street Journal,* September 2, 1998.

Skidmore, Dave. "Americans Raid Savings in September," Associated Press, November 2, 1998, AP Web site.

Slifman, L., and C. Corrado. "Decomposition of Productivity and Unit Costs." *Occasional Staff Studies* (Federal Reserve Board), November 18, 1996.

Social Security Trustees, OASHDI. *Annual Report of the Board of Trustees of the Old-Age and Survivors Insurance and Disabilities Insurance Trust Funds.* Washington, D.C.: U.S. Government Printing Office, 1995.

Solow, Robert M. "A Contribution to the Theory of Economic Growth." *Quarterly Journal of Economics,* vol. 70, no. 1 (February 1956).

"Special Report: How to Reshape the World Financial System." *Business Week,* October 12, 1998.

Staiger, Douglas, James H. Stock, and Mark W. Watson. "The NAIRU, Unemployment, and Monetary Policy." *Journal of Economic Perspectives,* pp. 33–50.

Starr-McClure, Martha. "Stock Market Wealth and Consumer Spending." *Finance and Economics Discussion Series,* 1998–20, Board of Governors of the Federal Reserve System, April 1998.

Stein, Herbert. "Spending and Getting." In *Contemporary Economic Problems, 1977,* edited by William Fellner. Washington, D.C.: American Enterprise Institute, 1977.

Stevenson, Richard W. "Greenspan Denounces Growing Protectionism." *New York Times,* April 17, 1999.

Stockman, David. *The Triumph of Politics.* New York: Harper & Row, 1986.

Sumrall, James B., Jr. "Diffusion of the Basic Oxygen Furnace in the U.S. Steel Industry: A Vintage Capital Model." Ph.D. dissertation, Boston College, 1977.

Sveikauskus, C.D., and L. Sveikauskus, "Industry Characteristics and Productivity Growth." *Southern Journal of Economics,* January 1982.

Teixeira, Ruy, and Joel Rogers. *The New Politics of Prosperity.* New York: Century Fund, forthcoming.

Terleckyi, Nestor. "What Do R&D Numbers Tell Us about Technological Change?" *American Economic Review,* May 1980.

Thurow, Lester. "Are Investments in Information Systems Paying Off?" *MIT Management Review,* Spring 1990.

———. "The Crusade That's Killing Prosperity." *American Prospect,* March–April 1996.

———. *Dangerous Currents.* New York: Oxford University Press, 1983.

———. "Gazing into the Crystal Ball: Pressures of Globalization May Help Keep Boom Going." *Boston Globe,* May 14, 1998.

———. *Generating Inequality: Mechanisms of Distribution in the U.S. Economy.* New York: Basic Books, 1975.

———. "Wages and the Service Sector." In *Restoring Broadly Shared Prosperity,* edited by Ray Marshall. Washington, D.C., and Austin: Economic Policy Institute and Lyndon B. Johnson School of Public Affairs, University of Texas, 1997.

Tobias, Andrew. "Take Control of Your Credit Card." *Parade,* November 1, 1998.

Tobin, James. "Inflation and Unemployment." *American Economic Review,* vol. 62 (March 1972).

Toffler, Alvin. *The Third Wave.* New York: William Morrow, 1980.

Uchitelle, Louis. "Why America Won't Boom." *New York Times,* June 12, 1994.

Ul Haq, Mahbub, Inge Kaul, and Isabelle Grunberg, eds. *The Tobin Tax: Coping with Financial Volatility.* Oxford: Oxford University Press, 1997.

Ullmann, Owen, Laura Cohn, and Michael Mandel. "The Fed's New Rule Book." *Business Week,* May 3, 1999.

U.S. Bureau of the Census. *Forecasts of the U.S. Population to 2050.* Washington, D.C.: Government Printing Office, 1997.

———. *Statistical Abstract of the United States.* Washington, D.C.: Government Printing Office, 1986, 1995, 1996.

U.S. Department of Labor, Bureau of Labor Statistics, *Industry Productivity Statistics,* April 22, 1997.

U.S. General Accounting Office. *Workers at Risk: Increased Number in Contingent Employment Lack Insurance, Other Benefits.* GAO Report HRD-91-56, March 1991.

Van Den Haag, Ernest. "In Praise of the Wage Gap." *Wall Street Journal,* June 26, 1996.

Waldstein, Louise. "Service Sector Wages, Productivity and Job Creation in the U.S. and Other Countries." In *Toward a High-Wage. High-Productivity Service Sector.* Washington, D.C.: Economic Policy Institute, 1989.

Walter, Norbert. "Deflating an Inflation Worry." *New York Times.* February 2, 1997.

Weiler, Paul. "Who Will Represent Labor Now?" *American Prospect,* Summer 1990.

Wessel, David. "Budget Seeks to Raise U.S. Living Standards and Reduce Inequality." *Wall Street Journal,* February 7, 1997, p. A1.

Wilke, John R. "Surge in Investments Changes U.S. Economy." *Wall Street Journal,* June 10, 1996.

Williamson, J. G., and P. H. Lindert. *American Inequality: A Macroeconomic History.* New York: Academic Press, 1980.

Wilson, William Julius. *When Work Disappears: The World of the New Urban Poor.* New York: Vintage Books, 1996.

Wolff, Edward N. "Recent Trends in the Size Distribution of Household Wealth." *Journal of Economic Perspectives,* vol. 11 (December 1997).

———. *Top Heavy: A Study of the Increasing Inequality of Wealth in America.* New York: Twentieth-Century Fund, 1995.

Woodward, Bob. *The Agenda.* New York: Simon & Schuster, 1994.

"Workaholics Anonymous: Why Do Americans Work So Hard?" *The Economist,* October 22, 1994.

World Bank. *World Development Report 1995.* New York: Oxford University Press, 1995.

Wysocki, Bernard, Jr. "The Mixed Blessings of Low Unemployment." *Wall Street Journal,* March 22, 1999, p. A1.

———. "Wealth of Notions: For This Economist, Long-Term Prosperity Hangs on Good Ideas." *Wall Street Journal,* January 21, 1997.

Yorukoglu, Mehmet. "The Information Technology Productivity Paradox." Department of Economics, University of Chicago, 1996.

Zachary, G. Pascal. "Asian Exports Haven't Flooded the U.S., But American Consumers Still Benefit from Lower Prices." *Wall Street Journal,* April 14, 1998.

Index

Page references followed by "n." or "nn." refer to information in notes.

Abramovitz, Moses, 107, 142
Accounting model of growth, 107–10, 209, 270n. 16
A-Corp firms, 250
Advances in knowledge. *See* Technological innovation
AFL-CIO, 123
African-Americans, 9, 46, 186–87, 199–200
Age of Diminished Expectations, The (Krugman), 2
Aggregate demand, 33–35, 154, 199, 200–201. *See also* Demand
Aggregate savings, 190, 291n. 9
Agriculture industry, productivity growth in, 71–72, 277–78n. 36
Airbus, 19
Akerlof, George, 294n. 27
Alesina, Alberto, 189–90
Altman, Robert, 131
Amazon.com, 256
American Online, 256
American Society for Training and Development, 224
Apparel Industry Partnership, 255
Appelbaum, Eileen, 221, 226–27, 304–5n. 31
Arrow, Kenneth, 77
Aschauer, David, 218, 219
Asian financial crisis
effects of, 247

Federal Reserve Board and, 295n. 29
interest rates and, 129, 177, 241n. 29
Japan and, 147
trade surplus in services and, 287n. 35
unemployment due to, 287–88n. 36
virtuous cycle instability and, 152
AT&T, 221, 306n. 49
Attewell, Paul, 68, 69
Automobiles, 227–28, 256, 288n. 42

Baby boom generation, 51, 86, 87, 246, 268n. 27
Balanced budget. *See* Budget, balanced
Banking industry
capital productivity in, 69
as capital source, 133, 134
crony capitalism and, 174
GDP and, 276n. 23
Barro, Robert J., 274–75n. 20
Bartik, Timothy, 219–20
Baumol, William, 60
Baumol's disease, 59–61, 63, 83
Becker, Gary, 168, 224
Bentsen, Lloyd, 120
Bernstein, Jared, 281n. 65, 282–84n. 78
Bhagwati, Jagdish, 174–75
Bingaman, Jeff, 259
Bishop, John, 224, 305n. 40
Black, Sandra, 221
Blacks. *See* African-Americans
Blair, Tony, 16
Blinder, Alan, 294n. 25
BLS (Bureau of Labor Statistics), 84, 96, 197

Bluestone, Barry, 280–81n. 65
  on all workers and hours worked,
    93–94
  data sources of, 284n. 79
  on earnings and inequality, 299n. 6
  household research of, 185–86
  on prime-age workers and hours
    worked, 92
Bluestone, Irving, 221
Boeing, 19
Bond markets, 22, 122, 133
Borjas, George, 196
Borland, 216
Boston, 267–68n. 24
Bostrom, Anne, 283n. 78
Brazil, 129, 290–91n. 66
Bretton Woods Articles of Agreement,
  135–36
Britain, 63–64, 214
Brown, Lynn, 292n. 16
Brynjolfsson, Erik, 79–80, 222, 280n. 60
Buchanan, Pat, 123
Buchele, Robert, 231
Budget, balanced
  dangers of, 166–69
  federal, 13–15, 23, 111–12, 119–22,
    239
Budget surpluses. *See* Surpluses, budget
Bureau of Labor Statistics (BLS), 84, 96,
  197
Bush, George Herbert Walker, 6, 119,
  120
Business Week, 6–7, 165, 266n. 12

CALSTART, 244
Capital
  accounting model and, 107
  cheap, 130
  human (*see* Human capital)
  mobility of, 130–35, 136, 162, 175,
    257–59, 290n. 54
  physical (*see* Physical capital)
  productivity growth and, 108–10

  sources of, 133, 134
  spending, 148–49
  in Wall Street model, 256
Capital markets, 135, 257–58. *See also*
  Stock market
Cappelli, Peter, 221
CBO (Congressional Budget Office), 7,
  28
CEA. *See* Council of Economic Advisers
  (CEA)
Census Bureau, 198
Center on Budget and Policy Priorities,
  299n. 5
Children's Defense Fund, 64
Christiansen, Jens, 231
Chrysler Corporation, 125, 146
Clinton, William Jefferson
  budget surpluses and, 167–68
  conversion to Wall Street model, 239,
    265n. 8
  on economic growth, 3
  economic program of, 23
  on education, 223, 244
  on government spending, 48
  NAFTA and, 288n. 39
  on public investment programs,
    119–20
  on Social Security, 242
COLA (cost-of-living adjustment),
  289n. 47
Coming Boom, The (Kahn), 2
Commission on Industrial Productivity,
  61–62
Communications Workers of America,
  306n. 49
Community colleges, labor force and, 7
Compa, Lance, 255
Comparative advantage theory, 124
Compound growth rates, 267n. 18
Computers. *See* Information revolution
Conditionality, 173
Congressional Budget Office (CBO), 7,
  28

Consumer price index (CPI), 275n. 22
Consumer spending, 148–49,
    286–87n. 24. *See also* Households
Consumption versus investment,
    292nn. 14, 16
Convergence, developing countries and,
    274–75n. 20
Cook, Philip J., 281n. 66
Corning, 221
Corrado, C., 276–77n. 25
Cost-of-living adjustment (COLA),
    289n. 47
Council of Economic Advisers (CEA)
    on economic growth, 7, 28, 31, 158,
        284n. 84
    on poverty rates, 198
Council on Competitiveness, 131
CPI (consumer price index), 275n. 22
CPS. *See* Current Population Survey
    (CPS)
Credit, effects of low-cost, 130, 144
Credit card debt, 181, 298n. 58
Currency devaluations, effects of, 172
Current Population Survey (CPS),
    281n. 68, 283n. 78, 284n. 79

David, Paul, 31, 72, 279n. 53
Davis, Bob, 7
Debt forgiveness, 310n. 26
Deflationary gap, 155
Deindustrialization, income inequality
    and, 193
Demand, 10. *See also* Aggregate demand
    discretionary management, 158
    elasticity of, 227
    export, 35
    investment and, 179–80
    Main Street model and, 248
    manufacturing and, 227–28
    neoclassical growth syllogism and,
        115
    New Growth theory and, 20–21,
        206, 225–26

post–World War II economic boom
    and, 33–35, 182
    for services, 228–29
    versus supply-side economics, 33,
        116
    virtuous cycle and, 117
    Wall Street model and, 151
Denison, Edward F., 209
    on advances in knowledge, 55, 142
    on aggregate potential national
        income in nonresidential business
        sector, 272n. 21
    on decline in productivity growth,
        53–54, 61
    definition of growth accounting, 44
    on GDP growth rate, 273n. 1
    on output per employee, 46–47
    on service-based economy, 59–60
Department of Defense, 12, 19
Developing countries
    conditional convergence and,
        274–75n. 20
    debt forgiveness and, 310n. 26
    growth industries in, 161
    labor rights and standards in, 253–54
    Wall Street model and, 173
Dicken, Peter, 130, 161
Dickens, William, 294n. 27
Diffusion curve, productivity lags and,
    78, 210
Discretionary demand management,
    158
Disembodied technical change. *See*
    Technological innovation
Disney, 255
Displaced workers, 284–85n. 87. *See
    also* Unemployment
Disposable personal income, 111
Dow Jones industrial average, 3, 293n. 18
Dreier, Peter, 269n. 5
Dual-earner families, 88, 185, 229,
    281n. 66, 299n. 9
Dunlop, John, 154

Earned Income Tax Credit (EITC), 121,
   248, 249, 302n. 45
Eatwell, John, 257–58
Economic Growth and Stability Act,
   289n. 52
Economic Policy Institute, 197
Economic Report of the President, 28, 155
Economics (Samuelson), 155–56
Economies of scale, 46, 55
Education
   budget surpluses and, 243–44
   demand for, 229
   government investments in, 167–68,
      223, 260–62, 308n. 3
   hours worked and level of, 94–95,
      97–98, 284n. 85, 299n. 9
   incomes and, 185–86, 191–93
   investments in New Growth theory,
      223–25
   of labor force (*see* Labor force:
      education of)
   national savings rate and, 148
   private sector investments in,
      223–24, 244, 306nn. 46, 47
   productivity growth and, 189
Eisner, Robert, 179
   on gross investments and gross
      savings, 286n. 16
   on gross national saving, 292n. 12
   interest versus investment, 291n. 4
   on investment versus consumption,
      292n. 14
   on paradox of thrift, 146–47
EITC. *See* Earned Income Tax Credit
   (EITC)
Elasticity of demand, 227
Elite, bond market and economic, 22–23
Elliott, Michael, 32
Employment
   decline in manufacturing, 228,
      288n. 36
   by government, 270n. 15
   rise in, 3, 41, 102, 269–70n. 5

   self-, 92
   trade deficit and, 287–88n. 36
Employment Act, Humphrey-Hawkins
   Full, 289n. 52
Employment Act of 1946, 36, 129
Employment Cost Index, 197
Employment/population ratio, 265n. 4
End of Affluence, The (Madrick), 2
Energy crisis, 59
Environment, economic growth impact
   on, 24
Equity markets, 133
Erenberg, Sharon J., 220
Eurodollar market, 130
Europe, 19, 63
European Union, 255
Expectations, role in growth, 261–62
Exports, 161, 169

Factor price equalization theory, 195
Family Leave Act, 121
Fast-track authority, 288n. 39
Fault-tolerant service, 78
Faux, Jeff, 218
Federal Express, 221
Federal Housing Administration (FHA),
   34
Federal Reserve Act of 1913, 129
Federal Reserve Board, 289n. 52
   Asian financial crisis and, 295n. 29
   on CEA GDP projections, 28
   inflation and (*see* Inflation: Federal
      Reserve Board and)
   interest rates and, 177
   Phillips curve and, 165
   Wall Street model and, 128–30, 153,
      154, 165
Federal surplus. *See* Surpluses, budget
Feedback, in technological innovation,
   77–78
Feldstein, Martin, 171–72
FHA (Federal Housing Administration),
   34

Fidelity, 134
Fieleke, Norman, 295nn. 32, 33
Financial services industry, 65–66. *See also* Banking industry
Forbes, Steve, 6
Ford Motor Company, 125, 145–46, 221
Foreign Affairs, 174
Foreign investment, 135, 136
Frank, Robert H., 194, 281n. 66
Fraumeni, Barbara, 108
Freeman, Richard, 196, 234
Free trade. *See also* North American Free Trade Agreement (NAFTA)
    income inequality and, 195
    inflation and, 15, 125
    Wall Street model and, 123–26, 169–75
Friedman, Milton, 153, 157

Galbraith, James, 158, 197–98, 302n. 45
Galbraith, John Kenneth, 265n. 7
Gallman, Robert, 31
Gap, The, 255
Garment Industries Training Corporation, 306n. 49
Garten, Jeffrey, 132
Gastil, Raymond, 275n. 20
GDP. *See* Gross domestic product (GDP)
Gender, wage gaps and, 9. *See also* Women
General Electric, 221
General Motors, 125, 134, 145, 230, 306n. 49
General Theory of Employment (Keynes), 155
Generation X, 88
Genetic engineering, 211–12
Gephardt, Richard, 309n. 21
Germany, 131, 132, 224, 282n. 77, 306n. 47
GI Bill, 34
Gingrich, Newt, 28, 121
Gini coefficient, 198, 201

Gleason, Joshua, 292n. 16
GNP (gross national product), 8
Goldin, Claudia, 262–63
Gollop, Frank, 108
Goods deficit, 287n. 35
Gordon, Frank, 160
Gordon, Robert J., 275n. 22, 294n. 25
Gore, Al, 239, 244
Government
    demand generation by, 34–35
    deregulation and income inequality, 194
    education and training investments of, 167–68, 223, 243–45, 308n. 3
    employment by, 270n. 15
    GDP projections of (*see* Gross domestic product (GDP): government projections of)
    growth collapse of, 39
    growth signals from, 234–35, 307n. 64
    information revolution origins and, 18–19
    investments and New Growth theory, 239–43
    Main Street model and, 12, 25–26, 249–50, 257–58
    post–World War II economic boom and, 36–39
    public infrastructure investment and, 218–20, 296–97n. 40
    regulation of wages and income inequality, 194
    regulations and growth, 55, 57–58, 250–52, 258–59
    research and development spending of, 18–19, 56–57, 215–18, 239–43
    spending and productivity growth, 58–59, 166, 189, 202
    theory of role in economy, 4–5, 19–20
    Wall Street model and (*see* Wall Street model: government policies and)

Gramlich, Edward, 296–97 n. 40
Great Depression, 32, 52, 144, 166
Greenberg, Stanley, 25
Greenspan, Alan, 15
    on economic growth, 102, 103
    on inflation, 13
    on interest rates, 128, 177
    on job insecurity, 94
    on negative productivity, 277n. 25
    on official productivity statistics, 66
    on Phillips curve debate, 165
    on stable prices, 115
    on stock market volatility, 153
    on stock market wealth, 286n. 22
    on surpluses, 113
    on trade expansion, 288n. 41
    on virtuous cycle, 117
    on wage dispersion, 193
Greenwood, Jeremy, 74, 75, 279n. 53
Greider, William, 145, 257, 285n. 7
Griliches, Zvi, 65, 109, 277–78n. 36
Gross domestic product (GDP)
    banking industry and, 276n. 23
    budget surpluses and, 167
    "creative destruction" and, 46
    expansion of, 2–3, 27
    government projections of, 7, 47–49,
        52, 100–101, 167, 280n. 63
    gross investment and, 110
    growth rate of, 8, 28, 29–32,
        272–73n. 1
    key ingredients in growth of,
        37–40
    long-term real, 31–32, 33
    post–World War II, 12, 30, 44
    prediction of, 40
    public and private sector
        contributions to, 38
    public sector investments and, 220,
        240–41
    saving rates and, 291nn. 8, 9
    slowdown in, 145–46
    trade deficit and, 170–71

    unemployment rate and, 91
Grossman, Gene, 105, 214
Gross national product (GNP), 8
Growth accounting, 43, 44

Hale, David, 290n. 61
Harrison, Bennett, 299n. 6
Harvard Business School Time Horizons
    Project, 131–32
Head Start program, 244–45
Health care, 148, 168
Helpman, Elhanan, 105
Hewlett-Packard, 221
Hitt, Lorin, 79–80, 222, 280n. 60
Hours worked per worker
    consumption demand and, 229
    decline in, 45
    decrease in, 96, 271n. 17
    education and (see Education: hours
        worked and level of)
    impact on labor force supply,
        284n. 80
    in Japan, 282n. 77
    job insecurity and, 94
    productivity growth and, 86–89,
        91–95
    rise in, 280–81n. 65, 282–84n. 78
    wage rates and, 88, 94, 163,
        267n. 21
    women and, 88, 92, 280–81n. 65
Households
    capital spending and, 148–49
    credit card debt of, 180
    improvements in income, 9–10
    median family income, 185–87,
        298n. 1
Howell, David, 192–93
Howes, Candace, 297n. 44
Human capital, in New Growth theory,
    213, 214. See also Labor force
Human Genome Project, 217
Humphrey-Hawkins Full Employment
    Act, 289n. 52

Illiteracy, labor force and, 99
ILO (International Labor Organization), 253, 309n. 19
IMF. *See* International Monetary Fund (IMF)
Immigration, 127, 195–96
Imports, 126, 169, 289n. 45
Improved resource allocation, 45–46
Income
  definitions of, 267n. 23
  disposable personal, 111
  distribution of, 63, 189
  education and, 185–86, 191–93
  government deregulation and inequality in, 194
  inequality and, 267n. 23, 299n. 5, 299nn. 5, 6, 301n. 38
  median family, 185–87, 298n. 1
  post-1973 inequality in, 184–87
  reasons for inequality in, 190–97
  rise in, 9–10, 182–83
  service-based economy and, 193, 274n. 13
  unions and, 194
India, 253
Industrial relations, in New Growth theory, 221
Industrial revolution, productivity growth lags in, 74
Inequality
  crime and, 189–90
  deindustrialization and income, 193
  economic growth and social, 1, 8–10, 24–25, 188–90, 203
  end of economic, 187–88
  free trade and income, 195
  government deregulation and income, 194
  incomes and, 184–87, 190–97, 267n. 23, 299n. 5, 299nn. 5, 6, 301n. 38
  rapid growth effect on income, 199–200

savings and, 190
sources behind surge in income, 190–97
technology and income, 192–93
trade deficit and income, 196
unions decline and income, 194
urban poverty and, 198–201
wage regulation and income, 194
Wall Street model and, 23, 202–4
winner-take-all society and income, 194–95, 281n. 66
Inflation, 6. *See also* Non-accelerating inflation rate of unemployment (NAIRU)
  in demand and supply-side economics, 117
  Federal Reserve Board and, 15, 22, 128–30, 139, 145–46, 177–79, 289n. 52, 294n. 25
  free trade and, 15, 125
  globalization and, 162, 295n. 32
  historical background of NAIRU and, 159–65
  in import-sensitive industries, 289n. 45
  interest rates and, 238
  labor and, 126, 127
  measurement of rates of, 275n. 22
  neoclassical growth syllogism and, 115, 139
  primer on theory of, 155–58
  theory of, 3, 4, 5, 296n. 38
  unemployment and, 15, 91, 155–57
  Wall Street model and, 13, 15, 16–17, 22, 113–14, 118, 154–55, 177–79, 238
Information revolution. *See also* Technological innovation
  government role in origins of, 18–19
  income inequality and, 192
  productivity growth and, 4, 7, 17–18, 66–69, 79–80, 179, 222, 237–38, 277n. 33, 280n. 60
  workplace reorganization and, 78

Infrastructure investment, public, 218–20, 239–43, 296–97n. 40
Inner cities, poverty and, 198–201
"Innovation index," 23
Intellectual property laws, 251–52
Interest rates
    Asian financial crisis and, 129, 177, 293n. 29
    decrease in, 121
    Federal Reserve Board and, 177
    Greenspan on, 128, 177
    inflation and, 238
    investments in physical capital and, 143–46
    savings and, 111–12, 146–50
    Wall Street model and (see Wall Street model: interest rates and)
Interindustry shifts, 59–60
International Labor Organization (ILO), 253, 309n. 19
International Monetary Fund (IMF), 135–36, 172–74, 257, 290–91n. 66
International Survey Research Company, 94
Investment
    versus consumption, 292n. 14
    in education of labor force (see Labor force: education of)
    foreign, 135, 136
    GDP and gross, 110
    global capital markets and, 135
    gross savings and gross, 286n. 16
    infrastructure, 218–20, 239–43
    Marx on, 285n. 7
    Multilateral Agreement on Investment, 134–35, 153, 252
    physical capital and, 143–46, 211, 214
    post–World War II virtuous cycle and, 35
    private, 223–24, 244, 306nn. 46, 47
    productivity growth and, 54, 67, 68, 108–9, 142–43

public infrastructure, 218–20, 239–43, 296–97n. 40
public sector (see Government)
    in research and development (see Research and development (R&D))
    savings rates and, 147–48
    service-based economy and, 295n. 33
    technical training, 23
    technological revolution and, 179–80

Japan
    Asian financial crisis and, 147
    decline in productivity growth and, 63
    gross domestic savings and GDP in, 291n. 8
    hours worked in, 282n. 77
    liquidity trap and, 144–45
    paradox of thrift and, 147
    private investments in, 306n. 47
    productivity growth and, 131
    productivity growth decline in, 132
    worker seniority in, 224
Job growth. See Employment
Job insecurity, hours worked and, 94
Johnson, Lyndon Baines, 36
Jorgenson, Dale
    accounting model of, 107–10
    on annual growth rate, 273n. 2
    on decline in productivity growth, 56
    New Growth theory and, 207–8
    on productivity decline, 273–74n. 11
    on technological progress, 141

Kahn, Herman, 2
Katz, Lawrence, 196, 302n. 45
Kemp, Jack, 6
Kemp-Roth tax cut, 119
Kennedy, John Fitzgerald, 36
Keynes, John Maynard, 155
Krugman, Paul, 2, 170
Kuhn, Thomas, 205

Kuttner, Robert, 300n. 18
Kuznets, Simon, 188–89, 207

Labor force
  community colleges and, 7
  costs of, 232–33
  education of, 99, 127, 223–25,
    245–46, 284n. 82, 305n. 40,
    306nn. 46, 47, 49
  flexibility of, 15, 126–28, 138–39,
    175–77
  global standards and, 254–55
  growth sources of, 87, 281n. 67
  hours worked (see Hours worked per
    worker)
  illiteracy and, 99
  organization of, 36
  participation in, 89–90, 97, 200,
    268n. 24, 271n. 17, 281n. 68,
    284n. 83, 308n. 11
  perfectly competitive labor markets,
    126, 212
  population growth and, 89, 95
  prime-age workers in, 87, 88, 92–93,
    97, 185
  productivity and, 17, 39–40, 43, 61,
    74, 141
  skilled, 45, 74, 225, 281n. 66
  supply, 85–86, 89–95, 246–47,
    296n. 36
  supply forecasts, 95–100
  underutilized, 98–99
  unions and, 36, 126–27, 164,
    306n. 49
  Wall Street model and, 126–28, 154,
    175–77
  women in, 36, 37, 51, 86, 87, 88,
    271n. 17
  workplace reorganization and,
    221–22
Labor laws, 127, 234, 248–49
  Labor rights, 253–55, 309n. 21
Labor standards, 255–56, 309n. 21

Learning curves, in technological
    innovation, 70, 77, 210, 279n. 53
Liquidity trap, 144–45
Lobbyists. See Special-interest groups
Los Angeles, 29
Lott, Trent, 121
Lotus, 216
Lucas, Robert, 293–94n. 24
Lynch, Lisa, 221

Mack, Connie, 289n. 52
Maddison, Angus, 31, 56, 272–73n. 1
Madrick, Jeffrey, 2
Magma Copper Co., 291n. 3
MAI (Multilateral Agreement on
    Investment), 134–35, 153, 252
Main Street model, 12
  definition of, 20–21
  demand and, 248
  government and, 12, 25–26, 249–50,
    257–58
  New Growth theory and, 235–36
  private sector and, 259–60
  unions and, 247–48
  wages and, 247–48
  Wall Street model versus, 261–62
Malaysia, 253
Malkiel, Burton, 21
Malthus, Thomas, 207
Mandatory retirement, 90
Mandel, Michael, 266n. 12
Mansfield, Edwin, 217
Manufacturing, 59–60
  demand and, 227–28
  employment decline in, 228,
    288n. 36
  productivity growth in, 72–73, 237,
    276n. 22
  versus trade and services productivity
    growth, 82
  wages in, 171, 197–98
Marginal product, 105
Marshall, Alfred, 50

Marshall Plan, 35
Marx, Karl, 105–6, 285n. 7
Massachusetts Financial Services, 134
Median annual household income. *See* Households
Medicaid, 121
Medicare, 121, 269n. 38
Medoff, James, 234
Mergers and acquisitions, 132
Mexico, 124–25, 172, 254–55, 256, 288n. 40. *See also* North American Free Trade Agreement (NAFTA)
Microsoft, 216
Minimum wage
  European, 233
  increases in, 15, 153, 163, 176, 249–50
Minorities, 199–200
Mishel, Larry, 276n. 22, 281n. 65, 282–84n. 78
Mokyr, Joel, 73
Monopolistic competition, 212
Motorola, 221
Multilateral Agreement on Investment (MAI), 134–35, 153, 252
Munnell, Alicia, 218–19
Murray, Alan, 23
Mutual fund industry, 134

NAFTA. *See* North American Free Trade Agreement (NAFTA)
NAIRU. *See* Non-accelerating inflation rate of unemployment (NAIRU)
National Association of Manufacturers (NAM), 6
National Income and Product Accounts, 275n. 22
National Institutes of Health, 168
National Labor Relations Act, 153–54
National Labor Relations Board (NLRB), 248–49
National savings rate
  aggregate savings, 190, 291n. 9
  education and, 148
  flaws in statistics on, 149
  gross savings rates and gross investment, 286n. 16
  inequality and, 190
  interest rates and, 111–12, 146–50
  mathematics of, 292nn. 12, 15
  in neoclassical syllogism, 110–13, 146–50
  spending rates and, 286n. 19
  theory of role in economy, 4, 5, 146–47
  World War II, 10, 34
Neighborhood effects, 189
Nelson, Richard, 80, 207, 209, 250
Neoclassical growth syllogism, 205
  demand and, 115
  flaws in, 140–51
  inflation and, 115, 139
  interest rates and physical capital investments in, 143–46
  national savings rate and, 110–13, 146–50
  primer on theory of, 104–6
  risks and, 26
  summary of faster growth principles of, 114–15, 150
  technological innovation and, 105, 106
Netscape, 256
Newcomen, Thomas, 73, 74
New Deal, 166
New Growth theory
  background of, 207–8
  definition of, 19, 205–6
  demand and, 20–21, 206, 225–26
  education and training investments in, 223–25
  historical evidence for, 214–15
  human capital in, 213, 214
  industrial relations in, 221
  Main Street model and, 235–36
  monopolistic competition in, 212

premises of, 208–13
public infrastructure investment and, 218–20, 239–43, 296–97n. 40
research and development spending in, 215–18, 239–43, 252
technological innovation and, 208–10, 309n. 17
wages and, 206, 232, 233–34
Wall Street model versus, 20, 225, 226, 235–36
workplace reorganization and, 220–22, 304–5n. 11
Nixon, Richard Milhous, 37
NLRB (National Labor Relations Board), 248–49
Non-accelerating inflation rate of unemployment (NAIRU). See also Unemployment
definition of, 157–58, 294n. 25
historical background of, 159–65
Noncorporate sector statistics, 276n. 25
Nonrival returns, 216, 251–52
Nordhaus, William, 148, 149, 292n. 15
North American Free Trade Agreement (NAFTA), 309n. 21
capital mobility and, 162
effects of, 124–25, 138
flaws in, 172
opposition to, 123
passage of, 288n. 39
purpose of, 15
tariff reduction and, 255

Okun, Arthur, 91, 189, 232, 275n. 20, 300n. 18
Okun's Law, 91, 281–82n. 73, 282n. 74
Older workers, 90
Oligopolies, 125
Oliver, Melvin, 187
Olson, Mancur, 62, 63, 64
OPEC. See Organization of Petroleum Exporting Countries (OPEC)

Organization of Petroleum Exporting Countries (OPEC), 32–33, 59, 125–26
Overworked American, The (Schor), 92

Paid Educational Leave (PEL) program, 306n. 49
Pakistan, 253
Panel Study of Income Dynamics (PSID), 284n. 79
Parks, Susan, 221
Part-time workers, 92, 284–85n. 87
Patent applications, 57
Pearlstein, Steve, 262
PEL (Paid Educational Leave) program, 306n. 49
Pentagon, 168
Perfectly competitive labor markets, 126, 212
Perot, Ross, 119, 120, 123
Perry, George, 294n. 27
Personal care expenditures, 149
Personal Responsibility and Work Opportunity Reconciliation Act of 1996, 250
Phillips, A. W., 155–56
Phillips, Kevin, 265n. 8
Phillips curve, 156, 157
globalization effect on, 161–62
labor supply effect on, 163
productivity growth and, 164–65
social protections effect on, 163–64
union power decline and, 164
Physical capital, 104–6, 141–46, 211, 214
Pieper, Ute, 173
Political Economy (Marshall), 50
Politicians, on economic growth, 6
Porter, Michael, 23, 131
Potential output, 33
Poterba, James, 131–32
Poverty, social inequality and urban, 198–201

Prime-age workers, 87, 88, 92–93, 97, 185

Private goods, 251

Private sector
budget surpluses and, 292n. 10
determinants of growth in, 39–42
education and training investments of, 223–24, 244, 306nn. 46, 47
GDP and, 38
Main Street model and, 259–60
productivity and government investments, 219
research and development in, 216–17
Wall Street model and, 204

Production function, 42–43, 271–72n. 18

Productivity growth
advances in knowledge and, 55, 57
in agriculture, 71–72, 277–78n. 36
antebellum United States and, 75–76
assumptions about, 48
Baumol's disease and, 59–61, 63, 83
capital and, 108–10
deficit in highly organized industries, 298n. 56
developing countries and decline in, 213
education and, 189
government GDP projections and (see Gross domestic product [GDP]: government projections of)
government regulations and, 55, 57–58, 251–52, 258–59
government spending and, 58–59, 166, 189, 239–43
historical cycles of, 66–69
hours worked per worker and, 86–89, 91–95
Industrial Revolution and, 74
information revolution and (see Information revolution: productivity growth and)
investment and, 54, 67, 68, 108–9, 142–43
job creation and, 228
labor and, 8, 17, 41, 53, 80–81
labor standards and, 231–32
lags in, 70–77, 78
managers effect on, 61
in manufacturing, 72–73, 254, 276n. 22
measurement problems of, 65–66, 275–76n. 22, 276–77n. 25
minimum wage and, 176
negative, 84
nonfarm corporate sector versus nonfarm nocorporate sector, 276n. 25
OPEC and, 59
Phillips curve and, 164–65
physical capital and, 141–42, 214
predictions for, 8
public sector, 270n. 16
reasons for slowdown of, 52–56, 66–69
recovery in, 3, 17, 80–84
research and development spending effect on, 56–57
responsibility for, 179–81
service-based economy and, 59–60, 81–83
slowdown of, 1–2, 41–42, 51–52
special-interest groups and, 62–64
standardization and, 78
taxes and, 58, 258–59
technological innovation and (see Technological innovation: productivity growth and)
unions and, 177, 234, 247–48
workers effect on, 61, 74
workplace reorganization and, 220–22

Property laws, 241–42, 309n. 17

PSID (Panel Study of Income Dynamics), 284n. 79

Public goods, 251
Public investment. *See* Government
Public policy. *See* Government
Public sector. *See* Government
Putnam, 134
Putting People First, 119

Queuing theory, 199–200

Railroad industry, 75–76
Rational expectations, 293–94n. 24
R&D. *See* Research and development
 (R&D)
Reagan, Ronald, 48, 265n. 7
Regulations, government
 of capital markets, 257–58
 growth and, 55, 57–58, 251–52,
  258–59
 special-interest groups and, 64
 of wages, 194
Reich, Robert, 120, 255, 268n. 26
Research and development (R&D)
 government role in, 18–19, 56–57,
  167–69, 215–18, 239–43
 New Growth theory and, 215–18,
  239–43, 252
 in private sector, 216–17
 productivity growth and decline in
  spending on, 56–57
 Wall Street model and, 12, 23
Retirement, 90
Ricardo, David, 124
Rifkin, Jeremy, 228
Roach, Stephen, 68
Robinson, John, 283n. 78
Rodrik, Dani, 189–90, 253
Rohatyn, Felix, 296n. 38
Romer, Paul
 on compound growth rates, 267n. 18
 on differential investment rates, 214
 on expectations, 261
 on government regulations, 250
 New Growth theory and, 19, 207

 on technological innovation, 208,
  209
Rose, Stephen, 280–81n. 65
 on all workers and hours worked,
  93–94
 data sources of, 284n. 79
 household research of, 185–86
 on prime-age workers and hours
  worked, 92
Rosenberg, Nathan, 71, 77
Rothstein, Richard, 269n. 5
Rubin, Robert, 120, 131
Russian financial crisis, 129, 152, 177

Sachs, Jeffrey, 171–72, 310n. 26
Safety net savings, 186–87
Salaries. *See* Wages
Samuelson, Paul, 155–56
Sargent, Thomas, 293–94n. 24
Savings rate. *See* National savings rate
Scherer, Frederick, 132
Schettkat, Ronald, 226–27
Schor, Juliet, 92, 282–84n. 78
Schroeder, Gerhard, 16
Schumpeter, Joseph, 46, 207, 212
Scott, Allen J., 308n. 6
Secrets of the Temple (Greider), 145
Self-employment, 92
Service-based economy
 assumptions about, 228–29
 demand and, 228–29
 globalization and, 162
 income and, 193, 274n. 13
 investment and, 295n. 33
 productivity growth and, 59–60,
  81–83
 surpluses and, 287n. 35
 wages in, 176, 231
Shapiro, Thomas, 187
Siemens, 221
Sierra Club, 64
Skilled versus unskilled workers, 45,
 74, 225, 281n. 66

Slifman, L., 276–77n. 25
Smith, Adam, 207
social protections, 163–64
Social rate of return, 216–17
Social Security, 90, 242, 269n. 38
Social Security Administration
  on economic growth, 7, 28–29
  forecasters on, 7, 266n. 16, 267n. 19
Social Security Trust Fund, 244,
  267n. 19
Software development, 211, 216
Sohn, Sung Won, 286n. 23
Solow, Robert
  on capital accumulation, 109
  on increased labor productivity,
    141
  neoclassical growth syllogism and,
    104
  on Phillips curve, 156
  on productivity growth and high-tech
    revolution, 67
  on technical innovation, 207–8
  on technological innovation, 105,
    106
South Korea, 257
Special-interest groups, 62–64, 274n. 19
Stable equilibria, 235
Staiger, Douglas, 158
Standardization, productivity growth
  and technological, 78
Steel industry, 268–69n. 32
Stein, Herbert, 59
Stern, Scott, 23
Stock, James, 158
Stockman, David, 119
Stock market
  as capital source, 133
  psychological aspects of prices in,
    151–52
  rise in, 3, 13, 293n. 18
  rise of, 122
  volatility of, 21, 27, 152–53
  wealth in, 286nn. 22, 23

Structural adjustment, 174
Summers, Larry, 5, 131–32, 136, 256
Supply-side economics, 2, 20, 32–33.
  See also New Growth theory
Surpluses, budget
  economic growth and, 112–13
  education and, 243–44
  GDP and, 167
  government investment and, 242
  private sector and, 292n. 10
  Wall Street model and, 167–68,
    239
Sweatshops, 255

Tax cuts
  Forbes on, 6
  Kemp-Roth, 119
  Kennedy and, 36
  Reagan and, 145
  Republicans on, 245
  the wealthy and, 202
Taxes, productivity growth and, 58,
  258–59
Taylor, Lance, 173
Technological innovation
  feedback loop in, 77–78
  income inequality and, 192–93
  learning curves and, 70, 77, 210,
    279n. 53
  in neoclassical growth syllogism, 105,
    106
  New Growth theory and, 208–10,
    309n. 17
  productivity growth and, 43, 47, 55,
    57, 67, 70–71, 108, 142, 180–81
  productivity lags and, 70–77
  Romer on, 208, 209
  Solow on, 105, 106
  theory of role in economy, 4, 18, 35,
    141–42
  versus Wall Street model, 179–81
Temin, Peter, 132
TFP (total factor productivity), 107–9

Thailand, 257
Third Wave, The (Toffler), 2
"The Third Way." *See* Wall Street model
Thrift, paradox of, 146–47. *See*
    National savings rate
Thurow, Lester, 98, 199, 232–33,
    293n. 24
Tobin, James, 258, 294n. 27
Tobin tax, 258–59
Toffler, Alvin, 2
Total factor productivity (TFP), 107–9
Trade balance, 170, 297n. 46
Trade barriers, 138
Trade deficit
    employment and, 287–88n. 36
    GDP and, 170–71
    with Mexico, 288n. 40
    reduction of, 297n. 44
    rise of, 123
    social inequality and, 196
    surplus and, 287n. 35
Trade protection, 63, 288n. 38
Transparency, 173
Trickle-down economics, 203
Triumph of Politics, The (Stockman), 119
"Twin-deficit" thesis, 171–72
Tyson, Laura, 120

UAW (United Automobile Workers),
    134, 230, 306n. 49
Uchitelle, Louis, 22
Underutilized workers, 98–99
Unemployment. *See also* Non-
    accelerating inflation rate of
    unemployment (NAIRU)
    decrease in, 3, 27, 41, 48, 102–3,
        128
    disguised rates of, 98
    due to Asian financial crisis,
        287–88n. 36
    growth and decrease in, 282n. 74
    historical background of NAIRU and,
        159–65

increase in, 89, 129, 160, 228
inflation and, 15, 91, 155–57
insurance, 163–64
manufacturing wages and, 197–98
Unions, 36
    cost-of-living adjustment and,
        289n. 47
    income inequality and decline of,
        194
    international labor standards and,
        253–54
    labor force and, 36, 126–27, 164,
        306n. 49
    Main Street model and, 247–48
    membership increases in, 248
    Phillips curve and decline in power
        of, 164
    productivity growth and, 177, 234,
        247–48
    reasons for, 126–27
    traditional workplace contracts and,
        230
    wages and, 126–27, 230
    Wall Street model and, 126–27,
        176–77
UNITE, 306n. 49
United Automobile Workers (UAW),
    134, 230, 306n. 49
United Nations Industrial Development
    Organization, 161
United Steelworkers, 291n. 3
University of Maryland, 281n. 78
University of Michigan Survey Research
    Center, 283n. 78

Veterans Administration, 34
Vietnam War, 37, 39
Virtuous cycle
    post–World War II, 11, 12, 35–37
    Wall Street, 13–14, 115–18, 139,
        151–53, 268n. 27
VisiCalc, 216
Volcker, Paul, 145, 177

Wage-led growth, 206, 226
Wages
  dispersion of, 193
  gender gaps in, 9
  globalization and, 162, 252–53
  government regulation of, 194
  hours worked and, 88, 94, 163,
    267n. 21
  inner city, 200
  international, 171, 233
  Main Street model and, 247
  in manufacturing, 171, 197–98
  minimum, 15, 153, 163, 176, 233,
    249
  New Growth theory and, 206, 232,
    233–34
  postwar boom and, 37, 182
  rise in, 9, 103, 197–98, 294n. 27,
    301n. 36
  in service-based economy, 176, 231
  Social Security and, 90
  unemployment and rise in, 160
  unions and, 126–27, 230
  Wall Street model and, 247
  of women, 267n. 21
Wagner Act of 1935, 248
Waldstein, Louise, 232–33
Wall Street, 5
Wall Street Journal, 7, 115
Wall Street model
  abandonment of, 238
  accounting model and, 107–10
  budget surpluses and, 167–68,
    239
  capital in, 256 (*see also* Capital)
  demand and, 151
  developing countries and, 173
  environment and, 24
  federal budget deficit and (*see*
    Budget, balanced: federal)
  Federal Reserve Board role in,
    128–30, 153, 154, 165
  fiscal policy and, 178

  flaws in, 16–17, 21–22, 139–40,
    151–55
  free trade and, 123–26, 169–75
  global capital mobility and, 130–35,
    136, 162, 175, 256–59, 290n. 54
  government policies and, 118,
    120–22, 153–55, 239, 265n. 8
  IMF and, 135–36, 172–74
  inequality and, 23, 202–4
  inflation and (*see* Inflation: Wall
    Street model and)
  interest rates and, 13, 15, 111–12,
    139, 143–46, 238, 268n. 27
  labor force and, 126–28, 154,
    175–77
  versus Main Street model, 261–62
  New Growth theory versus, 20, 225,
    226, 235–36
  origins of, 5–6, 12
  primer on conventional growth and,
    104–6
  principles of, 13–15, 268n. 26
  private sector and, 204
  research and development in,
    12, 23
  responsibility for growth and,
    179–81
  social inequality and, 23
  technological innovation versus,
    179–81
  unions and, 126–27, 176–77
  virtuous cycle (*see* Virtuous cycle)
  wages and, 247
Wall Street–Pennsylvania Avenue
    accord. *See* Wall Street model
Wal-Mart, 255
War on Poverty, 36
Watson, Mark, 158
Watt, James, 74
Wealth effect, 117–18, 152, 153, 201,
    203, 204
Welfare system reform, 15, 250
Wessel, David, 7

Wilson, William Julius, 199–200
Winner-take-all society, 194–95,
    281n. 66
Winter, Sidney, 80, 207, 209
Wolff, Edward, 186, 201, 302n. 46
Women
    hours worked, 88, 92, 280–81n. 65
    in labor force, 36, 37, 51, 86, 87, 88,
        271n. 17
    wages of, 267n. 21
Woodward, Bob, 121

Workplace reorganization
    information revolution and, 78
    New Growth theory and, 220–22,
        304–5n. 31
World Bank, 172–74, 257
World Trade Organization (WTO), 124,
    134, 253–54, 255, 309n. 19
WTO. See World Trade Organization
    (WTO)

Xerox, 221